# GENTRIFICATION

# GENTRIFICATION

LORETTA LEES, TOM SLATER,
AND ELVIN WYLY

Routledge
Taylor & Francis Group
New York   London

Routledge
Taylor & Francis Group
270 Madison Avenue
New York, NY 10016

Routledge
Taylor & Francis Group
2 Park Square
Milton Park, Abingdon
Oxon OX14 4RN

© 2008 by Taylor & Francis Group, LLC
Routledge is an imprint of Taylor & Francis Group, an Informa business

Printed in the United States of America on acid-free paper
10 9 8 7 6 5 4 3 2

International Standard Book Number-13: 978-0-415-95037-4 (Softcover) 978-0-415-95036-7 (Hardcover)

### Library of Congress Cataloging-in-Publication Data

Lees, Loretta.
  Gentrification / by Loretta Lees, Tom Slater, and Elvin Wyly.
    p. cm.
  Includes bibliographical references and index.
    ISBN 978-0-415-95036-7 (cloth) -- ISBN 978-0-415-95037-4 (pbk.)
    1. Gentrification. 2. Gentrification--Case studies. I. Slater, Tom. II. Wyly, Elvin K.
III. Title.

HT170.L44 2007
307.2--dc22                                                      2006103339

**Visit the Taylor & Francis Web site at**
**http://www.taylorandfrancis.com**

**and the Routledge Web site at**
**http://www.routledge.com**

# Contents

# Plates, Figures, Maps, and Boxes

## Figures

## Maps

## Boxes

# Acknowledgments

Writing this book has been a rewarding experience for all of us, not least because it has made us revisit many of the early writings on gentrification—which have taught us a lot.

*Our professional acknowledgments are as follows*:

*Loretta Lees*: I would like to thank Neil Smith for meeting with me in the Lower East Side back in 1988, just before the Tompkins Square Park riots when I was an undergraduate student embarking on my dissertation on gentrification. That meeting enthused me to continue studying and critiquing gentrification. A special thanks to Robert Beauregard and James DeFilippis for their supportive comments during the review process for this book and to Dave McBride for being so enthusiastic about the book. Thanks to Tim Butler, who has become a good friend and colleague, also to David Ley, Rob Imrie, Rowland Atkinson and Mark Davidson. Thanks to Peter Williams for reading and commenting on the discussion of fourth-wave gentrification in Chapter 5, David Reiss for hunting down back copies of *The Brownstoner*, and Dwight Demeritt for loaning me his mini-library on brownstoning. Finally, a very special thanks to Tom and Elvin for their wonderful work on this book.

*Tom Slater*: Gentrification has been part of my life since 1998, when I was displaced from my rented house in Tooting, south London, due to the landlord capitalizing on a gentrifying neighborhood, so I would like to thank that landlord for making me determined to do something about this disruptive process. For helping me to understand the global imprint of gentrification over the years, I thank all those activists, displaced tenants, and interested browsers for visiting Gentrification Web and contacting me with their locally embedded experiences. Rowland Atkinson, Gary Bridge, Winifred Curran, Mark Davidson, James DeFilippis, Dan Hammel, David Ley, Kathe Newman, Damaris Rose, Kate Swanson, and Alan Walks are good friends and colleagues who never fail to inspire me with their brilliance. Loretta and Elvin: thank you for making this project fun.

*Elvin Wyly*:

'I have gathered a posie of other men's flowers, and only the thread that binds them is my own'.

-**Montaigne**

I first encountered these words more than twenty years ago when I read the acknowledgments in Peter Gould's *The Geographer at Work*. Peter had first seen those lines four decades earlier in the title page of an anthology of poems committed to memory during the Second World War by Field Marshal A.P. Wavell (*Other Men's Flowers*, Putnam, New York, 1945). The words come back to me every single time I sign my name as an author. As I gather the posie of flowers from the women and men who have taught me so much, I realize that Montaigne and Gould taught me how to be a socialist scholar—a scholar who understands that knowledge is like language, community, urbanization, and real-estate value: it 'is socially created and not something that belongs to any individual' (see page 272 in this book). The value of my contribution to this project, then, comes from what I've learned from others. I'm deeply indebted for what I've learned from Tom and Loretta, brilliant and passionate co-authors. And I am also grateful to Dan Hammel, who first inspired a passion for mapping the frontiers of wealth and poverty as we walked through countless streets and alleys in Minneapolis, St. Paul, Philadelphia, Boston, Baltimore, Chicago, Detroit, and so many other cities. I've taken out scores of exotic low-downpayment, negative-amortization mortgages in an attempt to repay what I've learned about the unfinished research and resistance agenda on gentrification from Neil Smith, Kathe Newman, Jason Hackworth, and James DeFilippis—friends and colleagues with whom I have been privileged to collaborate. I am also indebted for all that I've learned from Mona Atia, Robert Beauregard, Keith Brown, Holly Foxcroft, Dennis Gale, George Galster, Ed Goetz, Bria Holcomb, Steve Holloway, David Imbroscio, Larry Keating, Bob Lake, Mickey Lauria, Liz Lee, David Ley, Peter Marcuse, Pat McCoy, Pablo Mendez, Chris Neidt, Jamie Peck, Kris Rengert, Matthew Rofe, Heather Smith, and Daphne Spain. And I've accumulated sizeable debts in what I have learned from those who might take issue with what I've written on the subject: John S. Adams, Brian J.L. Berry, Lance Freeman, John D. Kasarda, David Listokin, David Varady, and Vernon R. Wyly. Finally, parts of this book have benefited from extremely valuable critical comments and editorial advice from Tyler Pearce.

*On a more personal level*:

*Loretta Lees*: I would like to thank my partner, David Demeritt, who grew up as the son of a pioneer gentrifier in New York City and as such has long taken an interest in my work. I would like to thank my daughters, Meg and Alice, who continue to keep me grounded. I wish to dedicate this book to my late father, Arthur Lees.

*Tom Slater*: This book is for Sara, Zach, and Poppy, and also dedicated to David M. Smith, whose devastating undergraduate geography lectures opened my eyes to this wonderful subject and made me realize the role that geographers can play in addressing and challenging urban inequality.

*Elvin Wyly*: My love for the inner city came from voices I heard in the distance as a child. Robert S. Wyly and the late Florence A. Wyly built a wonderful, safe family life in the suburbs outside Washington, D.C. in the years when the 'voices of decline' about America's cities reached peak volume. But having 'The District' at a distance between 1966 and 1984 gave me an enduring passion ever since for going to the very heart of the city, any city. And now I've found a city of and for life, my District, my Dream City, my New Urban Frontier, my 'Peg, my Mission, my West End to Main Street: I'd like to dedicate this book to Jatinder Dhillon.

The authors would like to thank the following for cartographic and photographic help: To Peter Howard, photographer, Department of Geography, King's College London, for his expert help in getting all the images in this book ready for production. To Darren Smith for Plate 4.2, and Oleg Golubchikov for Plate 5.1. Map 1.1 was drawn by Roma Beaumont, cartographer (now retired), Department of Geography, King's College London. Map 7.2 was very kindly supplied by Ellen McElhinny, cartographer, Department of Geography, San Francisco State University. Map 7.3 was drawn by Eric Leinberger, cartographer, Department of Geography, University of British Columbia.

The authors and publisher would like to thank the following for granting permission to reproduce the material in this book:

Plate 1.1 Universal Press Syndicate
Plate 1.3 *The Brownstoner*
Plate 1.10 *The Phoenix*
Plate 2.2 *The New Yorker*
Plate 3.2 *Stay Free!* magazine (http://www.stayfreemagazine.org)
Plate 6.5 USA Today/Associated Press
Figure 2.1 was reproduced from M. Schill and R. Nathan, *Revitalizing Americas Cities: Neighborhood Reinvestment and Displacement*, p. 15, copyright State University of New York Press.
Figure B2.1a was reproduced from Blair Badcock, *Annals of the Association of American Geographers*, (79)1, p. 131, copyright Blackwell Publishing.
Figure B2.1b was reproduced from Eric Clark, *Geografiska Annaler*, B70, no. 2, p. 241, copyright Blackwell Publishing.
Figure B2.1c was reproduced from Dan Hammel, *Urban Geography*, 20, no. 2, p. 116, copyright Bellwether Publishing.
Figure B2.1d was reproduced from David O'Sullivan, *Journal of Geographical Systems*, 4, no 3, p. 251, copyright Springer Berlin/Heidelberg.
Figure B2.2 was reproduced from Luděk Sýkora, *Tijdschrift voor Economische en Sociale Geografie*, 84, no. 4, p. 286, copyright Blackwell Publishing.

Figure 2.4 was reproduced from Jason Hackworth, *Urban Affairs Review* 37, no. 6, p. 286, copyright Sage Publications.

Figure 4.2 was reproduced with permission from the Real Estate Board of New York.

Figure 5.1 was reproduced from Jason Hackworth and Neil Smith, *Tidschrift voor Economische en Sociale Geografie* 92, no. 4, p. 467, copyright Blackwell Publishing.

Box 6.1 was reproduced from Rowland Atkinson and Gary Bridge, eds. (2005), *Gentrification in a Global Context: The New Urban Colonialism*, p. 5, copyright Routledge.

# Preface

Gentrification is deeply rooted in social dynamics and economic trends. Its signs, effects and trajectories are to a large degree determined by its local context; the physical and the social characteristics of the neighbourhoods in question, the positions and the goals of the actors, the dominant functions of the city, the nature of economic restructuring and local government policy. The study of the city should pay heed to this complexity.... In the end, the 'why' of gentrification is less important than the 'how' and the repercussions of the process.

van Weesep (1994: 80)

Gentrification—the transformation of a working-class or vacant area of the central city into middle-class residential and/or commercial use—is without a doubt one of the more popular topics of urban inquiry. Gentrification has attracted widespread attention since its birth in London, England, and in a number of east coast U.S. cities in the 1950s and 1960s. It is a process that has attracted the attention of the media, national and local governments, urban planners, architects and developers, conservation/preservation groups, businesses (from utility companies to wine merchants), city boosters, and political activists. In the academic world it has been a central research theme in many subdisciplines of urban social science, capturing the attention of geographers, sociologists, anthropologists, housing economists, and political scientists, and resulting in a substantial and diverse international literature. Although there are numerous journal articles, a number of monographs and edited collections, and a 'Gentrification Web' (http://members.lycos.co.uk/gentrification/ 2007), surprisingly no textbook has ever been published on gentrification. We feel that there is a real need for a textbook on gentrification and one that is aimed at a broad range of readers.

Although the academic study of gentrification has been ongoing for the past forty years, the topic has seen a significant resurgence in recent years following a brief lull in the early 1990s. Much of this work has integrated gentrification theory and evidence into other important areas of urban research—globalization and world cities, changes in urban policy language and practice, social exclusion and polarization, debates on privatization, public space and citizenship, geographies of consumption, shifts in mortgage lending and housing policy, mechanisms of community organization, and the material effects of discourses of urban change. In short, gentrification has become a valuable lens through which to examine a variety of intersecting phenomena in a city and/or neighborhood context.

Why has 'gentrification' attracted such widespread interest? Chris Hamnett (1991: 173–174) outlines five reasons:

1. Gentrification has provided a novel and interesting urban phenomenon for geographers and sociologists to investigate.
2. Gentrification poses a major challenge to the traditional theories of residential location and social structure.
3. Gentrification is a political and policy-relevant issue as it is concerned with regeneration at the cost of displacement.
4. Gentrification has been seen as constituting a major 'leading edge' of contemporary metropolitan restructuring.
5. Gentrification represents one of the key theoretical and ideological battlegrounds in urban geography.

It is the last of these five reasons, gentrification's ideological and theoretical significance, that Hamnett (1991) places the most emphasis upon when explaining why gentrification has stimulated such widespread and sustained debate: 'The gentrification debate is one played for high theoretical and ideological stakes' (p. 174), he argues, and it has become an 'intellectual battleground between competing and radically opposed theoretical perspectives' (p. 175).

We would argue, however, that all of these reasons should be given equal weight but that some have been more important at certain times. For example, initially reason 2 was more important because gentrification challenged the historical specificity of traditional models of urban residential location, models such as those of Burgess (see Park, Burgess, and McKenzie 1925) and Hoyt (1939). Before the 1970s, it was generally accepted that these ecological models were fairly representative of urban structure; inconsistencies such as inner-city elite enclaves were usually dismissed as minor anomalies. Such models assumed an invasion and succession movement whereby more affluent households would move further and further out away from the inner city with their old houses being reoccupied by less affluent residents. Gentrification, by contrast, was the inverse of these traditional models in that it involved the middle classes moving back to the central city into working-class residential areas. As Walter Firey's (1947) study of Beacon Hill in Boston showed, older neighborhoods were being revitalized by citizens using private resources. But as Rose (1984: 47) notes, gentrification was seen as 'a temporary and small-scale aberration in what is seen as a … natural and dominant process of outward migration of people from inner cities'. Brian Berry (1980), for example, argued that gentrification would be short-lived because it was the result of a temporary squeeze or a cyclical housing squeeze, where there was an imbalance between the rates of new housing construction and new household formation. And over a decade later, during the worldwide economic recession of the early 1990s, Larry Bourne (1993a) too argued that gentrification was not long for this world. He said that a state of degentrification was emerging because

> the supply of potential young gentrifiers will be significantly smaller, given the passing of the baby-boom into middle-age, the declining rate of new household formation, and the general aging of [the] population. The expanding cohort of potential young gentrifiers will not be suffi-cient to compensate for the rapid decline in the younger cohorts. At the same time, given widespread macro-economic restructuring, corporate down-sizing and a persistent recession, we might also expect slower rates of employment growth in the service sector and associated occu-pations. (pp. 104–105)

Brian Berry and Larry Bourne were both wrong. Gentrification is still very alive and very well, so that over a decade later we can add the following to Hamnett's list:

6. Gentrification is the leading edge of neoliberal urbanism.
7. Gentrification has gone global and is intertwined with processes of globalization.
8. Gentrification is no longer confined to the inner city or to First World metropolises.

In late 1979, in the United States, President Jimmy Carter's Commission for a National Agenda for the Eighties suggested that central-city decline was inevitable; in their minds, the central city's destiny was death (Holcomb and Beauregard 1981). But in the following years, deindustrializing and depopulat-ing American cities tried to attract private development and investment into their downtown areas in the belief that demand for services would be boosted, spending would increase, jobs would be created, and a positive trickle down would help adjacent neighborhoods. Commonly, convention centers, new sta-diums and festival marketplaces were built and warehouses along rivers were redeveloped as shopping and leisure complexes, for example, South Street Seaport in New York City and Faneuil Hall in Boston. David Harvey (2000) writes in detail about such urban regeneration in Baltimore and, against the tide of city boosterism in the United States, tells a disturbing story in which Baltimore today is in more of a mess than in 1969, when he first saw the city. He asks, 'But how come it is that we are so persuaded that "there is no alterna-tive"?' (p. 155).

In 2007 in the United States and indeed around the world, these narratives of decline and death have been overtaken by a global neoliberal discourse of regeneration and renaissance. As Davidson and Lees (2005: 1167) argue,

> [A] gentrification "blue-print" is being mass-produced, mass-marketed, and mass-consumed around the world. As the urban-rural dichotomy has broken down … as a significant part of the world has become increasingly urbanized and desirous of an urban(e) lifestyle, the result seems to be that even some Third World cities and First World suburban and rural areas are experiencing gentrification.

Lagging somewhat behind the United States, at the end of the twentieth century in Britain, a New Labour government began to promote the 'urban renaissance' of British towns and cities. They prescribed concepts and ways of living that are closely tied to gentrification practices; in fact, Butler and Robson (2001a) have called their prescriptions 'a gentrifiers' charter', and Lees (2003a) 'text-book gentrification'.

The discursive construction of an 'urban renaissance' in the United Kingdom began in 1998, when the architect (and now Lord) Richard Rogers was asked by then Deputy Prime Minister John Prescott to head an Urban Task Force. Richard Rogers was to coordinate a group of experts from both the public and private sectors and a large number of working group members to identify the causes of urban decline in England and to 'recommend practical solutions to bring people back into our cities, towns and urban neighbourhoods' (Department of the Environment, Transport and the Regions [DETR] 1999: 1). As their mission statement explained,

> The Urban Task Force will identify causes of urban decline in England and recommend practical solutions to bring people back into our cities, towns and urban neighbourhoods. It will establish a new vision for urban regeneration founded on the principles of design excellence, social well-being and environmental responsibility within a viable economic and legislative framework. (p. 1)

As part of their research, the Urban Task Force visited not just English cities but also cities in Europe and the United States. The Urban Task Force's final report was published as *Towards an Urban Renaissance* (DETR 1999) and set out their urban vision for England. This is an explicitly pro-urban document that contains a plethora of exciting ideas about how to make cities in England better places. A year later, the government published its formal response to the Urban Task Force report, its 2000 Urban White Paper, *Our Towns and Cities—the Future: Delivering an Urban Renaissance* (DETR 2000a). This is the first white paper on urban policy in Britain since Peter Shore's *Policy for the Inner Cities* (Department of Environment 1977), and it stands as a statement of the centrality of cities in contemporary British life. The scope of the 2000 Urban White Paper is more comprehensive than that of the Urban Task Force report. The Urban White Paper draws on the Urban Task Force report, the work of the Social Exclusion Unit, and work such as *The State of the English*

*Cities* (DETR 2000b). As such, New Labour's concept of urban renaissance goes beyond physical environmental objectives to include concerns for social inclusion, wealth creation, sustainable development, urban governance, health and welfare, crime prevention, educational opportunity, freedom of movement, as well as environmental quality and good design. Whereas under Margaret Thatcher urban regeneration was the urban medicine for social *degeneration*, urban renaissance is New Labour's urban medicine for urban malaise. It is important to point out that the term 'gentrification' itself is not used in these policy documents. Instead, terms like 'urban renaissance', 'urban regeneration', and 'urban sustainability' are used in its place. These neutered terms politely avoid the class constitution of the processes involved. It's hard to be for 'gentrification', but who would oppose 'urban renaissance', 'urban regeneration', and 'urban sustainability' (Lees 2003a)?

On looking at the U.S. Department of Housing and Urban Development (HUD) report *State of the Cities* (June 1999), the issues and solutions discussed are very similar to those of the British Urban Task Force—the redevelopment of brownfield sites (abandoned and often contaminated industrial land), environmental sustainability, livability, and the decline in a sense of community. To counter the loss of middle-class families in the inner city, HUD argues for increased support for the revitalization initiatives of community-based organizations (read 'pro-gentrification groups'). As Wyly and Hammel (2005: 36) argue,

> [T]he most durable result of gentrification may be its effect on new priorities in the formulation of urban policy. Inner city land use decisions come to rely on considerations of middle-class market demand; gentrification underwrites new configurations of highest and best use, reallocations of neighbourhood public services, and realignments of police practices and public space regulation. The inherited landscapes and potential expansion of gentrification are now critical considerations in many domains of urban policy. To be sure, the word (which wealthy urbanites clearly understand as an epithet) almost never appears in the official discourse of renewal, revitalization, and market optimism. But the interests and priorities of gentrifiers are a foundational element of the post-industrial city as growth machine.

The latter is nowhere more obvious than in Richard Florida's (2003) much proclaimed book *The Rise of the Creative Class*, in which he argues that cities and regions can no longer compete economically by simply attracting companies or by developing mega-projects like sports stadiums and downtown development districts; rather, to capitalize on the new economy, policy makers must reach out to what he labels the 'creative class', that is gays, youth, bohemians, professors, scientists, artists, entrepreneurs, and the like. The creative class is seen to be the key to economic growth in the contemporary city or region (see http://www.creativeclass.com). Florida's 'creative class' has a lot in common with David Ley's (1980, 1994, 1996) gentrifying 'new middle class'. The interests and lifestyles of Florida's creative class and Ley's new middle class are different to the conservative middle classes whom cities have traditionally tried to attract but who preferred to live in the suburbs. The creative class (or Bobos—'bourgeois bohemians') manages to combine a bourgeois work ethic with bohemian culture. The creative class desires tolerance (Florida finds those cities most tolerant of, for example, the gay population will be more successful in attracting and keeping the creative class), diversity, bike paths, hiking trails, historic architecture, and so on. Florida's thesis, however, is an ambivalent one, as he himself recognizes that his model of urban and economic renaissance both invites gentrification and stifles the diversity and creativity that it seeks. In his 2005 book *Cities and the Creative Class*, he laments, 'With gentrification comes an out-migration of bohemians' (p. 25). Nevertheless, Florida's (gentrification) thesis has become big business. He has been invited all over the United States (and, indeed, outside the United States) to tell cities and states how to reinvent themselves and thus prosper. For example, in May 2004 almost 700 people from throughout Maine and other parts of New England came together at the Bates Mill complex in Lewiston, Maine, to explore the creative economy in Maine. The occasion was convened by Maine's state governor, John E. Baldacci. In his keynote address at the meeting, Richard Florida praised Maine's creative and entrepreneurial spirit, quoting his mentor Jane Jacobs, who said that 'new ideas require old buildings' (Maine Arts Commission 2004: 8). The belief that a creative workforce will lead the way in terms of urban and economic regeneration and development is so strong that in late 2004, Governor Baldacci accepted recommendations from a statewide committee to foster 'Maine's creative economy'. Governor Baldacci believes,

> The Creative Economy is a catalyst for vibrant downtowns, expanding cultural tourism, encouraging entrepreneurial activity and growing our communities in a way that allows us to retain and attract creative workers ... an investment in a stable workforce and competitiveness. (Maine Arts Commission 2004: 3)

As geographer David Harvey (1989a: 355) states, '[T]he production of images and of discourses is an important facet of activity that has to be analyzed as part and parcel of the reproduction and transformation of any symbolic order'. This book undertakes that task with respect to gentrification.

This textbook is timely for two related reasons. First, the process of gentrification has gone global (N. Smith 2002; Atkinson and Bridge 2005). It is no longer confined to North America and Europe; it now spans the globe and can be found in Mexico, Israel, Japan, South Africa, and New Zealand, and indeed in many other countries around the world too. Although gentrification in the United States has long been a feature of cities further down the urban hierarchy, in the United Kingdom this has not been the case until recently. Now gentrification can be found in provincial British cities such as Manchester, Sheffield, and Leeds. There is widespread scholarly agreement that gentrification is expanding dramatically. At the same time it is mutating, so that we now have different types of gentrification such as rural gentrification, new-build gentrification, and super-gentrification. This has raised all kinds of urgent questions about the implications of class transformations, working-class/low-income displacement and/or replacement, unequal experiences of the city, power and resistance, and how gentrification threatens 'cities for the many not the few' (Amin, Massey, and Thrift 2000). There can be little doubt that the gentrification literature is 'overwhelmingly critical' (Atkinson 2002), but this has had little effect in curbing the expansion of gentrification. We feel that one possible reason for this is that the literature has never been summarized in one comprehensive, accessible introductory volume (complete with case studies), and disseminated to a wide audience. This book, theoretically informed and empirically grounded, attempts to do just that.

Second, gentrification has worked its way into the planning manifestos of urban policy agendas to improve the economic, physical, and social outlook of disinvested central-city locations around the world. Often disguised as 'regeneration', 'renaissance', 'revitalization', or 'renewal', gentrification has become, in the words of one renowned gentrification scholar, 'a global urban strategy' and 'the consummate expression of an emerging neo-liberal urbanism' (N. Smith 2002). The British Government's Urban Task Force report (DETR 1999) and Urban White Paper (DETR 2000a) outlined above exemplify this new trend, and it is time for a coherent and sensitive assessment of the impact of gentrification on urban policy and vice versa. Given the scant regard exhibited by these urban manifestos for four decades of critical scholarship on gentrification, a dialogue between policy makers, planners, and academics seems of paramount importance, and this book will put the case forward for such a dialogue by critically reviewing a new body of work which has emerged to assess the gentrification–urban policy link (see Imrie 2004 for a sensible and informed review of the recent debates about the lack of engagement with policy in geography). In an article titled 'Geography and Public Policy', geographer Gilbert White (1972) said that he would not do research 'unless it promises results that would advance the aims of the people affected and unless [he was] prepared to take all practicable steps to help translate the results into action'; we would like this book to be one step in that direction.

### The Arguments

Unlike standard textbooks, which tend to regurgitate other authors' arguments, in this book we want to make a number of our own arguments too. In so doing, we want to challenge our readers to think critically about the gentrification process and to weigh up the arguments and debates presented. There are four lines of argument that flow through the book; these are not in any particular order, and to some degree they are interrelated.

First, we want to hold onto the label 'gentrification' in response to those who would argue that the term should be allowed to collapse under the weight of its own burden (e.g., Bondi 1999a) or that alternate words such as 'reurbanization' should be used instead (e.g.. Lambert and Boddy 2002). Rather, following Clark (2005), we advocate the idea of an elastic but targeted definition of gentrification. We argue strongly that the term 'gentrification' is one of the most political terms in urban studies (implying, by definition, class-based displacement), and to lose the term would be to lose the politics and political purchase of the term.

Second, we argue that the theoretical divisions between production and consumption explanations have been overdrawn and that most gentrification researchers now accept that production and consumption, supply and demand, economic and cultural, and structure and agency explanations are all a part of 'the elephant of gentrification' (see Hamnett 1991). As Clark (2005: 261) argues, '[N]either side is comprehensible without the other, and all present theories of gentrification touch bottom in these basic conditions for the existence of the phenomenon'. Following Beauregard (2003a: 999), we want to conceive of theory 'simply as knowledge that is consciously and explicitly positioned in a field of mutually referential texts'. As he argues, '[T]extual positioning is central to the contribution that theorists make and the recognition their theories receive' (p. 999). Furthermore, we agree with Atkinson (2003a: 2349), who argues that

> the problem of gentrification is less its conceptualisation and more about the need for a project which will begin to address the systematic inequalities of urban society upon which gentrification thrives.

Third, we argue that gentrification researchers' methods and methodologies are heavily implicated in the stories, explanations, theories, and conceptualizations of gentrification formulated. As Lees (1998: 2258) argues,

> The importance of methodology has seldom been stressed in studies of gentrification, despite the long-standing interest in the differing outcomes of different theoretical frameworks such as Marxism, humanism and postmodernism. But different methodological frameworks result in different outcomes of gentrification.

One result of this is that the scale and scope of gentrification are presented differently. Those interested in the humanist and sociocultural side of gentrification tend to present the process at the scale of the individual (for example, Butler 1997; Butler with Robson 2003; Ley 1996). Using survey and interview data, they connect gentrification to the individual decision maker and to small groups of people who share residential preferences. These approaches often make gentrification seem more chaotic and differentiated, with gentrifiers demonstrating important differences and distinctions (e.g., Butler with Robson 2003). By way of contrast, scholars interested in the politico-economic aspects of gentrification present the process as a much larger scale phenomenon. Rather than connecting gentrification to individuals and researching the phenomenon at that scale, they regard gentrifiers as a collective social group (class) bound by economic rationality (e.g., Hackworth 2002a; N. Smith 1996a). As such, they perceive no need to examine and explore the motivations of individual gentrifiers. Production-side scholars, therefore, use research methods which are adept at capturing the structural, large-scale aspects of gentrification, such as changing levels of capital investment and neighborhood class turnover.

Fourth, throughout the book but especially in the conclusion, we argue for a critical geography of gentrification, one that follows a social justice agenda and one that is focused on resisting gentrification where necessary. All three of us have been involved in antigentrification activities, mainly in North America; as such, we have had firsthand experience of the complexities of resisting such a hegemonic process. We demonstrate throughout the book that cities and neighborhoods do not move from a state of decline to renaissance naturally but that a plethora of key actors are involved in the process of gentrification—from individual gentrifiers to landlords, realtors, developers, the state, corporations, institutions, and so on—and they must be held accountable for their actions. We are not the first to advocate a social justice agenda with respect to gentrification. Back in 1981, in their monograph *Revitalizing Cities*, Holcomb and Beauregard's primary concern was with justice and equity, 'motivated by moral, philosophical, analytical, or practical imperatives' (p. iii). In particular, they were struck by the fact that the costs and benefits of gentrification were unevenly distributed relative to the needs of different urban groups. This is still the case today. Like Holcomb and Beauregard (1981: v), we too are skeptical of capitalism and supportive of economic and social democracy, and we want to challenge our readers' critical spirit and encourage further inquiry. We would like to see students, academics, and others involved in community projects associated with gentrification, because such a grassroots experience is invaluable in terms of a learning curve about this complex process and would aid in resisting the more pernicious aspects of the phenomenon.

We are also critical of British and American policy ideas about gentrification and social mixing and the Netherlands' policy of 'housing redifferentiation'. These policy ideas seek to socially mix neighborhoods, assuming that the benefits of gentrification (that is, middle-class residence in the central city) will trickle down to the lower and working classes, for example, that social capital will be passed from the middle classes to the working or lower classes through neighborly mixing. As Holcomb and Beauregard (1981: 3) note,

> Although it is often assumed that the benefits of revitalization will "trickle down" to the lower and working classes in a manner similar to that hypothesized for the housing market ... in fact they are often completely captured by the middle and upper classes.

Given that gentrification now seems rather inevitable given its mutating form, we want to be critical but also constructive; as such, we offer suggestions for making gentrification a more democratic and egalitarian process where possible. We do not want to suggest that the state should not invest in central cities; rather, we suggest that they need to look more closely at their policies and decision making. As Holcomb and Beauregard (1981: 70) argue, '[A]ttachment to place deserves recognition, and social networks should not be destroyed'. This is an argument that Dench, Gavron, and Young (2006) make in their book *The New East End*, where an affordability crisis due to gentrification in an already hot London property market and the particulars of council housing allocations mean that members of the same family can no longer reside in the same neighborhood/location and kinship networks are being destroyed forever. A socially just urban renaissance must seek to counter the negative aspects of gentrification; this requires the active support of local and national governments and committed political action by working-class communities and organizations. For example, governments need to exert stronger social control over developers—making sure not only that they fulfill their low-income housing quotas but also that the low-income housing they provide is of the same type and quality as the high-income housing, and that it is not segregated off but rather integral to the main development. The social, economic, and cultural segregation that exists in London's Docklands stands as a testimony to what happens when developer-led regeneration is allowed a relatively free rein. Local communities must be consulted about the regeneration of their local area, and this must be more than a form of participatory tokenism. However, low-income communities rarely have the education, networks, or finances to play a key role in such participation, and differences of opinion are always problematic to work through. Lessons can be learned from reading James DeFilippis and Peter North's (2004) participant observations on community organizing with respect to the regeneration of Elephant and Castle in central London. As Merrifield (2002a: 69) emphasizes, '[C]ommonality and togetherness in struggle has to be a prerequisite for any meaningful minority politics'; without it, resistance to capitalist urbanization is extremely difficult.

### The Audience

Our aim is to provide a textbook for upper undergraduate and master's students on the following courses (this is by no means an exclusive list): geography, sociology, urban studies, anthropology, housing studies, policy studies, urban planning, and political science. But we also want this book to be a useful resource for Ph.D. students, academics, researchers, planners, policy makers, and community organizations interested in gentrification. Like Andy Merrifield (2002a) in *Dialectical Urbanism*, we see ourselves as organic intellectuals, in that we want this text to speak to more than just university-based students and researchers. The key to targeting such a wide audience is by approaching the textbook in an interdisciplinary manner and concentrating on making the book widely accessible in style and content. As such, we adopt a bottom-up perspective and a style of writing that constitutes a critical geography that embraces ordinary experiences and commonsense viewpoints.

**How to Use This Book**

We have written *Gentrification* as a core text, and it can be used either as a resource for a full module on gentrification or for part of a module on, for example, urban geography or urban regeneration. The book has been written to be used not only by both students and academics but also by planners, policy makers, and community organizations interested in gentrification. The ways that these disparate readers use the book will be different.

For students and academics, we have included textbook-style features such as case studies, boxes, activities, and further reading. In fact, we begin the book with two detailed case studies because as well as outlining the theories and conceptualizations of gentrification, we want to tell the story of gentrification from the scale of the neighborhood up to the scale of the global. Gentrification began very much as a neighborhood process, but it is a process that has escalated up the spatial scale, so that much of the discussion these days is of a global gentrification. The boxes are learning aids, the activities are to get readers to reflect more on the material presented in the book, and the further readings are a mix of some of the works referred to in the chapter, so that students can read the most important ones in more detail, and new readings that back up the arguments in the text or offer alternative case studies.

When reading the book, please note where we direct the reader to discussions and arguments in different, usually (but not always) subsequent chapters. We have designed the book so that the arguments made build on each other throughout the book, hopefully strengthening our arguments as we go along. Some of the particular case studies of gentrification that we use are discussed not just in one chapter in the book but in a number of different chapters. For example, the case study of pioneer gentrification in Barnsbury in Chapter 1 is brought up-to-date in Chapter 4 in the discussion of the super-gentrification in Barnsbury. The case study of pioneer gentrification in Park Slope in Chapter 1 is brought up-to-date in Chapter 7 in a discussion of resistance to overspill gentrification in what realtors have dubbed 'South Slope' and 'Lower Slope'. The example of Newcastle's New Labour–led 'Going for Growth' urban regeneration strategy (thankfully now squashed) is used in both a discussion of new-build gentrification in Chapter 4 and a discussion of 'gentrification as a positive public policy tool' in Chapter 6. We feel that such a strategy makes the book more holistic by linking different chapters together.

For planners and policy makers, we suggest reading and thinking more about the positive and negative outcomes of gentrification (see in particular Chapter 6). It seems that the negative impacts outweigh the positive impacts at the neighborhood scale, but at the citywide scale this is not necessarily the case. We would like you to read, and think about, these words from Kate Shaw (2005):

> Progressive local governments can protect existing affordable housing, produce more social housing and encourage the production of affordable private housing. They can use the planning system to judiciously apply maximum standards in dwelling size and help to ensure a stock of relatively low-cost apartments. … Local governments can capitalize on their social and cultural diversity by engaging their lower-income residents in genuine consultative processes. They can provide leadership in values as well as practice, supporting a culture of openness to social housing, for example, and actively discouraging intolerance and prejudice. (pp. 182–183)
>
> Politicians, policymakers, planners and communities have to examine their commitments to multicultural, diverse, socially equitable and environmentally safe cities, because these elements do not persist or expand of their own accord. (p. 184)

For community organizations and activists, we suggest reading the book with a view to understanding the process of gentrification better—its *multiple* causes and impacts—so as to be able to better develop strategies to resist or, if that is not possible, ameliorate the process. It is now more difficult than ever to resist gentrification because it is no longer the result of individual middle-class actions (if it ever was); rather, it is the result of a number of actors and actions, the most important of which is now the state through the import of gentrification into urban policy, and indeed other public policy, worldwide. In Chapter 7 we outline a number of examples of attempts to resist gentrification, even if some of these have failed (and it is worth noting that Jan van Weesep [1994: 81] believes that nothing will halt gentrification); at least they have been instrumental in highlighting the problematic politics of gentrification.

### The Structure

A textbook like this cannot possibly cover all the literature on gentrification. The literature that has been selected is representative of the literature in general and of our main arguments in particular. As such, the book reflects our own intellectual predilections. The cases of gentrification discussed in detail tend to come from the United Kingdom, the United States, and Canada; this is not only because that is where the bulk of our research has been undertaken, but also because it is in these countries that the most detailed and systematic research has been undertaken to date. However, where possible, given word limits and other considerations, we discuss other cases of gentrification from around the world and provide the reader with plenty of alternative references.

The preface which you are reading now acts as the introduction to the book. Here we outline why gentrification is an important topic of social scientific inquiry, and we discuss the aims of the book and why we have written it the way we have.

Chapter 1 begins the book by discussing the birth of gentrification and the coinage, by the British sociologist Ruth Glass, of the term itself. It highlights the existence of a number of other urban processes that were gentrification or are considered by some to have been processes of gentrification. To some degree the emergence of the process of gentrification and the term itself are contemporaneous, but there are significant precursors to the coinage of the term. We then move on to discuss definitions of gentrification: the early definitions play off of Ruth Glass's definition, but later definitions (as we see in Chapter 4) try to accommodate the mutation of gentrification into different types. In Chapter 1 we discuss classical or first-wave gentrification in some detail, and we tell the empirical stories of two cases of classical gentrification—one in London and one in New York City—to highlight the importance of context in analyses of gentrification. We then turn to the early-stage models that were developed to explain the process. All the subsequent chapters play off, in different ways, of this chapter.

In Chapters 2 and 3, we discuss the main theoretical work on gentrification. Chapter 2 looks at the supply-side theories that have explained gentrification as a product of capitalist uneven development. Here we outline Neil Smith's (1979) rent gap thesis and some alternative rent gap models. We also consider the central and very important issue of displacement of low-income communities by the gentrifying middle classes. Of course, the explanations outlined here are only part of 'the elephant of gentrification'; and in highlighting the problems with production-orientated explanations, we point to the demand-side arguments in the next chapter, for as Merrifield (2002b: 25) argues in his book *Metromarxism*, '[E]verything is pregnant with its contrary'. We conclude the chapter with a discussion of resistance, asking what forms of resistance these particular explanations inform.

In Chapter 3, we turn to the consumption or demand-side explanations of gentrification that have explained gentrification as a consequence of changes in the industrial and occupational structure of advanced capitalist cities, ones which have engendered particular social and cultural changes too. We consider theses on the new middle class by authors such as Tim Butler (1997), theses in which politics and aesthetics are central. We outline David Ley's (1980) postindustrial and Chris Hamnett's (1994a) professionalization theses before paying attention to the roles of gender, sexuality, and ethnicity in gentrification, exploring Tim Butler's (1997) argument that gentrifiers seek to live amongst 'people like us'. As in the previous chapter, we highlight the problems and obfuscations engendered by these demand-side explanations, offering suggestions out of these problems where possible. Again, we conclude the chapter with a discussion of resistance, arguing that these explanations are more about personal resistance to, for example, suburbia or to the 'straight world' by gay gentrifiers.

In Chapter 4 we return to the definition of gentrification and ask, Is gentrification collapsing under the weight of its expanding definition? We look at how gentrification has mutated from its classical form into rural gentrification (which is not urban), new-build gentrification (which is not about renovating old houses), and the more recent super-gentrification (which stands against those stage models that assume an endpoint of mature gentrification in neighborhoods). In the light of all this, we argue very strongly that we must retain the term 'gentrification', despite the morphing of the process, because of the political value of the term itself.

In Chapter 5 we look at the main features of contemporary gentrification and how they differ from those of classical gentrification. We outline the characteristics of third-wave or postrecession gentrification and the way that gentrification has gone global. We discuss globalization, which to date, we feel, has been undertheorized in relation to gentrification. We relate the discussion of globalization and gentrification to the changing role of the state and the emergence of a local, national, and global neoliberalism. We identify a fourth wave of gentrification in the United States and discuss this in relation to the rebuilding of New Orleans. We conclude the chapter by promoting further research on 'the geography of gentrification', a geography which takes both space and the temporal dimensions of gentrification into consideration.

Chapter 6 asks two opposing questions: Is gentrification a negative neighborhood process? and, Is gentrification a positive neighborhood process? It weighs up the answers to both questions and relates them to the revanchist city thesis and the emancipatory city thesis respectively. Such questions are seldom asked outright, nor are the answers to them usually forthright.

Chapter 7 is the concluding chapter, and as well as pondering the future of gentrification it sets out more fully our social justice agenda. This agenda is first and foremost about resisting gentrification when and where necessary. We outline three case studies of attempts to resist gentrification demonstrating the different tactics that have been used, and then some of the strategies that low-income communities have developed to gain more control over, and ownership of, housing.

Finally, we hope that this book provides 'effective communication of what we already know' and stimulates 'principled public discussion about the nature of the cities we want to inhabit in the twenty-first century' (Shaw 2005: 184).

Plate 1.1 Gentrification

Dr. Dan explains gentrification in this cartoon by Garry Trudeau.

*Source: Doonesbury* © 1980 G. B. Trudeau. Reprinted with permission of Universal Press Syndicate.

# 1
# The Birth of Gentrification

> Sir, of all the tiresome emotive words coined by this generation "gentrification" must rank among the worst. By its implication of class ridden envy, peculiar I believe to this country and perhaps a symptom of our current malaise, fears of "gentrification" threaten plans for the rehabilitation of many derelict areas of "listed" housing in London.
>
> William Bell, member of the Greater London Council
> for Chelsea and chairman of the Historic Buildings Committee,
> in a letter to the *Times* ('Letters to the Editor' 1977)

More than forty years have passed since the term 'gentrification' was first coined by the British sociologist Ruth Glass. In this chapter we show that it is a slippery term, the problem being amplified by the preponderance of numerous alternative labels for gentrification. We also look at the birth of gentrification as a visible urban process. To some extent the coinage of the term and the birth of the process are contemporaneous (although Clark [2005] would argue otherwise). We also introduce the processes that are part and parcel of classical gentrification to our readers through two neighborhood-based case studies of *classic* gentrification in two different cities: New York and London. As a result, the stories told here are partial; we halt our stories just as gentrification becomes firmly anchored in these two neighborhoods, but we will return to the ongoing processes of gentrification in these two neighborhoods in Chapters 4 and 7 in the book. By choosing examples of classical gentrification from two different cities and countries, we demonstrate the necessary preconditions for gentrification and the contextual differences between these places (Carpenter and Lees 1995). We do not consider conceptual or theoretical debates about the process here; rather, we tell the empirical stories of the processes of gentrification in these different places. But it soon becomes apparent that gentrification is an economic, cultural, political, social, and institutional phenomenon—something that we argue more fully in Chapters 2 and 3. We tell the stories of how these two inner-city neighborhoods became devalorized/disinvested and how they subsequently became revalorized/reinvested. These stories involve various actors—from the state (who is implicated in the process as both disinvestor and investor from quite early on) to private institutions to pioneer gentrifiers. These stories demonstrate that processes of gentrification, even of classical gentrification, are complex and that they are closely related to the particular contexts of the neighborhoods and cities in which they are situated. We begin the book here by focusing on individual neighborhoods in First World cities; this is deliberate because gentrification began very much as a neighborhood-based process and a First World city process, but as we shall see later in the book this is no longer the case today. We end this chapter by outlining the early stage models that sought to explain gentrification before moving on to a more rigorous analysis of explanations of gentrification in Chapters 2 and 3.

**The Term 'Gentrification'**

As mentioned above, the term 'gentrification' was first coined by the British sociologist Ruth Glass in 1964, although it is rumored that she used the term 'gentrified' in an unpublished study of housing in North Kensington in 1959. Ruth Glass was a Marxist, a refugee from Nazi Germany, and one of the pioneers of urban sociology in Europe. She used the term 'gentrification' to describe some new and distinct processes of urban change that were beginning to affect inner London; the changes she described are now known as those of 'classical gentrification':

> One by one, many of the working class quarters of London have been invaded by the middle classes—upper and lower. Shabby, modest mews and cottages—two rooms up and two down—have been taken over, when their leases have expired, and have become elegant, expensive residences. Larger Victorian houses, downgraded in an earlier or recent period—which were used as lodging houses or were otherwise in multiple occupation—have been upgraded once again. Nowadays, many of these houses are being subdivided into costly flats or "houselets" (in terms of the new real estate snob jargon). The current social status and value of such dwellings are frequently in inverse relation to their status, and in any case enormously inflated by comparison with previous levels in their neighbourhoods. Once this process of 'gentrification' starts in a district it goes on rapidly until all or most of the original working class occupiers are displaced and the social character of the district is changed. (Glass 1964: xviii–xix)

Ruth Glass's definition of 'gentrification' has long offered some form of unity in the field. As Chris Hamnett (2003b) points out, Ruth Glass's use of the term 'gentrification' was deliberately ironic and tongue in cheek. It was rooted in the intricacies of traditional English rural class structure, the term was designed to point to the emergence of a new 'urban gentry', paralleling the 18th- and 19th-century rural gentry familiar to readers of Jane Austen who comprised the class strata below the landed gentry, but above yeoman farmers and peasants (p. 2401). So, literally, gentrification or 'gentry-fication' means the replacement of an existing population by a gentry. The term is also ironic in that it makes fun of the snobbish pretensions of affluent middle-class households who would still prefer a rural, traditional way of life if given the chance (just think of all those classic gentrifiers' homes with stripped wood floors, Aga stoves, open fires, and natural wood and material furnishings). There are parallels with notions of 'rustification' (that connects it through to the rural gentrification discussed in Chapter 4). Indeed, the antiurbanism of English culture was a recurrent theme in the writings of Ruth Glass. Glass identified gentrification as a complex urban process that included the rehabilitation of old housing stock, tenurial transformation from renting to owning, property price increases, and the displacement of working-class residents by the incoming middle classes.

In her discussion of gentrification in *London: Aspects of Change*, Glass went on to argue,

> While the cores of other large cities in the world, especially of those in the United States, are decaying, and are becoming ghettos of the "under-privileged", London may soon be faced with an *embarrass de richesse* in her central area—and this will prove to be a problem too. (1964: 141)

Glass here demonstrates her lack of knowledge of gentrification in the United States at this time. But her predictions for the future of London are spot on today, for the 2001 UK Census (National Statistics 2001) data shows that most of central London is now gentrified or gentrifying. And, as this book will argue, gentrification is a problem too.

### The Emergence of Gentrification

Gentrification, however, began before the term itself was coined. As Clark (2005: 260) points out, 'Ruth Glass did indeed coin the term in 1964, but it is careless to turn this into an assumption that we have here the origin of the phenomenon'. Neil Smith (1996a: 34–40) outlines some of its significant precursors, for example, the Haussmannization of Paris. Baron Haussmann, a member of Napoleon III's court, demolished the residential areas in which poor people lived in central Paris, displacing them to make room for the city's now famous tree-lined boulevards which showcase the city's famous monuments. Strict guidelines applied to new building along the boulevards, and the residences there became the most exclusive in the city. Gale (1984) argues that by the late 1930s, parts of New York, New Orleans, and Charleston, as well as the Georgetown area of Washington, D.C., were all experiencing gentrification. But the emergence of gentrification proper, we argue (contra Clark 2005), began in postwar advanced capitalist cities. Its earliest systematic occurrences were in the 1950s in large metropolitan cities like Boston; Washington, D.C.; London; and New York City. In both the United States and in Britain, postwar urban renewal meant the bulldozing of old neighborhoods to be replaced by modern housing and highways. As the destruction spread, so did the rebellion against it. In the beginning the protesters were mainly historians and architecture buffs, but slowly these were joined by young, middle-class families who bought and lovingly reconditioned beat-up, turn-of-the-century houses in 'bad' neighborhoods. In New York City, this was called 'brownstoning'; in Baltimore, 'homesteading'; in Toronto, 'whitepainting' or 'whitewalling'; and in San Francisco, 'red-brick chic'. As Williams (1986: 65) argued,

> Many American analysts have been uncomfortable with the term "gentrification" (with its obvious class connotations), preferring instead labels such as "back-to-the-city movement", "neighborhood revitalization", and "brownstoning", all of which were indicative of underlying divergences in what was believed to be central to this process.

Each term has its own little history. The term 'brownstoning', for example, came out of the brownstoning movement in New York City. A brownstone is a building constructed of, or faced with, a soft sandstone which weathers as a chocolate brown color (see Plate 1.2). The progentrification group the Brownstone Revival Committee was founded in New York City in 1968 by Everett Ortner, a pioneer gentrifier in Park Slope (see case study 2 in this chapter). The committee's magazine, *The Brownstoner*, advocated brownstone living, provided historical analysis and rehabilitation tips, and voiced news and

**Plate 1.2** Brownstone Houses in Park Slope, Brooklyn

These brownstones cost well over a million dollars each now.
*Source:* Photograph by Loretta Lees.

issues surrounding brownstones and their gentrification. Brownstoning was stylized as an act of love:

> I think one should approach the acquisition of a brownstone, the way one goes into a love affair: eyes open, but half closed too.... Pipes can be fixed, cracked walls repaired, painted woodwork stripped, old heating plants replaced. Those are only incidentals. What really counts is love.... To the non-lover it is merely a rowhouse. To the brownstone connoisseur, it is part of an architecturally homogeneous cityscape, scaled perfectly for its function, housing many but offering each person space and privacy and a civilized style of living. ('The Brownstoner' 1969; reprinted in 1991)

*The Brownstoner* got involved in the politics of gentrification. For example, in 1984 *The Brownstoner* published an article arguing, 'Gentrification is not "genocide" but "genesis"' ('Gentrification: Genesis Not Genocide'; see Plate 1.3).

In 1972, the annual Brownstone Conference was established by a Brooklyn realtor. Initially it was formed as a brownstone bank to alleviate the redlining (the refusal of banks and mortgage companies to finance mortgages in risky inner-city locations, granting mortgages on the basis of location rather than considering individual credit) of brownstones, then it ran an annual fair at the Brooklyn Union Gas headquarters and an annual ball at the Montauk Club in Park Slope. The Back to the City Conference established in 1974, also by Everett Ortner, set out to promote historic brownstone living. The first conference, held in New York's Waldorf-Astoria and sponsored by the Economic Development Council of New York City, the National Trust for Historic Preservation, the Municipal Art Society of New York, and Brooklyn Union Gas, followed the themes of preservation, finance, and promotion:

> The fact that the Brownstoners invested time and energy into using the media and government indicates that they had, on some level, grasped a basic fact about modern urban neighborhoods, namely that they exist within a larger framework. To establish social or geographic boundaries, neighborhood residents must have their claims recognized by external factors in the city's polity and economy. (Kasinitz 1988: 169)

*[handwritten margin note: Brownstoners used media & govt to est. social/geo boundaries]*

But what is particularly interesting is how the state in both the United States and the United Kingdom, for some time now, has refused to use the term 'gentrification', even when its policies were exactly that. As Neil Smith (1982: 139) has argued, 'A number of other terms are often used to refer to the process of gentrification, and all of them express a particular attitude towards the process'. In New York City, for example, in the 1970s the term 'homesteading' was often used in place of gentrification. Homesteading was a term derived from the U.S. Department of Housing and Urban Development's Urban Homesteading program that transferred vacant and abandoned

**Plate 1.3** Gentrification Is Not 'Genocide' but 'Genesis'

VOLUME 15 NUMBER 2 JULY 1984

# THE BROWNSTONER

NEWSLETTER OF THE BROWNSTONE REVIVAL COMMITTEE
200 MADISON AVENUE 3RD FLOOR NEW YORK, NEW YORK 10016

## Gentrification — Clarified

THE MYTH OF GENTRIFICATION has now been blasted by a new, 150-page report released (March 1984) by the New York Department of Planning. The report, ordered by the Mayor, is titled: Private Re-investment and Neighborhood Change, and does nothing less than document over and over again what City Planning sees as the benefits of the brown-stone movement, although that phrase never appears in its pages.

Another word that does not make an appearance is "gentrification", a word that has come to have a negative connotation in many circles. The City clearly prefers the word "reinvestment".

Gentrification describes areas in which development activity (whether private, government-aided or a combination of both) results in the displacement of low- or moderate-income families by those in higher income categories. This is regarded as desirable by some and undesirable by others. The study's findings, however, which are based on statistical analyses--mostly census data--provide some compelling support in favor of the gentrification process.

Park Slope neighborhood in Brooklyn and the Upper West Side in Manhattan were selected as subjects of this study. They were selected because of their visible private investment activity and their proximity to the city's two major parks, good public transportation and their resurgence of economic atmosphere. Gentrification is not "genocide" but "genesis".

## Florida Art Deco —

*Nathaniel Hendricks, President, Back to the City, Inc.*

THE 11TH ANNUAL BACK TO THE CITY CONFERENCE, sponsored by the Miami Design Preservation League, the Metro Dade Community & Economic Development, and Back to the City, Inc., was held April 13-15, 1984 in the Art Deco National Historic District, Miami Beach, Florida.

Historic structures always bring to mind inveterate images of colonial farmhouses, federal style city halls, and for me especially, Brooklyn brownstones and rowhouses. So it was a shock to see buildings of turquoise, yellow, pink and stainless steel when I entered historic Miami Beach for the 11th Annual Back to the City Conference.

continued on page 7

## Brownstone — The Real Thing

*This article by Ron Roth, a member who has studied architecture at the Columbia University Historic Preservation School, a Division of the Architectural School, is interesting and informative. He has also studied psychology and has been six years with the Landmarks Preservation Commission in research and design review. He is currently working on a book on "Starlight Park", an amusement park in the Bronx (1918-1946). One largely concrete building (now an MTA garage) still stands at Cross Bronx Expressway at 177th Street which is the geographic center of the Bronx, on the Bronx River.*

BROWNSTONE is a building quality sandstone composed of mineral grains held together by a cementing substance. It varies in structure and composition. Slabs are quarried from beds which range from fissile seams to seamless masses. As in other sandstones, false bedding or cross-grain is common to brownstone. False bedding causes a great deal of waste and makes the stone difficult to quarry and dress properly. Such stone nearly always has alternating streaks and patches of fine-grained and course-grained stone. Water in contact with brownstone can remove some of the cement and portions of the mineral grains which constitute the stone.

Like all other sandstones, the brownstones vary from textures like shales and slates, to the coarse conglomerate or pudding stone. Coarse-grained varieties look well in rock-face work. The finer grained varieties are better for fine carving or a tool-dressed surface, but can be adapted to rock-face work as well. The best texture is homogeneous throughout and not very coarse, but a uniformly coarse-grain is better than a mixture of fine and coarse. As a rule the coarse-grained sandstones are more porous and absorb water more freely, but less likely to be laminated or reedy, less liable to have clay seams, and generally are able to be worked more freely in all directions. The fine-grained sandstones are generally stronger, but less elastic, not so apt to disintegrate, but more apt to crack or shell. A rubbed surface is the most desirable finish for brownstone. Sand was used for the rubbing, or sand followed by grit.

As of 1896, reliable information on different brownstones was very scarce and widely scattered. It is believed that there is probably not another color common in building stones that is as permanent and as little liable to tarnish as brown. When brownstone is used to excess, particularly dark shades and along narrow streets, it can be gloomy and sombre. The darker shades, however, show dirt and stain less. 
continued on page 10

The Brownstone Revival Committee was adamant that gentrification was a positive thing.
*Source: The Brownstoner, 1984. Reprinted with permission of The Brownstoner.*

single-family houses to the city, who then offered them up for sale at a nominal sum, for example $1, to families willing to rehabilitate them and live in them for at least three years. This scheme was instrumental in the gentrification of neighborhoods like the Lower East Side in New York City (Lees and Bondi 1995). We return to the politics of the term 'gentrification' in more detail in Chapter 4.

## Definitions of Gentrification

Early definitions of gentrification by authors such as Neil Smith (1982: 139) were closely aligned to Glass's (1964) description:

> By gentrification I mean the process by which working class residential neighbourhoods are rehabilitated by middle class homebuyers, landlords and professional developers. I make the theoretical distinction between gentrification and redevelopment. Redevelopment involves not rehabilitation of old structures but the construction of new buildings on previously developed land.

By the early 1980s, the term 'gentrification' could easily be found in different dictionaries—and the definitions mirrored closely that of Smith above. The 1980 *Oxford American Dictionary* defined 'gentrification' as the 'movement of middle class families into urban areas causing property values to increase and having the secondary effect of driving out poorer families'; whilst the 1982 *American Heritage Dictionary* defined it as the 'restoration of deteriorated urban property especially in working-class neighborhoods by the middle and upper classes'. The 2004 *American Heritage Dictionary* has altered that definition only slightly: 'the restoration and upgrading of deteriorated urban property by middle class and affluent people, often resulting in displacement of lower-income people'. The 2000 *Dictionary of Human Geography*, however, in an entry written by Neil Smith, signified that the term itself was bound to change as the process evolved:

> **gentrification** The reinvestment of CAPITAL at the urban centre, which is designed to produce space for a more affluent class of people than currently occupies that space. The term, coined by Ruth Glass in 1964, has mostly been used to describe the residential aspects of this process but this is changing, as gentrification itself evolves. (N. Smith 2000: 294; emphasis in original)

It was apparent by the early 1980s that the residential rehabilitation that Ruth Glass had described was only one facet of the gentrification process. As cities sought ways to reimagine themselves out of deindustrialization, urban waterfronts were redeveloped, hotel and convention complexes were built, and retail and restaurant districts developed. These were deliberately constructed as middle-class spaces in the central city. This led Neil Smith (1986: 3) to argue that gentrification is

a highly dynamic process ... not amenable to overly restrictive definitions; rather than risk constraining our understanding of this developing process by imposing definitional order, we should strive to consider
the broad range of processes that contribute to this restructuring, and to
understand the links between seemingly separate processes.

In Chapter 4 we will look at how the term 'gentrification' has changed and
mutated over time to accommodate this dynamic and changing process, but
first we take a look in more detail at classical gentrification because it is against
this early form that all other types of gentrification are compared.

## Classical Gentrification

Classical gentrification is the type or wave of gentrification that Ruth Glass
(1964) based her coinage of the term on. Here, disinvested inner-city neighborhoods are upgraded by pioneer gentrifiers and the indigenous residents
are displaced. Working-class housing becomes middle-class housing. The
following two case studies of pioneer or classical gentrification, taken from
Lees (1994a), detail this process on different sides of the Atlantic, revealing the
multitude of actors, institutions, and processes involved.

### Case Study 1: Barnsbury, London

Barnsbury is a residential neighborhood in the north London borough
of Islington, located approximately two miles from the City of London
(see Map 1.1). Barnsbury was built as an upper-middle-class suburb around
1820 on hilltop fields stretching northwards; the housing is composed of
terraces and freestanding villas (see Plate 1.4):

> Unadorned Georgian streets lead to late Georgian stuccoed and balco-
> nied houses by way of unique squares—the expansive ovate Thornhill
> Square, the arcadian Barnsbury Square, the curiously Gothic Lons-
> dale Square, and the elegant Gibson Square from which the starkness
> of Milner Square's French Mechanical Style can be glimpsed. (Pring
> 1968/1969: 2)

But after the Second World War, Barnsbury went into decline, and its upper-
middle-class residents moved to the suburbs as swathes of suburban housing were built around London. This was a process similar to 'white flight' in
the United States, but whereas Americans fled from race (i.e., from people of
color), the residents of Barnsbury fled from the working classes: 'A combination of class fear and railway engineering turned a vast stretch of residential
London into a no-mans land.... Camden Town, Holloway, Islington, were
abandoned to the hopelessly entrenched working class' (Raban 1974: 80).

As in the United States, the suburbanization of London was facilitated by the
state. Abercrombie's *Greater London Plan* (1944), which became the blueprint
for the postwar reconstruction of London, institutionalized the valorization

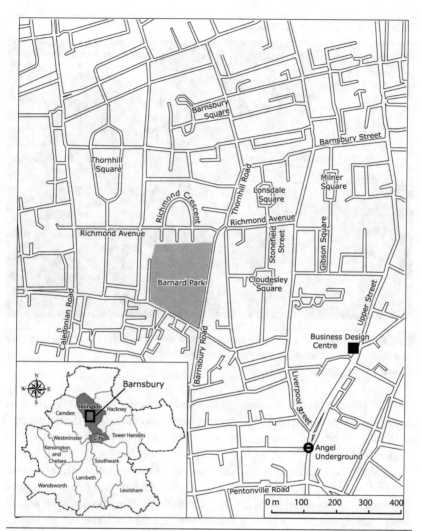

**Map 1.1** Barnsbury, Islington, London

of the suburbs and the devalorization of the inner city. This was further entrenched by the 1952 New Town Development Act, which exported 30,000 Londoners to expanded towns such as Bury St. Edmunds. The properties they left behind rapidly went into multioccupation. In postwar London, the demand for housing was greater than the available supply, but the pressure caused by demand was differential throughout London. In Barnsbury the pressure was great due to its large stock of privately rented accommodation located minutes from central London. Those demanding housing in Barnsbury were too poor to buy and did not qualify for council (social) housing. In 1961 13 percent of the population were born in Ireland, Malta, Cyprus, and the British Caribbean.

**Plate 1.4** Thornhill Crescent, Barnsbury

Barnsbury has a number of squares and crescents, all of which have distinctive architectures. This architectural aesthetic attracted pioneer and later waves of gentrifiers.
*Source:* Photograph by Loretta Lees.

Statistically Barnsbury was one of the areas of greatest housing stress in London. In 1961 62 percent of Barnsbury's households lived in shared accommodation in comparison to only 30 percent in the County of London (London Borough of Islington 1966: 6). In a 1968 pilot survey in Matilda Street, Barnsbury, by the London Borough of Islington, out of 160 households interviewed, 127 had no access to a bath, 138 shared a toilet, 15 had no kitchen sink, and 25 were living in overcrowded conditions (1969: 13). Barnsbury was an area of severe housing stress, as this vignette from the Matilda Street survey shows: '[O]ne old lady of nearly 80 could only manage to go to the outside WC by going down the 4 or 5 steps on her backside. The highest hopes she had were that the council were going to provide her with a commode'. The degree of overcrowding found in Barnsbury illustrates the housing stress at the time, and the decline in overcrowding is directly linked to gentrification. In 1961, 20.8 percent of households lived in rooms of more than 1.5 people; in 1971, 12.4 percent; in 1981, 6.4 percent; and in 1991, only 1.8 percent.

Pioneer gentrifiers began moving into Barnsbury in the late 1950s. However, 'it was extremely difficult to obtain funds during the 1950s and 1960s.... [F]or house purchases, success in obtaining them was largely a reflection of personal connections' (Williams 1976: 76). There was little private finance in Barnsbury until the late 1950s, when the 1959 Housing Purchase and Housing Act made

£100 million available to building societies to increase owner-occupation and invest in old property (Williams 1976: 74). This shift can be associated with the beginnings of gentrification in Barnsbury. The main influx of middle-class people occurred from 1961 to 1975, when Barnsbury's professional managerial class increased from 23 to 43 percent (UK Census). These pioneer gentrifiers were architects, planners, university lecturers, comprehensive school teachers, social workers, the police, and medical photographers, and they were overwhelmingly Labour voting (Bugler 1968). As one pioneer gentrifier put it,

> I like the place because there's such a lack of the products of English public schools. My man, and all that. People aren't affected here as they are in Chelsea, Hampstead or South Kensington. (Anthony Froshang, graphic designer, in Carson 1965: 395)

But building societies only really began to take an interest in Islington after 1972, when increasing numbers of the middle classes bought homes in the area (Williams 1978: 23–24). One board of directors visited an architect's rehabilitated house to see what their loan had achieved; they were impressed, and situations like this increased their confidence in the area (Williams 1976).

The rapid tenurial transformation that occurred in Barnsbury between 1961 and 1981 is quite striking; owner-occupation increased from 7 to 19 percent, furnished rentals declined from 14 to 7 percent, and unfurnished rentals from 61 to a mere 6 percent (UK Census). Hamnett and Randolph (1984, 1986) analyzed this tenurial transformation—the 'flat break-up market' in central London—which emerged as part of a broader national trend where blocks of privately rented apartments were sold for individual owner-occupation in a wave of conversions from the 1960s through the 1980s. These changes were not purely the result of the actions of individual gentrifiers. Hamnett and Randolph's (1986) 'value gap' thesis (see Box 2.2) emphasizes the political and institutional context shaping the actions of developers, landlords, buyers, and renters in central London at this time. It was the 'value gap' (the relationship between a building's tenanted investment value and its vacant possession value, the former being a measure of the rented building's annual rental income, and the latter a measure of the property's future sale price when it is converted into owner-occupation—the landlord sells off the building when the gap widened sufficiently) and its attendant tenurial transformation that was the main 'producer' (see Chapter 2, on production explanations) of gentrification in Barnsbury. The value gap became important in Barnsbury in the late 1950s and especially the 1960s, for landlords were getting a decreasing return on their rented property (due to new rent control and occupancy regulations) and developers were realizing capital gains of £20,000 or so by buying up rented property, evicting the tenants, and selling it in a vacant state. The middle classes were a captive market, and building societies were releasing more funds to inner-city property (Pitt 1977: 9). The turning point for Barnsbury was associated with the 1957 Rent Act, which decontrolled unfurnished tenancies during a time of increasing home ownership. Before the act, rents were controlled at an arbitrary level, and the act was introduced to alleviate the poor condition of housing and its poor investment value. It allowed the landlord to change the market price of any property let after the act, and those with security of tenure lost it if they moved out of their controlled tenancies. The act made it legal, in London houses with a rateable value of over £40, to give most rent-controlled tenants six months to quit after a standstill period of fifteen months, or they could increase the rent. As a result Barnsbury suffered many cases of winkling, where tenants were forced to leave because of bribery and harassment.

In a report titled *David and Goliath*, Anne Power (1973) recites the story of Redsprings Property Company, who launched their property empire by buying a number of tenanted properties on Stonefield Street in Barnsbury from the Dove Brothers landlords for £2,000 (see Plate 1.5). They had to remove the tenants to realize their vacant value of £10,000–12,000. Tenants were bribed with sums of £250–900, some moved out of London, and others were rehoused by Islington Borough Council. In one severe case of winkling, two tenants had a bulging wall, and whilst they were out builders demolished the outer wall of their living room and bedroom, providing a full view to the street. A steel support was erected from the middle of one bed to the ceiling, and a note attached to it read, 'You dirty filthy bastard'! That same evening the law center worker who was chairman of the Tenants Association took out an injunction to prevent the landlords from undertaking any more building work. A screen was eventually placed over the gap, and six months later the wall rebuilt. The wall became 'a symbol in Stonefield Street of the tenants' determination and the landlords' not-so-kid-glove winkling tactics' (Power 1973, cited in Lees 1994a:140). There were other cases of 'Rachmanism'. Rachmanism refers to the unscrupulous tactics of the landlord Peter Rachman, who operated in London in the 1960s (see Green 1979). His name is synonymous with winkling at this time. The Rachman exposé came out of the Profumo sex scandal of 1963, and led to the Milner Holland *Report of the Committee on Housing* in 1964. Landlord David Knight was Barnsbury's Rachman. He evicted a twenty-three-year-old teacher from her flat on Barnsbury Road. She had reported him to a rent tribunal to get her rent reduced, and in response he cut off her electricity, locked her out, and threw out her belongings. She received a letter in which he said he would shoot her dead, then a week later a car pulled up to her and shone a light in her face, and the next day she got a note saying, 'Cop it kid, we shot at you, we missed by half an inch'! A telling sign of the times was a *London Property Letter* that stated, 'Properly done, conversions are the next best thing to counterfeiting for making money' (cited in Counter Information Services

**Plate 1.5** Stonefield Street, Barnsbury

In this street, and in many others, unscrupulous landlords tried to winkle tenants out of their homes.

*Source:* Photograph by Loretta Lees.

1973: 42). The Greater London Council (GLC) eventually jumped on the improvement bandwagon, too, and developed its own brand of 'welfare winkling'. A group of houses in Cloudsley Street and Batchelor Street were bought by the GLC for £90 each in 1966 and 1970, rehabilitated, and re-let to high-income tenants at £15 a week. Many of the original tenants were 'moved into appalling short life houses in North Islington and left to rot in the midst of slum clearance for over four years' (Cowley et al. 1977: 179). Then in the mid-1970s, the houses were offered to new tenants for £20,000 each.

Returning back to Hamnett and Randolph's (1986) 'value gap thesis' (see also Chapter 2), this is a useful one for explaining why different parts of Barnsbury gentrified at different times:

> In Barnsbury lease reversion assumed a particular importance for the gentrification process. Different properties in the area belonged to different landowning estates and their leases closed at different times, depending on when the estates were built.... The leases from the older estates owned by aristocratic or institutional landlords folded between 1920 and 1940. These owners sold their freeholds to private landlords because ground rents which had been high in the 19th Century had been eroded by 20th century inflation, because the landowner's capital was tied up and yielding no return, the security of tenure had been

extended to lessees, and the big freeholders were being condemned as slum landlords. It was the new freeholders, the private landlords, who were to profit from the flat break-up in central London after 1966, when private rented flats were sold into owner occupation and gentrification. Developers and private individuals waited in anticipation. The *London Property Letter* (February 1970) circulated amongst estate agents referred to Barnsbury as a "healthy chicken ripe for plucking". (Lees 1994b: 202)

The 1969 Housing Act demonstrated a new commitment from government to rehabilitation instead of just renewal. The act provided local authorities with the power to allocate discretionary improvement grants. The improvement grants were £1,000 and £1,200 for conversions (tax-free and per dwelling unit created). As the grants had to be met pound for pound by the improver, they automatically favored the more well-off improver or developer (Hamnett 1973: 252–253) and aided the gentrification process in Barnsbury. Initially there were no restrictions on the improvement grants; as such, a property could be sold immediately after rehabilitation/conversion with vast profits being realized. In 1971 56 percent of all Islington's improvement grants went to the wards of Barnsbury and St. Peters (Power 1972: 3), revealing the extent of renovation activity in the area at this time. Williams (1976: 74) found that up to 90 percent of those properties sold by estate agencies in Islington in the 1960s were of rented property converted into owner-occupation. By 1972 nearly 60 percent of Barnsbury's housing had been rehabilitated, and the new households consisted predominantly of middle-class owner-occupiers (Ferris 1972: 95). House prices had risen significantly over this period: for example, a house in Lonsdale Square which had cost £9,000 in 1966 cost £18,000 in 1969 and £35,000 in 1972 (nearly a fourfold increase in just six years). In 1974 Islington Council placed restrictions on its improvement grants so that applicants had to remain in their improved property for at least five years after rehabilitation.

Other government schemes which aided the gentrification process were the designation of parts of Barnsbury as a General Improvement Area and a Housing Action Area. The former aimed to encourage voluntary action in improving areas of private property by providing higher grants for properties and encouraging local authorities to undertake environmental improvements, and the latter sought rapid improvement through voluntary action by increasing the improvement grants allocated to these areas. But the pioneer gentrifiers themselves were also instrumental in blocking local authority redevelopment initiatives in the area and promoting private rehabilitation instead. They did this through the Barnsbury Association, which they formed in 1964. This amenity society wanted a policy of environmental improvement that would preserve and enhance Barnsbury's unique nineteenth-century townscape.

With contacts in Fleet Street and Whitehall, the Barnsbury Association was able to get its approach accepted as official planning policy for the area:

> The Barnsbury Association rapidly became the heroes of the planning pundits; "this is the way to improve a twilight area" wrote expert Professor Peter Hall. Not one of the planning experts who commented on the widely publicized Barnsbury Planning Exhibition in 1968 asked who was Barnsbury being improved for. (Cowley et al. 1977: 178)

The media connections of North London's pioneer gentrifiers were epitomized in the cartoon strip *Life and Times in NW1*, which first appeared in the *Listener* in 1967 and was featured in a pocket cartoon by Marc Boxer in the *Times* from 1969 to 1983.

After attaining conservation status in 1971, finance for repairs in Barnsbury was also available from the National Heritage Memorial Fund, from the Architectural Heritage Fund, and from various Housing Act grants (see Plate 1.6 for an example of an Islington Conservation and Maintenance Guide). But by the time the Barnsbury Action Group formed in 1970 as the 'official' opposition to the Barnsbury Association, the future of the area had already been determined (Cowley et al. 1977: 179). The Barnsbury Action Group was a small pressure group of about twenty-six people whose tactics included political lobbying, designing petitions, letters to the press, and so on (see Chapter 7 on resisting gentrification). They drew attention to the consequences of 'improvement' in Barnsbury, but in community organizing terms were not an unqualified success.

The social change that took place in Barnsbury was stark. During the late 1960s and early 1970s, when the most active and visible gentrification was occurring, class differences were overt:

> One of the tips of that whole iceberg of social pressures which is London is to be found in the Barnsbury district of Islington. Conflict is anachronistically visible there in the outward appearance of houses side by side with one another—some with all the marks of grey poverty; their neighbours smartly repainted and with all the externals of wealth. Whole streets in Barnsbury show these signs of transition; and neighbouring squares can there find themselves each in a different camp—whether of middle class contentment, or of slums. (Ash 1972: 32)

Space was one exemplar of class difference. Pitt (1977) mentions four houses in Lonsdale Square: two contained single-family middle-class owner-occupants, whilst the other two provided accommodation for forty-eight single working-class tenants in the furnished rented sector. Many of the working class 'resented the influx of "Chelsea-ites", that is, middle-class immigrants with totally different

**Plate 1.6** An Islington Conservation Guide

CONSERVATION AND MAINTENANCE GUIDE

# THE
# MID VICTORIAN VILLA
# 1850–1870

LONDON BOROUGH OF ISLINGTON

The villas in Alwyne Road,
London N1, have been taken
as examples for this leaflet, but
there may be differences or
variations with your property.

This leaflet sets out to illustrate the common architectural
and design features of the mid-Victorian villa, and suggests what
features are important to retain, restore and reinstate in order
to improve the value of the property and the street.

These guides (this one is from the late 1980s) are provided to all the residents living in conservation areas in Islington. They have become more detailed and regulatory over time. Individual neighborhoods with conservation status now have their own guides too.
*Source:* Islington Council.

lifestyles and value orientations' (Ferris 1972: 44). Some disliked the pioneer gentrifiers as much as they disliked ethnic minorities:

> I used to live in Barnsbury. I never did like the n-----s even though I work with them and lived next door to one. Then Barnsbury types moved in and started preaching to us we shouldn't be prejudiced and should love the blacks and then the b-----ds turned right round and kicked them out and then us after. (Power 1972, cited in Lees 1994a: 209 )

As gentrification progressed, those tenants in bad housing who felt threatened by the winkler were appalled to see the council spending money on a traffic scheme, tree planting, and new iron railings in smarter squares. Local residents were resentful that their children could not afford to live locally in houses that they had 'saved' during the war. They wanted to keep small industrial units in Barnsbury, whereas the incomers preferred antique shops and small offices that offered no employment to the locals (Pitt 1977: 9). Some of the pioneer gentrifiers wanted to live in a socially mixed neighborhood (see also Chapter 6 on gentrification and social mixing):

> The present trend towards a rising proportion of the middle classes in the population will continue. This will help create a better social balance in the structure of the community, and the professional expertise of the articulate few will ultimately benefit the underprivileged population. (Ken Pring, Barnsbury pioneer gentrifier and architect, quoted in Pitt 1977: 1)

Other gentrifiers, however, were much more negative about social mixing: 'I like to smile at them and stop for a talk. But I don't want to have tea with them'; and 'I don't think they quite understand why we want to pay so much money and go to so much trouble to live in these houses, which they don't like very much. All they want to do is leave them, and live out of London' (Bugler 1968: 228).

By the late 1970s, property speculation had dampened significantly as gentrification became firmly anchored in Barnsbury. In the 1980s, larger conversions were replaced by smaller-scale conversions, for example the conversion of single-family townhouses into one- or two-bed flats. We continue the story of gentrification in Barnsbury in Chapter 4.

*Case Study 2: Park Slope, New York City*

Park Slope is located in the Brooklyn borough of New York City (see Map 1.2). Park Slope was one of the first residential suburbs in New York City and experienced considerable growth in the last two decades of the nineteenth century due to the settlement of merchants, lawyers, doctors, and other professionals able to commute to Manhattan over the Brooklyn Bridge, which was completed in 1883. Park Slope soon became an elite residential

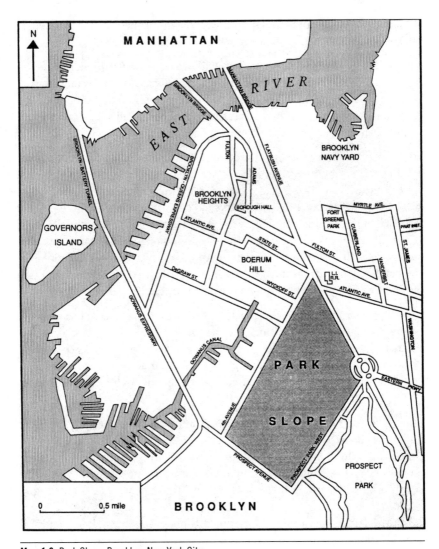

**Map 1.2** Park Slope, Brooklyn, New York City

community, second only to Brooklyn Heights in Brooklyn status, 'a magnet for Brooklyn's well-to-do, a retreat for those who wished to live lavishly' (Jackson and Manbeck 1998: 165) away from the increasing density of Manhattan. The upslope sections of the neighborhood have long contained the more expensive residences that housed this elite: architecturally distinctive 3–4-story single-family brownstones, some of the finest Romanesque Revival and Queen Anne houses in the United States (see Plate 1.7). Further down the Slope, more modest brownstones, brick-fronted properties, and 2–3-story wood frame row houses were built to house Eastern European and Irish servants, store owners,

**Plate 1.7** 6th Avenue and Berkeley Place, Park Slope

These large brownstone single-family houses were some of the first properties to be gentrified in Park Slope. For example, pioneer gentrifiers Everett and Evelyn Ortner bought in Berkeley Place. *Source:* Photograph by Loretta Lees.

dockland workers, and workers at the Ansonia Clock factory on 7th Avenue—the largest of its kind in the world by 1890 (see Plate 1.8).

Suburbanization affected Park Slope early, in the first decade of the twentieth century, when the middle classes moved to the then suburb of Flatbush. The brownstones they left behind became 'genteel' rooming houses and later, with the advent of the Great Depression in the 1930s, low-class rooming houses occupied predominantly by the Irish and Italian community. Over time landlords closed these buildings or let them decline into disrepair, and in the 1930s social planners began to call Park Slope a 'slum'. In the 1940s and 1950s, approximately 75 percent of Park Slope's housing stock was rooming houses with absentee landlords. The sections near Prospect Park retained their high-rent status, yet this area experienced the largest amount of subdivision (Justa 1984). After the Second World War, another wave of suburbanization ensued aided by the construction of the Long Island Expressway (see Seiden Miller 1979: 29) and the Verrazano Bridge, which opened in 1965 (facilitating the suburbanization of Staten Island), and the federal mortgage programs which made new suburban homes available for young families with little or no down payments. There was a white flight from Brooklyn of some 682,000 whites between 1940 and 1970 (Seiden Miller 1979: 26–32). 'White flight' away from Park Slope was taking place at a time of a significant increase in black and

**Plate 1.8** Wood Frame Row Houses in Park Slope

Wood frame row houses located mostly in the southern and eastern sections of Park Slope were for the most part gentrified later than the brownstone properties.
*Source:* Photograph by Loretta Lees.

Hispanic (especially Puerto Rican) settlement in the neighborhood, especially in the sections closer to the Gowanus Canal. In 1950, Park Slope was 99 percent white; by 1990, it was 52 percent white. Frank Torres, resident of Park Slope, summarizes the events of the time:

> [A] lot of people round here were civil servants—policemen, token clerks—and around the middle 60s their salaries became nicer, they started making $15,000 a year and they really thought they had made the big time and right away they had to buy a house with a garage and chimneys.... They went to Long Island and New Jersey—if they went to New Jersey they really wanted to go to California—and after the Verrazano Bridge was built they went to Staten Island, but they all left at the same time, when the blacks and the Puerto Ricans moved in during the early 60s. That chased even the poor white people out.... And the landlords who were getting $45 to $50 rents from working class people found out they could get $150 to $175 from welfare recipients. (Hodenfield 1986: 8)

In the United States up until the Second World War, less than half of the population was owner-occupiers and less than half of the available housing was single-family units. The years 1948–1960 saw a massive increase in home ownership following tax subsidies for owner-occupancy. Indeed, since the New Deal there had been attempts to increase owner-occupancy in the hope that it would act as a social stabilizer (Berry 1980: 10–11). At this time, as in Britain, there was a bias towards investment in new construction, rather than investment in old property; this was a function of federal tax codes. Suburbanization was part and parcel of the home ownership move in the United States, and highway construction facilitated the process.

In 1965 the *New York World Telegram* called Park Slope '[t]he run down area of downtown Brooklyn' (Watkins 1984). Systematic disinvestment locked the neighborhood into a spiral of economic decline and devalorization, resulting in physical deterioration and residential abandonment which reached a peak in Park Slope in the mid-1970s, particularly during the 1975–1977 fiscal crisis of New York City (Carpenter and Lees 1995: 293). One resident, Michael Eugenio, remembers, 'If you had anything worthwhile in your house, you had break-ins, they'd rob you blind. Your car wasn't safe in the street, tires would be missing, batteries would be missing' (Hodenfield 1986: 8). In 1972, there was vicious gang warfare in Park Slope between the Italian 'Golden Guineas' and the Puerto Ricans who moved into the area, some of whom set up dope rackets. That summer, dozens of people were assaulted, an eighteen year old had his legs blown off with a double-barreled shotgun, and a police car was overturned and hit with Molotov cocktails. Squatters and drug dealers moved into the abandoned buildings in the area, and candy stores did business behind bulletproof shields:

> Right across from where I live I watched them sell, shoot up, keel over from overdoses, and there were shootings, everybody diving under cars. We were prisoners in our houses and we started fighting. (Lew Smith of Berkeley Place, in Hodenfield 1986: 9)

In the midst of all this, pioneer gentrifiers or brownstoners began to move into Park Slope, but in fact a matrix of groups, underpinned by state and federal government legislation which encouraged reinvestment in 'rundown' neighborhoods (Squires 1992), were responsible for reinvestment in Park Slope. Pioneer gentrifiers, neighborhood groups and organizations, public utility companies, and property developers all contributed to the revalorization of Park Slope (Carpenter and Lees 1995: 295). In the pioneer phase of gentrification, many gentrifiers undertook their own work; this was known as 'sweat equity'. 'Sweat equity' was a loan provided to finance some of the rehabilitation costs of a property, where the prospective owners do much of the work themselves. 'Homesteading' was another term for it. Brownstoning in Park Slope was initially undertaken often without financial assistance; indeed, in the 1960s and 1970s there was active redlining of the area. Jan Maruca (1978: 3) sums up the problem of gaining access to a mortgage for Park Slope property in the 1970s: '[G]etting a mortgage might be compared to going on a

Big Game Safari: it requires careful advance preparation, proper equipment, skilful tracking—and still you may come home with an empty bag'.

In 1966, a group called the Park Slope Betterment Committee bought houses and began to advertise them through brokers to 'white collar workers'; their aim was to stabilize the area. This was heralded as 'private initiative' (*Civic News* 1969: 9). They were one of the first progentrification groups to emerge in Park Slope; their founder, Everett Ortner, had moved from Brooklyn Heights to Park Slope in 1963. He said, 'I realized that unless other people learned an appreciation for the community and began moving in, the area would eventually die'. Their sole ambition was to 'drum up business' and recruit like-minded others to establish Park Slope as a solid and vital community (Milkowski 1981). Initially each member pledged $250, and the money went towards putting up binders for the purchase of houses that the committee thought would interest young couples and for advertising the virtues of the neighborhood. By way of example, a four-story brownstone came up for sale on 6th Avenue; Joseph Ferris, then president of the Park Slope Betterment Committee, immediately placed a binder on the house and called two friends—Everett Ortner and Robert Weiss, a publishing executive. They called several friends, and the house was bought for $18,000 by friends of Weiss (Monaghan 1966). They sent brochures to Brooklyn Heights, Greenwich Village, and the West Side of Manhattan, obviously having a particular set of people in mind—gentrifiers. They gained the support of the Park Slope Civic Council, a not-for-profit organization that grew out of the South Brooklyn Board of Trade, which was concerned with civic issues in the area. The Park Slope Civic Council had already organized house tours in Park Slope: the first occurred as early as 1959, and such tours were effectively a form of public real estate promotion (see Plate 1.9).

In the early days, gentrification in Park Slope was not just about making profit. One journalist commenting on brownstoning in Park Slope noted, 'No one recommended buying brownstones as an investment per se. Most people noted that if they put their money into US treasury notes, if not Big Mac bonds, they would realize at least the same return with less effort' (Gershun 1975: 28). Gentrification was not just about economics, as Plate 1.10 shows. The new breed of middle-class brownstone owner in Park Slope was characterized as 'idealistic, unprejudiced, adventurous and energetic' (Holton 1968). Rothenberg (1995) discusses how Park Slope became home to one of the largest concentrations of lesbians living in the United States (see Chapter 3 on gay gentrification). Her account reveals the relationship between the neighborhood's gentrification and the well-educated liberal politics of the 'alternative' people who moved in during the 1970s. She tells how lesbians were attracted to the neighborhood's cheap housing and alternative community, and how mainly through word of mouth (Rothenberg's work is tellingly titled '"And She Told Two Friends"…'), Park Slope became a supportive, liberal, and tolerant queer space.

**Plate 1.9** An Advertisement for a Park Slope House Tour

# PARK SLOPE: THEN AND NOW

## 32nd Annual House Tour
## Sunday, May 19, 1991 Noon to 5 P. M.

Advance Tickets: $8.00

Weekdays – Art Bazaar, 197 Seventh Ave. (Between Second & Third St.)
Weekends – Key Food, Corner of Carroll St. & Seventh Ave.

Day of Tour Tickets: $10.00

Art Bazaar, also Ninth St.
and Seventh Ave., Northwest Corner

presented by the Park Slope Civic Council -- For More information call (718) 788-9150

These fliers were sent out by the Park Slope Civic Council in order to promote real estate and therein gentrification in their neighborhood.
*Source:* Park Slope Civic Council.

Ironically, given the displacement that occurred, Park Slope's pioneer gentrifiers were interested in keeping a socially mixed neighborhood and were concerned with homelessness and public or low-rent housing (see Chapter 6 on gentrification and social mixing). Nevertheless, in the early 1970s there was a

**Plate 1.10** Brownstone Brooklyn: 'A Place for All Reasons'

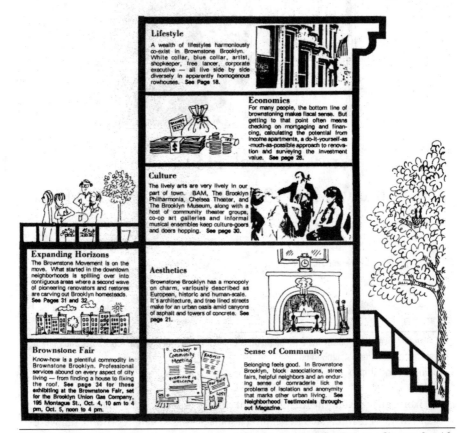

We get a clear sense here of the economic and cultural dimensions of gentrification—see Chapters 2 and 3.
*Source: The Phoenix,* 1975. Reprinted with permission of *The Phoenix.*

dual real estate market in Park Slope (O'Hanlon 1982: 145), one for blacks and one for whites. Blockbusting realtors would send out information on houses being for sale that were not for sale to stimulate turnover in the neighborhood, and brokers would buy houses from families in the poorer area west of 7th Avenue and sell them to blacks and Hispanics at twice the price.

Public utility companies were also active in the gentrification of Park Slope in an attempt to stabilize the area. Their initiatives were part of the 'greenlining' movement designed to persuade banks to cooperate in the restoration of Brooklyn's neighborhoods by providing mortgages and other loans. As early as 1965, Brooklyn Union Gas restored a four-story brownstone in Park Slope which was too large to be revitalized by the public. At this time there was no government aid for revitalization; therefore, people in Park Slope approached Brooklyn Union Gas for help. The Brooklyn Union Gas Company 'saved' Prospect Place, between 6th Avenue and Flatbush Avenue, by adapting three old abandoned stores into one-story residences and renovating the exteriors of other buildings on the block, including the trompe l'oeil paintings on the sides of three of the buildings (Muir 1977: 33). The scheme was financed by Greater New York Savings Bank and the Federal Housing Association. This and other projects were referred to as the 'Cinderella Schemes': 'What was sound and sturdy was restored! What was ugly was made beautiful—just like Cinderella' ('Civic News' 1972: 10–13). The Cinderella schemes attempted to bring about change by stimulating the private sector to invest in the revitalization of threatened neighborhoods. Brooklyn Union Gas also opened the Brownstone Information Center, which gave the public information on the basics of reno- vation and rehabilitation and sponsored workshops in conjunction with the Park Slope Civic Council's annual house tours. In the early 1970s, William E. Hand of Brooklyn Union Gas said, 'One of the vital signs of a healthy New York City is the incredible rebirth of decrepit blocks into attractive middle income neighborhoods' ('Civic News' 1973: 4). It was no coincidence though that such revitalization stabilized Brooklyn Union Gas's customer base and helped profit margins in decaying neighborhoods—note the references to gas in this description of the restorations in the Prospect Place project mentioned earlier: 'The gas-lit outside appeal of the new homes is complemented by the comfort features inside: year round gas air conditioning and plenty of living space that spills over into free-form backyard patios dotted with evergreen shrubbery and gas-fired barbeques' ('Civic News' 1972: 12).

Park Slope attained landmark status in 1973—the landmark conservancy offered tax rebates on building restoration and maintenance or a tax remis- sion to save certain landmarked buildings (see Map 1.3). Landmark status was secured due to the activities of pioneer gentrifiers and the Park Slope Civic Council. Evelyn Ortner, wife of Everett Ortner, documented the architecture and history of Park Slope and sent this to the Landmarks Preservation Com- mittee for scrutiny before landmark status was awarded.

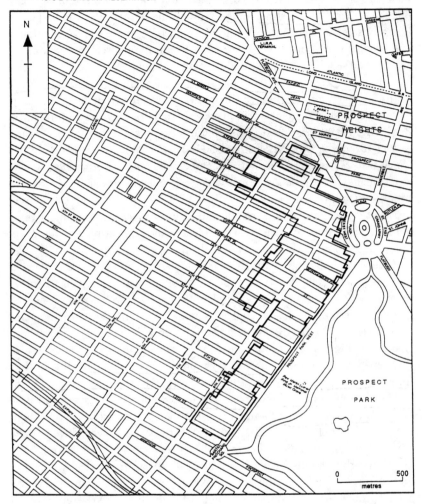

─── - 1973 LANDMARK PRESERVATION

**Map 1.3** The Park Slope Landmark District, 1973

If one adopts Neil Smith's (1979) 'rent gap schema' (see Chapter 2; see also N. Smith, Duncan, and Reid [1989], who operationalized it using tax arrears data) to establish the turning point at which disinvestment was succeeded by reinvestment in Park Slope, it was 1976, for that year had the highest rate, 7.1 percent, of buildings 5+ quarters in tax arrears (calculated from data on tax arrears for 1970–1980 in O'Hanlon 1982: 200). That cooperative (also known as 'co-op') and condominium conversions began in 1977 (New York City Department of City Planning 1985: 12) cannot be considered a coincidence, given there was no real interest from developers in undertaking such conversions before 1977, that is, before the closure of the 'rent gap'. Co-ops became very visible in the north and central Slope in the early

1980s (Griffin 1982: 26). The three census tracts that border Grand Army Plaza, Prospect Park West, 1st Street, and 6th Avenue, had 72 percent of Park Slope's conversion filings from the late 1970s to the mid-1980s. Indeed, between 1977 and 1984, applications were filed for 130 conversions; this made up 21 percent of the applications from the Borough of Brooklyn alone (Lees 1994b: 148).

During this first anchoring phase of gentrification, redlining was still rife; in one such example, in 1977 Bart Meyers and Alice Radosh wanted to buy a four-story brownstone in Park Slope, which they planned to upgrade and convert. The house cost $79,000; they had a deposit of $20,000 in cash, an annual income of over $30,000, and no credit problems. They got the $59,000 mortgage they needed only after going to sixty-one banks, and then only because of a personal connection (Fried 1978: 23). Private mortgages and cash were consistently used to buy property in Park Slope between 1965 and 1988, but bank mortgages became more important after 1975, probably due to the 1977 Federal Community Reinvestment Act, which outlawed the discrimination caused by redlining undertaken by specific financial institutions, and the fact that in 1978 the act became state law in New York State. Probably affected by the 1977 act and 1978 law and by grassroots pressure, local commercial and savings banks initiated liberal mortgage programs in Park Slope after 1978 (O'Hanlon 1982: 150). Chase Manhattan Bank produced the Urban Home Loan Program, which was designed to booster the rehabilitation of vacant 1–4-family homes, offering acquisition, construction, and permanent financing in one package at its prime lending rate. Citibank became the main lending institution; in fliers, it laid claim as 'the bank that helped preserve Park Slope's history', and it even designed a Citibank tote bag with a distinctive Park Slope logo. Although there were numerous federal programs at the time providing capital for property rehabilitation (see Lees 1994b: 201–203), most of the reinvestment in Park Slope seems to have occurred without the assistance of public subsidies. Indeed, following on the heels of the Cinderella scheme discussed earlier, another utility company, Con Edison, offered similar help in the form of its 'Renaissance' housing rehabilitation programs. One example was the former Higgins Ink building on 8th Street between 4th and 5th Avenues, which was converted into ten middle-income co-op apartments. Paul Kerzer, an early coordinator of Con Edison's Renaissance program, said, 'We believe Brooklyn has embarked on a major renaissance of neighborhood stability and of rebuilding our major preservation efforts' ('The Brownstoner' 1981: 9). The Renaissance program was designed to make more co-op apartments available and offered legal, architectural, and financial services to the community. The state was also a player in the process of gentrification in New York City and Park Slope at this time with federal policies such as Section 203(k) Rehabilitation Mortgage Insurance, Community Development Block Grants, and the like, and state government programs such as New York City's J-51 Program (which gave tax exemption and tax abatement), which was used to rehabilitate 9.7 percent of Park Slope's multifamily units between 1970 and 1980 (Lees 1994b: 210–211).

During this anchoring phase of gentrification, active displacement occurred. For example, in 1981 the tenants of a Garfield Place apartment block due to be renovated into six co-ops were harassed by the landlord cutting off their heat and hot water for ten days in October, sealing off the basement, and denying them access to fuse boxes and the backyard. One tenant said, 'There is a large displacement going on in Park Slope and people don't have any place to turn' (Goodno 1982: 1). The politics of gentrification in the area were complicated—the main grassroots actor in the area was, and still is, the Fifth Avenue Committee, which was/is prorehabilitation but antigentrification (see Chapter 7 for a detailed case study of the Fifth Avenue Committee):

> There are few options for improving the quality of life in the neighborhood beyond bringing in capital. ... But the question remains for whom. We want to attract capital into the area but we don't want to be washed out with it. (Fran Justa, former president of the Fifth Avenue Committee, quoted in DeRocker 1981: 6)

From the mid-late 1980s onwards, a more mediated form of gentrification became apparent when co-op and condo conversions began to dominate—the developer as gentrifier was more noticeable, and 'Ready Maders' were created (Draper 1991: 177–178) where the purchaser would buy a property with a ready-made image. This marked the end of pioneer or classical gentrification in Park Slope. By this stage, the elite housing on Park Slope's upper slope was pretty much thoroughly gentrified. Later processes were quite different—by the mid-1990s, the upper slopes were experiencing 'super-gentrification' (Lees 2000), a topic discussed in Chapter 4, and the much cheaper lower slopes were experiencing overspill gentrification (see Chapter 7).

### Early Stage Models

The early stage models of gentrification developed in the 1970s and 1980s to both explain the process and predict the future course of gentrification mirrored Glass's definition of classical gentrification and generally described the changes as a filtering process in the manner of some of the early ecologists.

Clay (1979) produced one of the first major studies of gentrification. Undertaking a survey of expert informants, he found that private urban reinvestment had occurred in all of the largest U.S. cities in the late 1970s. Most of the American gentrified neighborhoods that he found were at least seventy-five years old, the houses were usually Victorian and occupied by working-class families, and some properties were abandoned. Clay (1979: 57–60) developed one of the first stage models of gentrification; he outlined a schema from stage 1 (pioneer gentrification) to stage 4 (maturing gentrification) (see Box 1.1).

---

**Box 1.1**

**Clay's (1979) Stage Model of Gentrification**

**Stage 1**

[A] small group of risk-oblivious people move in and renovate proper-ties for their own use. Little public attention is given to renovation at this stage, and little displacement occurs because the newcomers often take housing that is vacant or part of the normal market turnover in what is often an extremely soft market. This pioneer group accepts the risks of such a move.

Sweat equity and private capital are used almost exclusively, since conventional mortgage funds are unavailable. This first stage is well under way before it receives any public recognition, although even at this early stage the grapevine is spreading the word. The first efforts are con-centrated in very small areas, often two to three blocks. The first group of newcomers usually contains a significant number of design profession-als or artists who have the skill, time, and ability to undertake extensive rehabilitation. (In Boston, San Francisco and other cities, respondents suggested it was the homosexual community who made up the popula-tion. They seek privacy and have the money and the taste to take on this challenge. One observer suggested that "Smart money will follow homo-sexuals in cities.")

**Stage 2**

[A] few more of the same type of people move in and fix up houses for their own use. Subtle promotional activities are begun, often by a few percep-tive realtors. Small-scale speculators may renovate a few houses in visible locations for resale or rental. Rarely does a large speculator come in at this stage, because capital for investors and residents is still scarce. Those who come in at this stage seek units that are relatively easy to acquire—vacant buildings owned by absentee landlords, city-owned or tax-foreclosed properties.

Some displacement occurs as vacant housing becomes scarce. Those who come in stages one and two will later be considered the old-timers in this new neighborhood.

If the neighborhood is to have its name changed, it often happens at this stage. New boundaries are identified, and the media begin to pay attention to the area....

In some neighborhoods mortgage money becomes available, but the loan is more often secured by other property, given by the seller, or given for a relatively low percentage of the total investment. Renovation spreads to adjacent blocks.

## Stage 3

[A]t this stage major media or official interest is directed to the neighborhood. The pioneers may continue to be important in shaping the process, but they are not the only important ones. Urban renewal may begin ... or a developer ... may move in. Individual investors who restore or renovate housing for their own use continue to buy into their neighborhood. The trend is set for the kind of rehabilitation activity that will dominate. Physical improvements become even more visible because of their volume and because of the general improvement they make to the whole area. Prices begin to escalate rapidly.

Displacement continues. ...

The arrivals in this third stage include increasing numbers of people who see the housing as an investment in addition to being a place to live. These newer middle-class residents begin to organize their own groups or change the character of the pioneers' organization.

The organized community turns outward to promote the neighborhood to other middle-class people and to make demands for public resources. It turns inward to exert peer influence on neighbors and to shape community life. Tensions between old residents and the gentry begin to emerge. Social service institutions and subsidized housing are resisted with passion. Protective or defensive actions against crime are taken. If the new residents, especially the most recent arrivals, are less tolerant of lower or working-class behavior, these tensions may become serious. Banks begin to greenline the area, looking for spatial patterns of reinvestment and then making loans to middle-class buyers and investors within the limited area. ...

The popular image of the process of change at this stage is clearly gentrification and is treated as such by the media. The neighborhood is now viewed as safe for larger numbers of young middle-class professionals.

## Stage 4

[A] larger number of properties are gentrified, and the middle-class continues to come. What is significant about the new residents is that more are from the business and managerial middle class than from the professional middle class. ...

Efforts may be made to win historic district designation or to obtain other stringent public controls to reinforce the private investment that has taken place.

Buildings that have been held for speculation appear on the market. ... Small, specialized retail and professional services or commercial activities begin to emerge, especially if the neighborhood is located near the downtown or a major institution. Rapid price and rent spirals are set off. Displacement now affects not only renters but some home owners as well. Additional neighborhoods in the city are being discovered to meet the increasing demand of the middle class. While some controversy emerges, especially related to displacement, relatively little is done to dampen middle-class reinvestment.

*Source:* This is an abbreviated version of Clay (1979: 57–59).

He based his model on observations and data from a number of cities, including Boston's South End, Philadelphia's Society Hill, San Francisco's Western Addition, and Washington's Capitol Hill. He stated, 'The following elaborated typology of stages in the development of gentrification neighborhoods is useful for predictive purposes' (p. 57). But given that Clay's (1979) model was developed in the early days of the process, it is heavily skewed towards descriptions of pioneer or first-wave gentrification (see Chapter 5 for a more recent stage model). Clay recognizes this; as he says,

> This short summary of the process is all that the present set of cases allows. But this is not the end of the story. Not all the units have been taken by the middle class, and price and demand are still high. There is room for substantial growth of the middle class population within the present gentrification areas.... Because relatively few neighborhoods have actually completed gentrification, the mature gentrified neighborhood cannot be described as confidently as the process. (p. 59)

As such, it is much less useful as a tool for describing later processes of gentrification in the 1980s and 1990s. Do note the assumption that the neighborhoods will move towards a stage of complete gentrification, for in Chapter 4 we will discuss new processes of gentrification that are occurring that contradict such predictions of an endpoint of mature gentrification. Clay's model is also a very American model—as such, some of the elements are not ones that would have been found in the United Kingdom, or elsewhere, at that time. But perhaps what is most striking about Clay's model is that it states Richard Florida's (2003) thesis on the creative class (see Preface) twenty-three years before it was developed! And contra the new policy ideas about gentrification and social mixing in the United Kingdom and elsewhere (see Preface and Chapter 4), stage 3 suggests not harmonious mixing but actual conflict!

Writing at the same time, Gale (1979) formulated a classic gentrification model that underlined class and status distinctions between old and new residents in a gentrifying neighborhood. He drew on research in three areas at different stages of the gentrification process in Washington, D.C. Unlike with 'incumbent upgrading', where residents rehabilitate their own homes without an associated population turnover, Gale's model of classical gentrification emphasized population change in terms of the displacement of former working-class residents. The gentrifier type is described by Gale as follows:

> The most typical such household is childless and composed of one or two white adults in their late twenties or thirties. College educated, often possessing graduate education, the household head is most likely a professional or (less commonly) a manager. The annual household income … is likely to range between $15,000 and $30,000 (the US median was about $14,900 in 1977) with several resettlers earning more than $40,000. (1979: 295)

The differences between Clay's (1979) and Gale's (1979) stage models of gentrification indicate how different emphases and interests in gentrification research lead to different 'pictures' or 'stories' of the process (as we shall see in Chapters 2 and 3).

One of the reasons that stage models of gentrification were developed was to cope with the temporal variations in gentrification that were already apparent in the 1970s. Gentrification stage models were designed to represent gentrification in an orderly, temporal, sequential progression. Risk is center stage in these models, for in the first stage or pioneer stage, risk-oblivious households are seen to move into risky neighborhoods. The pioneer gentrifier works in the cultural professions, is risk oblivious, wants to pursue a nonconformist lifestyle, wants a socially mixed environment, and rehabilitates his or her property using sweat equity. Then more risk-conscious mainstream professionals move in, some with young families. Realtors and developers start to show an interest, and as property prices increase the original residents might be pushed out. Over time, older and more affluent and conservative households move in, attracted to what is now a safe investment. Eventually, gentrification is seen to stabilize at an endpoint of mature gentrification.

Rose (1984) was one of the first people to question the way that gentrification was being conceptualized. She was concerned about the generalized descriptions of typical gentrifiers and typical gentrified neighborhoods. Rose (1984) criticized stage models for lumping together different processes and effects; she preferred to see gentrification as a 'chaotic concept' in which different actors, housing tenures, motives, and allegiances coexisted. For Rose, 'the terms "gentrification" and "gentrifiers" … are "chaotic conceptions" which obscure the fact that a multiplicity of processes, rather than a single causal process, produce changes in the occupation of inner-city neighbourhoods from the lower to higher income residents' (1984: 62). Interestingly, despite her criticisms, Rose has a go at defining gentrification based on population turnover defined on the basis of residents' incomes. At the end of Chapter 4, we discuss the conceptualization of gentrification as 'chaotic' and outline a less chaotic take on the process, drawing on Clark (2005).

## Summary

In this chapter, we looked at the birth of gentrification as a process and the coining of the term. We looked at different definitions of the process and different terms for the process. The two case studies of classical gentrification—one in London and one in New York—show in detail the neighborhood trajectories from disinvestment to reinvestment that are the focus of the production explanations in Chapter 2. Barnsbury illustrates the 'value gap', and Park Slope illustrates the 'rent gap'. The activities of pioneer gentrifiers that are the focus of the consumption explanations in Chapter 3 are also listed in detail—their sweat equity, the politicization of interest groups and their greenlining activities, and their commitment to a new urbane way of life. We conclude the chapter with a look at the early stage models that were developed to try to explain the process before turning to explanations in more detail in Chapters 2 and 3, and updating these stage models in Chapter 5.

## Activities and Exercises

- Watch the movies *Batteries Not Included* (1987; director: Matthew Robbins; presented by Steven Spielberg) and/or *High Hopes* (1988; director: Mike Leigh).
- Think about how Clay's (1979) gentrification stage model corresponds to the case studies presented here of Barnsbury and Park Slope.
- Read the critique of stage models of gentrification in Damaris Rose (1984), 'Rethinking Gentrification: Beyond the Uneven Development of Marxist Urban Theory,' in *Environment and Planning D: Society and Space*.
- Read some different stories of pioneer gentrification: on the Lower East Side, see Abu-Lughod (1994) and Neil Smith (1996a); on Kitsilano in Vancouver, see Ley (1981, 1996); on the Lower East Side and Park Slope, see Lees and Bondi (1995); and on Society Hill in Philadephia and False Creek in Vancouver, see Cybriwsky, Ley, and Western (1986).
- Read the conference papers in van Weesep and Musterd (1991), *Housing for the Better-Off: Gentrification in Europe*, to learn about gentrification in different parts of Europe and how it might differ from the cases shown here. On Amsterdam, read Neil Smith (1996a: 166–173).

- Read Joseph Barry and John Derevlany (eds.), *Yuppies Invade My House at Dinnertime: A Tale of Brunch, Bombs, and Gentrification in an American City* (1987; Hoboken, NJ: Big River Publishing). This book is a collection of letters from the *Hoboken Reporter* that are testimony to the intense gentrification that Hoboken, New Jersey, underwent in the 1980s.

## Further Reading

Badcock, B. (2001) 'Thirty years on: Gentrification and class changeover in Adelaide's inner suburbs, 1966–96', *Urban Studies* 38:1559–1572.

Carpenter, J., and L. Lees. (1995) 'Gentrification in New York, London and Paris: An international comparison', *International Journal of Urban and Regional Research*, 19, 2: 286–303. Reprinted in M. Pacione (ed.) *Land-Use, Structure and Change in the Western City*, vol. 2 of *The City: Critical Concepts in the Social Sciences* (London: Routledge) 544–566.

Caulfield, J. (1989) *City Form and Everyday Life: Toronto's Gentrification and Critical Social Practice* (Toronto: University of Toronto Press).

Glass, R. (1989) *Clichés of Urban Doom* (Oxford: Blackwell). (Read pp. 132–158 and 159–183.)

Holcomb, H. B., and R. A. Beauregard (1981) *Revitalizing Cities* (Washington, DC: Association of American Geographers).

Lees, L. (1994b) 'Gentrification in London and New York: An Atlantic gap?' *Housing Studies* 9, 2: 199–217.

Lyons, M., and J. Gelb (1993) 'A tale of two cities: Housing policy and gentrification in London and New York', *Journal of Urban Affairs* 15, 4: 345–366.

van Weesep, J., and S. Musterd (1991) *Housing for the Better-off: Gentrification in Europe* (Utrecht, the Netherlands: Stedelijke Netwerken).

Zukin, S. (1982) *Loft Living: Culture and Capital in Urban Change* (Baltimore: John Hopkins University Press).

**Plate 2.1** 'Landlord Wants Us Out or Dead', Lower East Side, 1988

Evictions and displacement were high in the Lower East Side during the mid- to late 1980s as landlords and developers sought to close the rent gap.
*Source:* Photograph by Loretta Lees.

# 2

# Producing Gentrification

The urban wilderness produced by the cyclical movement of capital and its devalorization have, from the perspective of capital, become new urban frontiers of profitability. Gentrification is a frontier on which fortunes are made. From the perspective of working-class residents and their neighborhoods, however, the frontier is more directly political rather than economic. Threatened with displacement as the frontier of profitability advances, the issue for them is to fight for the establishment of a political frontier behind which working-class residents can take back control of their homes: there are two sides to any frontier.

N. Smith (1986: 34)

Forty years after Ruth Glass coined the term 'gentrification' to describe the class transformation of urban space, the politics of naming seemed to enter a new, self-consciously satirical phase. One prominent epicenter of this shift was New York City—birthplace of catchy monikers like SoHo, the area South of Houston Street on the southern edge of Greenwich Village, which had inspired countless imitations in other cities from the 1970s through the 1990s. After an unusual recession in 2001 that was marked by especially fast house price increases amidst falling interest rates, the speed of gentrification in New York intensified the competition to identify and name the latest, hippest edges of the frontier. Among the most memorable (if annoying) labels that appeared were Mea-Pa, the Meatpacking District, with NoMeat just to the north; Rambo, Right Across the Manhattan Bridge Overpass (next to Dumbo, Down Under the Manhattan Bridge Overpass, so known thanks to years of promotion by a single powerful developer); SoHa, South Harlem; and, perhaps most remarkably, SoBro, the South Bronx urban disaster memory of arson fires in the 1970s now celebrated on the front page of the *New York Times* as follows: 'hundreds of artists, hipsters, Web designers, photographers, doctors and journalists have been seduced by the mix of industrial lofts and nineteenth-century rowhouses' (Berger 2005a: A1). Before long, humorists at the *New Yorker* found the name game irresistible: in a short piece titled 'Top Brokers Spot the Hot New Neighborhoods', Bruce McCall (2004: 28) profiled the city's leading fictional brokers at the most pretentious firms, including The Tweedy Group, Frick-Carnegie Homes, and Muffy St. Barnabus and Partners (Plate 2.2). Brokers extolled the virtues of WoFa, the old South Flushing site of the 1964 World's Fair, for 'refugees priced out of Dumbo'; while other buyers were encouraged to consider Whog (between the Whitestone and Throgs Neck Bridges), BruBou (the Bruckner Boulevard school bus parking lot), or MausoQuee (Mausoleums in

**Plate 2.2** From Soho to SoBro and WoFa?

TOP BROKERS SPOT THE HOT NEW NEIGHBORHOODS BY BRUCE McCALL

*Marcy Spence-Brearley,*
*The Tweedy Group*

"There's vibrant new life among the ruins in **WoFa**, the trendy South Flushing area cobbled into being on the site of the 1964-65 New York World's Fair by refugees priced out of Dumbo. The formerly forlorn gaggle of abandoned structures and cracked asphalt is a humming habitat for young artists, complete with all the amenities that define the bohemian life style: no Starbucks, no running water, no street cleaning, and no convenient subway stops."

GREATER NEW YORK AREA

*Wally Simpson-Windsor,*
*Watercress-Sherry*

"To increasing numbers of discriminating and unsentimental home buyers, the occasional fine for tomb desecration seems a small price to pay for the Gilded Age splendor on offer in **MausoQuee**, in the sylvan hush of sprawling New Calvary Cemetery, in Queens. All-granite construction, marble floors, stained-glass windows, and perpetual lawn care make mausoleum living gracious living, and it all comes with a sense of privacy meant to last through the ages."

*Cindy Whitebread,*
*Mayflower & Standish*

"Until last week, **Whog**, a stretch of shoreline between the Whitestone and Throgs Neck bridges, was little more than scrub grass and mud lapped by flotsam-littered tides. Now it has leaped to life as a pioneering outpost for New York's surprisingly populous and literally swinging bungee-jumping set, drawn by the proximity of two towering bridges and plentiful ambulance routes. There's nothing like a Sunday saunter along **Whog**'s waterside, where young daredevils gather to gaze skyward, amid hoarse choruses of 'Jump!' or softly murmured 'Uh-oh!'s."

*Chip Thurn und Taxis,*
*Muffy St. Barnabas & Partners*

"**UnGeoWa** is still more beachhead than neighborhood, but that hasn't deterred its growing population of New Jerseyites so eager for a Manhattan address that they're willing to swim the Hudson and set up house in old piano crates under the George Washington Bridge. Where else but **UnGeoWa** offers instant Manhattan prestige, sweeping river views, and home prices in the low three figures?"

*Freddie Bullion,*
*Frick-Carnegie Homes*

"The weed-choked rectangle of asphalt that they're calling **BruBou** is catching on fast with upper Manhattan's colorful bands of gypsies. Situated on the vast Bruckner Boulevard parking lot, where hundreds of roomy school buses (lots of windows!) sit empty between the hours of 5 P.M. and 6 A.M., **BruBou** is just the place for the peripatetic transient who doesn't mind moving in every night and moving out every morning. A tip for prospective **BruBou** homesteaders: never buy a school bus from a gypsy if he offers to throw in his niece."

Queens' New Calvary Cemetery). But the very hottest listings were trumpeted by Chip Thurn und Taxis:

> UnGeoWa is still more beachhead than neighborhood, but that hasn't deterred its growing population of New Jerseyites so eager for a Manhattan address that they're willing to swim the Hudson and set up house in old piano crates under the George Washington Bridge. Where else but UnGeoWa offers instant Manhattan prestige, sweeping river views, and home prices in the low three figures? (McCall 2004: 128)

It soon became clear, however, that the most bizarre images on the gentrification frontier were not fictional at all. After adjusting for inflation, condo prices in Manhattan stood at 138 percent of their level near the peak of the 1980s real estate bubble—and the figure topped 225 percent for single-family homes, duplexes, and other housing types (Bhalla et al. 2004: 95). The share of home owners in the Bronx spending more than 60 percent of their income on housing costs shot up from 11.3 percent to 20.0 percent between 1999 and 2002, and more than a fifth of all renters in the city devoted more than half of their income to rent (Bhalla et al. 2004: 115). Between 1999 and 2002, at least 2,000 New York renters were forced to move by landlord harassment, more than 2,900 were evicted, about 600 were displaced by highway construction or other government activities, more than 5,000 were displaced by other private action, and more than 39,000 moved because they needed a less expensive residence or had difficulty paying the rent (U.S. Bureau of the Census 2002). And in early 2006, the Associated Press reported a proposal to redevelop the old Brooklyn House of Detention (shuttered in 2003) as a mixed-use project with retail, housing, perhaps a hotel, and modernized cell blocks. The idea was proposed by Borough President Marty Markowitz, who said, 'I've already called developers, and there is an interest' (Caruso 2006). New condos are under construction not far from the old jail, and brownstones in the vicinity are going for more than $1.5 million; Markowitz argued, 'It would be foolish if the city does not take advantage of this super-hot real-estate market' (Julian 2006: 27). The *New Yorker* observed that Harlem's

---

**Plate 2.2 (Continued)** New York's Soho, an acronym for an area south of Houston Street that saw dramatic reinvestment beginning in the 1960s, inspired countless imitators in many cities. The tradition of creative names to promote the hottest, hippest new address has become especially competitive in recent years, with accelerated gentrification in places like Dumbo (Down under the Manhattan Bridge Overpass), NoMeat (North of the Meatpacking District), SoHa (Southern Harlem), and even SoBro—the South Bronx, a place once firmly entrenched in the American imagination as a desolate wasteland of poverty, abandonment, and arson. This satire, which appeared in the *New Yorker* in late 2004, captures some of the irrational exuberance that infected the competition to coin the newest, most marketable names for the edges of the gentrification frontier. Production accounts of gentrification emphasize that inner-city neighborhood transformation cannot be understood simply as the product of consumer preference or middle-class demand; the need to pursue profits plays a crucial role in the actions of developers, investors, and many other powerful groups involved in the urban land market.

*Source: McCall/The New Yorker, ©2004 Condé Nast Publications, Inc.*

Parkside Correctional Facility is already going condo as '10 Mount Morris Park West', and thus offers valuable lessons 'for anyone interested in breaking into the correctional-conversion sector' (Julian 2006: 27). First lesson:

> Pick the right neighborhood. Prisons aren't usually in affluent residential districts, so if the housing is to be high end (most of the Mount Morris condominiums will list for more than a million dollars) it will need to be in a neighborhood (like the Mount Morris Park Historic District) that is already being gentrified. (Julian 2006: 27)

These images constitute a tiny sample from the multitude of vignettes of contemporary gentrification, which 'has become not a sideshow in the city, but rather a major component of the urban imaginary' (Ley 2003: 2527). And it is central not only to the urban imaginary but also to the hard-edged calculus of speculation, risk, profit, and loss—and to the strong sense of entitlement expressed by Andres Duany's (2001) defense of the 'natural' process of home price appreciation. In this chapter, we consider the implications of Neil Smith's (1986: 34) insistence that gentrification is a 'frontier on which fortunes are made', and we scrutinize the motivations and logic followed by aggressive developers, flamboyant real estate brokers, savvy buyers in the market for million-dollar condos, and budget-conscious government officials. We examine production explanations—theories that explain how the possibility of winning enormous fortunes provides powerful incentives that shape the behavior of individuals, groups, and institutions that have a stake in what happens on the urban frontier. Although individuals and organizations certainly consider a wide variety of factors when they make the kinds of decisions that can affect a neighborhood, many of the constraints that narrow the field of attractive choices can be traced to fundamental rules of economic production in market economies. Production explanations show how neighborhood change is connected to underlying rules of the game—economic relations, legal principles and practices, institutional arrangements, and pure political struggles—in which value and profit are produced and distributed.

In this chapter, we begin by tracing how production explanations emerged in the 1970s in response to widespread popular fascination with an urban 'renaissance'. Many of the urgent questions people ask today about gentrification have been shaped in profound ways by the legacy of a previous generation of scholars—and developers, policy makers, and investors as well as displacees, activists, protesters, and community organizers. We need to consider the history of how certain urban processes have been understood at various points in time—while avoiding the temptation to see the history of ideas as a neat, orderly march of paradigms. Even today, perspectives on gentrification and neighborhood change remain the site of considerable disagreement. We then examine the single most influential production explanation, Neil Smith's rent gap framework, and its position in broader political–economic theories of the circulation of capital in the urban environment. Next we consider how problems with measuring and interpreting the rent gap and other aspects of production explanations inaugurated a series of vibrant debates over the meaning and significance of neighborhood transformation. Finally, we explore a new generation of studies that analyze the evolving dynamics of the production of gentrified landscapes.

## Back to the City? The Limits of Neoclassical Economics

In the late 1970s, the future of old industrial cities seemed uncertain and precarious. Especially in the United States, urban centers had been battered by deindustrialization and suburbanization since the 1950s. Suburbanization accelerated in the 1960s, when many middle- and working-class whites fled as African–Americans sought to challenge police brutality, housing and school discrimination, and other mechanisms of racial segregation and stratification (Jackson 1985; Sugrue 2005). At the same time, however, small pockets of the old inner city showed signs of reversal: in some places, government-driven urban renewal programs had created new offices, malls, or upscale residential developments for middle-class, mostly white households. Elsewhere, there seemed to be signs of 'spontaneous' neighborhood revitalization by middle-class households, many of them young, white, and well educated. After a massive spike in gasoline prices in 1973 (a shock that was repeated six years later), commuting costs spiraled for suburbanites even as the combined effects of recession, inflation, and high interest rates played havoc with housing market activity. All of these trends seemed to call into question the survival of the 'American dream' of owning the single-family suburban house.

In the midst of this gloomy picture, signs of change in several inner-city neighborhoods seemed to offer hope for a brighter urban future. Popular media observations of inner-city change led scholars and policy analysts to see an encouraging 'back to the city' movement that might be able to reverse the effects of decades of white flight suburbanization. In 1977, Everett Ortner (the Park Slope gentrifier we met in Chapter 1), the managing editor of *Popular Science Monthly*, claimed that '[b]ack to the city is an important movement that is going on in every city in the country' (quoted in Beauregard 2003b: 207). That same year, in one of the first widely cited scholarly analyses of gentrification, Gregory Lipton (1977) suggested that

> [w]hile the dominant pattern may involve the loss of a middle- and upper-income, predominantly white population from the center and their replacement by lower-income, predominantly black and other minority populations, a fairly large number of cities are experiencing some population changes running counter to this major trend. (p. 137)

Most observers saw the changes underway as the result of middle-class lifestyle changes that were altering locational preferences. For Lipton and many others, the distinctive features of the baby boom generation (postponed marriages, fewer or no children, and rising divorce rates) combined with the rising costs in money and time spent for commuting all served to 'decrease the relative desirability of single-family, suburban homes compared to central city multiple-family dwellings' (Lipton 1977: 147). A flood of statements appeared soon afterwards with the back-to-the-city theme, predictably accompanied by euphoria over a timely possible remedy to decades of decay. In 1977, for example, Baltimore's Mayor Fred Schaefer trumpeted that 'people are starting to come back and live here ... they're beginning to find out there is something alive here. They're coming back for ... life, pride, activity' (quoted in Ley 1996: 33). And for the preface of an edited collection titled *Back to the City* (Laska and Spain 1980), former New Orleans Mayor Moon Landrieu declared,

> Americans are coming back to the city. All across the country, older inner-city neighborhoods are exhibiting a new vitality and a renewed sense of community. (Laska and Spain 1980: ix)

This type of view had become mainstream through the 1970s. Although the fate of the city was uncertain, the conventional wisdom held that a growing wave of young, well-educated professionals were choosing to come back to the city—and the choices of these 'urban pioneers' were helping to spur renewal, renovation, revitalization, and perhaps a full-fledged urban renaissance. At the time, these sunny, optimistic terms overshadowed the cumbersome, class-laden word 'gentrification'. Years later, Neil Smith reflected on his experience coming from small-town Scotland to Philadelphia in 1976:

> In those days I had to explain to everyone—friends, fellow students, professors, casual acquaintances, smalltalkers at parties—what precisely this arcane academic term meant. Gentrification is the process, I would begin, by which poor and working-class neighborhoods in the inner city are refurbished via an influx of private capital and middle-class home-buyers and renters.... The poorest working-class neighborhoods are getting a remake; capital and the gentry are coming home, and for some in their wake it is not an entirely pretty sight. Often as not that ended the conversation, but it also occasionally led to exclamations that gentrifica-tion sounded like a great idea: had I come up with it? (Smith 1996a: 32)

### Challenging the Sovereign Consumer

This sunny view of 'revitalization' and 'renaissance' ignored the harsh realities of poverty, displacement, and chronic shortages of affordable housing. And the popular debate began to expose fundamental flaws in the dominant framework used to study cities and urban problems. Press accounts and quick-turnaround tabulations of census data were producing a vast literature that for the most part *described* changes in lifestyle, demographic conditions, and locational patterns—while appealing to self-evident *explanations*. But if there was a back-to-the-city movement driven by changes in locational preferences, *why* were middle-class preferences changing? There was a palpable sense of surprise and shock during these years, because gentrification was not at all what neoclassical urban theory had predicted.

By the time Neil Smith was being asked at parties if he had invented gentrification, the dominant perspective in urban studies was a blend of the social and spatial theories of the Chicago School of Sociology, and the methods and assumptions of neoclassical economics. These frameworks portrayed the suburbanization of middle-class and wealthy households as the driving force of urban growth, suburban expansion, and overall metropolitan housing market change. Among the many legacies of the Chicago School, one of the most enduring was the idea that the urban environment tends towards equilibrium much as an organism does, with individuals and groups sorting themselves into 'natural areas' that constituted a city symbiotically balanced between cooperation and conflict (see Hiebert [2000] for a concise summary of the Chicago School's influence on geography). This logic laid the foundation for ideas of spatial equilibrium and economic competition that were used to develop neoclassical models of urban land markets in the late 1950s and early 1960s (Alonso 1964; Muth 1969). These models explained suburbanization in terms of an overriding consumer preference for space, combined with differences in the ability of high- and low-income households to engage in locational trade-offs between access to centralized employment and the cheaper land prices available on the lower-density urban fringe. Measuring these trade-offs in terms of the costs per unit of area, the neoclassical models seemed to account for the spatial paradox of the U.S. city: middle-class and wealthy households living on cheap suburban land, and poor and working-class households forced to crowd into dense apartment blocks on expensive, centrally located inner-city land. Layered on top of these models was the concept of residential 'filtering,' advanced by Homer Hoyt based on his analysis of new kinds of housing statistics first collected by government agencies in the 1930s and 1940s. Hoyt observed that new houses and new neighborhoods were almost always built for higher-income households, and that as homes (and neighborhoods) aged, they 'filtered down' and became more affordable for progressively poorer groups (Hoyt 1939).

As the influence of neoclassical economics grew in the 1960s, many of the descriptive and qualitative accounts of the Chicago School came to be formalized and expressed in increasingly sophisticated mathematical and quantitative terms. In the course of creating these formal models, however, the neoclassical urbanists had built everything on the foundations of equilibrium and consumer sovereignty (Lake 1983). The form and function of the city, the argument went, could be understood as the result of choices made by innumerable individual decision makers. Consumers rationally choose amongst available options in order to maximize satisfaction or 'utility,' subject to the constraints of their available resources. Firms compete to serve the needs of these utility-maximizing consumers, and in the case of neighborhoods and housing, the resulting market will yield the spatial trade-offs between space and accessibility that structure different residential patterns. If such a competitive market is allowed to operate free of cumbersome regulations and other distortions, the neoclassical reasoning continues, the incentives for both producers and consumers to optimize their behavior will push the urban environment towards an equilibrium—such that there will be no systematic shortages of housing, for example—while yielding the maximum amount of utility for the maximum number of people. The conceptual simplicity of such arguments—along with the confidence of their moral implications and the mathematical sophistication of their expression in textbooks and articles—has allowed neoclassical economics to play a decisive role in discussions among urban scholars and government officials with the power to shape the rules of the game of urban life. As new sources of data on urban population and housing proliferated, developments in computer technologies and applied multivariate statistics made it possible for the neoclassical urbanists to provide increasingly detailed measures, simulations, and predictions. Government planning efforts expanded, and neoclassical frameworks that had been devised to *explain* urban structure came to be *imposed on* cities in the form of planning and zoning regulations, transportation investments, and housing policies (Metzger 2000). Together, all of these dominant tendencies in 1960s urbanism created a compelling narrative—making it appear that suburban wealth and growth juxtaposed with inner-city poverty and decline were all natural, logical, and inevitable (Beauregard 1993; Harvey 1973; Hiebert 2000; Metzger 2000).

Gentrification directly contradicted this narrative. The appearance of substantial pockets of gentrification in dozens of cities rendered consumer sovereignty explanations deeply problematic—challenging the foundational assumptions of spatial preferences and filtering, and perhaps the axiom of individual consumer choice itself. On the one hand, initial proclamations of a back-to-the-city movement were contradicted by evidence that gentrifiers came mostly from other central-city locations (and not the suburbs). As Beauregard (2003b) pointed out when discussing the late 1970s, 'Amid the good news about population growth in the cities, middle-income households were still fleeing to the suburbs' (p. 209). On the other hand, attempts to refine the standard neoclassical models raised even more fundamental questions of interpretation. Gentrification certainly could be predicted with the standard approach if the model assumptions were revised—to consider the effects, for example, if wealthier households become more sensitive to the transportation expenses of the suburbs (Kern 1981; LeRoy and Sonstelie 1983; Wheaton 1977). Schill and Nathan (1983: 15) offered the most explicit attempt to rework the Alonso–Muth bid-rent models:

> Although these land use models have most frequently been used
> to explain the creation of affluent suburbs, they can also explain the

location of affluent neighborhoods near the central business district. Economists would say that in such neighborhoods the bid rent curve of the inmovers must be steeper than the curves of both the poor who live in the central city and the inmovers' suburban counterparts. That is, the well-to-do people who move into revitalizing neighborhoods value both land and accessibility, and can afford to pay for them both. They thus outbid all other groups for land close to the urban core.

Following this logic, gentrification is the natural outcome of shifts in the trade-offs between accessibility and space that make inner-city locations more attractive for wealthier households. It's just a new spatial equilibrium (see Figure 2.1). But revising assumptions on consumer choices left critics wondering how useful the neoclassical models really were: was this *explanation* or *description*? And if so many consumers were changing their decisions in response to new conditions, why not reconsider the ideology of consumer 'choice' and examine the role of those constraints instead? What about the

---

**Figure 2.1** Gentrification as Bid-Rent Consumer Sovereignty. Neoclassical theory explains gentrification as the equilibrium solution to a change in the housing and transportation trade-offs made by middle- and upper-income consumers.

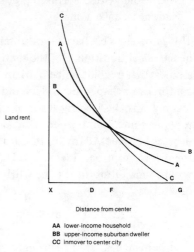

In *Revitalizing America's Cities*, Schill and Nathan (1983) revised the dominant bid-rent model (Alonso, 1964; Muth, 1969) to incorporate different assumptions on the preference for space and accessibility among higher-income consumers. In the standard formulation, middle-class and wealthy households have a preference for spacious residential environments, and can easily afford the transportation expenses of distant, low-density suburbs. Upper-income households thus outbid lower-income households in the suburbs, while lower-income households crowd into centrally located land in order to be closer to work, which in the traditional model is assumed as the central business district. Schill and Nathan (1983, p. 15) continue: 'Curve AA represents a lower-income household's bid rent curve, BB represents an upper-income suburban dweller's, and CC the inmover's. If X denotes the center of the city, the inmigrant will consume land denoted by segment XD, the poor household will locate on segment DF, and the upper-income suburban household will live on land to the right of point F. Before reinvestment, the poor would have consumed segment XF.' Similar neoclassical accounts of gentrification include Kern (1981), LeRoy and Sonstelie (1983), and Wheaton (1977). Updated and refined versions of the approach include Brueckner et al. (1999), Brueckner and Rosenthal (2005), De Bartolome and Ross (2002), De Salvo and Huq (1996), Glaeser (2000), and Kwon (2006).

*Source*: M. Schill and R. Nathan *Revitalizing America's Cities: Neighborhood Reinvestment and Displacement*, pp. 15–16. © 1983 State University of New York Press.

choices available to the poor and working classes? Perhaps it would be best to consider the limits on individual choice, the boundaries set by inequalities of wealth and power.

### 'We Wish the Theory to Become Not True'

Neoclassical theories continue to dominate urban theory and urban policy, and several economists have worked to refine bid-rent models to chart gentrification and other shifts in the contours of urban spatial structure (Brueckner et al. 1999; Brueckner and Rosenthal 2005; De Bartolome and Ross 2002; DeSalvo and Huq 1996; Glaeser, Kahn, and Rappaport 2000; Kwon 2005). Yet Chris Hamnett's (1992: 116) merciless caricature of the approach sums up the frustration of many urbanists:

> It is only necessary to attend a few economics conferences or to read some of the neoclassical literature to realize that this perspective is as vibrant and ill-informed as ever. The recipe is simple. Take a set of behavioral outcomes, add a handful of socio-economic predictor variables, whisk the mixture thoroughly until it has a thick consistency, insert a regression equation for half an hour until half baked, garnish the results with a sprinkling of significance tests and serve with consommé à choix. Voila!

This is surely a bit harsh—an unfair distortion of some of the work in the neoclassical tradition. But the sentiment was behind a sea change in urban studies that revolutionized urban thinking beginning in the 1970s and continues to shape our understanding of cities today (Zukin 2006). David Harvey was the leading force of a new perspective that went back to the roots of contemporary neoclassical theory—the classical political economy debates between Adam Smith, Ricardo, Malthus, and Marx—to understand the origins of urban inequality. Harvey's (1973) *Social Justice and the City* was the manifesto of this new urban studies, which sought to understand how cities

> are founded upon the exploitation of the many by the few. An urbanism founded on exploitation is a legacy of history. A genuinely humanizing urbanism has yet to be brought into being. It remains for revolutionary theory to chart the path. (Harvey 1973: 314)

Harvey offered a panoramic view of urbanism and society, and in later work he outlined a comprehensive analysis of economic, urban, and cultural change (Harvey 1982, 1985, 1989a, 2000, 2003; see also Zukin 2006). But his attack on the dominant neoclassical explanation of inner-city decline and ghetto formation is crucial for our analysis of gentrification. Harvey took aim at the models of urban structure that Alonso (1964) and Muth (1969) had built using the principles of agricultural land-use patterns that had been devised by a Prussian landowner, Johann Heinrich von Thünen (1793–1850):

> After an analytic presentation of the theory, Muth seeks to evaluate the empirical relevance of the theory by testing it against the existing structure of residential land use in Chicago. His tests indicate that the theory is broadly correct, with, however, certain deviations explicable by such things as racial discrimination in the housing market. We may thus infer that the theory is a true theory. This truth, arrived at by classical positivist means, can be used to help us identify the problem. What for Muth was a successful test of a social theory becomes an indicator of what the problem is. The theory predicts that poor groups must, of necessity, live where they can least afford to live.
>
> Our objective is to eliminate ghettos. Therefore, the only valid policy ... is to eliminate the conditions which give rise to the truth of the theory. In other words, we wish the von Thünen theory of the urban land market to become not true. The simplest approach here is to eliminate those mechanisms which serve to generate the theory. The mechanism in this case is very simple—competitive bidding for the use of the land. (Harvey 1973: 137)

This is part of the context that shaped Neil Smith's reaction to the optimistic, uncritical celebrations of an urban renaissance in the late 1970s. And it is acutely relevant today, when neoclassical assumptions have been revitalized and hijacked by the political triumphs of neoliberalism, such that city governments now act less as regulators of markets to protect marginalized residents and more as entrepreneurial agents of market processes and capital accumulation (Harvey 1989b; Peck 2007; see Chapter 5). One of the recent descendants of the back-to-the city tradition, for example, models high-income households' locational choices as a function of spatial variations in the age of housing, and calibrates equations to develop projections for the future magnitude of gentrification: 'Such predictions are crucial for local policymakers and real-estate developers who must plan for the future despite their limited ability to predict the city's evolution' (Brueckner and Rosenthal 2005: 1; see also Vigdor 2002; Massey 2002; Rivlin 2002). There is a remarkable continuity in the internal dynamics of the neoclassical approach, but the context of policy and politics has dramatically increased the risks for poor and marginalized residents facing gentrification pressures. Unfortunately, estimating complex models to show how elite locational preference narrows the options for lower-income households distracts our attention from the fundamental inequalities of class power. There is nothing natural or optimal about gentrification, displacement, and neighborhood polarization. *Who* stands to profit from these geographies of inequality? *Why* has consumer preference changed in such a way that gentrification has swept across so many cities for nearly forty years? Neil Smith took a knife to the soft underbelly of mainstream thinking when he approached these questions:

> In the decision to rehabilitate an inner city structure, one consumer preference tends to stand out above the others—the preference for profit, or, more accurately, a sound financial investment. ... A theory of gentrification must therefore explain why some neighborhoods are profitable to redevelop while others are not. *What are the conditions of profitability? Consumer sovereignty explanations took for granted the availability of areas ripe for gentrification when this was precisely what had to be explained.* (Smith 1979: 540–541; emphasis added)

### Development, Disinvestment, and the Rent Gap

> The logic behind uneven development is that the development of one area creates barriers to further development, thus leading to under-development, and that the underdevelopment of that area creates opportunities for a new phase of development. Geographically this leads to the possibility of what we might call a "locational seesaw": the successive development, underdevelopment, and redevelopment of given areas as capital jumps from one place to another, then back again, both creating and destroying its own opportunities for development. (N. Smith 1982: 151)

Geography creates powerful contradictions for capital investment. Particularly in the urban realm, massive investments are required to create the places that must exist in order for profits to be made—offices, factories, shops, homes, and all the rest of the infrastructure that makes up what is often called the 'built environment'. Yet once these investments are committed and quite literally put in place, capital cannot be quickly or easily shifted to newer, more profitable opportunities elsewhere. Technological change and expanding networks of trade, migration, and settlement—in short, every element of economic development—can threaten and undermine the profitability of previous investments. Individual investors committed to older technologies in older places lose out to those able to take advantage of new development in new places, while *as a group* capitalists are always forced to choose between investing to maintain the viability of previous capital commitments or exploiting new opportunities (and neglecting or abandoning the old). Moreover, capital investment is always animated by a geographical tension: between the need to equalize conditions and seek out new markets in new places, versus the need for differentiation and a division of labor that is matched to various places' comparative advantage. The result is a dynamic 'see-saw' of investment and disinvestment over time and across space, in an ongoing process of uneven geographical development (Smith 1982, 1984; Harvey 1973, 1982, 2003). Capitalism is always creating new places, new environments designed for profit and accumulation, in the process devalorizing previous investments and landscapes. This paradox of development fascinated Marx and generations of political economists, and the process was distilled beautifully in the early twentieth century by Joseph Schumpeter's (1934) concept of creative destruction. But Neil Smith was the first to connect these fundamental dynamics of capitalist development to the fine-grained circumstances of individual land parcels in the inner city, where gentrified wealth collides with disinvested poverty.

In a competitive market economy, new urban development is geared to maximize profit: landowners, developers, and everyone else involved in the development process all have incentives to use a particular land parcel for the most profitable function possible, given the available construction technology, prevailing regulations, building styles and fashions, nearby competitors, and local urban context. For some parcels, the economically optimal use—what planners and economists call the 'highest and best use'—will be high-end retail; for others, upper-middle-class residential. Location is obviously crucial in deciding the highest and best use for a particular parcel—and once a structure is built, it is quite literally anchored to its location. The *value* of a house, shop, condominium, or any other structure is the total labor invested to create it, given a society's prevailing technologies, wage rates, and so on. But if the structure is sold, the transaction *sales price* will also depend on the relative attractiveness of the land where the structure is situated. Land itself, though, has very little intrinsic value: particularly in the urban environment, the attractiveness of land is based mainly on location, accessibility, and the labor and technology devoted to improving a site. This means that the value of urban land is primarily a collective social creation: if a tiny piece of land located in the heart of a large, vibrant, growing city commands a premium on the market, it is because (1) centrality and accessibility are valued in the society, and (2) collective social investments over time produced a large, vibrant city. Private property rights, however, allow landowners to capture most of this social investment in the form of *ground rent*, which is simply the charge that owners are able to demand for the rights to use their land (Ball 1985; Krueckeberg 1995; Blomley 2004). For landlords, ground rent is received primarily as a stream of payments from tenants. Owners who prefer not to be landlords forego this stream of payments, but they can replace it by engaging in economic activity on the site (essentially paying rent to themselves). And whenever an owner sells a piece of land, the price will incorporate buyers' expectations of the future stream of payments for the rights to use the land. Ground rent, therefore, is capitalized for each owner through some combination of tenant payments, entrepreneurial activity, and asset appreciation captured at resale.

**Figure 2.2** The Depression Cycle and the Rent Gap

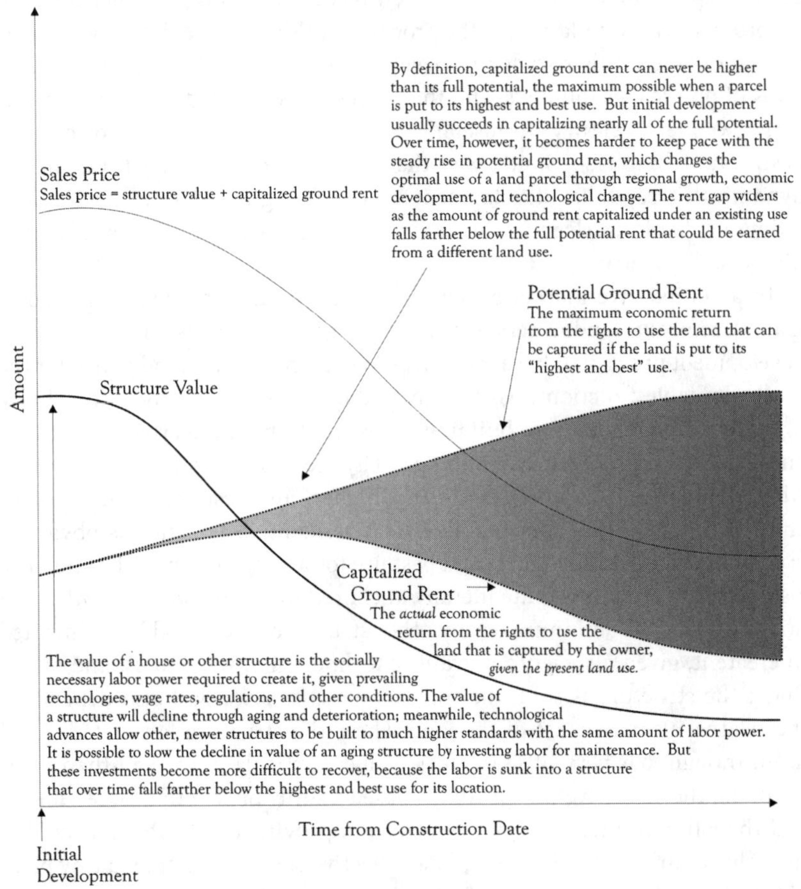

By definition, capitalized ground rent can never be higher than its full potential, the maximum possible when a parcel is put to its highest and best use. But initial development usually succeeds in capitalizing nearly all of the full potential. Over time, however, it becomes harder to keep pace with the steady rise in potential ground rent, which changes the optimal use of a land parcel through regional growth, economic development, and technological change. The rent gap widens as the amount of ground rent capitalized under an existing use falls farther below the full potential rent that could be earned from a different land use.

Sales Price
Sales price = structure value + capitalized ground rent

Potential Ground Rent
The maximum economic return from the rights to use the land that can be captured if the land is put to its "highest and best" use.

Amount

Structure Value

Capitalized Ground Rent
The *actual* economic return from the rights to use the land that is captured by the owner, *given the present land use.*

The value of a house or other structure is the socially necessary labor power required to create it, given prevailing technologies, wage rates, regulations, and other conditions. The value of a structure will decline through aging and deterioration; meanwhile, technological advances allow other, newer structures to be built to much higher standards with the same amount of labor power. It is possible to slow the decline in value of an aging structure by investing labor for maintenance. But these investments become more difficult to recover, because the labor is sunk into a structure that over time falls farther below the highest and best use for its location.

Time from Construction Date

Initial
Development

The rent gap, shown in the shaded area, is the shortfall between the actual economic return from a land parcel given its present land use (capitalized ground rent) and the potential return if it were put to its optimal, highest, and best use (potential ground rent). Nearly every aspect of urban growth, innovation, and technological development will change the urban landscape of accessibility and activity, producing mismatches between existing land uses and optimal, highest, and best uses. Urban investment and growth thus inevitably produce disinvestment and rent gaps for older portions of the urban fabric. As the rent gap grows larger, it creates lucrative profit opportunities for developers, investors, home buyers, and local governments to orchestrate a shift in land use—for instance, from working-class residential to middle- or upper-class residential.
*Source:* Adapted from Neil Smith (1979).

All of these elements change over time with urban development, spatial restructuring, and advances in technology (see Figure 2.2). When a land parcel is newly developed, all actors in the development process work to maximize profitability: competition amongst and between buyers and sellers, and renters and landlords, ensures that the rights to use a particular land parcel are capitalized as nearly as possible up to the full potential. But the capital invested to develop a place is now anchored there, and thus it is vulnerable to anything that alters the urban-economic circumstances of that place. For a few years, intensified development nearby may make it more accessible and desirable—thus allowing an owner to demand higher ground rent. But the investment in a particular land use will eventually face an unavoidable depreciation: buildings and other infrastructure age, and require ongoing labor and capital for maintenance and repair. As new urban growth adopts better construction and design technologies, land uses developed in previous generations become less competitive and less profitable. With each passing year, we are a bit more likely to see a divergence between 'capitalized ground rent' (the actual rent captured with the present land use) and 'potential ground rent' (the maximum that could be appropriated based on the highest and best use). Capitalized ground rent is constrained by the terms and conditions of previous investments and commitments of labor, and is undermined by the mounting costs of repair and maintenance. Potential ground rent, by contrast, almost always increases steadily over time: so long as an urban region enjoys some combination of population growth, employment expansion, and technological innovation, any particular location will become more highly valued over time if an owner is willing to put the land to its optimal, highest, and best use.

This cycle of depreciation and disinvestment is urban creative destruction with a vengeance. New development undermines older investments, and ongoing depreciation forces owners to consider carefully before sinking more capital into aging land uses. When the contrast between old and new tends to have a clear spatial imprint—older land uses and structures near the core, for instance, and newer development on the fringe—then disinvestment can become increasingly logical, rational, and attractive for those saddled with older commitments. Landlords in poorer inner-city neighborhoods, for example, are holding investments in buildings that may have represented the highest and best use of a century ago; spending money to maintain these assets as low-cost rental units becomes ever more difficult to justify, since the investments will be difficult to recover from low-income tenants. It becomes rational and logical for landlords to 'milk' the property, extracting capitalized ground rent from the tenants, spending the absolute minimum to maintain the structure, and waiting as potential ground rent increases in the hopes of eventually capturing a windfall through redevelopment. In the early stages, disinvestment is extremely difficult to detect: we are not accustomed to taking notice when an owner does not repaint the house, replace the windows, or rebuild the roof. But gradually the deferred maintenance becomes apparent: people with the money to do so will leave a neighborhood, and financial institutions 'redline' the neighborhood as too risky to make loans. Neighborhood decline accelerates, and moderate-income residents and businesses moving away are replaced by successively poorer tenants who move in. In any society where class inequalities are bound up with racial–ethnic divisions or other sociocultural polarization, this turnover almost invariably unleashes racist and xenophobic arguments that a particular group is 'causing' neighborhood decline. But poorer residents and businesses can only afford to move in *after* a neighborhood has been devalorized—after capital disinvestment and the departure of the wealthy and middle classes.

The disinvestment dynamic explains the apparent contradiction of poverty-ridden inner cities across so much of the developed world—the paradox of poor people living on valuable land in the heart of large, vibrant cities (Alonso 1964; Harvey 1973; Knox and McCarthy 2005: 132–135). Ground rent capitalized under an existing land use (e.g., working-class residential) falls farther below the growth- and technology-driven increasing potential that could be captured under the optimal, highest, and best use—for instance, if the land could be used for luxury residential or high-end retail. This divergence between capitalized and potential ground rent is the rent gap, and it is fundamental to the production of gentrified landscapes. As Smith puts it, 'Only when this gap emerges can gentrification be expected since if the present use succeeded in capitalizing all or most of the ground rent, little economic benefit could be derived from redevelopment' (N. Smith 1979: 545). Changing the land use—so that a landowner can chase that ever-rising curve of potential ground rent—can involve wholesale redevelopment on a neighborhood scale:

> Gentrification occurs when the gap is wide enough that developers can purchase shells cheaply, can pay the builders' costs and profit for rehabilitation, can pay interest on mortgage and construction loans, and can then sell the end product for a sale price that leaves a satisfactory return to the developer. The entire ground rent, or a large portion of it, is now capitalized: the neighborhood has been 'recycled' and begins a new cycle of use. (N. Smith 1979: 545)

But redevelopment can also proceed block by block or house by house—the 'spontaneous' revival that attracts so much popular attention—as middle-class 'pioneers' venture into poor neighborhoods in search of historic structures that can be renovated and restored. Moreover, the rent gap is often closed with heavy assistance and subsidy by government action—clearing old land uses through various forms of urban renewal, upgrading streets and other public infrastructure, and providing incentives for developers, new businesses, or new middle-class residents. As we have seen in Chapter 1, the specific form of reinvestment, the physical appearance or architectural style, and the particular coalitions of individuals involved vary widely with the context of different neighborhoods, cities, and national circumstances; but one common element across all of these variations is the fundamental structure of incentives in the capitalist city. Urban growth and neighborhood change proceed with the dynamics of profit and accumulation, and so the calculus of capital becomes interwoven with the entire range of social and cultural dimensions of individuals' choices of where and how to live in the urban environment. Even the most apparently individual, personal decisions turn out to be bound up with larger social and collective processes. An individual home buyer, for example, will carefully consider resale value when deciding how much to offer for a house; the buyer is not simply expressing an independent consumer preference, then, but is negotiating the tension between personal or family needs and the broader social relations of what a house means as an asset—as a vehicle for long-term savings and wealth accumulation.

One of the most important implications of the rent gap theory, then, involves the way we understand the individual consumer preferences at the heart of neoclassical theory and in the glare of media fascination with the latest neighborhood 'frontier.' The rent gap places the experience of individual land market actors in the context of collective social relations. In capitalist property markets, the decisive consumer preference is the desire to achieve a reasonable rate of return on a sound financial investment. And the rent gap shows how this preference, once seen as impossible in the inner city, can be satisfied there once the process of devalorization is driven far enough by metropolitan growth and suburbanization. As Neil Smith (1979: 546) sums up,

> [G]entrification is a structural product of the land and housing markets. Capital flows where the rate of return is highest, and the movement of capital to the suburbs, along with the continual depreciation of inner-city capital, eventually produces the rent gap. When this gap grows sufficiently large, rehabilitation (or, for that matter, renewal) can begin to challenge the rates of return available elsewhere, and capital flows back.

### The Rent Gap Debates

Distilled to a potent ten-page essay in the October 1979 issue of the *Journal of the American Planning Association*, Smith's rent gap hypothesis was a provocative intervention in urban theory. Years later, Smith reflected, 'Long after it was dispatched to an interested editor, my advisor delivered his own verdict on the paper: "It's OK," he muttered, "but it's so simple. Everybody knows that"' (N. Smith 1992a: 110). Perhaps not. The rent gap has been at the center of intense debate for more than a quarter century, which is appropriate if we consider the etymology of 'gap'—from the Old Norse for 'chasm', denoting a breach in a wall or fence, a breach in defenses, a break in continuity, or a wide difference in ideas or views. The rent gap is part of an assault to breach the defensive wall of mainstream urban studies, by challenging the assumption that urban landscapes can be explained in large part as the result of consumer preferences, and the notion that neighborhood change can be understood in terms of who moves in and who moves out. Scholars, therefore, take its implications very seriously.

Disagreement persists in three areas. *First*, there are concerns over terminology. Some of these appear minor at first, but hint at deeper issues. Smith's approach to the centuries-old literature on land rent led him to base his concepts on Marx's labor theory of value, and so he was cautious to avoid the common phrase 'land value' because housing is usually bought and sold together with the land it occupies (although not always in the U.K.; see Lees 1994b), and land itself is not produced by human labor: 'Here it is preferable to talk of ground rent rather than land value, since the price of land does not reflect a quantity of labor power applied to it, as with the value of commodities proper' (N. Smith 1979: 543). The ground shifted quickly, however, as most of the subsequent work on the topic dropped 'ground rent' in favor of 'capitalized land rent' and 'potential land rent'. Other ambiguities crept in with concepts like Hamnett and Randolph's (1986) 'value gap' (which we turn to later in this chapter), which in technical terms should really be called a 'price gap'. And some of the confusion over terminology has become quite serious. Steven Bourassa (1990, 1993: 1733) challenged the entire rent gap framework, largely on neoclassical economic grounds, and accused Smith of misusing 'terms that have well-established meanings in the land economics literature (Marxian as well as neoclassical)'. Bourassa argued instead for definitions that would distinguish accounting, cash-flow concepts from the economic notion of opportunity cost. Smith (1996b: 1199) fired back at Bourassa,

> The first response to Bourassa's argument has to be a certain incredulity at its own terminological confusion. Here, for example, is a partial list of the terms for *rent*, *ground rent*, and *land price*—crucial but different concepts in the rent gap theory—that show up in the first four pages of the text alone: actual rent … actual land rent … actual ground rent … potential rent … potential land rent … potential value … ground rent … potential ground rent … land rent … land value … opportunity costs … latent opportunity cost … cash flows … accounting cash flows … accounting rent … economic rent … actual cash flows … contract rent … capitalized ground rent … annual site value.

This struggle over words might seem obscure or tedious, stranding us 'on the desert island of terminological debate' (N. Smith 1996b: 1203). But words are important (as we argue in Chapter 4 with respect to the term 'gentrification'): it is only a slight exaggeration to say that the difference between 'regeneration' and 'gentrification' is akin to the gap between 'terrorist' and 'freedom fighter'. Moreover, this terminological struggle blurred into a *second* set of more conceptual disputes. Chris Hamnett (1984) suggested that the rent gap was nothing new, while Steve Bourassa (1993) claimed it was an unnecessary departure from conventional economic concepts with no legitimate precedent. But Eric Clark (1988) had already provided a concise review of several alternative formulations of the basic idea, in the classical and neoclassical tradition as well as Marxist thought going back to Engels's *The Housing Question* in 1872:

> The expansion of the big modern cities gives the land in certain sections of them, particularly in those which are centrally situated, an artificial and often enormously increasing value; the buildings erected in these areas depress this value, instead of increasing it, because they no longer correspond to the changed circumstances. They are pulled down and replaced by others. This takes place above all with centrally located workers' houses, whose rents, even with the greatest overcrowding, can never, or only very slowly, increase above a certain maximum. They are pulled down and in their stead shops, warehouses, and public buildings are erected.... The result is that the workers are forced out of the center of the towns towards the outskirts. (Engels 1872/1975: 20, quoted in Clark 1988: 244)

As Clark (1988: 245) concluded, 'Engels and Marshall were early to articulate the idea; Smith and Asplund et al. retrieve it from oblivion a century later'. But a century of scholarship failed to produce any consensus on Engels's comment that 'the buildings erected in these areas depress this value'. Bourassa argued that in classical economic theory, land rent is *independent of land use*—invalidating Smith's definition of capitalized ground rent. But the difficulty of distinguishing 'pure' land rent from returns on capital invested in buildings had long obsessed the classical political economists; the puzzle led von Thünen to use the illustrative case of a fire sweeping through farm buildings—immediately completing the disinvestment process and allowing pure land rent to determine the optimal land use without the distortions created by sunk costs in outdated buildings. He noted, 'Fire destroys at once. Time too destroys buildings, though more slowly' (von Thünen 1966: 21; cited in Clark 1995: 1498). Sadly, such hypothetical experiments often shape the everyday lives of residents in urban disaster zones—most recently in New Orleans, where local experts have been surprised at the prices paid for flood-damaged properties by investors moving into the market less than a year after Hurricane Katrina (Saulhy 2006; see Chapter 5).

Yet the conceptual difficulty of land rent and land use *does* have a solution. Hammel (1999b) noted that in his original formulation, Smith examined capitalized ground rent only at the level of the individual land parcel, and potential ground rent at the metropolitan scale. But capitalized ground rent can also be influenced by conditions in the surrounding neighborhood:

> In urban areas, we have created a pattern of land use that, despite the pace of change, is often remarkably permanent. Inner-city areas have many sites with a potential for development that could return high levels of rent. That development never occurs, however, because the

perception of an impoverished neighborhood prevents large amounts of capital from being applied to the land. The surrounding uses make high levels of development infeasible, and the property continues to languish. Thus, the potential land rent of a parcel based on metropolitan-wide factors is quite high, but factors at the neighborhood scale constrain the capitalized land rent to a lower level. (Hammel 1999a: 1290)

This integration of the rent gap with theories of scale resolves a number of crucial difficulties. Scale effects provide one way of explaining why the tendency for capitalized ground rent to fall over time—with the aging of buildings and the rising costs of maintenance and repair—can be resisted: if a sufficient number of property owners have the wealth to reinvest, and if this continued investment in the building stock is geographically concentrated, the formation of the rent gap will be minimized and delayed. Even cities with vast areas of poverty and disinvestment also usually have old, elite neighborhoods with many of the city's wealthiest families.

But in the absence of an agglomeration effect among wealthy households strongly committed to a particular neighborhood, the devalorization cycle will push capitalized ground rent farther below its potential. And here, scale effects also help to resolve certain questions about where gentrification is most likely to take place. Although we might expect gentrification to begin where the gap is greatest—where the potential for profit is maximized—in most cities gentrification follows a different path: it often begins in a relatively depressed, devalorized, working-class part of the city—but *not* the absolute epicenter of the region's worst poverty and disinvestment. The very poorest districts have the largest rent gap measured at the parcel level in relation to the metropolitan level—but not when we consider effects at the neighborhood scale. Neighborhood effects—entrenched regional perceptions of an area, the physical location of social services and nonprofits serving the poor and the homeless, and the real and perceived risks of crime—all of these and many other factors mediate the operation of the rent gap. In other words, neighborhood effects determine whether it will be possible to close the gap between a parcel's capitalized ground rent and the broader, metropolitan-wide potential ground rent. In New York, gentrification began in Greenwich Village and the Lower East Side—not the far poorer (but more isolated and stigmatized) neighborhoods of Harlem, the South Bronx, Bushwick, or Bedford-Stuyvesant. In Chicago, gentrification did not begin in the heavily disinvested South Side; rather, it began first in a small pocket of poverty and disinvestment in the Near North Side, then expanded with heavy public subsidy to a somewhat larger poverty-ridden area just west of downtown. But many things have changed at the neighborhood scale in both of these cities, including major government action to demolish low-income housing projects and disperse the residents into private-market rentals (see Chapter 6). And so now, once these neighborhood-scale barriers are coming down, gentrification is moving into parts of Chicago's South Side (see Plate 2.3), and further into New York's Harlem, Bed-Stuy, and SoBro, and even onto the edges of the dirty industrial Gowanus Canal, where one of the members of the Community Planning Board refuses to be diplomatic: 'They call it gentrification, I call it genocide. They're killing neighborhoods' (Berger 2005b).

Still, a *third* point of disagreement persists in the rent gap literatures. How do we translate all the concepts involved in the theory into 'an easily applied language of observation' (Clark 1995: 1493)? As David Ley (1987a) has emphasized, empirical tests are essential to maintain accountability in our theorizing and our thinking (but see Smith's 1987 response to Ley [1986] and Clark [1995]). Unfortunately, the rent gap involves concepts that are extremely hard to measure: nothing close to the phenomenon of capitalized ground rent appears in any public database or accounting ledger. To measure the rent gap properly, a researcher has to construct specialized indicators after sifting through decades of land records and becoming familiar with the details of historical market conditions, neighborhood settings, tax assessment practices, the provisions of government subsidies, and other factors. It's not surprising that very few researchers have invested the time and effort (see Box 2.1). The results of these studies do provide qualified support for the rent gap thesis, with certain modifications and adjustments for local and historical context; additional support for the framework comes from empirical studies that measure other aspects of urban investment and disinvestment (Engels 1994; Hackworth 2002a; N. Smith 1996a; N. Smith and DeFilippis 1999). Nevertheless, conceptual and terminological debates over the rent gap persist, and empirical research is unlikely to reconcile the fundamental interpretive differences between those steeped in the neoclassical economics tradition versus those working in the Marxist vein (Clark 1988, 1995). Moreover, debate over the rent gap has been complicated by the introduction of apparently similar hypotheses—Hamnett and Randolph's (1986) theory of a 'value gap' driving the conversion of London rental flats to owner-occupation (see Chapter 1 on Barnsbury), and Sýkora's (1993) notion of a 'functional gap' describing the mismatch between urban core land uses under state-socialist conditions in Prague as market conditions created a land market gradient in the early 1990s (see Box 2.2). Finally, the conceptual architecture of the rent gap—with its emphasis on landowners' absolute control over the rights to use and profit from land—has to be adapted to consider the different legal and political circumstances of different historical periods, as well as different countries. A new wave of empirical research from Eastern Europe and Sweden is providing new insights even as it raises new questions, and Adam Millard-Ball (2000: 1689) is surely right to identify 'the need for a wider conceptual framework for production-side explanations of gentrification in countries with different economic systems'.

**Plate 2.3** New Luxury Condominiums on the South Side of Chicago, 2006

The rent gap suggests that gentrification provides one way to increase capitalized ground rent on parcels that have been devalorized by obsolete land uses and years of suburbanization. One of the major debates over the rent gap, however, has involved the empirical observation that gentrification often begins not in the very poorest districts, but areas just a bit better off—for instance, mixed working-class and poor neighborhoods that are not far from downtown employment centers, and not too isolated from remaining middle-class enclaves in the central city. Hammel (1999b) suggests that geographic scale helps to explain this anomaly. Capitalized ground rent for an individual parcel is influenced by neighborhood effects—by the social, institutional, and physical circumstances of surrounding land uses. Thus, a land parcel may have an enormous rent gap when its capitalized ground rent is measured against a steadily rising potential ground rent at the metropolitan scale, but redevelopment will only be feasible if the negative barriers *at the neighborhood scale* can be overcome. In the case of Chicago, gentrification in the 1960s and 1970s began not in the city's poorest, heavily disinvested South Side, but closer to downtown in a smaller pocket of disinvestment on the Near North Side. But over the years, gentrification has expanded around all sides of the downtown core, while the Chicago Housing Authority has used federal funds to demolish many low-income public housing projects and disperse the residents to the private rental market. In short, the neighborhood scale has begun to change dramatically, and now new luxury homes are sprouting across Chicago's South Side. Some neighborhood effects persist, however: real and perceived concerns about crime on the South Side prompted this developer to assure prospective buyers that the building security system is 'linked to [the] police department 24 hours a day'.
*Source:* Photograph by Elvin Wyly.

| Box 2.1 |
|---|

| **Measuring the Rent Gap** |
|---|

The rent gap explains gentrification as the product of investment and dis-investment in the urban land market. Over time, urban development and expansion create a tension between 'capitalized ground rent'—the economic return from the rights to use land, given its present use—and 'potential ground rent', the return that could be earned if the land were put to its optimal, highest, and best use. As the gap between potential and capitalized ground rent widens, it provides an ever more powerful incentive for land-use change; residential gentrification is one way of closing the rent gap.

The rent gap has been one of the most hotly debated themes in the entire study of gentrification, inspiring controversy that is perhaps second only to the cultural and class implications of the term 'gentrification' itself. Why such dispute? First, the hypothesis draws direct links between many local empirical cases of neighborhood change—specific spaces undergoing complex transitions and tensions—and the broad forces of urban development and the uneven development of capitalism itself. Many people, therefore, view it as an implicit claim that all cases of gentrification can, in one way or another, be tied back to the workings of urban land markets under capitalism. This perception makes the thesis a high-stakes battle between interpretations of dualisms—between the unique and the universal, between human agency and structured constraint, and between individual choices and collective social forces. And the perception lends urgency to the second reason for continued dispute: the extreme difficulty in operationalizing the concepts in order to provide empirical tests for the hypothesis.

It's surprising that there have been so few detailed empirical studies that operationalize the rent gap. At first glance, this seems rather curious, because the rent gap was first developed more than a quarter century ago. To be sure, quite a few studies *do* offer fine-grained analyses of the gentrified landscapes produced through the dynamics of urban property markets: to cite only a few of the best examples, we can point to Ley's (1986) multivariate analysis including ratios between inner-city and metropolitan house values and rents for twenty-two Canadian urban regions, Neil Smith's (1996a) use of property tax delinquency to map the turning points from disinvestment to reinvestment in parts of Manhattan (see also N. Smith and DeFilippis 1999), Engels's (1994) rich analysis of the links between mortgage-lending practices and redlining in a gentrifying inner suburb of Sydney, Hackworth's (2002b) diagnosis of several real estate indicators in several New York neighborhoods, and Hamnett's (2003b) examination of a variety of indicators for London's housing market. But none of these studies directly captures the elements of the rent gap thesis.

The concepts of capitalized and potential ground rent are extremely difficult to measure. We can easily find a treasure trove of data on things like home sales prices, but these data are useless for distinguishing ground rent—the economic returns from the use of the land—from house price; also, house prices are notoriously sensitive to such things as mortgage interest rates, and house prices do not measure house value, which in the rent gap framework is defined as the socially necessary amount of labor power invested in construction, periodic maintenance, and major renovations. Getting at these key indicators requires an enormous investment of time to collect fugitive information, adjust it for variations in lot sizes and other factors, and organize it in a way that allows analysis of potential and capitalized ground rents over long periods of time. Quite simply, it takes years of painstaking work to sift through specialized historical archives, gain knowledge of representative case studies of transformation, or develop alternative ways of gaining insight into the contours of investment and disinvestment. The best evidence we have on the dynamics of rent gaps comes from Luděk Sýkora's (1993) analysis of the market transition and the emergence of a land price gradient in Prague, Czech Republic (see Box 2.2); Blair Badcock's work in Adelaide, Australia (see Figure B2.1a); Eric Clark's work in Malmö, Sweden (see Figure B2.1b); Dan Hammel's work in Minneapolis, in the United States (see Figure B2.1c); and David O'Sullivan's microscale simulation model relating changes in individual buildings and lots to those of their immediate neighbors in an area of Hoxton in inner East London (see Figure B2.1d). Each of these studies provides strong evidence that the trajectory of capitalized and potential ground rent does indeed follow the general tendency theorized by Neil Smith (1979); but context also matters, and we should not be surprised that the lines do not always trace out perfect lines that suggest a trigger mechanism that can be used to 'predict' gentrification. Individual and collective decisions matter. But the evidence, despite its conceptual and empirical limitations, does support many of the claims and implications of the hypothesis.

Still, there is much that we do not know about the empirical facets of the rent gap: we need to understand how developers, investors, and gentrifiers respond to rent gaps in different cities; to determine how their perceptions of prices, appreciation rates, and other market indicators compare to the concepts of potential and capitalized ground rent; and to undertake comparisons of rent gaps for properties in areas that did experience gentrification versus properties in areas that have not yet witnessed reinvestment. Finally, we need research to measure how the concepts of potential and capitalized ground rent themselves are altered when a significant fraction of housing market activity involves buyers and sellers working or moving across international boundaries. Is potential ground

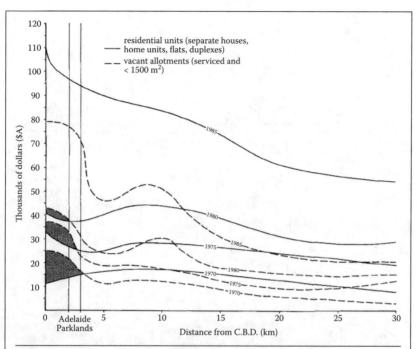

**Figure B2.1a** The Contraction of Adelaide's Rent Gap between 1970 and 1985
*Source:* Blair Badcock, An Australian view of the rent gap hypothesis, *Annals of the Association of American Geographers*, 79(1), p. 131. © 1989 Blackwell Publishing.

rent itself, for instance, becoming globalized as local property transactions are tied into world financial markets? Some indicators suggest that perhaps it is. In 2005, the *Economist* (in 'The global housing boom') noted that the combined value of all residential property in the world's developed economies shot up by some $30 trillion over a five-year period, and adjusting for the total size of all these economies, the resulting bubble exceeded the stock market booms of the 1920s and the 1990s.

Blair Badcock (1989) assembled data on the average prices paid for vacant lots, and for housing of all types, in each of the thirty local government areas in Adelaide, Australia. His reasoning was that the price paid for a vacant lot represents the expected future income from its use, and thus can be understood as potential ground rent; he suggested that the house price data, by contrast, measure capitalized ground rent while unfortunately also mixing in the value of improvements. Badcock then plotted these figures by distance from the central business district (CBD), with separate curves for different time periods, and interpreted the cases where vacant lot prices exceeded dwelling prices (shaded in gray) as clear evidence of an inner-city rent gap. Badcock's analysis provides compelling

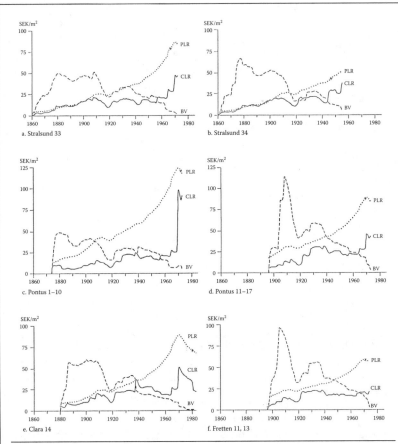

**Figure B2.1b** Rent Gaps for Six Redevelopment Areas in Malmö, Sweden
*Source:* Eric Clark, The rent gap and the transformation of the built environment:
case studies in Malmö, 1860–1985, *Geografiska Annaler*, B70, 2:241–254. © 1988
Blackwell Publishing.

support for the existence of a substantial rent gap in inner Adelaide in
1970, and its closure by the early 1980s. But Badcock's data sources do
not correspond precisely to the rent gap hypothesis, because they measure
averages for different parts of the city, and measure lots and houses of different types and sizes; a more precise measure would involve tracking both
capitalized and potential ground rent over time for the same parcels.

Eric Clark (1988) has produced the definitive work on the history,
theoretical roots, and empirical expression of rent gaps. His empirical
work is based on the long-term changes observed in several specific properties in inner-city Malmö that were first developed in the late nineteenth
century, and subsequently demolished to make way for new construction,
mostly in the 1960s and 1970s. To measure capitalized land rent (CLR),

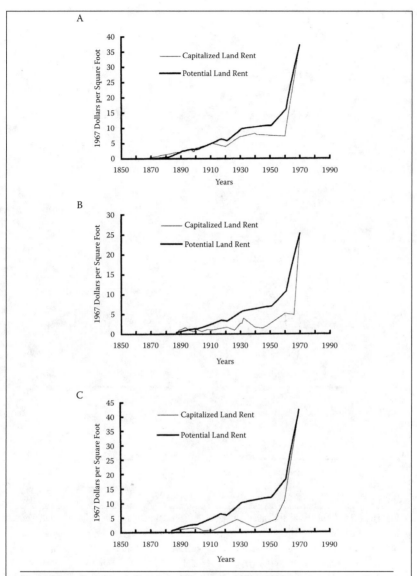

**Figure B2.1c** Rent Gaps in Downtown Minneapolis, 1870s–1960s
*Source:* Dan Hammel, Gentrification and land rent: a historical view of the rent gap in Minneapolis, *Urban Geography*, 20, 2, 116–145. © 1999 Bellwether Publishing.

he combined several data sources to balance the strength and weakness of each, separating estimates for the assessed value of buildings (BV) and the land they occupy while adjusting for inflation, the size of the lots, and other important factors. To measure potential land rent (PLR), he used bills of sale for vacant land parcels just prior to development and

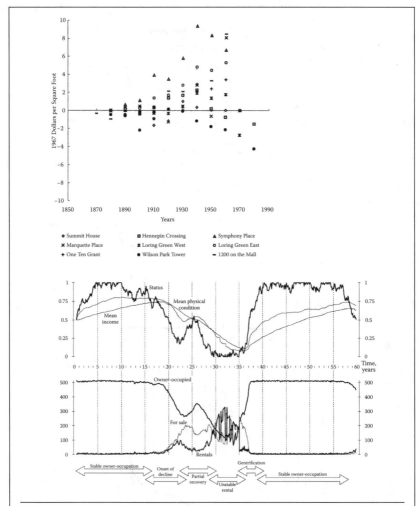

**Figure B2.1d** A Microspatial Simulation Model of Disinvestment and Gentrification in Hoxton, Inner East London
*Source:* David O'Sullivan Toward micro-scale spatial modeling of gentrification, *Journal of Geographical Systems*: 4, 3:251–274. © 2002 Springer Berlin/ Heidelberg.

adjusted the figures to account for metropolitan population growth and total property value inflation. Clark offered detailed historical analyses of the development and redevelopment circumstances of each of the cases, showing how the particular experiences of individuals and institutions working in particular neighborhood settings at various times will produce different kinds of rent gaps; in other words, the rent gap is not a mechanistic device, but rather a general structural tendency that follows different

paths depending on human agency and context. Yet despite these variations, there is 'a rather clear picture of the rent gap. The building capital
fixed to a piece of land in connection with initial development maintains a
fair degree of appropriateness to its site over a period of time', but in

> increasingly changed circumstances, the buildings become increasingly
> anachronistic. Other forms of building capital would be better suited
> to realize a growing potential land rent, while the existing building
> capital tends to hold down the site's level of realizable land rent: a rent
> gap emerges. The property owner may either attempt through further
> investments to keep the building appropriate to its site, or withhold
> investment, minimize maintenance and variable costs, and milk it as it
> stands, resulting in a broadening of the rent gap. ... Eventually, the rent
> gap reaches a level when development firms find the property attractive.
> This signals the beginning of an upward trend in capitalized land rent,
> resulting in a narrowing of the rent gap. (Clark 1988: 252)

Dan Hammel (1999b) studied the history of nine groups of parcels that
were assembled and redeveloped for middle-class and luxury apartments
in the 1960s. Adapting Eric Clark's approach, Hammel combined data
from tax assessments and deeds of sale to measure capitalized land rent
and potential land rent for each property from initial development in the
1870s and 1880s. He found substantial rent gaps for nearly all of the parcels. The properties showing the clearest trends appear in Figure B2.1c,
and led Hammel to suggest that rent gaps could develop not only through
absolute devalorization and falling capitalized rents, but also through stable or slightly rising capitalized rents that failed to keep pace with rapid
increases in potential land rent. Many of the other parcels Hammel studied, though, illustrated more complex rent gap patterns that could only
be understood by considering the specific local history of each property.
Nevertheless, the general pattern is clear, with rent gaps growing wider
through the middle decades of the twentieth century until redevelopment
in the 1960s. Hammel emphasized that the rent gap hypothesis does not
lend itself to questions of precise prediction of the location and timing of
redevelopment:

> [G]entrification derives much of its significance from its links to the
> process of urban restructuring and uneven development. The rent gap
> hypothesis is useful in understanding gentrification not because it
> provides precise prediction ... but because it provides a theoretical link
> between gentrification and these larger processes. This study suggests
> that at least part of that linkage can be seen in the land-rent histories of
> gentrified parcels in Minneapolis. (Hammel 1999b: 142)

Remarkably, the long history of multivariate quantitative analysis that was so pervasive in urban geography in the 1960s, and that persists today in urban economics and regional science, has been rare in gentrification research. There are almost no multivariate studies. David O'Sullivan's work (2002) is a recent exception, and offers a fine-grained view of the complex interactions of different actors involved in urban real estate markets who look closely at what's happening to individual houses, those next door, and those down the block. O'Sullivan develops something called a 'cellular automaton' spatial model, which is essentially what happens if you mix geography and algebra: you get a series of rules that govern what happens to a property based on the condition and events observed for neighboring properties. O'Sullivan's model relates several measures of property condition and value with resident income levels for particular properties, and is designed to relate changes in overall neighborhood conditions over time with model parameters that capture specific aspects of how the market operates. For example, how fast does a decline in property values lead to a corresponding decline in the incomes of buyers and renters who move into the next vacant home in the area? And when and where will the cycle of disinvestment produce spatial pockets where it is profitable for entrepreneurial types to take the risks of redevelopment to earn the profits of gentrification? O'Sullivan's model translates these kinds of rules into a series of equations that simulate the long-term evolution of the rental and ownership segments of the market in Hoxton, inner East London. His results describe a complex, long-term trajectory of disinvestment and resurgence:

From the 30th to the 35th years the neighborhood is very unstable with large numbers of rental properties, large numbers of sales, and continuing decline in mean household income and in the physical condition of properties. At the end of this period, properties start to return to owner occupation and the fall in both incomes and the conditions of buildings is halted. These effects combine to see the neighborhood's status sharply rise, and mean household incomes subsequently rise sharply. Within a matter of only 3 years virtually all properties are back in owner-occupation. (O'Sullivan 2002: 268)

In the end, O'Sullivan's approach offers a rare analysis of the dynamics of extremely local events in property markets, and sheds light on the dynamics of scale in neighborhood change; but he also notes that this spatial resolution comes at the price of certain simplifying data assumptions that make it impossible to capture the precise categories of potential and capitalized ground rent.

| Box 2.2 |
|---|
| **Other Gaps?** |

In 1979, the *Journal of the American Planning Association* published Neil Smith's 'Toward a Theory of Gentrification: A Back to the City Movement by Capital, Not People'. Smith's specific explanatory mechanism, the rent gap, instantly became influential in the study of gentrification. But Smith's explanation was based on theories in classical political economy and land rent that had been discussed since the middle of the nineteenth century. Eric Clark (1988) has traced the history of both neoclassical and Marxian efforts to come to terms with the discontinuous, uneven process of adjustment over time and space, as urban development, technological change, and the depreciation of aging structures interact to create localized mismatches between current and optimal land uses. Smith's conception is unique for its explicit consideration of gentrification, and for its connections to broader processes of uneven urban development; but it is not without precedent.

And it has also inspired other efforts to capture different kinds of mismatches or disjunctures. Hamnett and Randolph (1986), for instance, developed a complementary alternative to the rent gap, proposing that a **value gap** could explain the pressure to convert rental housing to owner-occupancy (see the case study of Barnsbury in Chapter 1). Hamnett and Randolph analyzed the historical politics and economics of the 'flat break-up market' in central London, which emerged as part of a broader national trend where blocks of privately-rented apartments were sold for individual owner-occupation in a wave of conversions from the 1960s through the 1980s. Market conditions in Britain had created two distinct methods of valuing residential property—one based on the stream of rental income a potential buyer/landlord could expect from a particular property, and the other based on the sale value for owner-occupation; 'where the two sets of values diverged … a value gap could open up, thereby creating the possibility of a profitable transfer of residential property from one tenure to another' (p. 133). And these values did diverge in the middle decades of the Twentieth Century. Owner-occupancy began to receive larger tax and interest-rate subsidies, while tenant rent controls and occupancy regulations made it harder for landlords to earn expected rates of return on investments. Landlords responded with disinvestment through under-maintenance—until it became possible, thanks to the expansion of mortgage credit through building societies, to sell flats either to existing tenants or to other prospective owner-occupiers. The resulting divergence in the economics of the two sectors 'had a fundamentally debilitating effect on the viability of the private rental sector' (p. 133) and culminated in 'the wholesale loss of rented accommodation through its transfer to owner-occupation' (p. 135).

Implicit in all of this, of course, is that the basic processes at the heart of the rent gap are expressed differently in the urban landscape, depending upon the kinds of rules governing a specific property market. Zoning regulations, tax rates for different land uses, tax incentives designed to encourage redevelopment, and other factors all help to shape the way devalorization works in a particular city, in a particular regional and national context. Loretta Lees (1994b), for example, shows that neighborhood change in London and New York (cr. Chapter 1) follows different paths, what she terms an **Atlantic Gap**, thanks to contrasts in the rules of property transfer, the capitalization of property through the housing finance system, and in conservation and historic designation. She concludes that 'The rent gap is a more appropriate theorisation of gentrification in the US than the value gap because of its focus on land, abandonment and place, alongside relevant legal and political differences' (p. 216).

These legal and political differences are absolutely crucial. As an explanatory tool and a framework for political–economic analysis, the rent gap is a glimpse at one facet of the workings of capitalist property markets. It is thus not surprising, then, that Millard-Ball (2000: 1688) finds the rent gap and value gap of limited use in understanding the effects of state intervention and housing allocation policies in Stockholm: 'Much gentrification in Sweden appears to rely on non-market or quasi-market processes, which gap theories, based as they are on the operation of market forces and rational economic behavior, are ill-suited to analyze'.

Elsewhere, these 'market forces' began to transform the urban environment with the fall of repressive state-socialist regimes in the Soviet Union and Eastern Europe. With the collapse of centrally-planned systems for housing and land allocation, cities in these settings began to change rapidly with the emergence of sharp land-value gradients. Luděk Sýkora (1993) examined the effects of market transition in Prague in the early 1990s, and was able to measure the average prices paid per square meter at a privatization auction (see map below). The extreme center-to-edge variations 'reflect both the value of the location and the unnatural character of the artificially equalized price of land or rent under the socialist system' and this 'emerging price gradient' builds pressure to change land uses. Sýkora (1993: 287–288) drew a distinction between short-term adjustments in occupancy and use of existing structures—what he called a **functional gap**—and longer-term rent-gap pressures to reconfigure, rebuild, or redevelop: 'Functional gaps are caused by the underutilization of available land and buildings relative to their current physical quality.

When centrally planned allocation of resources is replaced by allocation ruled by market forces, freely set rents influence the distribution of
functions in space. Thus, functions with an inefficient utilization of space
may soon be outbid by more progressive functions with a highly intensive
space utilization. In this way, the functional gaps can be closed in a very
short time without making huge investments'.

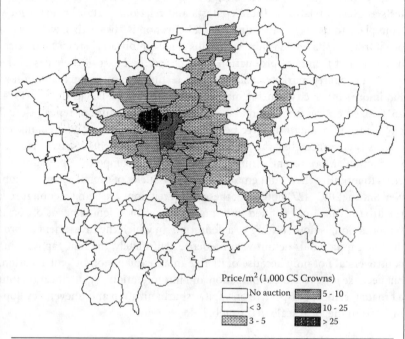

Price/m² (1,000 CS Crowns)
No auction    5 - 10
< 3           10 - 25
3 - 5         > 25

**Figure B2.2** Average Prices Paid for One Square Meter of Nonresidential Premises at
Privatization Auctions in 1991–1992, Prague
*Source:* Luděk Sýkora, City in transition: the role of the rent gap in Prague's
revitalization, *Tijdschrift voor Economisce en Sociale Geografie,* 84(4), p. 286, © 1993
Blackwell Publishing.

## Gentrification and Uneven Development

Millard-Ball (2000: 1673) notes that 'production-side explanations have come
to be virtually synonymous with 'gap' theories of gentrification', and Redfern
(1997: 1277) observes, 'Normally, rejection of Smith's rent-gap model would
appear implicitly or explicitly to mean endorsement of the consumption-oriented
accounts'. But the minutiae of the rent gap debates—important though they
may be to land rent specialists and empirical researchers—should not distract
us from the 'wider conceptual framework' for production explanations. Neil
Smith (1996b: 1202) emphasized that his original theorization was deliberately

simplified: 'If the rent-gap theory works at all, it works because of its simplicity and its limited theoretical claims. It should certainly be subjected to theoretical criticism, but I do think that this will be useful only if the theoretical premises are taken seriously from the start'. And the central theoretical premise concerns the fundamentally social and political dimensions of economic power in urban land markets: all the lines in those graphs and curves of potential and capitalized ground rent (see Figure 2.2) are the outcome of political contests and class relations. These contests and relations certainly vary widely from place to place, but the fundamental question is always this: who gets to profit from capitalized ground rent? This is not simply an abstract theoretical discussion of factors of production, but goes to the heart of the rules of the game in property markets. Analyzing the terrible racism and exploitation in Baltimore's inner-city housing market in the early 1970s, David Harvey (1974: 251) seized on the fundamental social and political nature of rent: '[A]ctual payments are made to real live people and not to pieces of land. Tenants are not easily convinced that the rent collector merely represents a scarce factor of production'. More recently, surveying the growing competitive pressures for cities to mobilize their built environments as vehicles of capital accumulation, Neil Smith (2002: 427) notes that these social relations are being reconfigured: the urban scale, once defined in terms of the locally oriented needs of social reproduction, is now shifting to a definition 'in which the investment of productive capital holds definitive precedence'. Ultimately, the rent gap remains controversial not only because of its role in an explanation of gentrification, but because it weaves the explanation and interpretation of gentrification into a broader, critical perspective on capitalist urbanization and uneven development from the local scale to the global.

*Spatial Fixes and Circuits of Capital*
Recall that urbanization involves massive capital investments that, once committed, are tied up in buildings and other facilities for long periods of time, creating barriers to new kinds of investment in these places. Geographical expansion provides a 'spatial fix' to this dilemma, allowing capital investment to gravitate to new markets in new *places* that can be built with the most current and advanced (and thus most profitable) technologies. But as we have already seen, this spatial expansion accelerates the devalorization of previous investments in older parts of the urban fabric: 'The movement of capital into suburban development', Smith observed, 'led to a systematic devalorization of inner and central city capital, and this, in turn, with the development of the rent gap, led to the creation of new investment opportunities in the inner city precisely because an effective barrier to new investment had previously operated there' (N. Smith 1982: 149). As it turns out, new investment opportunities are crucially important in the periodic crises that punctuate the boom-and-bust cycles of capitalism.

When rates of profit begin to fall in the major sectors of industrial production—the 'first circuit' of capital investment—investors and financial institutions seek out more profitable opportunities in other sectors. At this point, the 'second circuit'—real estate and the built environment—becomes an especially attractive vehicle for investment. Capital switches away from goods- and service-producing industries into construction and real estate, driving building booms and rapid inflation in real estate markets until here, too, overaccumulation drives down the rate of profit (Harvey 1978; Beauregard 1994; Charney 2001, 2003; Lefebvre 1991). In the most extreme cases, property booms are leading indicators of recession, appearing as a 'kind of last-ditch hope for finding productive uses for rapidly overaccumulating capital' (Harvey 1985: 20).

Recessions and depressions ultimately require and allow spatial restructuring of the urban economy. On the one hand, suburbanization created an unprecedented spatial fix for the crisis of the Great Depression in the 1930s, with government-subsidized investment in highway construction and cheap mortgages encouraging massive new residential development—creating additional new markets for automobiles, consumer durables, and petroleum products (Walker 1981). On the other hand, inner-city devalorization created rent gaps, creating the conditions for a locational switch of capital that seemed to accelerate gentrification during times of recession in the 1970s and 1980s in the United States and Canada. For Smith, then, 'the gentrification and redevelopment of the inner city represent a linear continuation of the forces and relations that led to suburbanization' (N. Smith 1982: 150). Ultimately, then, gentrification is tightly bound up with much larger processes: it is the leading edge of the spatial restructuring of capitalist urbanization, and it

> is part of a larger redevelopment process dedicated to the revitalization of the profit rate. In the process, many downtowns are being converted into bourgeois playgrounds replete with quaint markets, restored townhouses, boutique rows, yachting marinas, and Hyatt Regencies. These very visual alterations to the urban landscape are not at all an accidental side-effect of temporary economic disequilibrium but are as rooted in the structure of capitalist society as was the advent of suburbanization. (N. Smith 1982: 151–152)

And this also means that the negative consequences of gentrification—the rising housing expense burden for poor renters, and the personal catastrophes of displacement, eviction, and homelessness—are not simply isolated local anomalies. They are symptoms of the fundamental inequalities of capitalist property markets, which favor the creation of urban environments to serve the needs of capital accumulation, often at the expense of the needs of home, community, family, and everyday social life.

## The Problems with Production Explanations

We've deliberately simplified this overview of production theories. We've tried to accentuate the key challenges to the mainstream assumptions of consumer preference, individual behavior, and benign spatial equilibrium. But in the last twenty years, production narratives have evolved in much more subtle and nuanced directions in order to consider the interplay and mutual constitution of production and consumption (Beauregard 1986; Clark 1995; Hamnett 1991; Ley 2003; Rose 1984; N. Smith and DeFilippis 1999; N.Smith 2002). These efforts—variously understood as reconciliation, integration, or complementarity—are the result of production theorists' dialogue with social and cultural theorists studying a new middle class that seems to have distinctive values and political sensibilities that favor gender, racial, sexual, and class diversity at the neighborhood scale. These social and cultural theories, which we examine more closely in the next chapter, are quite distinct from the neoclassical economic tradition. But both approaches share a reverence for understanding the motivations and decisions of individual actors, including gentrifiers. As the ambassadors of the ruling conventional wisdom of policy and politics, neoclassical analysts have rarely felt the need to respond directly to production-side challenges—although Berry (1999) unsheathed his sword when insurgents rewrote his 'Islands of Renewal in Seas of Decay' to describe public-housing projects surrounded by reinvestment as 'Islands of Decay in Seas of Renewal' (see also Byrne 2003; Vigdor 2002). The result is a curious state of affairs: an intense, rich, and theoretically astute debate on the left, amongst those who generally agree on the inadequacy of the neoclassical approach, the significance of gentrification, and its costs and inequalities. The key point of disagreement is the causal explanation: why? When? Where?

It's a fairly simple matter to summarize the problems that have been associated with production explanations. First, the measurement and verification problems of the rent gap debates look settled by comparison with the controversy over attempts to document capital switching and other facets of uneven economic development. Second, both Marxist and neoclassical accounts rely on the axiom of economic rationality, and downplay the significance of individuals who (intentionally or not) defy the norm. And third, for many readers, drawing a direct link between so many diverse local cases of gentrification and the entire anatomy of global capitalism seems to imply that individual gentrifiers behave first and foremost as ruthless capital accumulators. Some do. But many are in contradictory class positions (to borrow the terms of the sociologist Eric Wright) shaped by inequalities of gender, race, ethnicity, and sexual identity (Freeman 2006; Rose 1984; Lauria and Knopp 1985); we should always be careful, then, to focus criticism on the rules and inequalities of *property* and to think very carefully before villainizing the *individual people* who are playing by those rules (Krueckeberg 1995; Lees 1994b; Blomley 2004). When gentrification inflates home prices in once-disinvested neighborhoods, it is common to find that poor home owners are suddenly eager to cash out on the appreciation by selling and moving away; we should be sympathetic to this kind of accumulation, even as we remember that low-income renters don't have the same opportunity. Similarly, it is possible even in the tightest housing markets to find individual landlords who actually know their low-income tenants as individuals—and who therefore resist the incentives to raise rents or evict a vulnerable household (Newman and Wyly 2006). Consumption theorists are right: individual choices do matter in what happens in gentrifying neighborhoods. But so are production theorists: a few landlords keeping rents below rising market rates do not fundamentally alter the meaning of the renter–landlord relation, and do nothing to advance us to a long-term solution that would protect what Chester Hartman (1984) famously described as the 'right to stay put', or what David Imbroscio (2004) has proposed as a full-fledged political philosophy for the 'right to place'.

These kinds of conversations, though, become unproductive (pardon the pun) as soon as a certain word is used. Production theorists are attacked for their *determinism*. This is a prima facie irony, since if we are trying to determine what causes something, determinism is precisely what we need. But the critics do have an important point. Drawing on her research that showed how lower-middle-class women found the inner city more supportive than the patriarchal low-density suburbs, Damaris Rose (1984: 56) tried diplomatically to remind us that 'gentrifiers are not the mere bearers of a process determined independently of them'. But Chris Hamnett (1992: 117) opted for flowery prose with sharp thorns, charging that Smith's 'opposition to any form of agency explanation reveals him as a structuralist for whom individual agency is reduced to the role of flickering shadows cast by the light of capital's fire'. And Chris Hamnett wasn't convinced by Neil Smith's attempts to consider the interplay of production and consumption: 'I sought to show that his later writing is still unduly economist and deterministic and that he is unwilling to accept that individuals may have any significant role in shaping their environment outside influencing the colouring on the cake' (Hamnett 1992: 117). Smith lit a Molotov cocktail and tossed capital's fire back at Hamnett, suggesting that Hamnett had abandoned an earlier concern for class injustice in favor of a pro-gentry methodological individualism; perhaps this was part of 'the transformation from the "young Hamnett" to the "old Hamnett", as it were' (N. Smith 1992: 114). Smith went on to advocate a 'non-essentialist' way of understanding gentrification by using class as the 'point of entry' into the constellation of social relations and social identities involved (N. Smith 1992: 114; see also Graham 1990 and Gibson-Graham's 1993 recipe for smashing capitalism while working at home in your spare time). Still, the contingency of difference and identity should not blind us to the fundamental importance of class:

[L]et's for a moment assume the priority of individual preference. Now let us ask: who has the greatest power to realize their preferences? Without in any way denying the ability of even very poor people to exercise some extent of preference, I think it is obvious that in a capitalist society one's preferences are more likely to be actualized, and one can afford grander preferences, to the extent that one commands capital. We may regret that economics so strongly affects one's ability to exercise preferences, but it would hardly be prudent to deny it; preference is an inherently class question. (N. Smith 1992: 114)

Many consumption theorists are still not convinced. We'll see why in the next chapter. But what we need to confront here is the matter of context. Theoretical purity in the pages of academic journals, text con text jousting with charming, erudite wit is one thing; the lives of the poor and working classes whose homes, communities, and lives are gentrified are another matter entirely. In the years since the production–consumption debates reached the peak of sophistication and intensity in the late 1980s and early 1990s, each of the major criticisms of production theories has been subverted by dramatic shifts in political context. Social inequalities have worsened with the consolidation of neoliberalism as a triumphant political movement that has been able to implement specific policy templates that dictate 'market justice'—the principle that free markets are and should always be the undisputed arbiter of social outcomes (Jessop 2002; Kodras 2002; Peck 2007; see Chapters 5 and 6). As the 'cultural turn' has become more influential among scholars, economic trends and national and city politics have gone in precisely the opposite direction. And so we have three profound ironies:

1. Consumer sovereignty has become urban policy. As more scholars have rejected the deterministic assumptions of economic rationality as a way of understanding social and cultural change, right-wing political movements have implemented neoliberal policies explicitly based on these assumptions (Jessop 2002; Kodras 2002; Mitchell 2003). Throughout the Global North, many national governments are pursuing policies that restrict the rights of individuals as *citizens*—redefining rights instead in terms of *consumers* and *investors* as cities seek to attract wealthy home owners and free-spending tourists. In the Global South, many of these principles are imposed by the 'structural adjustment' dictates of the International Monetary Fund and other transnational financial institutions. Consumer sovereignty is becoming policy—summarized best perhaps by George W. Bush's notion of the 'ownership society'—such that individuals face increased penalties if they do not behave as *Homo economicus* in planning their home purchase, their retirement, and even the expenses of their own health care. In overheated real estate markets, the concept of

'neighborhood' is increasingly viewed in terms of the potential for capital accumulation; and new sources of information may accelerate the competitive dynamics in areas of reinvestment (see Figure 2.3). The charge of determinism may well have been justified in seeking causal explanations for the emergence of gentrification in the 1960s, but in today's climate such criticisms miss the mark. Gentrification is a fact of urban life, and its consequences take place in a political context that is quite deterministic. At a panel discussion in the 2002 meeting of the Association of American Geographers, Harvey was criticized for presenting an account of American imperialism that was 'a totalizing discourse'. Without missing a beat, Harvey replied, 'Well, it's a totalizing system'.

2. Capital switches have become 'mind-boggling' (Blackburn 2006; The Economist 2006). After many critics abandoned production explanations because of the mixed empirical results on rent gaps, capital switching, and other facets of uneven urban development, an accelerating wave of innovation in financial markets produced a much larger menu of complex financial instruments that operationalize many of these principles. These mechanisms have transformed much of the system of housing finance at large, and they have also lubricated the process of unequal reinvestment and polarizing gentrification in the inner city (Ashton 2005; Hackworth 2002a, 2002b). When Harvey pointed out in 1978 that capital switching 'cannot be accomplished without a money supply and credit system which create "fictional capital" in advance of actual production and consumption' (p. 103), it was extremely difficult to find specific evidence on the neighborhood-level spatial dimensions of these dynamics. This has changed. In the last generation, fictional capital has expanded dramatically with the proliferation of new types of hedge funds, real estate investment trusts, risk-partitioned mortgage-backed securities, automated loan-underwriting systems, credit-scoring algorithms tied to risk-based pricing schemes, collateralized debt obligations, and so on; 'credit' has an increasingly complex vocabulary (Blackburn 2006; Fabozzi 2001). A new wave of research is documenting how at least some of these instruments of capital accumulation mediate the dynamics of gentrification and the political strategies of those who stand to profit from it (Hackworth 2002a, 2002b; Lake 1995; Hackworth and Smith 2001).

3. The politics of methods have displaced attention from those displaced by gentrification. The displacement of poor- and working-class residents was once a prominent concern across much of the political spectrum in gentrification research (Hartman 1984; Laska and Spain 1980: chs. 15–19; Schill and Nathan 1983: ch. 5). But a

widespread backlash against the model-intensive flavor of neoclassical urban economics turned off many political economists to quantitative research, and the trend has accelerated as the 'cultural turn' focused new interests in the construction of identity, difference, and community for people living in gentrifying neighborhoods. This social and cultural research is certainly important. Unfortunately, even the most sophisticated ethnographic accounts of the changes underway in dynamic inner-city neighborhoods cannot be used to gain generalizable knowledge of certain consequences of gentrification: anyone who participates in an interview or focus group in a gentrifying neighborhood has, by definition, not yet been displaced. Very few gentrification researchers are able to integrate quantitative

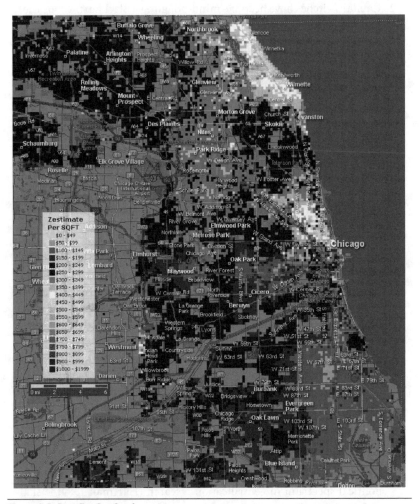

**Figure 2.3** Rent Gap Dot Com?

and qualitative methods (but see Lees 2003b; Ley 2003; N. Smith and DeFilippis 1999). Even fewer have the specialized expertise to engage neoclassical analysts on the terrain of multivariate modeling and longitudinal sociospatial analysis. As a consequence, when a series of

---

**Figure 2.3 *(Continued)***

Drawing connections between gentrification and urban property markets invariably raises controversial issues over the politics of data and methods. These politics have been the subject of academic debate for many years, but some facets of the disputes may be shifting in curious ways with the dramatic expansion of the use of internet data providers. Back in 1986, David Ley examined the factors correlated with gentrification in 22 Canadian metropolitan areas, and he included two measures intended to measure the rent gap—the ratio of inner-city to metropolitan house values, and the ratio of inner-city to metropolitan rental costs—and ultimately found no support for the hypothesis. Neil Smith (1987: 463–464) did not react kindly: 'The clumsiness of this translation from concept to operational variable is astonishing ... this indicator does not refer to rent, nor does it even postulate an economic gap in the central city. Both ingredients are missing in a two-ingredient recipe. Ley is untroubled by the emptiness of his bowl, however, merely assuring us that the postulated ratios do represent "one valid measure of the rent gap"....'. Ley (1987: 468) tried to make a case that the measures did capture the essence of the theory, and then went on to lampoon Smith's use of the rent gap to predict where reinvestment was most likely to begin: 'The devalorization cycle and the mystique around the rent gap now become unnecessary baggage. All that is now required for gentrification to occur is the potential for profit'. Two decades later, this spirited and charming academic debate now takes place amongst homeowners and realtors. Zillow.com, a Seattle-based startup that attracted nearly 2.8 million visitors to its web site after its launch in February, 2006, devised what it called 'zestimates', using models of local price trends to estimate property values for more than 40 million homes nationwide. Heavy use by residents, journalists, and anyone else with an interest in property values led the *San Diego Union-Tribune* to quip that 'the term "to zillow" has joined such phrases as "to google"' (Showley, 2006). Millions of people can look up the zestimate for their home simply by typing in the address, and 'While they are at it, users are looking up friends, neighbors, ex-spouses, family members, bosses. It is also a gold mine of celebrity trivia, if you know the celebrity's address' (Blanton, 2006). But when Zillow took the next step—aggregating its zestimates to create 'City Heat Maps' of the estimated property value per square foot for homes—the result comes tantalizingly close to measuring the spatial imprint of devalorization. To be sure, the measure captures neither capitalized nor potential ground rent, nor their changes over time in the devalorization cycle; the measure also seems to blend house price and lot price. Nevertheless, with a standard per-square-foot indicator, the maps clearly highlight pockets of the city with low values surrounded by much 'hotter' areas. The image above is a black-and-white version of the online color map, but in general, dark areas have relatively low per-square-foot values, while the brighter areas have higher values; note the patchwork of dark and light areas near the downtown core and extending to the northwest. It's not clear how individual consumer behavior may change with the diffusion of this kind of information, which was until recently only available to professionals or researchers willing to sift through specialized local property records. 'The launch of Zillow comes as homeowners' emotions are running high and house prices have begun to soften after years of rapid appreciation', reports the *Boston Globe*. 'The site's Zestimates also have become a point of contention for real estate agents who feel threatened by Zillow's free access to information previously available only to professionals' (Blanton, 2006).

*Source:* Zillow (2006).

studies based on government housing databases seemed to provide evidence that gentrification was not actually displacing low-income renters in gentrifying neighborhoods, few researchers were able to respond (Freeman and Braconi 2002; Freeman 2005; Vigdor 2002). These studies received enormous press coverage, punctuated by a headline in *USA Today*: 'Gentrification: A Boost for Everyone?' (see Plate 6.5) Many community activists shouted, 'No!' and provided detailed accounts of the individual experiences of poor people whose lives were damaged by gentrification. But in mainstream public and policy discourse, such cases are always dismissed as 'anecdotal'.

*Producing New Inequalities, New Scales, and New Struggles*

Gentrification is nothing more and nothing less than the neighborhood expression of class inequality. It should thus come as no surprise that recent paths of neighborhood change reflect the well-documented increase in social polarization in urbanized societies throughout the world. Production accounts draw attention to three important shifts in the nature and implications of gentrification in these times of worsened inequality.

First, local rent gap dynamics have become much more tightly intertwined with transnational processes. In theoretical terms, of course, the rent gap has always been inextricable from global uneven development and circuits of capital. And for many years, major international developers have been key players in the production of large-scale gentrification landscapes (most famously in the development of London's Canary Wharf by the Canadian firm Olympia & York). But in the last decade or so, other facets have been transnationalized as well. The vast majority of residential mortgages are now bought and sold repeatedly in pools of securities on world financial markets, such that local devalorization cycles and rent gap dynamics are lubricated by shifts in interest rates, currency fluctuations, government budget deficits, and investor sentiment. These trends have been particularly pronounced in the United States, where home-equity loans and 'exotic' mortgage products have turned houses into virtual automatic teller machines; as the economist Paul Krugman (2006) quips, '[W]e became a nation in which people make a living by selling one another's houses, and they pay for the houses with money borrowed from China'. This financial integration affects all kinds of neighborhoods, but there is evidence that it is particularly important in lubricating rent gap reinvestment in the gentrifying inner city. Meanwhile, key segments of local labor markets in large cities are now interwoven into a world urban system: local clusters of transnational corporate services and headquarters not only generate demand for local gentrified residential space, but also serve to weave this local demand into transnational circuits of labor migration amongst itinerant professionals on short-term assignments or freelance employment contracts. Matthew Rofe (2003) goes so far as to suggest that we are seeing the emergence of a distinct gentrifying class, part of an elite global community in which the construction of identity is increasingly commodified and tied to specific neighborhoods in the competitive real estate markets at the top of the world urban hierarchy. This commodification, he argues, erodes the symbolic significance of local gentrification processes: 'In order to maintain a distinctive identity, numerous gentrifiers are projecting their identity from the scale of the local onto the scale of the global. In doing so, these individuals actively position themselves as a global elite community' (Rofe 2003: 2511).

Second, the leading edge of uneven urban development has expanded dramatically *inside* gentrifying cities. In other words, reinvestment has moved beyond the comparatively small enclaves of gentrification, and is moving deeper into other parts of the devalorized urban environment (see Chapters 4 and 5). In many cities, this move supplies an endless stream of raw material for journalists, investors, and community residents trying to figure out precisely where the frontier is this month. The local details always vary, but the expansion is the logical extension of the rent gap framework (see Figure 2.4). As Jason Hackworth (2002b: 825) observes, '[H]ousing markets are in flux as the reinvested core—the area close to the CBD [central business district] that experienced the bulk of real estate investment during earlier waves of gentrification—shoves the once-monolithic belt of disinvestment (the land value valley) outward from the urban core' to more distant parts of the central city, and into the inner-ring suburbs as well.

Third, the politics of urban property markets have altered the terrain for opposition and resistance. Gentrification now receives more explicit governmental support, through both subsidies to large corporate developers and targeted policies designed to attract individual gentrifiers. Expanded reinvestment has displaced and dispersed more and more low-income renters, effectively displacing opposition and resistance itself (DeFilippis 2004; Hackworth 2002b; Hackworth and Smith 2001; Goetz 2003). But for low-income home owners and institutional property owners that serve working-class or poor clients, the expansion of gentrification is bittersweet: quite literally, these individuals and institutions must decide whether and when to sell out and leave. In this sense, gentrification is more than ever driven by the politics of property rights—the social relations that underpin the entire rent gap framework and the struggles of who gets enriched by capitalized ground rent. Unfortunately, property rights have become so deeply enmeshed into social and cultural traditions in many capitalist societies—values and symbols of individualism, freedom, and the 'dream' of homeownership, for instance—that house price appreciation is now regarded as an individual entitlement or an inalienable right of citizenship. Urban politics have thus become much more vicious in terms of any issue believed to enhance or threaten property values. In American housing markets, this has traditionally meant upper-middle-class white suburbanites using 'property values' as code for racist practices of exclusion

**Figure 2.4** Evolving Land Value Surfaces and the Expansion of Gentrification

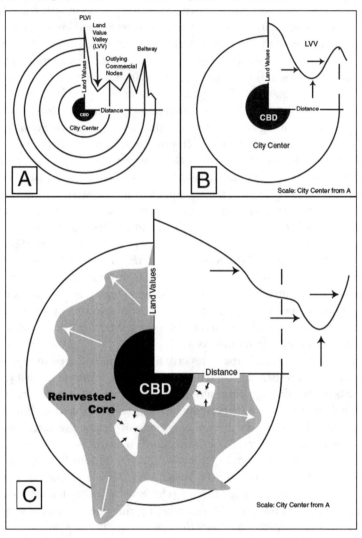

Since the initial linkage between industrialization and urbanization in the nineteenth century, land values have been closely tied to centralization (A). Industrialization typically created a 'peak land value intersection' (PLVI) in a city's central business district (CBD), with later suburbanization creating smaller peaks at commercial nodes and along major transportation corridors. Suburbanization and the devalorization cycle, however, gradually created what Homer Hoyt (1933) called a 'land value valley' (LVV) near the city center (B); the LVV gradually moves outwards as various parts of the urban environment are devalorized. After several decades of gentrification, the land value surface is a complex mosaic of disinvestment and reinvestment (C).

*Source:* Jason Hackworth, Post recession gentrification in New York City, *Urban Affairs Review*, 37(6), p. 826, © 2002 Sage Publications, Inc.

and discrimination. But these practices are becoming increasingly common among working-class home owners in aging inner-ring suburbs that are now facing intensified devalorization and disinvestment (N. Smith et al. 2001). Indeed, there is evidence that the desire to protect property values is forging a new kind of progentrification coalition in declining industrial suburbs in the United States. Christopher Niedt draws on interviews, archival research, and participant observation in a suburb of Baltimore, Maryland; he concludes that white working-class home owners and community organizations in these places support gentrification efforts and the resulting renter displacement, because 'many of them have drawn from a resurgent national conservatism to explain decline as an effect of government subsidies and "people from the city"' (Niedt 2006: 99). Moreover, gentrification can produce physical landscapes that even steadfast tax-cutting, antigovernment conservatives regard as attractive and successful; home owners who are otherwise ideologically opposed to government programs will thus support publicly financed gentrification 'as a growth strategy that supposedly improves places by removing problem people and land uses and replacing them with better ones' (Niedt 2006: 116).

We should not underestimate the stakes in these conflicts, and we must not ignore the fundamentally political questions that masquerade as neutral rules and laws governing urban property markets. Property is about power, control, and the right to exclude. And as the philosophy of market justice has been used to justify extremes in wealth and power across more and more domains of society, those who stand to benefit from gentrification have become bolder in their claims. The clearest statement comes from Andres Duany, a prominent architect and leader of the 'new urbanist' design movement who has become a key figure in the production of many gentrified landscapes in the United States. In an essay published by a right-wing think tank, Duany offers 'Three Cheers for Gentrification':

> These days, whenever more than a handful of middle-income people move into a formerly down-at-the-heels neighborhood, they are accused of committing that newest of social sins: "gentrification". This loaded term—conjuring up images of yuppies stealing urban housing from rightful inhabitants—has become embedded in the way many activists understand urban evolution. And the thinking behind it has become a serious obstacle to the revival of American cities.... Gentrification rebalances a concentration of poverty by providing the tax base, rub-off work ethic, and political effectiveness of a middle class, and in the process improves the quality of life for all of a community's residents. It is the rising tide that lifts all boats....
>
> [P]eople should not be prevented from profiting on the natural appreciation of their neighborhoods. Not in America. (Duany 2001: 37, 39)

This kind of reasoning—sort of a trickle-down theory applied to housing and neighborhoods—has become the most powerful ideological weapon among developers, speculators, wealthy home owners, and other advocates of gentrification (see Chapter 6). And the argument works by ignoring or suppressing the fundamental question posed by production theorists: what produced the 'down-at heels neighborhood' that subsequently becomes a popular place to invest and speculate? Ignoring the process of disinvestment and the creation of rent gaps allows advocates of gentrification to present reinvestment and redevelopment—the closure of rent gaps—as nothing more than common sense and good planning.

Unfortunately, the tax base benefits of gentrification invariably subsidize more the gentrifiers or the institutions that serve them. The poor and working classes have no less of a work ethic than today's gentrifiers, many of whose main source of wealth is the 'natural' house price appreciation that comes from that collective social creation—urbanization itself. The politically effective middle classes have been more willing in recent years to villainize renters, the poor, the homeless, and any other individuals whose presence might possibly undermine property values. And improvements in the quality of life for a community's residents simply cannot be enjoyed by those who lose out on the right to be community residents. In recent years, these rights become more tenuous, as gentrification has accelerated and undermined the security of marginalized renters in many cities. But these rights are always bound up with the politics of production and consumption in the urban environment, creating possibilities for change.

## Summary

In this chapter, rather than just outlining production explanations per se, we situated them in debates from the early 1970s onward about the back-to-the-city movement of middle-class gentrifiers in the United States. Of course, the history of production explanations about the back-to-the-city movement was not one that could be neatly ordered, for different explanations held purchase at the same time. There was no simple Kuhnian paradigm shift from one explanation to another. This state of affairs mirrors the situation today, where there are many different explanations of gentrification. In the chapter we focused our lens on the most influential production explanation, Neil Smith's rent gap thesis; we situated this thesis within wider political–economic theories about the circulation of capital in the city, especially the theory of uneven development. We discussed how the problems of measuring and interpreting the rent gap and other aspects of production explanations lit a series of important debates about the meaning and significance of neighborhood transformation. The chapter was very much focused on production explanations with reference to the United States, but we pointed to some of the production explanations that have emerged outside the United States, for example, Hamnett and Randolph's 'value gap' in London and Sýkora's 'functional gap' in Prague. We pointed to some of the problems with production explanations, especially those that the consumption explanations in the next chapter focus on. In so doing we highlighted some of the fiery words that were thrown back and forth amongst gentrification researchers in the 1980s and 1990s, words which attacked and defended production (and consumption) explanations. We ended the chapter by exploring a new generation of work on production explanations, and we argue that production accounts are still very important today, especially in highlighting the increasing social injustice/inequality in cities around the world.

### Activities and Exercises

- Read Harvey's (1973) *Social Justice and the City*. Focus on two arguments: first, Harvey's argument that geography (and social science more generally) cannot remain 'objective' in the face of urban inequality; and, second, his Marxist argument that production is the decisive phase but that it is determined by the demands of consumption.
- Compare Smith's 'rent gap' thesis to Hamnett and Randolph's 'value gap'.
- Compare Smith's 'rent gap' thesis to Sýkora's 'functional gap'.
- Study N. Smith, B. Duncan, and L. Reid (1989), 'From Disinvestment to Reinvestment: Tax Arrears and Turning Points in the East Village', *Housing Studies*, 4, 4: 238–252. This is one of the few pieces of work that operationalizes the rent gap.
- Try to think about what kinds of data one would have to collect to show the operation of the rent gap in a city of your choice.
- Before turning to Chapter 3, read J. Duncan and D. Ley (1982), 'Structural Marxism and Human Geography: A Critical Assessment', *Annals of the Association of American Geographers* 72:30–59. This article is a nice summary of the issues that gentrification authors such as David Ley had with Marxist-structuralist interpretations of the city. In particular, it argues that capital is more conservative than most structuralists would have us believe, and that inner-city reinvestment would appear too risky for entrepreneurs until market demand establishes itself.

### Further Reading

Badcock, B. (1989) 'An Australian view of the rent gap hypothesis', *Annals of the Association of American Geographers* 79: 125–145.

Clark, E. (1988) 'The rent gap and the transformation of the built environment: Case studies in Malmö 1860–1985', *Geografiska Annaler* 70B: 241–254.

Clark, E. (1991) 'Rent gaps and value gaps: Complementary or contradictory?' in J. van Weesep and S. Musterd (eds.) *Urban Housing for the Better Off: Gentrification in Europe* (Utrecht, the Netherlands: Stedelijke Netwerken) 17–29.

Hammel, D. J. (1999a) 'Re-establishing the rent gap: An alternative view of capitalized land rent', *Urban Studies* 36, 8: 1283–1293.

Hammel, D. J. (1999b) 'Gentrification and land rent: A historical view of the rent gap in Minneapolis', *Urban Geography* 20, 2: 116–145.

Hamnett, C., and B. Randolph (1986) 'Tenurial transformation and the flat break-up market in London: The British condo experience', in N. Smith and P. Williams (eds.) *Gentrification of the City* (London: Allen and Unwin) 121–152.

Millard-Ball, A. (2000) 'Moving beyond the gentrification gaps: Social change, tenure change and gap theories in Stockholm', *Urban Studies* 37, 9: 1673–1693.

Rose, D. (1984) 'Rethinking gentrification: Beyond the uneven development of Marxist urban theory', *Environment and Planning D: Society and Space* 1: 47–74.

Smith, N., B. Duncan, and L. Reid (1989) 'From disinvestment to reinvestment: Tax arrears and turning points in the East Village', *Housing Studies* 4, 4: 238–252.

Sýkora, L. (1993) 'City in transition: The role of rent gap in Prague's revitalization', *Tijdschrift voor Economisce en Sociale Geografie* 84, 4: 281–293.

Wyly, E., and D. Hammel (1999) 'Islands of decay in seas of renewal: Housing policy and the resurgence of gentrification', *Housing Policy Debate* 10, 4: 711–771.

**Plate 3.1** 'A Vegetarian Diet for Your Dog' in the Gentrifying Lower East Side, 1988

This image shows nicely the new cultures of consumption of the 'new' middle class, or yuppies as some have called them. Note the irony of concern over feeding your dog a vegetarian diet when homeless people and heroin addicts are on your doorstep in the Lower East Side at this time.

*Source:* Photograph by Loretta Lees.

# 3
# Consumption Explanations

> The crucial point ... is that "gentrifiers" are not the mere bearers of a process determined independently of them. Their constitution, as certain types of workers and as people, is as crucial an element in the production of gentrification as is the production of the dwellings they occupy.
>
> Rose (1984: 56)

At the end of the 1980s, the decade when the term 'yuppie' came into widespread use on both sides of the Atlantic, John Short (1989: 174) summarized the emergence of what he called 'the new urban order':

> In summary there has been a loss of manufacturing employment and an increase in service employment all against a background of rising unemployment. The social effects have been a reduction in the power of the traditional male working class, an increase in female employment and the emergence of a new middle class. These trends have been given popular recognition in the terms yuppie and yuffie, themselves part of a plethora of new words coined in the 1980s including buppies, swells and (my favourite) lombards. A yuppie is a young upwardly mobile person though the u can also denote urban. Yuffies are young urban failures. If the yuppies are the successful new middle class, yuffies are the stranded and blocked working class. The other terms? Buppie is the yuppie's black equivalent, swell is single women earning lots in London, a term which summarizes the rise of the female executive and perhaps the beginnings of the end for the monopoly of the male domination of senior and responsible positions. Lombard is lots of money but a right dickhead, a term of abuse whose real quality is only recognized if you know that one of the main streets in the City of London is Lombard Street.

Short worried that his paper would immediately become a victim of history and that the amusing terms above may have 'a very short shelf-life'. Whilst most of the terms listed by Short have indeed disappeared from view, 'yuppie' has proven to be remarkably tenacious, not least because it is a key weapon in struggles against gentrification, used to identify unwelcome new arrivals in neighborhoods whose spending power threatens community, the longevity of affordable housing, and valued local amenities. Yet perhaps the most famous critic of gentrification, Neil Smith, has warned that 'the difficulty in identifying this new middle class, especially in economic terms, should give us pause before we glibly associate yuppies and gentrification' (1996a: 104). Beauregard (1990: 856–857) takes this warning further:

> To attribute gentrification solely to yuppies is to eliminate quite complex processes and to shift the burden of the negative consequences of gentrification away from factions of capital (for example, developers) who often are responsible. Such a focus robs analysis of its structural and political perspective.

This chapter explores the consumption-side theories that have explained gentrification as a consequence of changes in the industrial and occupational structure of advanced capitalist cities. This is the 'loss of manufacturing employment and an increase in service employment' described by Short, which led to an expansion in the amount of middle-class professionals with a disposition towards central-city living and an associated rejection of suburbia. In other words, our purpose is to introduce and analyze a vast (and still expanding) literature that has explored questions of class constitution such as 'Who are the gentrifiers?' 'Where do they come from?' and 'What draws them to live in central-city neighborhoods?' For some time now, there has been wide agreement that class should be the undercurrent in the study of gentrification (Hamnett 1991; Smith 1992a; Wyly and Hammel 1999), and the research response has been to find out about the behavior of the middle classes, particularly why they are seeking to locate in previously disinvested neighborhoods. This is a surprisingly complex issue, and the reasons vary from place to place. Over the years, there has been increasing theoretical sophistication in research undertaken in many different countries that seeks to understand middle-class gentrifiers—a very diverse, ambivalent group that cannot be reduced to conservative, self-interested yuppies, not least because the negative connotations of that term are at odds with the 'marginal' position of some gentrifiers (Rose 1984), and the left–liberal politics that many gentrifiers espouse (Ley 1994). If one thing above all was clear from the 1970s debates over a back-to-the-city movement across North America (see Chapter 2), it was that more sophisticated theoretical treatments of the production of gentrifiers were needed if the consumption aspects of gentrification were to have explanatory merit.

### The Production of Gentrifiers : The Postindustrial and Professionalization Theses

In the summer of 1972, a young urban geographer called David Ley arrived in Vancouver to take up his first academic appointment at the University of British Columbia (where he remains today). That autumn, at a local church, he met a widow in her seventies, Mrs. Edna Shakel, who had just been evicted from her three-room apartment on a street in the gentrifying Fairview district that was experiencing rapid condominium development. To remain in that area, Mrs. Shakel had to downgrade to a single-room apartment with a shared bathroom (see Ley 1996: 1–3 for a fuller discussion). This encounter stimulated Ley's lengthy research project on gentrification in Canadian cities, still ongoing (see Ley 2003). The story of Ley's career to date has in fact been one of 'peopling' human geography—he is a key figure in what became known as 'humanistic geography', which calls for a more sensitive incorporation of human agency into geographical research focused on structural issues, especially structural Marxist work (Duncan and Ley 1982). This commitment to researching the 'everyday lives' of people in geographical contexts shows no sign of weakening—a recent paper by Ley (2004) attempts to 'bring the issue of human agency to a globalisation discourse that has frequently been satisfied with speaking of a space of networks and flows devoid of knowledgeable human agents' (p. 152).

The year after Ley arrived in Vancouver, the American sociologist Daniel Bell published *The Coming of Post-Industrial Society* (Bell 1973), which became extremely influential to Ley's interpretation of gentrification—so much so that it is often referred to as Ley's 'postindustrial thesis' on gentrification (see Box 3.1). Bell's work was subjected to intense criticism, especially by scholars on the left, who questioned the politics of an account which emerged to challenge Marxist theories of societal development. In one scathing critique, Walker and Greenberg (1982) called the postindustrial thesis 'a rather broad and vacuous set of generalizations' stemming from 'a fundamentally empiricist approach to social history in which overt "facts" are taken as the whole of reality, rather than as the products of causal mechanisms or structural

---

| Box 3.1 |
| --- |
| **Daniel Bell's Post-industrial Thesis** |
| Daniel Bell argued that there are four key features of a 'post-industrial society' in emergence:<br><br>• a shift from a manufacturing to a service-based economy<br>• the centrality of new science-based industries with 'specialized knowledge' as a key resource, where universities replace factories as dominant institutions<br>• the rapid rise of managerial, professional, and technical occupations<br>• artistic avant-gardes lead consumer culture, rather than media, corporations, or government<br><br>*Source:* Bell (1973). |

relations which give rise to sensible phenomena' (pp. 17–18). Today, however, it would take a brave voice not to accept that many of Bell's arguments were remarkably prescient. The growth of professional and managerial employment is now a well-known fact; even David Harvey (1989a), one of the highest-profile Marxist voices, conceded that Bell's treatment of cultural transformation was 'probably more accurate than many of the left attempts to grasp what was happening' (p. 353).

From 1972 onwards, David Ley sought to understand gentrification in the context of the emergence of the postindustrial city in a project that was at once historical and contemporary, and particularly concerned with the cultural politics of gentrification, but not at the expense of economic change in Canadian cities, as many researchers incorrectly stated. Ley argued that postindustrial society had altered the rationale behind the allocation of land use in urban contexts in Canada, as new middle-class professionals (what he called a 'cultural new class') were an expanding cohort with 'a vocation to enhance the quality of life in pursuits that are not simply economistic' (1996: 15). Ley argued that gentrification represented a new phase in urban development where consumption factors, taste, and a particular aesthetic outlook towards the city from an expanding middle class saw an 'imagineering of an alternative urbanism to suburbanization' (p. 15) which could not be captured by explanations of the process that privileged structural forces of production and housing market dynamics.

In the 1990s, Ley's arguments were advanced further by another geographer, Chris Hamnett, who was impressed by how Ley's postindustrial thesis was 'clearly rooted in the deeper changes in the structure of production, the changing division of labour, and the rise of a locationally concentrated service class' (Hamnett 1991: 177). As we saw in Chapter 2, Hamnett has been consistently and highly critical of Neil Smith's claim that the rent gap thesis is integral to any explanation of gentrification (Hamnett 1984, 1991, 2003b). For Hamnett (1991), '[I]f gentrification theory has a centrepiece it must rest on the conditions for the production of potential gentrifiers' (p. 187). Soon after this 1991 article was published, Hamnett began a sustained assault on Saskia Sassen's renowned work on global cities (Sassen 1991), with the production of potential gentrifiers playing a lead role. He was bothered by Sassen's thesis of 'social polarisation' in global cities, which holds that changes in the industrial and employment structure have produced growing occupational and income polarization, or, in Sassen's (1991) words, 'a high-income stratum and a low-income stratum of workers' (p. 13), with fewer jobs in the middle. Hamnett argued that this thesis not only was a 'slave' of New York and Los Angeles, but also contradicted other (and, in his view, more theoretically and empirically valid) work on urban social change, especially Bell's arguments on the emergence of a postindustrial society and Ley's grounding of those arguments in Canadian cities. Using evidence from London, one of Sassen's

global cities, Hamnett came up with a 'professionalization thesis' to counter
Sassen's polarization thesis:

> [T]here is evidence that a process of professionalisation is concen-
> trated in a number of large cities with a strong financial/producer
> service base. ... London experienced an increase in the proportion of
> professional and managerial workers in 1961–1981, while the numbers
> and the shares of all other groups declined. There is no evidence for
> absolute social polarisation in London in the 1960s and 1970s, and the
> 1991 census is most unlikely to reveal a sudden reversal of fortune.
> (1994b: 407)

Hamnett's prediction of further professionalization evidence from the 1991
UK Census was indeed accurate (Hamnett 1996)—but how is this often rather
numbing debate relevant to gentrification? The answer can be found in the fact
that these professional and managerial workers are gentrifiers, and a rapidly
expanding group exerting huge influence on housing markets and neighborhoods. In Hamnett's view, gentrification is a product of the transformation of
western cities from manufacturing centers to centers of business services and
the creative and cultural industries, where associated changes to the occupational and income structure produce an expanding middle class that has
replaced (not displaced) the industrial working class in desirable inner city
areas. In sum,

> Not surprisingly in a market economy, the increase in the size and
> purchasing power of the middle classes has been accompanied by an
> intensification of demand pressure in the housing market. This has been
> particularly marked in inner London as it is here that many of the new
> middle class work, and this, combined with a desire to minimise com-
> muting time, and greater ability to afford the cultural and social attrac-
> tions of life in the central and inner city, has been associated with the
> growth of gentrification. (Hamnett 2003b: 2424)

Ley's postindustrial and Hamnett's professionalization theses are tightly
linked, and have proven very important in consumption explanations of
the process (see Munt's 1987 study of Battersea, London, which is rooted
in these explanations). With increased recognition that any explanation of
gentrification must incorporate both production- and consumption-side
explanations (Clark 1992), it would take a determined structuralist not to
grapple with the theses! At this stage in our discussion, we know why the
new middle class is an expanding group, and that many of them are not
returning from the suburbs but choosing not to locate in the suburbs. However, what we need to examine now is the vast body of literature which seeks
to explain *why* gentrifiers gentrify.

## The New Middle Class

> People like us live in the inner London suburbs really. We wanted to live somewhere that was mixed and various and vibrant; full of young middle class people doing places up.

Stoke Newington gentrifier (quoted in Butler 1997: 124)

In 1991, the British sociologist Alan Warde observed,

> The fragmentation and fluidity of the middle-classes [are] a structural base for a great variety of consumption practices.... To tie down the details of consumption behaviour to closely specified fractions of these classes is probably impossible. (p. 228)

While Warde was correct to note a great variety of consumption practices among a differentiated middle class, the second part of this quotation today seems a bizarre statement, as so much work has appeared since 1991 along *precisely* the lines that Warde thought impossible. A newcomer to the gentrification literature will soon encounter a substantial literature on the characteristics of different types of gentrifiers, and their reasons for gentrifying—often expressed in gentrifiers' own words, as a number of researchers have undertaken qualitative work to track the movements and aspirations of the new middle class. In this section we break down this work into several themes, by no means disconnected from each other, but a reflection of what can be found in the literature on the gentrifying new middle class.

### Countercultural Identities, Politics, and Education

In April 2002, Air Canada's monthly magazine, *enRoute*, ran an article entitled 'Canada's Top Ten Coolest Neighbourhoods'. Criteria for entry in the top ten of coolness, selected by a panel of thirty-eight prominent Canadians, were set out as follows:

> When today's archetypal young graphic designer leaves home, he [*sic*] is looking for something different than what his parents may have sought. Often, he will look for a "young" place inhabited by his peers. He will seek out a "fun" place, where he can indulge in his favourite leisure activities. But most of all, he will look for an area that makes him feel distinct and at home at the same time, a neighbourhood that reflects his tastes—a place that is cool. (p. 37)

*enRoute*'s top ten coolest neighborhoods in Canada are listed in Figure 3.1. If we dispense with the arbitrary association of graphic designers with coolness, the striking feature of this list is the fact that every single neighborhood on it has experienced gentrification. In addition, arguably the two most famous gentrified neighborhoods in Canada occupy the top two slots. These ten neighborhoods, where gentrification is generally well advanced, have interesting

1. Queen Street West, Toronto
2. Le Plateau Mont-Royal, Montréal
3. Vieux-Montréal, Montréal
4. West-End, Vancouver
5. Little Italy, Toronto
6. Old Strathcona, Edmonton
7. The Exchange District, Winnipeg
8. Lower Water Street, Halifax
9. Inglewood, Calgary
10. Le Vieux-Québec, Québec City

**Figure 3.1**  *enRoute's* Top Ten Coolest Neighbourhoods (2002)

and unique histories, but for our purposes we must note what they share. From the late 1960s onwards, they became arenas for the expression of the countercultural politics of the emerging new middle class. Thus, a suitable starting location for exploring the characteristics of gentrifiers is Canada, and particularly the work of Jon Caulfield and, again, David Ley.

Gentrification accelerated across Canada in the 1970s during what has become known as the 'reform era' of Canadian urban politics (see Harris 1987). For Caulfield (1994), 1970s and 1980s gentrification in Toronto was a very deliberate middle-class rejection of the oppressive conformity of suburbia, modernist planning, and mass market principles, 'oriented toward reconstituting the meanings of old city neighbourhoods towards an alternative urban future' (p. 109). The process was portrayed as a highly critical middle-class reaction (what he termed a 'critical social practice') to the city's postwar modernist development. Toronto's expanding middle-class intelligentsia was instrumental in the reorientation of the city's identity away from suburbia and back towards the central city. For the best part of two decades, Toronto's gentrification was in every sense a deliberate operation of resistance to everything that characterized urban development in the 1960s, and thus a practice 'eluding the domination of social and cultural structures and constituting new conditions for experience' (Caulfield 1989: 624). In his interviews with the gentrifiers of Toronto, Caulfield observed that their affection for Toronto's 'old city neighborhoods' was rooted in their desire to escape the mundane, banal routines that characterized suburbia:

> Old city places offer difference and freedom, privacy and fantasy, possibilities for carnival.... These are not just matters of philosophical abstraction but, in a carnival sense ... the force that [Walter] Benjamin believed was among the most vital stimuli to resistance to domination. "A big city is an encyclopaedia of sexual possibility", a characterization to be grasped in its wider sense; the city is "the place of our meeting with the other". (Caulfield 1989: 625)

This issue of 'the place of our meeting with the other' will be taken up in Chapter 6; here, it is necessary to register that Caulfield's point was that gentrification could not be separated from reform-era middle-class resistance to political and structural domination.

A similar argument emerges from Ley's (1996) coverage of the intertwining of gentrification and reform-era urban politics. Post 1968, the year when the student protests against the repressive colonization of everyday life by an overregulated society reached their peak all over the world (Watts 2001), many centrally located neighborhoods in urban Canada saw their social and economic status elevate as the central city became the arena for countercultural awareness, tolerance, diversity, and liberation. This occurred in the context of a laissez-faire state, the rapidly changing industrial and occupational structure described earlier (where 'hippies became yuppies', as Ley so tellingly put it, in the shift towards a postindustrial city), welfare retrenchment, a real estate and new construction boom, the advent of postmodern niche marketing and conspicuous consumption (Ley and Mills 1993), and the aestheticization and commodification of art and artistic lifestyles (Ley 2003). In the 1970s, neighborhoods such as Yorkville and the Annex in Toronto, Kitsilano and Fairview Slopes in Vancouver, and Le Plateau Mont-Royal in Montréal became hotbeds of 'hippie' youth reaction against political conservatism, modernist planning, and suburban ideologies.

But what were the politics of these youth once they grew up and became gentrifiers? What happens to voting behavior as social status rises? Suspicious of the empirical accountability of arguments from the United States which alluded to a conservative 'adversarial politics' among middle-class gentrifiers, Ley (1994) provided evidence from 1980s electoral returns in the three largest Canadian cities (Toronto, Montréal, and Vancouver) to demonstrate that the principal gentrifying districts in each city in fact contained an electorate which predominantly sided with more left–liberal reform politics. Reform politics in Canada prioritize a more 'open' government concerned with neighborhood rights, minority rights, improved public services (especially housing and transportation), and greater attention to heritage, environment, public open space, and cultural and leisure facilities. In one famous gentrifying district, Kitsilano in Vancouver, '[R]eform politics were retained through the gentrification cycle' (Ley 1996: 283); in another, Don Vale in Toronto, '[S]upport for reform candidates ... rose steadily, with the most concentrated support occurring in the 1978 election and after, coinciding with the second stage of gentrification and the emergence of professionals as the dominant group' (p. 288). In all three cities under scrutiny, there was 'no significant tendency overall for social upgrading in the city centre to be associated with [adversarial] conservative politics' (Ley 1994: 70).

In short, Ley argued that the values of the countercultural youth movements of the late 1960s 'diffused and evolved among receptive and much larger segments of the professional middle class along an identifiable occupational continuum' (1996: 210), and these are not the self-interested yuppie conservative values commonly attributed to gentrifiers. For Ley (and Caulfield), collective new middle-class disdain for the monotony of suburbia, and for the mass organization and repetition of postwar Fordism and its crushing of individualism and difference (and entire neighborhoods, through freeway construction), could not be divorced from the *explanation of gentrification* in general, and the *politics of gentrifiers* in particular. Furthermore, this discussion should not be treated as specific to the changing social status of Canadian urban neighborhoods. There is evidence from cities in other parts of the world that left–liberal politics characterize the new middle-class professional, not least in Melbourne, Australia (Mullins 1982; Logan 1985), and in many British cities (Savage 1991). In London, the gentrifiers interviewed by Tim Butler (1997) in Hackney demonstrated a *Guardian*-reading, Labour-voting, leftist ideological orientation. A commonly held view there was 'that a high level of consumption is acceptable but that one should be taxed to pay for a safety net', as evidenced by this gentrifier's comment:

> I am not sure that I buy the argument that I actually have to give up my Persian carpets for those people who are living under Waterloo Bridge to have homes. I am prepared to be taxed more heavily than I am and of course one is better off and it is difficult to see how one would feel if one didn't have this money. (Georgina, quoted in Butler 1997: 152)

These accounts challenge popular assumptions of gentrifiers as yuppie 'space invaders' (N. Smith and Williams 1986), and thus, as the quotation from Robert Beauregard highlights at the start of this chapter, demonizing gentrifiers for the negative effects of the process is probably unwarranted (although this must come with the caveat that care must be taken not to claim that all gentrifiers are tolerant liberals!). As Rofe (2003) has recently shown in a study of Sydney, the gentrifying elite are cosmopolitan, politically progressive, and supportive of antiracism, aboriginal rights, and social justice movements—indeed, many 'lamented a growing backlash of bigotry and xenophobia perceived to arise from a fear of global integration … thereby distancing themselves further from a myopic mainstream Australian culture' (p. 2520).

The quotation which began this section contains a phrase commonly heard among the gentrifiers of London (and probably elsewhere)—'people like us'. This has been the focus of work by Tim Butler, who has extensively researched the gentrifying middle classes in London. Butler (1997) noted how many of his respondents wanted to live amongst 'like-minded' people, seeing themselves as part of a middle-class community of couples and families finding ways to negotiate and adapt to various aspects of life in a global city. In more recent work, Butler with Robson (2003) looked at six different neighborhoods in London and found that these take on different meanings and associations that attract potential residents and then act on those who settled there, terming this the formation of a 'metropolitan habitus'. They researched how gentrifiers 'acted in different ways to ensure their hegemony over the localities in which they have settled', and how, because of living in unstable economic times and facing various structural constraints, gentrification should be seen as a middle-class 'coping strategy' (p. 27). The most pressing issue to cope with was explained as follows:

> Having taken the decision not to flee to the suburbs, living in the inner city presents the middle classes with a number of problems—particularly if there are children. The main issue that needs to be confronted is education and the fact that London's schools perform badly—particularly at secondary level. The necessary strategies to cope with this demand a huge investment of time, emotional energy and resources. (p. 29)

Butler with Robson (2003) have shown how social relations in gentrifying neighborhoods are often governed by the performance of local schools:

> Education markets are now rivalling those in housing and employment as determinants of the nature, extent and stability of middle-class gentrification of inner-city localities. The reported instability of Brixton is not because of its status as a centre for international hedonistic youth but because it doesn't provide the infrastructure for middle-class family life. ... Although there is a high-performing primary school, it has not become the middle-class school and does not provide either the basis of long-lasting social networks or the necessary route map to plan appropriate secondary education pathways. ... [M]iddle-class incomers have managed the classic manoeuvre of gentrification: coupling a necessary spatial proximity to other urban groups while strategically maintaining and protecting their material and cultural distance from them. (pp. 157–158)

Education is explained as a parental strategy deployed to ensure that children will also be middle class—will also become 'people like us'—and thus plays 'a fundamental role in processes of cultural and social class reproduction' (p. 159). Butler's work helps us to understand how gentrification in London is a response to various constraints in the form of housing, employment, consumption, and especially education. Gentrifiers are usually well educated, but these authors show that it is through looking at the education of their children that we can understand the process of gentrification. In the contemporary global city, the housing market trajectories of whom Butler (2003) has most recently called 'embattled settlers' are governed by 'the imperatives of everyday life (work and consumption) and intergenerational social reproduction (schooling and socialisation)' (p. 2484). Given the difficulties involved in coming to terms with living in London, it is hardly surprising that many gentrifiers eventually choose to leave the city for rural locations, giving rise to 'rural gentrification', which we discuss in Chapter 4.

*Gender*

In the early 1980s it was recognized that, through their increasing participation in the labor force, women were playing an active and important role
in bringing about gentrification (Markusen 1981; Holcomb and Beauregard
1981)—but the reasons for this lacked adequate conceptualization. This was
first noted by Damaris Rose in a pathbreaking article published in 1984. Rose
is a socialist–feminist urban geographer who, along with many others at the
time, was involved in a long struggle to get 1970s Marxists (e.g., Castells 1977)
to take the issues of social reproduction more seriously, rather than conflate
them with issues of consumption, which had the effect of 'obscuring the active
work of household members in reproducing both labour power and people'
(Rose 1984: 54). Rose thus argued that it was 'crucial to explore the relationships between gentrification, social and spatial restructuring of waged labour
processes, and changes in the reproduction of labour power and of people' (p.
48). Her 1984 paper was the first attempt, albeit tentative at the time (as she
acknowledged), to explore these relationships.

Rose emphasized the growing importance of both single women professionals and dual-earner couples in gentrification and argued that inner
cities may be more propitious spaces than suburbs for working out equitable
divisions of domestic labor. This followed up a claim first made by Ann
Markusen:

> [G]entrification is in large part a result of the breakdown of the patri-
> archal household. Households of gay people, singles, and professional
> couples with central business district jobs increasingly find central
> locations attractive. ... Gentrification ... corresponds to the two-income
> (or more) professional household that requires both a relatively central
> urban location to minimize journey-to-work costs of several wage earn-
> ers and a location that enhances efficiency in household production
> (stores are nearer) and in the substitution of market-produced com-
> modities (laundries, restaurants, child care) for household production.
> (Markusen 1981: 32)

Rose was heavily influenced by the notion of the 'chômeur(euse) instruit(e)',
an educated but unemployed male (female), developed by Francine Dansereau
and colleagues in work on housing tenure in Montréal (Dansereau et al. 1981).
This led to Rose's coinage of the phrase 'marginal gentrifier', later bolstered
by empirical research in that city (Rose and LeBourdais 1986; Rose 1989). It
refers to the fact that marginally employed professionals, prominent among
whom were women, single parents, and those receiving moderate incomes,
were attracted to central-city neighborhoods due to the range of support services they offered—which were unavailable in the suburbs. For example, the
worry of precarious employment could be eased by networking and holding
more than one job; and by minimizing space–time constraints, lone female

parents could combine paid and unpaid (domestic) labor with greater ease than in suburban locations:

> [It] is now becoming clear that many who become gentrifiers do so substantially because of the difficulties, not only of affording housing, but also of carrying on their particular living arrangements in conventional suburbs. ... [M]any existing older inner-city neighbourhoods ... facilitate access to community services, enable shared use of facilities, provide an efficient and nonisolating environment for reproductive work, and enhance opportunities for women to develop locally based friendship networks and a supportive environment. (Rose 1984: 63–64)

Rose was one of the first scholars to note that 'gentrifiers' were a differentiated group, and she concluded her article by calling for an approach to gentrification which explores 'the actual processes through which those groups we now subsume under the category "gentrifiers" are produced and reproduced' (p. 69).

A later paper documented the importance of professional women who were single parents in the process of gentrification, from research undertaken in Lower Outremont in Montréal (Rose and LeBourdais 1986). This was followed by an attempt to develop a theoretical framework that linked wider economic restructuring to labor force restructuring at the metropolitan scale (Rose 1989), showing how the latter is mediated by restructuring of social and economic relations at the household and individual scale. These efforts were paralleled by those of Robert Beauregard (1986), who, like Rose, viewed gentrification as a 'chaotic' concept, with so many themes and issues vying for attention that just one or two factors could not possibly explain the process. Beauregard viewed it as essential to link the consumption practices of gentrifiers with their decisions on biological reproduction, and it is worth quoting him at length on this important issue:

> The postponement of marriage facilitates this consumption, but it also makes it necessary if people are to meet others and develop friendships. Persons without partners, outside of the milieu of college, must now join clubs and frequent places (e.g. "singles" bars) where other singles (both the never-married and the divorced) congregate in order to make close friends. Couples (married or not) need friendships beyond the workplace and may wish to congregate at "public" places. These social opportunities, moreover, though possibly no more numerous in cities than in suburbs, are decidedly more spatially concentrated and, because of suburban zoning, tend to be more spatially integrated with residences. Clustering occurs as these individuals move proximate to "consumption items" and as entrepreneurs identify this fraction of labor as comprising conspicuous and major consumers. Both the need to consume outside of the home and the desire to make friends and meet sexual partners,

either during the now-extended period of "search" before marriage or a lifetime of fluid personal relationships, encourage the identification with and migration to certain areas of the city. (p. 44)

Reading this twenty years later, it is by no means out of date; indeed, Beauregard could well be describing the background to the popular TV series *Sex and the City*, which focuses on the life and times of four professional Manhattan-based women whose conspicuous consumption, fluid personal relationships, and congregation in clubs and singles bars made compelling viewing for many millions worldwide. Not surprisingly, numerous commentaries on *Sex and the City* focus on its contribution to feminist discourse, and how its four stars have become feminist icons. The city as a site of women's education, liberation, and expression in the context of gentrification was noted by, inter alia, Briavel Holcomb (1984) and then Peter Williams (1986) over twenty years ago:

Many of the female (and male) gentry were beneficiaries of the boom in tertiary education in the 1960s and 1970s. They were also in many cases the children of the middle-class suburbanites. Attending universities and colleges not only allowed many women to exercise choice over what roles they took on subsequently (including a working career), but also allowed many of them to experience a very different urban environment. Subsequently, having become familiar with the apparently more solid, intimate and accessible world of the inner city, many were encouraged to reject suburbia physically (just as they were rejecting it mentally) and opt for the world they now understood and preferred. For women, that decision gave them ready access to relatively well paid jobs, a supportive environment and the opportunity to imprint themselves and their new-found status upon the landscape. (Williams 1986: 69)

Perhaps the best example of this, among many, is the 'postmodern landscape' of Fairview Slopes in Vancouver, where Mills (1988) found that 'beliefs and practices centred around divided gender roles are fairly uncommon' (p. 181; see Chapter 4).

As the literature on gender and gentrification grew, it became characterized by research that looked at gender as a *social relation* in the context of the gentrifying household. Alan Warde (1991) argued that 'to explain "who are the gentrifiers?" the best approach is by way of understanding gender divisions, rather than class divisions' (p. 223). For Warde, gentrification was less about class expression and landscape aesthetics, and more about household composition and organization in the context of patriarchal pressures and the ways in which women adapt to new patterns of employment. For the two types of 'gentrifier' household—one single, the other dual-earner/family—he claimed that, among the former, 'access to commercial alternatives to services typically provided by women in family households can be readily obtained [in gentrifying neighborhoods]', and the location of the latter 'is a solution to problems of access to work and home and of combining paid and unpaid labour' (p. 229). In short, Warde believed that both kinds of living arrangement are best understood as a function of women reorienting their behavior to domestic and labor market pressures. This was also the tenor of an important intervention by Liz Bondi (1991), who believed that further research on gender and gentrification needed to move beyond its treatment of gender relations as primarily economic, and consider how 'changes in the sexual division of labour in the workplace, the community and the home ... are negotiated through cultural constructions of femininity and masculinity' (p. 195), and how gender positions are expressed and forged through gentrification.

The arguments of Warde in particular were called into question by Butler and Hamnett (1994), who were bothered by how he 'dispensed' with the key role of class in gentrification. The example of Hackney in east London, where Butler undertook research in the late 1980s, was used to challenge Warde. Heavily influenced by the work of Savage et al. (1992) on how the middle classes are fragmented and differentiated according to their access to educational and cultural capital, Butler and Hamnett (1994) used evidence from Hackney to assert that it is the *interaction* between class (governed by both occupation and education) and gender which is crucial to the explanation of gentrification in that neighborhood. These authors conclude that gentrification is 'not solely a class process, but neither is it solely a gender process. It involves the consumption of inner-city housing by middle-class people who have an identifiable class and cultural formation, one of whose major identifying characteristics centres around the occupational identity of its female members' (p. 491). It was largely the daughters of middle-class families who benefited from the expansion of educational opportunities during the postwar decades, and the purchasing power of these professional women (even in the context of continuing gender inequality within households) was crucial to the early gentrification of Hackney. The basic point being made was that social class background is vitally important in gentrification, and heavily influences the role played by gender.

In perhaps the most recent contribution of key theoretical significance to the literature on gender and gentrification, Bondi (1999b) argues that contra Butler and Hamnett, gender practices cannot simply be 'read-off' from socioeconomic or demographic variables (p. 263), and that the London inner-urban experience is not easily transportable to other contexts. She instead focuses on the centrality of the patterning of *life courses* in the articulation of class and gender practices, drawing on a mixed-methods study conducted in three neighborhoods in Edinburgh (two inner urban and one suburban). Three key issues emerged from this research:

1. Gentrification is not just about a particular strand of the professional middle class. More significance needs to be accorded to financially independent middle-class women whose occupations are not classified as 'professions' but whose lifestyles and outlooks are broadly the same as those of professional middle-class men.
2. Local context is crucial to the relationship between gender and gentrification. It was only in one of the neighborhoods studied (higher-status, inner-urban Stockbridge) that proximity to family was not of much importance to interviewees, so there is much differentiation *between* middle-class professional women in that city.
3. Perceptions of future life courses were woven into gentrifiers' discussions of their prospective housing careers, and were anchored in intergenerational class mobility. In the other inner-urban neighborhood, Leith, some gentrifiers had working-class backgrounds; upward social mobility had enabled them to return to their place of origin after residence elsewhere.

Five years earlier, in a study of a gentrifying neighborhood in west London, Gary Bridge (1994) noted that there was 'a general stage-in-the-lifestyle effect in that there was a reliance on social relations in the neighbourhood that might be more explicable by gender, age and family status, rather than by social or spatial solidarity groups' (p. 46–47). Bondi's (1999b) paper takes this further and calls for further research on gender and gentrification that pays attention to the shaping of life courses and the specifics of place—a still somewhat unexplored area of investigation (but see Karsten [2003] for a detailed study of these issues in Amsterdam).

*Sexuality*

> In this country, in America, there's plenty of pie for everybody to make it. ... The fact that we [gay people] have money, the fact that we spent it—that's an economic contribution.

> Gay speculator (quoted in Knopp 1990: 347)

A different kind of life course in specific urban places has been the focus of studies which have examined the changing geographies of sexuality in the inner city, especially those studies which have explained the role of gays and lesbians in the gentrification process. Without question the most famous of these studies is Manuel Castells's account of the formation of the gay community in San Francisco, a chapter in his landmark book on urban social movements, *The City and the Grassroots* (1983). Castells pointed out that it was the spatial concentration of gays which made it possible for the gay liberation movement in that city (and elsewhere) to gather momentum—as Harry Britt, the political leader of the city's gay community at the time, told Castells,

'When gays are spatially scattered, they are not gay, because they are invisible' (p. 138). This spatial concentration was instrumental to the gentrification of certain San Francisco neighborhoods; some brief background is needed to explain sexuality and gentrification in this context.

San Francisco was a major port city in World War II; homosexuality was illegal in the military, so many gays serving in the Pacific region were discharged and ordered to disembark into the city. As many did not return home due to the stigma of homosexuality, meeting points emerged among those who had discovered their sexual and cultural identity, such as bars in disinvested parts of town, around which gay networks were constructed. The 1950s and 1960s were a time of immense countercultural uprising in San Francisco, exemplified by the renowned Beatnik network, which emerged in reaction to the heterosexual institutions of the family and, crucially, suburbia. The subversive literary prowess of Jack Kerouac and Allen Ginsberg, among others, created a climate of tolerance for homosexuality, and once the media covered this 'deviance', the attraction of alternative San Francisco to isolated gays all over the United States became magnetic. Following the watershed of the Stonewall Riots of 1969, when police raided a gay bar in Greenwich Village in New York City and met determined resistance, newly liberated gays continued to flock to San Francisco because of its reputation as a sympathetic milieu.

Post 1969, Castells noted,

> The gay movement realized that between liberation and politics it first had to establish a community in a series of spatial settings and through a network of economic, social and cultural institutions. (p. 143)

This community centered around the Castro neighborhood, an area characterized by Victorian townhouses vacated by the Irish working class who moved to the suburbs—thus, there was much affordable housing to buy and rent. From the mid-1970s onwards, the Castro gay 'ghetto', as Castells called it, expanded in all directions, and a 'very dense gay network of bars, health clubs, stores, businesses, and activities developed on the basis of a growing population' (p. 156). Castells argued that gentrification 'has been largely, although not exclusively, triggered by gay people' and 'has greatly helped San Francisco to preserve its historical heritage of beautiful old Victorian buildings' (p. 158). He found three ways in which the gentrification process involved the gay community (pp. 158–159):

1. Affluent gay professionals bought inexpensive properties and hired skilled renovators to improve their use and exchange value.
2. Gay realtors and interior decorators used their commercial and artistic skills and bought property in low-cost areas, and repaired and renovated the buildings in order to sell them at a profit.

3. Less affluent gays formed collectives to either rent or buy inexpensive buildings, and fixed them up themselves (this was the most common form of gentrification).

Explaining what constituted these 'collectives', Castells noted that 'many were single men, did not have to sustain a family, were young, and [were] connected to a relatively prosperous service economy ... [which] made it easier for them to find a house in a tight housing market' (p. 160). This was also noted in an important article by Lauria and Knopp (1985):

> [B]eing a gay male in this society is economically advantageous. Males make more money than their female counterparts in every sector of the economy, and gay males tend to have fewer dependents than straight men. This means that many gay men are in an excellent position to become gentrifiers. (p. 161)

Demographics aside, however, what is particularly striking in the Castells study is not just how the gay community's early efforts at forging an identity in a spatial setting in the most trying of circumstances led to rampant gentrification, but also how the expanding Castro is a contradictory, ambivalent space—it was vital to an oppressed group seeking liberation, but the gentrification that followed oppressed other groups:

> [T]here has been little urban improvement for the black families forced to move out from the Hayes Valley, or help for Latinos suffering high rents along the Dolores corridor because of real estate speculation from the increasing influx of gays. (Castells 1983, p. 167)

So, while gay gentrification might be explained, in Lauria and Knopp's (1985) words, by 'the need to escape to an oasis of tolerance ... an opportunity to combat oppression by creating neighbourhoods over which they [gays] have maximum control' (p. 161), it can lead to another form of oppression—the displacement of low-income minorities and/or the working class. As is usually the case with gentrification, surface appearances (beautiful Victorian buildings and famous gay neighborhoods, now often tourist attractions) mask underlying injustices and tensions.

Larry Knopp has been at the forefront of the analysis of gay gentrification in the context of booming urban land markets (e.g., Knopp 1990, 1997), particularly emphasizing the class interests involved in the process, something on which Castells was rather silent. In a discussion of 1960s and 1970s gentrification in the Marigny neighborhood of New Orleans, Knopp (1990) explained that the earliest gentrifiers were predominantly gay middle-class professionals, that the leaders of the historic preservation movement in Marigny during the 1970s were openly gay, and, crucially, that the speculators and developers who entered the scene in the mid-1970s, accelerating gentrification, were mostly gay men. On this last point, Knopp identified the role of a real estate firm which became a community institution in its own right, one that, often through illegal means (bribing appraisers employed by financial institutions), 'helped members of the local gay community to secure financing for virtually the entire purchase price of homes' (p. 345). This was followed by a development corporation owned by a gay man with close ties to New Orleans' conservative business community; this corporation tried to develop a distinctively affluent gay community in Marigny—in the words of the owner, 'an environment of pools and jacuzzis and … free love … essentially a gay enclave of fairly wealthy people' (quoted on p. 346). Contrary to what Knopp was expecting to discover, rather than gentrifying as a collective response to oppression, gay gentrification in New Orleans was primarily 'an alternative strategy for accumulation', one of 'overcoming institutional obstacles to investment in certain parts of the city' (p. 347). Knopp therefore insisted that any understanding of gay gentrification must consider questions of class interests as well as gay identity construction.

One of the more controversial aspects of Castells's study of San Francisco was his general contention that it is only gay men who form residential concentrations in urban neighborhoods. However, the work of Tamar Rothenberg (1995) in Park Slope, New York City (see Chapter 1), on lesbian gentrifiers illustrates that it is not just gay men who have an innate 'territorial imperative', as Castells put it. Park Slope has probably the heaviest concentration of lesbians in the United States, and Rothenberg noted that the establishment of a loosely defined lesbian community there was related to the timing of both the women's movement and early gentrification, where political activists were attracted by the idea of 'sweat equity' housing. But the reasons for their continuing concentration in Park Slope are somewhat different from those concerning the gay men outlined by Castells and Knopp:

> Word-of-mouth, not statistical information, is what lures women to a "lesbian neighbourhood". What matters to the people who live in a community is their experience of the place, how they feel walking down the street, the services available to them. (Rothenberg 1995: 169)

Whilst a number of Rothenberg's interviewees stopped short of describing Park Slope as a true lesbian community, all of them affirmed the spatial significance of a large population of lesbians in Park Slope, and how this population has grown due to 'the power of lesbian social networking' (p. 177). To capture this networking, Rothenberg refers to a 1980s TV shampoo commercial which held the repetitive slogan, 'And she told two friends, and she told two friends…' so that many more women eventually knew about the quality of the shampoo. Rothenberg points out how this slogan captures the social networking among the lesbian gentrifiers of Park Slope—but with the outcome that huge pressures are placed on the local housing market, and rising rents lead to the displacement of many lesbians to adjacent neighborhoods. Rothenberg's study thus supports Knopp's insistence that a study of sexuality and gentrification must pay attention to housing market dynamics as well as the formation of gay identities.

The presence of a gay population in economically thriving urban neighborhoods has recently become a high-profile urban policy issue in North America, attributable to the enormous influence of Richard Florida's creative class thesis in policy circles. We introduced his thesis in the Preface to this book, explaining its implications for gentrification—our purpose here is to zoom in on one of Florida's observations, namely, that the conspicuous presence of gays and lesbians is vital to urban economic development. Florida (2003) has stated that the 'engines of economic development' are the three 'T's': technology, talent, and tolerance. On tolerance, he says the following:

> I think it's important for a place to have low entry barriers for people, that is, to be a place where newcomers are accepted quickly into all sorts of social and economic arrangements. Such places gain a creativity advantage. All else being equal, they are likely to attract greater numbers of talented and creative people—the sort of people who power innovation and growth. (p. 250)

Later on in a book characterized by 'excruciating details of his own biography, lifestyle and consumption habits ... [and] less-than-analytical musings [that] descend into self-indulgent forms of amateur microsociology and crass celebrations of hipster embourgeoisement' (Peck 2005: 744–745), Florida (2003) shows just how crucial gays are to his creativity bandwagon:

> In travelling to cities for my speaking engagements, I have come up with a handy metric to distinguish those cities that are part of the Creative Age from those that are not. If city leaders tell me to wear whatever I want, take me to a casual contemporary café or restaurant for dinner, and most important encourage me to talk openly about the role of diversity and gays, I am confident their city will be able to attract the Creative Class and prosper in this emerging era. If on the other hand they ask me to "please wear a business suit and a tie", take me to a private club for dinner, and ask me to "play down the stuff about bohemians and gays", I can be reasonably sure they will have a hard time making it. (p. 304)

Among a bewildering set of indices drawn up in his book to rank cities' creativity, there is a 'Gay Index'. Developed by his colleague Gary Gates, it uses residential data from the U.S. Bureau of the Census to rank regions by their concentrations of gay people. Together, Florida and Gates noted that the same places that were popular among gays were also the ones where high-tech industry located. Florida (2003) summed up as follows:

[A] place that welcomes the gay community welcomes all kinds of people. ... [G]ays can be said to be the "canaries of the Creative Age". For these reasons, openness to the gay community is a good indicator of the low entry barriers to human capital that are so important to spurring creativity and generating high-tech growth. (p. 256)

Florida's message, backed up by suggestive statistical correlations, is simple and attractive to urban policy makers—be tolerant of gays, and your city will 'succeed and prosper economically'. Furthermore, if cities are not open, inclusive, and diverse, 'they will fall further behind' (p. 266). What is never mentioned among all this enthusiastic rhetoric about gays and economic development is the role of gays in facilitating gentrification. On the issue of gentrification, Florida, presumably to preempt any criticism, appears worried:

[T]he current round of urban revitalization is giving rise to serious tensions between established neighborhood residents and newer, more affluent people moving in. In an increasing number of cities, the scales have tipped from revitalization to rampant gentrification and displacement. Some of these places have become unaffordable for any but the most affluent. ... While the technological downturn of the last few years relieved some of this pressure on urban housing markets, gentrification in major urban centers continues to threaten the diversity and creativity that have driven these cities' innovation and growth in the first place. (pp. 289–290)

These are astonishing words from someone who has been promoting the attractions of gentrified/gentrifying neighborhoods in a number of American cities for the best part of a decade. The contradictions are glaring—technology (high-tech industry) is seen to be one of the three fundamental assets any city should have to attract creative types, yet when there is a technological downturn, housing in that city becomes more affordable to them. Furthermore, the very process in which the creative class takes part—gentrification—threatens the longevity of the diverse and creative conditions which attracted them. This points to some serious problems with Florida's thesis (Peck 2005).

*Ethnicity*

Without question, until recently, the most neglected area of inquiry in research that asks, 'Who are the gentrifiers?' is the existence of gentrifiers who are non-white but share all the other characteristics of the new middle class. The image most people have of gentrifiers is of white yuppie 'pioneers' moving into low-income neighborhoods with dense concentrations of ethnic minorities. This image was neatly captured by a satirical magazine entitled *American Gentrifier* (see Plate 3.2) with a picture of a white professional couple on the front, with baby, accompanied by amusing contents listings such as 'Bed-Stuy—Still Too Black?' (Bed-Stuy is Bedford-Stuyvesant, a onetime highly segregated and very

**Plate 3.2** The American Gentrifier

American Gentrifier

Brooklyn Edition Winter 2005

10 VIOLENT CRIMES YOU
CAN LIVE WITH

LOCAL DELIS NOW
STOCKING BRIE

BED STUY: STILL
TOO BLACK?

PLUS: WHEN TO
START THE KIDS ON
ANTIDEPRESSANTS

Look at this wholesome image of the American gentrifying family. What does it say about the process of gentrification?
*Source: Stay Free!* magazine, 2004. Reprinted with permission of *Stay Free!* magazine.

poor African–American neighborhood in Brooklyn, New York City, which is now experiencing gentrification.)

But what about the black middle class, many of whom possess precisely the same educational, occupational, and income characteristics as gentrifiers? In the United States, the demographic expansion of the black middle class is very well documented, but usually in the context of their mass exodus from ghetto neighborhoods to suburban areas, with devastating consequences for those left behind (e.g., W. J. Wilson 1996). Until recently very few studies have looked at the black middle class who remain in, or move into, central-city neighborhoods and contribute to the gentrification process, which has been happening in many cities across the country. An exception is the work by Bostic and Martin (2003), who provided a useful (quantitative) scoring technique for identifying gentrified neighborhoods in the United States, and found that during the 1970s, black home owners were of significant gentrifying influence, but less so in the 1980s (due to the impact of fair-lending and antidiscrimination efforts that allowed black home owners into more affluent suburban areas, rather than gentrifying areas). But whilst valuable in a broad sense, quantitative longitudinal studies do not help us to learn about the local (neighborhood) impacts of black gentrification, for which we have to turn to the smaller-scale work of a more qualitative nature. Furthermore, Bostic and Martin's findings sit uneasily with work that does show that black gentrification greatly affected some high-profile neighborhoods in the 1980s.

Harlem in New York City is doubtless the most famous African–American neighborhood in the United States. The Harlem Renaissance of the 1920s, a local flowering of art, literature, and music that had international influence, was followed by decades of systematic disinvestment poetically captured by Kenneth Clark's *Dark Ghetto* (1964). So devastated was Harlem that a ripple of astonishment was felt when Richard Schaffer and Neil Smith (1986) pointed to it as a candidate for gentrification, albeit with a question mark. A key finding was as follows:

> At present it is clear that despite prominent press reports featuring individual white gentrifiers in Harlem ... the vast majority of people involved in rehabilitation and redevelopment in Central Harlem are black. (p. 358)

Monique Taylor (1992), a graduate student when Schaffer and Smith's article was published, decided to research the black middle class in Harlem from 1987 to 1992, and found that gentrifiers were 'strongly motivated by a desire to participate in the rituals that define daily life in this (in)famous and historically black community' (p. 102). Taylor found black gentrifiers confronting what she called a 'dilemma of difference' during their transition from outsider to insider in a place where their class position and lifestyle are so distinct from those of other blacks, but also when constructing a black identity distinct from the white world of the workplace (this is also memorably depicted in the Spike Lee film *Jungle Fever* [Lee 1991]). Economic factors are not ignored in this study, but for Taylor, black gentrification was also 'a strategy of cultural survival rooted in the search for the positive meaning and support that the black community might provide' (Taylor 1992: 109). Home owners in Harlem were seen to be bridging the dual worlds of race and class that they were defined by—the difference of race defined their marginal status in the workplace, but the difference of class defined their 'outsiderness' in Harlem. In her book-length treatment of these issues (Taylor 2002), one of Taylor's respondents described the class conflict giving rise to this outsiderness:

> The other people [nongentrifiers] ... they've been lied to for so long and here's people like myself have come in. We're making some bread. We get the best apartments that they weren't even thinking about.... So then that makes them a little angry, which I can understand. You got this division, in a sense, in an area like this, between people who have some money and people who don't have some money. ... [T]here's this friction. (p. 91)

The arrival of the so-called Second Harlem Renaissance (gentrification) is well documented by Taylor—125th Street, Harlem's symbolic commercial strip, has all the hallmarks of advanced gentrification, including a Starbucks, unthinkable in recent memory. Particularly relevant to our discussion is how the black middle class paved the way for accelerated gentrification by the wealthier, white middle class that followed, making the words of Schaffer and Smith (1986) very prescient:

> The inescapable conclusion is that unless Harlem defies all the empirical trends, the process might well begin as black gentrification, but any wholesale rehabilitation of Central Harlem would necessarily involve a considerable influx of middle- and upper-class whites. (p. 359)

Lance Freeman (2006) has also written about black gentrification in Harlem and in Clinton Hill, Brooklyn. Unlike Taylor (2002), who focused on the black gentry, Freeman aims to provide a better understanding of gentrification from the vantage point of the indigenous residents living in these neighborhoods. His focus, then, is on the impacts of gentrification on nongentrifiers, a research strategy that Slater, Curran, and Lees (2004) called for. However, he cannot escape discussing the black middle class too:

> In some ways, however, the gentrification of black neighbourhoods is liberating in ways not imagined by Ley and others. That is, the process may be liberating for eclectic-minded segments of the black middle class as well who see in gentrification an opportunity to carve out their own space without having to conform to the precepts of white America or the conservative ethos that dominates much of black America. Gentrifying black neighbourhoods like the ones examined here represent spaces where the black identity is celebrated, the norm and not considered the "other". Several observers have noted that for some middle class blacks, the legacy of the civil rights era was not integrating into white neighbourhoods

but having the wherewithal to create desirable black neighbourhoods. (p. 196)

Yet black gentrification can be something far removed from the positive force with which it is often portrayed, as Michelle Boyd (2000, 2005) has shown in the South Side of Chicago. An ethnographic study of the creeping black gentrification of the Douglas/Grand Boulevard neighborhood, a place even more devastated by institutional racism and disinvestment than Harlem, revealed that many existing residents and community organizers (and the powerful local planning commission) were receptive to the idea of attracting the black middle class to an economically impoverished part of the city. Indeed, it was seen as a strategy for 'racial uplift', to elevate the status and self-esteem of the black community, best exemplified by renaming the area 'Bronzeville', the name the area was given by St. Clair Drake and Horace Cayton in their monumental 1945 study, *Black Metropolis*. Not only was the black middle class expected to interact with all community members—but it was also assumed that the tax base improvements brought by the black middle class would benefit all black people in the neighborhood. But as Boyd (2005) points out,

> By homogenizing the needs and interests of the black poor and the black elites, promoters of black gentrification mask the extent to which their strategies differently and disproportionately threaten lower income residents. ... [T]he race uplift framework justifies gentrification but it does so using a different logic.... [It] creates the illusion that gentrification strategies are implemented both in the interests of, and with the approval of, the poor black residents it displaces. (pp. 285–286)

A revealing quote came from a member of the powerful local planning commission: '[We] don't mind gentrification. But we want to minimize displacement' (Boyd 2005: 116). The fact that these are two sides of the same coin was not even recognized. As Wyly and Hammel (2000) have pointed out, Chicago's historic black ghetto, once dominated by public housing but now being demolished for mixed-income settlements, is in the quite bizarre situation of being a place where generations of racial prejudice, segregation, and containment have led to the most attractive land in the city for development and middle-class colonization—resulting in low-income displacement.

### Class Constitution and the Gentrification Aesthetic

Earlier in this chapter, we explained how David Ley (1996) pointed out that consecutive waves of the new middle class in Canada viewed the central city as 'a mark of distinction in the constitution of an identity separate from the constellation of place and identity shaped by the suburbs' (p. 211). But how is this social distinction marked out on the streets of gentrifying neighborhoods?

How do gentrifiers distinguish themselves from other social class groups? A gentrifying or gentrified neighborhood has a certain 'feel' to it, a certain look, a landscape of conspicuous consumption that makes the process readily identifiable (see Plates 3.3 and 3.4). This has become known as the *gentrification aesthetic*, and as Jager (1986) pointed out,

> [T]he aesthetics of gentrification not only illustrate the class dimension of the process but also express the dynamic constitution of social class of which gentrification is a specific part. ...
>
> Slums become Victoriana, and housing becomes a cultural investment with façadal display signifying social ascension. (pp. 78–79)

Jager's essay was the first widely cited analysis of the architectural and internal decorative aesthetics of gentrified buildings and neighborhoods. His research on the landscapes of 'Victoriana' in inner Melbourne revealed that by 'buying into history', the new middle class was expressing its social distance from not just the working class, but also the old middle class. With respect to the former, this was Jager's reasoning:

> The effacing of an industrial past and a working-class presence, the whitewashing of a former social stain, was achieved through extensive remodelling. The return to historical purity and authenticity (of the "high" Victorian era) is realized by stripping away external additions, by sandblasting, by internal gutting. The restoration of an *anterior* history was virtually the only manner in which the recent stigma of inner areas could be removed or redefined. It is in the fundamental drive to dislodge, and symbolically obliterate, the former working-class past that the aestheticization of Victoriana took off. (p. 83)

On the latter, Jager writes,

> What characterizes this new consumption ... is an emphasis on aesthetic-cultural themes. Leisure and relative affluence create the opportunity for artistic consumption, and art becomes increasingly integrated into the middle-class pattern of consumption as a form of investment, status symbol and means of self-expression. The difference between this consumption model and a more traditional middle-class one is marked. (p. 86)

Victoriana in Melbourne was, for Jager, a process of urban conservation that reused and recycled history in a deliberate process of new middle-class demarcation and distinction. But even if Melbourne's gentrifiers sought to individualize history's mass production through the consumption of time, this aestheticization eventually led to a 'gentrification kitsch', where imitation took precedence over authenticity in the necessity to compensate for market

**Plate 3.3** Elm Grove, Toronto

Pregentrification.
*Source:* Photograph by Tom Slater.

consumption and produce profit from a repackaged past. Cultural difference becomes mass produced as gentrification advances, as N. Smith (1996a), drawing on Jager's work, explains:

> As the choicest structures are converted and open sites become increasingly conspicuous, as well as expensive, in otherwise gentrified neighbourhoods, the infill is accomplished by new construction. Here the architectural form provides no historical meaning that can be reworked into cultural display, and the appeal to the kitsch of gentrification is therefore more extreme. Where such modern infill occurs in gentrifying neighbourhoods ... the impression is one of having come full circle, in geographical and cultural

**Plate 3.4** Elm Grove, Toronto

Postgentrification.
*Source:* Photograph by Tom Slater.

as well as architectural terms. This infill gentrification is accomplishing a suburbanization of the city. (p. 115)

This can be clearly seen in Plate 3.5.

Munt's (1987) study of gentrification in Battersea paid more attention to the *interiors* of the Victorian houses in that neighborhood than Jager's exterior focus:

[O]stentatious display and exhibitionism require a stage. The creation and alteration of space allow this. … [A]ll the interviewees had inherited from previous gentrifiers or provided themselves with an extended kitchen and

**Plate 3.5** Harbourside Development near Bristol Bridge

Note the choicest structures on the left, and the infill on the far right, appealing to the kitsch of its neighbors.
*Source:* Photograph by Tom Slater.

open lounge. The walls are torn down and the through-lounge becomes an extended showcase of the gentrifiers' aesthetic and cultural consumption. This is made visible to those outside by the absence of netted curtains, thus allowing the gentrifiers to flaunt their wealth and to express a social status. (p. 1193)

Similar observations are made in a study of New York, London, and Paris by Carpenter and Lees (1995), who note that 'it is the interiors that really mark out a gentrifier's status in all three cities' (p. 299), and provide a detailed summary of the aesthetic signifiers of upward social mobility and how they contribute to the process of gentrifiers 'reclaiming space'. Caroline Mills (1988) described the gentrification aesthetic in Fairview Slopes, Vancouver, as a 'postmodern landscape' that expressed the neighborhood by a striking intermixture of past and present architectural forms, or, in realtors' terms, 'an eclectic fusion of classical and contemporary details' (p. 176). But what is behind this particular gentrification aesthetic, this particular set of 'tastes' among the new middle class, and how is it translated into commodity? And, what happens to the gentrification aesthetic once it is commodified?

Gary Bridge (1995, 2001a, 2001b) has explored these issues in some detail in his ongoing investigations of class constitution and gentrification. Bridge's key contribution to this debate has been to note that the majority of class-constitutive effects 'occur outside of the gentrified neighborhood (division of labour and workplace relations) or before the process has taken place (socialization of lifestyle and taste)', which necessitates a view of residence that encompasses the entire metropolitan area, not just individual neighborhoods (1995: 245). For Bridge, what scholars such as Jager had missed among the imposing neighborhood Victoriana was that prior educational experience is crucial to the gentrification aesthetic:

> The influence of education might help explain the existence of the gentrification aesthetic in terms of the acquisition of "good taste" through middle-class background and/or a middle-class (higher) education. The gentrification aesthetic does not arise spontaneously from reaction to a working-class environment. (pp. 243–244)

This possession of cultural capital came up again in a later paper on gentrification in Sydney, where Bridge (2001a) looked at the role of estate agents in the gentrification aesthetic, and drew on the work of Pierre Bourdieu to show how they 'negotiate the boundaries of class demarcation and distinction' in the conversion of cultural capital (taste) into economic capital (price) (p. 89). Typically they have to move between working-class vendors and middle-class purchasers, as one estate agent based in the neighborhood of Glebe showed:

> [A] lot of our clients ... they've been to university so they have an academic, more sophisticated background, more cultural background than the average suburb has. ... [They] don't have a lot of money but they have knowledge, they also have the ability to convert these old homes which were, 20 years ago, turned from beautiful old Victorian homes to just money earning, devoid of character, aluminium-windowed properties and they convert them back into the Victorian home. It's a difference between, it's a different social class, it's a gentrification of it. A lot of the people in Glebe aren't as wealthy as they'd like to be but culturally they're very wealthy. (p. 90)

Yet the gentrification aesthetic is not an end-stage, static phenomenon. For Bridge, it is constantly on the move as gentrification intensifies, with its boundaries being tested 'in the acquisition of modern goods on one side and the identification of historical symbols on the other' (2001b: 214). He argues that this balancing act is important in understanding how gentrification continues and thrives, as 'aesthetic display formed a way of coordinating rational expectations such that the new set of strategies [in Sydney] were successful as a wider class movement in as much as taste then converted into price in the market values of the properties' (p. 213). This conversion of cultural capital into economic capital as gentrification proceeds has also been noted by Ley (2003) in a Bourdieu-influenced discussion of artists and the gentrification aesthetic in Canada. Here the conversion is done not just by estate agents but also by 'a cadre of cultural intermediaries in real estate, travel, cuisine, the arts and home decorating ... [that] disseminates knowledge about neighbourhood sites and the rules, resources and rituals of the gentrifier's lifestyle' (p. 2538). The outcome of this economic valorization of the gentrification aesthetic is an increase in property prices which leads, ironically, to the displacement of artists, those very people whose aesthetic dispositions helped to initiate the influx of middle-class professionals. One of the most commonly noted trends in the process of gentrification is that places and people once deemed hip, authentic, trendy, and subversive quickly become appropriated, manufactured, and mass-produced kitsch for higher-earning groups. Thus, if we speak of a gentrification aesthetic, we must remember that this aesthetic is far from frozen, and leads to enormous profits as cultural capital becomes economic capital.

This leads our focus onto a particular form of gentrification that has transformed the landscapes of so many cities across the globe with declining manufacturing bases. No discussion of the gentrification aesthetic can ignore the phenomenon of 'loft living' in the warehouses of former industrial districts. The most influential study of this phenomenon came from Sharon Zukin in her classic work *Loft Living: Culture and Capital in Urban Change*, first published in 1982. In the second edition, Zukin (1989) explained how derelict manufacturing spaces in the Soho (South of Houston) district of New York City attracted artists in the 1960s and 1970s and thereafter provided a cultural impetus for the commercial redevelopment of Lower Manhattan. Arguably the most important concept introduced in this book, and central to Zukin's explanation of gentrification, is what she called the artistic mode of production (AMP), quite simply an attempt by large-scale investors in the built environment to ride out and to control a precarious investment climate, using the culture industries as a tool for attracting capital (p. 176). Zukin demonstrates that precarious economic conditions were highly conducive to 'a seemingly modest redevelopment strategy based on the arts and on historic preservation' (p. 176). In short, large-scale investors were forced to redirect their attentions towards a strategy of cultural consumption if profits were to be extracted from the built environment. In another example of the conversion of cultural capital into economic capital, Zukin showed how capital incorporated culture to open up devalorized industrial land markets to more market forces—what she memorably called a 'historic compromise' between culture and capital in the urban core.

In her discussion of consumer demand for lofts, Zukin was particularly astute on the emergence of the gentrification aesthetic:

[P]erhaps there is an aesthetic component to the demand factor—a *zeitgeist* that finds expression in the old factory spaces and thus identifying in some existential way with an archaic past or an artistic style of life. If this is true, then the question of timing becomes crucial. Sweatshops existed for many years, and no-one had suggested that moving into a sweatshop was chic. ... So if people found lofts attractive in the 1970s, some changes in values must have "come together" in the 1960s. There must have been an "aesthetic conjuncture". On the one hand, artists' living habits become a cultural model for the middle class. On the other hand, old factories became a means of expression for a "post-industrial" civilization. A heightened sense of art and history, space and time, was dramatized by the taste-setting mass media. (pp. 14–15)

In keeping with the restless gentrification aesthetic, once this 'dramatization' occurred, loft residence quickly moved away from its bohemian, marginal, artist 'live–work' roots into a commodity, a way of life for the wealthy urban professional. The undeniably striking cast-iron façades and columns lining Soho's cobbled streets (see Plate 3.6) are now more likely to house ostentatious celebrities than bohemian artists, just as the lofts in London's Clerkenwell and Shoreditch house corporate executives rather than, say, musicians. Field and Irving (1999) explain:

**Plate 3.6** Greene Street, Soho, Manhattan

Look at the architecture and the streetscape.
*Source:* Photograph by Tom Slater.

While the first loft dwellers had, in the main, been engaged in the creative arts, owners of loft buildings soon realized that they could market the image and ambience of the brilliantly expressive artist to members of the public who had little or no direct involvement in the arts world. ... From their original function as sites of light-manufacturing production, to their role as sites of "artistic" production, these lofts thus assumed a further role as psychologically dynamic spaces in which the loft buyer, so the developers' marketing brochures claimed, could express and fulfil their personality. (p. 172)

This creation of a loft identity has been astonishingly successful—'New York-style' lofts are now marketed in cities all over the world; the market leader in London is, tellingly, the *Manhattan Loft Corporation*, which ironically claims to 'address the needs of individuals rather than "the market"' (http://www.manhattanloft.co.uk). Julie Podmore (1998), in her study of loft living in Montréal, calls this the 'SoHo syndrome', where 'loft spaces depend on their resemblance to SoHo lofts for their legitimacy as "avant-garde" domestic spaces and sites of identity construction' (p. 284). Unlike Zukin, she uses Bourdieu's concept of habitus—the location in which class constitution is produced by linking aesthetic dispositions and social practices—to explain the diffusion of the loft aesthetic away from Soho. Local media discourses in Montréal linked the Soho experience to the postindustrial landscape of that city, building connections between space, aesthetics, and identity. Surveying media articles, Podmore found 'patterns of taste, lifestyle, location and the use of space which revealed the practices and judgements that constitute the loft *habitus*' (p. 289). She distinguishes between loft dwellers, who use lofts solely as domestic spaces, and loft artists, who live and work in their lofts—whereas the former value large loft spaces for their work, the latter give such spaces aesthetic values, and view them as central to the 'real' (Soho-inflected) loft experience, seeing it as more authentic:

We were looking for something really big so size was important. Something with big windows, something with potential. Places that were already fixed up were too expensive. This place actually had less potential than others we saw but it was really cheap at the time. The fact that it was an authentic loft. It's a sweatshop that we turned into a loft. It's not just a place where you tear down some walls and you call it a loft. It's an actual industrial building. It has an authentic elevator that came right up into the space and that was sort of a cool feature. (Loft dweller, quoted in Podmore 1998: 297)

Perhaps the power of the loft habitus, and the gentrification aesthetic, is revealed in this quotation—the industrial past is romanticized (some would say erased), the building somehow authentic, and thus it has (presumably market) 'potential'. But as Zukin (1989) pointed out, 'Only people who do not know the steam and sweat of a real factory can find industrial space romantic or interesting' (p. 59).

### The Problems with Consumption Explanations

It should be clear by now that a huge literature exists on the production of new middle-class gentrifiers, and the reasons for their location in central-city neighborhoods. In recent years, especially in the United Kingdom, this literature has simply exploded—so many articles have appeared with gentrifiers occupying center stage, as exemplified by the special issue of *Urban Studies* on gentrification, published in November 2003 with the title 'The Gentry and the City'. But as a collective, this literature must not be viewed uncritically. Aside from the obvious criticisms that central issues such as the production of space; the role of real estate developers, mortgage financiers, and global capitalists; and the propitious role of the local and national state are all sidelined by consumption accounts, we argue here that a key problem is that the focus on the constitution and practices of middle-class gentrifiers—one of the *beneficiary* groups of gentrification—has arguably shifted attention away from the negative effects of the process.

For example, the work explaining how gentrification is anchored around the intersection of housing and education markets (e.g., Butler with Robson 2003; Hamnett 2003b) is devoid of any careful qualitative consideration of working-class people and how the gentrification-education connection affects them. If the working class is mentioned at all, it is usually in the form of how the middle classes feel about 'others', or neighbors not like them. These feelings are often rather depressing, as evidenced by Tim Butler's study of gentrification in Barnsbury, London:

> Gentrification in Barnsbury (and probably London) is therefore apparently playing a rather dangerous game. It values the presence of others—that much has been seen from the quotations from respondents—but chooses not to interact with them. They are, as it were, much valued as a kind of social wallpaper, but no more. (Butler 2003: 2484)

Yet despite the obvious intellectual rigor and major contribution to the literature Butler has made, might it be an equally dangerous game for him to call gentrifiers 'embattled settlers' when the structural constraints on their own lifestyle preferences comprise a far less worrying problem than being priced out of a city altogether, as has happened to so many worse-off Londoners in the last twenty years? We must also question the language Butler with Robson (2003) use to describe the gentrification of a global city—'a middle class coping-strategy'. While there is no doubt that the middle classes have to confront difficulties in the fields of education, housing, work, and consumption, there are many groups in London who have to cope with the *consequences* of gentrification, such as the astoundingly rapid erosion of affordable housing in that city, and the possibility of eviction and displacement.

Our purpose here is not to criticize research (or researchers) that seeks to understand the urban experiences of more advantaged social groups, and certainly not to demonize gentrifiers, whose identities are multiple and whose ambivalent politics often contradict assumptions of a group intent on booting out extant low-income groups from their neighborhoods (Bridge 2003; Ley 2004). We simply wish to point out that next to nothing has been published on the experiences of nongentrifying groups living in the neighborhoods into which the much-researched cosmopolitan middle classes are arriving en masse (see Freeman [2006] for a recent exception). Instead, academic inquiry into gentrification has provided a closer view of the issues that confront the middle classes when choosing where to live. It is as if those middle classes are the only characters occupying the stage of gentrification, with the working-class backstage, both perennial understudies and perennially understudied. This is particularly disappointing, for middle-class gentrifiers are, of course, only one part of a much larger story (Slater, Curran, and Lees 2004). One of the more worrying aspects of some research into gentrifiers is that it ends up empathizing with their plight, rather than thinking of the wider conditions which allow them to gain privileged access to more desirable parts of the city.

Some scholars also take issue with accounts of hipsters, artisans, and bohemian types which include uncritical acceptance of the language of 'urban pioneers' and 'pioneer gentrification', which is the case in articles too numerous to list. Neil Smith (1996a) sums up the problem of seeing the gentrifying middle class as brave explorers:

> The idea of "urban pioneers" is as insulting applied to contemporary cities as the original idea of "pioneers" in the US West. Now, as then, it implies that no one lives in the areas being pioneered—no one worthy of notice, at least. (p. 33)

Smith has shown that the language of pioneering, often woven together with the language of an advancing 'frontier' of 'revitalization', simply serves and feeds real estate and policy interests, forming an ideology justifying 'monstrous incivility in the heart of the city' (p. 18) in the form of gentrification, class conquest, and community upheaval. Contemporary parallels can now be drawn with the boosterism surrounding urban 'regeneration' and 'renaissance' in the United Kingdom, or, in the United States, 'mixed-income communities' that obfuscate the reality of gentrification, capital reinvestment, and the displacement of public housing tenants through HUD's HOPE VI Program (see Chapter 6).

Another problem with consumption explanations, specifically the highly influential postindustrial thesis, is that it suggests a city is devoid of industrial land uses and the working-class labor that still-existing industries support. This has been the focus of recent work by Winifred Curran (2004), who has studied the displacement of work (rather than residence) in the neighborhood of Williamsburg in New York City. She argues that gentrification serves as the justification for the creative destruction of the urban landscape of industrial production:

> In the case of industrial uses and blue-collar workers, a narrative of obsolescence has been created which makes the removal of industrial work and workers politically palatable. Constructing industrial space as obsolete makes the removal of industrial factories and warehouses that remain in central cities, as well as the jobs they provide ... a pragmatic response to global economic change. ... Those industrial uses that remain are framed not only as obsolete but also as dirty barriers to progress and a more beautiful urban landscape. ... [G]entrification ... plays a crucial role in displacing industrial uses that do remain in areas of a city newly defined as desirable. (p. 1245)

Curran notes that New York City, commonly labeled 'postindustrial', still supports 250,000 manufacturing jobs employing workers who are lesser educated than those in other sectors, and who are particularly vulnerable to gentrification and displacement. In Williamsburg, small businesses are being displaced and jobs lost because of the conversion of manufacturing space to other uses (usually high-end residential loft space). Interestingly, of the owners of displaced businesses that Curran interviewed, 'all but one cited eviction by the landlord in order to convert the space or the lack of affordable space in which to expand as the reason for their moves' (2004: 1246). Curran's main argument is that consumption explanations rooted in the postindustrial thesis advanced by Daniel Bell and David Ley tend to conceal the industrial activity that still exists in central cities (for the locational benefits of being integrated into the globalized urban economy). Without understanding how gentrification displaces work as well as residence, Curran argues that the understanding of the process cannot be complete.

*Informing Resistance*

Due to their focus on the practices and politics of the new middle class, consumption explanations have not been very influential in strategies to resist gentrification. This is evident in the fact that so much resistance to gentrification is centered on simplistic slanders of 'yuppies', slanders that are seemingly oblivious of the frequent observation that gentrifiers are a hugely diverse group that cannot be reduced to this label. That said, the potential for informing dissent and protest is not great when considering those consumption accounts that end up empathizing with gentrifiers whilst they decide where to live and where to send their children to school. We therefore feel it is essential that research into gentrifiers must be critical as well as theoretically sophisticated. This should

not be an invitation to criticize gentrifiers and blame them for the process—
'a misplaced charge' (Ley 2003: 2541)—but rather an invitation to understand the broader mechanisms that allow some people to become gentrifiers,
whilst others will never stand a chance of becoming 'professionalized' and
simply feel the negative effects of professionals moving into low-income
neighborhoods.

Currently, the sort of resistance that consumption explanations inform is
not really resistance to gentrification, but resistance to the blandness, conformity, patriarchy, and straightness of suburbia. There is no question that
when viewed as a collective, the work discussed in this chapter has one theme
in common—the central city is the antithesis of suburbia for the new middle
class. It is an arena for counterculture, for 'raging against the machine', for
female liberation, for gay expression, for aesthetic creation, and for artistic
experimentation. The strip mall is rejected in favor of the boutique and the
delicatessen, the home as a site of female domestic labor is rejected in favor
of the city as a place where women make inroads into a male-dominated
world, and the closeted space of the gated community is rejected in a process of coming out together in a gay community. These are without question
major interventions in the history of unequal capitalist urbanization, progressive moments of liberation surprisingly facilitated by gentrification. Yet crucial questions remain—who does not benefit from these interventions? What
happens to housing markets and rents in the process? What about the many
thousands of urban dwellers who are not among Hamnett's professionalized?
And the many thousands of workers who cannot, and would not, claim mem-
bership of Ley's new middle class?

## Summary

This chapter summarized a huge literature on the production of gentrifiers.
We began by looking at the work of David Ley and Chris Hamnett, whose
post-industrial and professionalization theses have explained gentrification as
a consequence of major changes in the industrial and occupational structure
of advanced capitalist cities, resulting in the growth of middle-class professionals. We then broke down the research on the 'new middle class' into several themes; countercultural identities (using the example of Canadian cities),
politics and education, gender, sexuality, and ethnicity. The purpose was to
recognize the important research undertaken to explore and conceptualize
these themes with respect to gentrification; to tie the process to important
changes in society, varying in different geographical contexts; and to show
how these changes cannot be divorced from the upward economic trajectory
of urban neighborhoods. We then explored class constitution and the gentrification aesthetic, explaining how the 'look' of gentrified neighborhoods can
tell us much about the process, and particularly gentrifiers. We concluded by
introducing some of the problems with this literature, particularly how an

empathetic focus on gentrifiers can divert attention away from the injustices of the process, and showed how consumption explanations teach us less about resistance to gentrification than about resistance to suburbia.

## Activities and Exercises

- Reread the section above, 'Class Constitution and the Gentrification Aesthetic'. Take a walk around some central-city neighborhoods in the city where you live (or nearest to where you live), and in a notebook jot down some of the possible signifiers of gentrification. Have you spotted the aesthetic?
- Watch the PBS documentary *Flag Wars* (2003), by documentary filmmakers Linda Goode Bryant and Laura Poitras, on the gentrification of a deteriorating community in Columbus, Ohio, by gay men and lesbians. The 'flag wars' of the title take on more than one meaning. First, it refers to the rainbow flags that hang outside some gay and lesbian homes, and the response to these by the nongay residents in the neighborhood. It also refers to the burning of a rainbow flag that had been flying outside of the Ohio statehouse.
- Watch the KQED documentary *The Castro* (1997), part of KQED's *Neighborhoods: The Hidden Cities of San Francisco* series. The resource guide and other material to supplement this documentary can be found at http://www.kqed.org/w/hood/castro/resourceguide/index.html.
- Watch a few episodes of *Sex and the City*. Does it support the views of Holcomb, Beauregard, and Williams that the gentrified city is a site of education, liberation, and expression for middle-class women?
- After reading Chapters 1 and 2 of Monique Taylor's book *Harlem: Between Heaven and Hell* (2002), watch the Spike Lee movie *Jungle Fever* (Lee 1991), particularly the scenes involving Wesley Snipes, who plays a black middle-class gentrifier living in Harlem but working as an architect in a very white corporate environment. How does he confront the dualities of race and class in this context?
- Watch the scene in *Boyz N the Hood* (1991, John Singleton) in which Furious Styles (Laurence Fishburne), a self-styled street intellectual, explains the process of gentrification and neighborhood decline in black neighborhoods to an 'old head' and a group of youths congregating on a street corner. (Read also Freeman 2006: 118–119.)

## Further Reading

Bondi, L. (1999b) 'Gender, class and gentrification: Enriching the debate', *Environment and Planning D: Society and Space* 17: 261–282.

Boyd, M. (2005) 'The downside of racial uplift: The meaning of gentrification in an African-American neighborhood', *City & Society* 17: 265–288.

Bridge, G. (2001a) 'Estate agents as interpreters of economic and cultural capital: The gentrification premium in the Sydney housing market', *International Journal of Urban and Regional Research* 25: 87–101.

Butler, T., with G. Robson (2003) *London Calling: The Middle-Classes and the Remaking of Inner London* (London: Berg).

Castells, M. (1983) *The City and the Grassroots: A Cross-Cultural Theory of Urban Social Movements* (London: Arnold). (See Chapter 14.)

Caulfield, J. (1994) *City Form and Everyday Life: Toronto's Gentrification and Critical Social Practice* (Toronto: University of Toronto Press).

Freeman, L. (2006) *There Goes the 'Hood: Views of Gentrification from the Ground Up* (Philadelphia: Temple University Press).

Hamnett, C. (2000) 'Gentrification, postindustrialism, and industrial and occupational restructuring in global cities', in G. Bridge and S. Watson (eds.) *A Companion to the City* (Oxford: Blackwell) 331–341.

Jager, M. (1986) 'Class definition and the aesthetics of gentrification: Victoriana in Melbourne', in N. Smith and P. Williams (eds.) *Gentrification of the City* (London: Unwin Hyman) 78–91.

Knopp, L. (1990) 'Some theoretical implications of gay involvement in an urban land market', *Political Geography Quarterly* 9: 337–352.

Ley, D. (1996) *The New Middle Class and the Remaking of the Central City* (Oxford: Oxford University Press).

Rothenberg, T. (1995) 'And she told two friends: Lesbians creating urban social space', in D. Bell and G. Valentine (eds.) *Mapping Desire: Geographies of Sexualities* (London: Routledge) 165–181.

Taylor, M. (2002) *Harlem: Between Heaven and Hell* (Minneapolis: University of Minnesota Press).

Zukin, S. (1989) *Loft Living: Culture and Capital in Urban Change* 2nd ed. (New Brunswick, NJ: Rutgers University Press).

**Plate 4.1** New-Build Gentrification along the Thames

This image shows new-build gentrification along the Thames juxtaposed with (architecturally) classic gentrification.
*Source:* Photograph by Mark Davidson.

128

# 4

# The Mutation of Gentrification

Gentrification was initially understood as the rehabilitation of decaying and low-income housing by middle-class outsiders in central cities. In the late 1970s a broader conceptualisation of the process began to emerge, and by the early 1980s new scholarship had developed a far broader meaning of gentrification, linking it with processes of spatial, economic and social restructuring. Gentrification emerged as a visible spatial component of this transformation. It was evident in the redevelopment of waterfronts, the rise of hotel and convention complexes in central cities, large-scale luxury office and residential developments, and fashionable, high priced shopping districts.

Sassen (1991: 255)

In this chapter, we look at the mutation of gentrification, capturing the temporal and spatial changes to the process. In this, we look at recent derivatives of the term 'gentrification' and the expansion of the term's meaning to encompass the middle-class (re)settlement of rural areas (questioning the spatial determinism of inner-city gentrification), 'new-build' developments (questioning the historic built environment of gentrification), and supergentrification (questioning the assumption in stage models of an endpoint to gentrification). We cast light on contemporary concerns that commentators are stretching the term 'gentrification' too far, and in so doing we examine whether the political salience of 'gentrification' is collapsing under the weight of its expanding definition.

## A Mutating Process

As the process of gentrification has mutated over time, so have the terms used to explain and describe it. Most of the terms that have been coined are derivatives of the term 'gentrification'. Perhaps the first derivative was the term 'rural gentrification' or what has more recently been called 'greentrification' (Smith and Phillips 2001). The term 'rural gentrification' can be traced back to Parsons (1980). The term refers to the gentrification of rural areas, and it studies the link between new middle-class settlement, socioeconomic and cultural transformations of the rural landscape, and the subsequent displacement and marginalization of low-income groups. Studies of rural gentrification note the parallels between such rural transformations and similar processes in an urban context. Given the spread of the urban (not only physically but also socially and culturally; see Amin and Thrift 2002), rural gentrification shares the urban(e) characteristics of gentrification in cities. This dialectical play between urban and rural is not new, for as we saw in Chapter 1, the term 'gentrification' played ironically off the eighteenth- and nineteenth-century English rural gentry. As Ruth Glass argued, 'Urban, suburban and rural areas have thus become encouraged to merge into one another; and they have lost some of their differentiating features' (1989: 137).

The next derivative was probably new-build gentrification. As Sharon Zukin (1991: 193) explained, as real estate developers woke up to the opportunity of offering a 'product based on place', notions of gentrification expanded to include a varied range of building forms, some of which were newly constructed townhouses and condominiums. Such buildings are obviously at odds with the classic gentrification notion of a rehabilitated 'old' property. In the Netherlands, such new-build development is part of a policy of 'housing redifferentiation' that is nothing less than a policy of gentrification (see Uitermark, Duyvendak, and Kleinhans 2007; see also Chapter 6). Not all authors, however, agree that inner-city new-build developments are a form of gentrification—some prefer to term them 'reurbanisation' (e.g., Lambert and Boddy 2002; Boddy 2007; Buzar, Hall, and Ogden 2007).

A more recent derivative is super-gentrification, or financification (Lees 2000, 2003b; Butler and Lees 2006). Here we find a further level of gentrification which is superimposed on an already gentrified neighborhood, one that involves a higher financial or economic investment in the neighborhood than previous waves of gentrification and requires a qualitatively different level of economic resource. This gentrification is driven largely by globally connected workers employed in the City of London or on Wall Street.

In this chapter, we focus our lens on these three mutations of gentrification because they seem at odds with the classical notion of gentrification and as such it is important to debate them as processes. However, there are many more derivatives of the term 'gentrification', most of them are fairly recent, and they are a product of the massive expansion and changes associated with gentrification in its third wave (for a more detailed discussion of third-wave gentrification, see Chapter 5)—for in its third wave, gentrification has moved away from its classical referent, the historic built environment of the metropolitan central city.

Before turning to rural gentrification, new-build gentrification, and super-gentrification, we touch on some other mutations to demonstrate the new definitional fluidity of the term 'gentrification'.

'Studentification', first termed by Darren Smith (2002), is one such term. Studentification refers to the process of social, environmental, and economic change effected by large numbers of students invading particular areas of the cities and towns in which popular universities are located. In many ways the massive expansion of higher education in Britain over the last decade has given rise to such a process. Though originating in Britain, studentification has also recently been adopted in American English to refer to similar problems arising from the overpopulation of many U.S. 'college towns'. Studentification is framed as a 'gentrification factory' in that studentifiers 'represent a potential grouping of future gentrifiers' (D. Smith 2005: 86) or what D. Smith and Holt (2007) term 'apprentice gentrifiers'. This work extends temporal analyses of the life courses of gentrifiers to their formative years and looks at their cultural and residential predilections over time and space.

Thus far all the examples of gentrification have been residential, but gentrification has long been commercial too. In our case studies of gentrification in Chapter 1, Upper Street in Barnsbury and Seventh Avenue in Park Slope began to gentrify not long after pioneer gentrifiers moved into those neighborhoods. 'Commercial gentrification' refers to the gentrification of commercial premises or commercial streets or areas; it has also been called 'boutiqueification' or 'retail gentrification'. In the early days of gentrification in Park Slope (see Chapter 1), the state was heavily implicated in commercial gentrification. Through what became known as 'shopsteading' (the residential version was called 'homesteading'; see Chapter 1), the City of New York sold off vacant commercial premises along 7th Avenue in Park Slope for a nominal sum on the condition that the new owners would renovate the premises and set up new businesses. Zukin (1990) discusses the way that gentrification's spatial form is obvious in consumption spaces along streets that have changed to cater to gentrifiers' tastes. Ley (1996) discusses the way that 'hippy' retailing was initially significant in the gentrification of Kitsilano in Vancouver, as pioneer gentrifiers sought craft shops that were anti-mass merchandise. Bridge and Dowling (2001) discuss the retail fabric of four inner Sydney neighborhoods and argue that restaurant eating and individualized rather than mass consumption are the main consumption practices associated with gentrification in these neighborhoods. Here, consumer demands and individual preferences are the key.

'Tourism gentrification' is a term used by Gotham (2005) in a case study of the sociospatial transformation of New Orleans' Vieux Carre (French Quarter). He defines 'tourism gentrification' as the transformation of a neighborhood into a relatively affluent and exclusive enclave in which corporate entertainment and tourism venues have proliferated. In arguing that the growth of tourism has enhanced the significance of consumption-orientated activities in residential space and as such encouraged gentrification, Gotham contests explanations, such as those of David Ley, that view gentrification as the outcome of consumer demands (see Chapter 3). The gentrification that emerges is both commercial and residential, and, as he argues, it reflects new institutional connections between the local institutions, the real estate industry and the global economy. Thus, the phenomenon of tourism gentrification presents a challenge to traditional explanations of gentrification that assume demand-side or production-side factors drive the process. Gentrification is not an outcome of group preferences nor a reflection of market laws of supply and demand. One particular myth is the claim that consumer desires are forces to which capital merely reacts. Consumer taste for gentrified spaces is, instead, created and marketed, and depends on the alternatives offered by powerful capitalists who are primarily interested in producing the built environment from which they can extract the highest profit. (Gotham 2005: 1114)

In many ways, Gotham is outlining the intricacies of third-wave gentrification (see Chapter 5), a gentrification that not only is connected to processes of globalization but also has new institutional connections. This leads Gotham to conclude,

The pretentious and widely promulgated claim that the "creative class" and "cultural intermediaries" drive gentrification elides the complex and multidimensional effects of global-level socioeconomic transformations and the powerful role corporate capital plays in the organization and development of gentrified spaces. (p. 1114)

In many ways linked to tourism gentrification, Griffith (2000) discusses how culturally distinct sections of coastal cities are threatened with 'coastal gentrification'. This is because coastal cities are sources of capital investment primarily for construction and tourism. Brighton and Hove on the south coast of Britain have been gentrified over the past decade or so (see Plate 4.2), and indeed their authorities have been heavily involved in making these places where the 'urbane' middle classes would want to live.

Gotham (2005) connects tourism gentrification in New Orleans to global socioeconomic transformations. Indeed Neil Smith (2002: 80) argues that gentrification is a 'global urban strategy' that is 'densely connected into the circuits of global capital and cultural circulation'. Such 'global gentrification', or what Atkinson and Bridge (2005) call 'the new urban colonialism', is the leading edge of neoliberal urbanism (see Chapter 5), an urbanism that is affecting cities worldwide. As N. Smith (2002) argues, the process of gentrification has gone global—it is no longer restricted to western cities—as can be seen in Atkinson and Bridge's (2005) edited collection that brings together a number of essays on gentrification from around the world. Despite the recent assertion of links between gentrification and globalization, the analysis of these links has actually been quite limited. It is often conjectural and empirically unsubstantiated. The studies of super-gentrification outlined later in this chapter force us to think about the links between gentrification and globalization in more detail.

**Plate 4.2** Gentrification in Brighton

Gentrification in Brighton began as a sweat equity process in its commercial and residential center not far from the seafront, the results of which are shown here, but the City Council is now adopting a much more showy form of 'regeneration' with various projects on their books.
*Source:* Photograph by Darren Smith.

In contrast to the new emphasis on the global in the gentrification literature, there have also been attempts to insist that gentrification in global cities, such as London and New York, is different from gentrification in provincial cities. These debates about 'provincial gentrification' have been especially important in the United Kingdom in the context of a nation dominated by its capital city—London (where until recently most of the studies of gentrification had been located) and in the context of New Labour's urban renaissance agenda outlined in the Preface to this book. There are now a number of studies of gentrification outside of London, for example Paul Dutton (2003, 2005) on Leeds and Gary Bridge (2003) on Bristol. British authors argue that the process of gentrification in provincial cities came after gentrification emerged in London, and that the process in London cascaded down to smaller cities throughout Britain. London in this sense is an incubator for gentrification. Such an idea of gentrification cascading down the urban hierarchy can, however, be refuted in the context of the United States. For example, in a case study of Portland, Maine, Lees (2006) shows that gentrification in this small city, down the urban hierarchy, was happening pretty much at the same time as, if not before, gentrification in the nearby, much larger cities of Boston and

New York. The problem with the work on provincial gentrification to date is that it often confuses the notion of a global city with that of a metropolitan city. A small city can be metropolitan but not global, for example Bristol and Edinburgh in the United Kingdom.

The recent provincial gentrification in the United Kingdom is often 'state-led gentrification' or 'municipally managed gentrification' (see Chapter 5). The state first supported gentrification in its first wave, as we saw in the case studies of Barnsbury and Park Slope in Chapter 1, because it was too risky at this early stage for the private sector to be attracted. More recently, the state has become involved again in the third wave, as the discussion of New Labour's vision of urban renaissance for English towns and cities in the Preface reveals. At this stage, state involvement is about attracting the middle classes back to the central city and keeping them there. Authors like Cameron (2003) and Slater (2004b) have shown how local authorities or municipalities can be key actors in the gentrification process. Slater (2004b) argues that certain bylaws introduced by the City of Toronto, for example those that prohibit rooming house/bachelorette development or conversion, are heavily implicated in the municipal promotion and management of gentrification in South Parkdale in Toronto.

State involvement in gentrification has gone one step further in Burnley, Blackburn/Darwen, Hyndburn, Pendle, and Rossendale, old declining mill towns north of Manchester. It has entered the territory of celebrity make-overs! Elevate East Lancashire, a government-funded housing market renewal pathfinder charged with finding innovative solutions to the problems of low demand, negative equity, and housing market collapse, hired Anthony Wilson and his partner Yvette Livesey to imagineer the regeneration of this part of northern England. Anthony Wilson set up the legendary Factory Records; launched the careers of Joy Division, New Order, and the Happy Mondays; and opened the legendary Hacienda nightclub in Manchester immortalized in the film *24 Hour Party People*. Their report, 'Dreaming of Pennine Lancashire', proposes a 'fashion tower' (a vertical story of the industrial revolution to get the chattering classes talking, incubator units for new fashion-based businesses, and a school of fashion and design), 'chic sheds' designed by Philippe Starck (allotment sheds to make gardening fashionable to the young creatives that they want to attract), a canal-side curry mile like the one in Manchester, and a football theme park. The authors claim that Pennine Lancashire could use the acronym 'PL' in the same way that Los Angeles is known as 'LA'. This is no ordinary regeneration paper; it is 'epigrammatic, self-mocking, occasionally pretentious, arch, knowing, amusing, surprising and quite often inspirational' (Carter 2005). The authors have swallowed Richard Florida hook, line, and sinker, for as Wilson says, '[I]t is only with the bohemian culture you create the living environment for the creative class—the only way forward for the old smoke stack towns' (Carter 2005). For more detail on this report and actual regeneration activity in East Lancashire, see http://www.elevate-east-lancs.co.uk.

As we can see, then, gentrification has mutated into a number of different types over time, and authors have played off of the term 'gentrification' to explain and describe these different types. These different types of gentrification all share something in common—a socioeconomic and indeed cultural transformation due to middle-class colonization or recolonization. We turn now to look at three of these types in more detail, focusing on how they differ from the classical gentrification outlined in Chapter 1 and indeed from many of the theories of gentrification outlined in Chapters 2 and 3.

## Rural Gentrification

> Although gentrification has been the subject of widespread attention and heated debate, one of the most striking features of the debate has been its urbanity, and how this urbanity has proceeded virtually without comment.
>
> Phillips (2002: 284)

For so many, the term 'gentrification' relates exclusively to cities. It was first observed and coined in an urban context, and has been extensively researched in urban neighborhoods. The influential theories which have emerged to explain it, and the major struggles over its negative effects, are all rooted in urban settings. But this should not be taken as confirmation that the process is specifically urban. As Darling (2005) has argued, '[U]rban and rural scholars tend largely to keep to their own epistemological pumpkin patches, comfortably sequestered in the midst of their respective canons, despite the myriad ontological ties which bind such landscapes together' (p. 1015). A process of 'rural gentrification' was first observed by Parsons (1980) in the United Kingdom, and other work followed in that decade to address the issue of class transformation in UK rural villages (e.g., Pacione 1984; Little 1987; Thrift 1987; Cloke and Thrift 1987). Darling (2005) notes that the literature on rural gentrification is more fully developed in the United Kingdom and lists four 'shifts' which constitute its collective focus:

1. Shifts in the class structure of rural Britain, focusing on the colonization of the British countryside by an exurban or suburban middle class of home owners seeking the 'rural idyll' and the 'consumption of nature' (Thrift 1987), and the displacement of working-class rural residents through rising house prices
2. Shifts in the rural capital accumulation process, and the theorization of a 'postproductivist' rural landscape in which industry and agriculture give way to service-oriented development (often, real estate conversions)
3. Shifts in the composition of the rural British housing stock, including patterns of ownership and changing housing policies

4. Shifts in how rural gentrification can be theorized in relation to urban gentrification, centered on, inter alia, the production–consumption debates (see Chapters 2 and 3)

Martin Phillips has worked on the last shift above, for example—he studied four villages in the Gower Peninsula in South Wales, situating the findings within the major debates of the urban gentrification literature (see Phillips 1993). In this study, he found that 'there might be a significant difference between urban and rural gentrification, at least in terms of the integration of class positions within households and the influence of patriarchal gender identities' (p. 138). In his study sites, he noted that contrary to the arguments of Rose (1989) and Bondi (1991) (see Chapter 3), there was household asymmetry in terms of labor, which actually contributed to the movement of middle-class families into these villages; women were choosing reproductive labor (the bringing up of the family) and wanted a safe, supportive, rural community in which to nurture children, thus subsidizing male professional–managerial careers. So, contrary to Ann Markusen's (1981) claim that gentrification is a result of 'the breakdown of the patriarchal household', Phillips argued that in this rural context gentrification is a result of the continuity of the patriarchal household.

But rural gentrification should not necessarily be seen as something completely different from its urban relation. In later works, Phillips (2002, 2004) documents a crucial parallel between rural and urban gentrification—both reflect distancing from suburban space and suburbia. In this study of two Berkshire villages, he noted that just like urban gentrifiers, rural gentrifiers wished for social distinction in a conscious rejection of postwar mass-produced suburban housing:

> I wanted something turn of the century or First World War at the latest. Because I feel that those houses have been built with a lot more character. ... Anything sort of Second World War onwards, I would find generally, yeah, lacking in the sort of individuality and character that we'll have. Yeah, Second World War onwards we tend to have mass housing building came on and repetition. (Respondent, quoted in Phillips 2002: 301)

Another similarity between rural and urban gentrification was discovered by Darren Smith and Deborah Phillips (2001) in their study of the Hebden Bridge district of West Yorkshire (a bastion of 'Pennine rurality'). While the key difference is the fact that rural gentrifiers stressed the demand for (and perception of) 'green' residential space (Smith and Phillips term the process 'greentrification'), these gentrifiers had a lot in common with their urban counterparts:

> The attraction of Hebden Bridge as a district has much to do with its historical significance as a place, renowned for its radicalism, non-conformity and tolerance of "otherness". The location has long provided

a magnet for those in pursuit of "difference", including "hippies" in the past, and more recently artists, craft-workers and "new age travelers". (p. 460)

So, it would seem that the 'greentrifiers' of the Pennines have a lot in common with the gentrifiers discussed by David Ley and Jon Caulfield in the context of urban Canada (see Chapter 3). While reasons for moving to this area included practically the entire gamut of rural life, everything from the 'authenticity' of working farms to the presence of sheep (p. 460), the existence of strong countercultural values among a diverse group of gentrifiers—many of them 'escaping' from large cities—suggests that rural gentrification should not be seen as the opposite of its urban form, but perhaps as another illustration of a mutating process operating along a rural–urban continuum.

Smith and Phillips's paper is very much geared toward a consumption-side explanation of gentrification—in fact, they disregard calls to integrate consumption with production approaches by arguing that 'a consumption-led focus within a gentrification framework provides an effective start-ing point to illuminate the differences between processes of revitalization within and between rural locations' (p. 466). A sensible remedy to this one-sided view (and also to the awkward interchanging of gentrification and 'revitalization') is provided by Eliza Darling (2005) in her study of rural gentrification in New York State's Adirondack State Park, a popular tourist retreat. From the outset, whilst not disregarding consumption factors, she is keen to fill in the gaps left by British research by examining 'the significance of the material production of nature by the state management of the local landscape in creating the conditions within which investment and disin-vestment in the rural built environment occur in the first place' (p. 1018). Darling, who prefers the term 'wilderness gentrification' (to set it apart from the 'rural gentrification' described in Britain), explains that whilst there are fundamental commonalities with urban gentrification, the process in the Adirondack State Park differs due to the local particularities of the rent gap (see Chapter 2):

It is a different story in the wilderness, largely because of the kind of rent that is being capitalized. What gets produced in the process of urban gentrification is residential space. What gets produced in the process of wilderness gentrification is recreational nature. (p. 1022)

Darling explains that much of the housing in the region lies empty for the majority of the year due to the absence of tourists; thus, the geographical expression of the rent gap is different: '[U]ndercapitalized land in the wilder-ness might instead be defined as undeveloped shorefront property, or, alter-natively, developed shorefront property that is rented year round to the local workforce for low house rents rather than seasonally to tourist consumers for higher house rents' (p. 1023). It is interesting to note how the rent gap is closed given the clear lack of significant local disinvestment:

> For a developer who typically deals with high-priced real-estate trans-actions in places like New York City or the Hamptons, the bargain-base-ment property prices typically found across the Adirondack Park must make the entire place seem disinvested and indeed, New Jersey fast-food tycoon Roger Jakubowski called Adirondack real estate "the last nickel bargain in America". (p. 1028)

Yet Darling's work shows that despite some differences in the character of gen-trification between cities and the wilderness, it is the underlying logic of the process of capital accumulation which unites the urban and rural, and the gentrification of both.

Also in the United States, Rina Ghose (2004) has studied rural gentrifi-cation in the western part of the state of Montana (her Ph.D. thesis [1998] was imaginatively entitled 'A Realtor Runs through It'!). She found that Real-tors—key agents in the gentrification process in this context—are 'selling not just homes, but a "Montana Dream", "a log cabin getaway", "country style comfort", and "room for horses ... rural yet minutes from the city"' (p. 537). The new construction marketed this way in the wilderness surrounding the town of Missoula was leading to a dramatic rise in house prices (the bottom end of the market saw prices triple in the 1990s), so that the average Missou-lan could 'scarcely afford such prices and [is] being pushed out of the hous-ing market' (p. 538). An interesting irony emerged from her research, in that the wilderness dream marketed to the gentrifiers was under threat from all the new construction taking place to house them! Long-term residents spoke of loss of open spaces, the emergence of uncontrolled sprawl, overcrowding, the destruction of wildlife habitats, and so on—hardly a wilderness setting! Furthermore, the destruction of community and local identity was occurring under gentrification; this was met with anger by local people unable to afford the expensive consumption lifestyles led by the gentrifiers—yet another echo of the urban form of the process. In sum, the work of Ghose and others dis-cussed above suggests that rural gentrification is best viewed as a close relative of urban gentrification, rather than a distant cousin.

### New-Build Gentrification

When luxury condos are built on reclaimed industrial land, does it count as gentrification? These are not old houses, and there is no displacement of a low-income community. Gentrification authors have long been aware of such a question, but there have been few attempts to outline the competing argu-ments and their implications. In this chapter we analyze the relationship between new-build developments and earlier definitions of gentrification. We draw on case studies of new-build gentrification in Vancouver, Canada, and Newcastle and London in the United Kingdom.

Most gentrification authors would now agree that certain new-build developments should be characterized as gentrification, but there are still a minority who believe they should not. The fact that today gentrifiers' residences are 'as likely to be smart new townhouses as renovated workers' cottages' (Shaw 2002: 42) has led authors such as Neil Smith to change their definition of gentrification (see his earlier definition of gentrification in Chapter 1), so that he now argues that a distinction can no longer be made between classical and new-build gentrification. He argues that gentrification has departed from Glass' description and refers to a much broader phenomenon:

> How, in the large context of changing social geographies, are we to distinguish adequately between the rehabilitation of nineteenth-century housing, the construction of new condominium towers, the opening of festival markets to attract local and not so local tourists, the proliferation of wine bars—and boutiques for everything—and the construction of modern and postmodern office buildings employing thousands of professionals, all looking for a place to live? ... Gentrification is no longer about a narrow and quixotic oddity in the housing market but has become the leading residential edge of a much larger endeavour: the class remake of the central urban landscape. (N. Smith 1996a: 39)

New-build residential developments, nevertheless, stand in stark contrast to the renovated Victorian and Georgian landscapes of classic gentrification texts (e.g., those of Glass [1964] and N. Smith [1982]). This has led housing researchers such as Christine Lambert and Martin Boddy (2002: 20) to question whether new-build, city center residential landscapes can in fact be characterized as gentrification at all:

> [W]e would question whether the sort of new housing development and conversion described in Bristol and other second tier cities, or indeed the development of London's Docklands, can, in fact, still be characterised as "gentrification"—post-recession or otherwise. There are parallels: new geographies of neighbourhood change, new middle class fractions colonising new areas of central urban space, and attachment to a distinctive lifestyle and urban aesthetic. But "gentrification", as originally coined, referred primarily to a rather different type of "new middle class", buying up older, often "historic" individual housing units and renovating and restoring them for their own use—and in the process driving up property values and driving out former, typically lower income working class residents. Discourses of gentrification and the gentrification literature itself do represent a useful starting point for the analysis of the sort of phenomenon discussed above. We would conclude, however, that

to describe these processes as gentrification is stretching the term and what it set out to describe too far.

Debating these positions, Davidson and Lees (2005) drew up the cases for and against new-build gentrification (see Box 4.1). They found more evidence for 'the case for'. In 'the case for', they argue that as in traditional notions of gentrification, capital is reinvested in disinvested central-city locations, even if the product is a new-build development. Like in classic gentrification, the people attracted to these developments are the urban-seeking middle classes. And the end result is the same, too—displacement of lower-income people by an incoming middle class—even if the processes of displacement are perhaps less overt. Davidson and Lees argue that although direct displacement cannot occur because the site is brownfield and as such has no resident population, indirect displacement—lower-income displace-ment in adjacent residential communities—is likely to occur instead. The indirect displacement might take the form of 'exclusionary displacement' or price shadowing, where lower-income groups are unable to access prop-erty due to the gentrification of the neighborhood. It might also cause sociocultural displacement as the incomers take control of the community apparatus in the area. Importantly, Davidson and Lees (2005) point out that unlike the direct displacement tied to traditional processes of gentrifica-tion, indirect displacement can avoid legislation (planning or other, e.g., antiwinkling laws) that seeks to protect poorer inner-city residents from displacement.

| Box 4.1 |
|---|
| **The Cases for and against New-Build Gentrification** |
| **The Case for** <br> • It causes displacement, albeit indirect and/or sociocultural. <br> • In-movers are the urbane new middle classes. <br> • A gentrified landscape/aesthetic is produced. <br> • Capital is reinvested in disinvested urban areas (often on brownfield sites, but not always). <br><br> **The Case against** <br> • Preexisting populations are not displaced. <br> • The process does not involve the restoration of old housing by individuals. <br> • It is a different version of urban living. <br><br> *Source:* Davidson and Lees (2005: 1169–1170). |

The case against new-build developments in central cities being characterized as gentrification includes the argument that this is not a process involving the loving restoration of old housing by gentrifiers rich in social and cultural capital and, as with pioneer gentrifiers, poor in economic capital. Rather, the developer produces a product and lifestyle to be bought by those with sufficient economic capital to afford these new developments. According to Lambert and Boddy (2002: 21), the purchasers are buying into a different version of urban living. The crux of Lambert and Boddy's (2002: 18) argument is that because these new houses are built on brownfield land, they do not displace a preexisting residential population; as such, they argue that with respect to new-build developments, 'Gentrification in the sense of a process of social change based on "invasion and succession" is, therefore, a misnomer'. They argue instead that such developments are better termed 'reurbanisation'. Nevertheless, the empirical evidence supports Davidson and Lees (2005) and Davidson (2006), who show that displacement does occur and that new-build developments act as beachheads from which the tentacles of gentrification can spread into the surrounding neighborhoods, depending on the particular histories and contexts of those neighborhoods.

Although new-build gentrification has really taken off in the postrecession or third-wave era—as Sassen's quote at the beginning of this chapter and Caroline Mills's work (below) on new-build gentrification in Vancouver, Canada, show—new-build gentrification first emerged in the 1980s. The difference between these two time periods is that in the 1980s the state was a background actor in new-build gentrification, whereas in contemporary, third-wave gentrification the state is a key actor. Moreover, new-build gentrification is not always located on ex-industrial brownfield sites; some new-build gentrification is located on preexisting residential sites, as the cases of Fairview Slopes in Vancouver, Canada, and Newcastle, United Kingdom, below, demonstrate. In addition, the actors involved in new-build gentrification are usually more varied than those in classical gentrification, including architects and developers as well as the state.

*Case Study 1: The Postmodern Landscape of Fairview Slopes, Vancouver, Canada*

Caroline Mills (1988, 1989, 1993) analyzed the newly built postmodern landscape of Fairview Slopes, a small neighborhood in inner-city Vancouver. It stands on a steep hill, above False Creek South, overlooking downtown Vancouver (see Plate 4.3). There, developers, architects, and marketing agents created a new landscape of gentrification, one that demonstrated processes of capital reinvestment, social upgrading, and middle-class colonization. In the first decade of the twentieth century, Fairview Slopes was developed with modest wood frame houses housing professionals, tradespeople, and workers in the shipbuilding, sawmill, and steel plants along False Creek. The area became a mix of residential and industrial use, and in the 1960s, as deindustrialization

**Plate 4.3** Fairview Slopes, Vancouver

When Fairview Slopes first gentrified, the gentrification of downtown Vancouver and the wholesale redevelopment of the North Shore of Vancouver, which it overlooks, was only just beginning.
*Source:* Photograph by Loretta Lees.

hit home in Vancouver, many houses were converted into rooming houses or communal homes. Much of the housing was rental, and the area developed a reputation as countercultural or, in some accounts, as a slum. But over a fifteen-year period, the neighborhood was redeveloped. The instigator for the redevelopment of Fairview Slopes was the City Council's redevelopment of the adjacent False Creek South from industrial to residential and amenity uses in 1972 (see Cybriwsky, Ley, and Western 1986; Ley 1987b). Here, the newly elected TEAM (The Electors Action Movement), educated liberals who promoted the idea of a 'livable city', shifted planning philosophy in City Hall so that it was politically progressive: aesthetically and socially inclusive. Fairview Slopes was rezoned as a medium-density residential and commercial neighborhood, speculative activity increased in anticipation of redevelopment, and developers became involved, attracted by bonus densities which could be earned for good designs.

Mills' research was concerned with the specifics of cultural issues in the gentrification process (see Chapter 3). For Mills (1989: 390), following Cosgrove and Jackson (1987: 95), 'Culture is not a residual category, the surface variation left unaccounted for by more powerful economic analyses; it is the very medium through which social change is experienced, contested and constituted'. Mills was influenced by the emergence of a 'new cultural geography' in which the metaphor of text underscored the symbolic qualities of landscape. Mills used Geertz's (1973) ethnography as a method through which to analyze the landscape of Fairview Slopes as a cultural form. She analyzed the textual landscape of gentrification in Fairview Slopes by analyzing (1) advertising imagery, (2) the postmodern style of the gentrified landscape, and (3) the practice of gentrification in terms of the texts of the producers and consumers of this gentrified landscape. In so doing she looked at cultural 'texts' such as advertising, planning and architectural design, and details about the everyday lives of residents drawn from interviews with them. She began her analysis by looking at the planning of the neighborhood, and then extended this account outwards to consider the postmodern design of the neighborhood and the stories of those individuals involved in the production and consumption of the landscape.

Mills was one of the first authors to look at the marketing of a gentrifier lifestyle, from 'open house' displays of rooms to advertising brochures. In her discussions of advertising imagery, Mills argued that advertising was the conduit along which cultural meaning flowed: 'From the culturally constituted world, meaning is transferred into consumer goods; the fashion and advertising systems are two strategies by which this is achieved. Then individuals draw that meaning from the goods by various rituals, including those of possession, exchange and grooming' (Mills 1988: 170). From advertising imagery, Mills teased out the nuances of a lifestyle language and looked at how gentrification could be understood in terms of capital accumulation and the cultural 'meaning' of living in an inner-city neighborhood.

Mills remains one of the few authors to investigate the architecture of gentrification in any detail. According to Mills the developers, with encouragement from the state, were creating new kinds of commodities with a supposedly discriminating edge to them. In analyzing the architectural style of the new-builds, Mills found differences between the first and second phases of development in the 1970s and 1980s. For Mills, these differences represented the two faces of postmodernism—the architecture of the everyday (it was suggestive of history and context, at human scale, and clustered organically around courtyards) and a pandering to the culture of consumption (local themes were played against themes from elsewhere; classical detail mixed with contemporary; and there were columns, arches, and Palladian windows) as developers moved away from TEAM's 'livable city' agenda.

Throughout her research on Fairview Slopes, Mills was interested in the lives of 'real gentrifiers'. Following Geertz, she interrogated 'the dialogue of text and context, cultural practices and social life', through a method of 'thick description' which aimed 'to excavate the multiple layers of meaning that actions have to social actors' (Mills 1988: 171). She got the bulk of her data on the producers and consumers of this gentrified landscape through two series of interviews—first with the key producers of the landscape (designers and developers, real estate agents, etc.), and then with the key consumers (the residents of the new buildings in Fairview Slopes). Mills did not find that developers unilaterally 'produced' the new landscape of Fairview Slopes; rather, she found it to be a process of negotiation 'to which the changing mindsets of its potential consumers were pivotal' (1988: 180).

Interestingly, Mills questioned whether the redevelopment of Fairview Slopes was gentrification at all: 'Yet Fairview Slopes does not fit the usual image of a gentrified neighbourhood. It is a landscape of redevelopment, and renting is probably still as common as owner occupancy'. Nevertheless, she answered the question assertively by saying yes, indeed, it is gentrification—but it is a gentrification aesthetic that has moved on from classical gentrification, as she argued:

> Just as blue jeans became the international uniform of the new class …
> so gentrified housing became its international neighbourhood. … Iron-
> ically, as blue jeans turned into a new conformity, so does the landscape
> distinctiveness of the gentrified neighbourhood. (1988: 186)

*Case Study 2: Regenerating Newcastle*

In a more recent discussion of new-build gentrification, Stuart Cameron (2003) discusses Newcastle City Council's citywide regeneration strategy named 'Going for Growth' that sought to 'remodel' low-demand housing areas in inner-city Newcastle. Its explicit objective was to rebalance the population of disadvantaged and stigmatized communities by building housing that would attract the middle classes into these areas. Here new-build gentrification was not to take place on brownfield sites; rather, like in Fairview Slopes, it was to take place on preexisting residential land. The new-build gentrification here was about social engineering—trying to attract the middle classes to parts of inner-city Newcastle to socially rebalance these areas. As such, it was connected to national government urban policy prescriptions, such as the Urban White Paper (DETR 2000a) discussed in the Preface, in terms of attracting the middle classes back to the central city in the hopes that social mixing would mean the transference of social capital from the social capital rich to the social capital poor (see Chapter 6 on 'positive gentrification').

The aim of Going for Growth was to bridge the gulf between suburbanites with jobs and inner-city residents without jobs, and to counter central-city population loss and its impact on the local tax base and the local economy. In many ways, the story of Newcastle's decline was like the American doughnut effect—the hollowing out of the urban core economically, socially, and culturally. In the United States, cities have long tried to address these issues through a range of initiatives—from festival marketplaces to stadiums, waterfront development, and more recently the gentrification of social housing (see Chapter 6). Indeed, Cameron (2003: 2372) states that Going for Growth seems to have more in common with the model of gentrification linked to the urban renewal found in U.S. cities in the 1950s. British cities have been well behind American cities in countering the doughnut effect—and indeed, it is only really in the last 5–10 years that cities like Manchester, Sheffield, and Newcastle have actively pursued policies and practices aimed to attract the middle classes to live and play in their central cities. Interestingly, in earlier papers on new city center and waterfront redevelopments in Newcastle, Cameron (1992; see also Cameron and Doling 1994) argues that these should not be viewed as gentrification because they have not involved the displacement of, or other negative impacts on, the existing low-income resident population. But he changes his mind; by way of contrast, Cameron (2003) argues with respect to Going for Growth that existing low-income residents would be displaced and that this would be especially sharp for those with histories of antisocial behavior, for they would not be rehoused readily:

> This perhaps suggests a particularly sharp form of displacement and exclusion affecting those who are seen as a threat to the attraction of a new, middle class population. It is possible to see here Smith's … notion of a "revanchist city" with a punitive response to the poor. On the other hand, some existing residents as well as incomers may welcome this form of action against anti-social behaviour. (p. 2372)

Indeed, one of the city's oldest working-class communities no longer figured in the civic plans for a twenty-first-century Newcastle. Luckily, however, Going for Growth had barely gotten off the ground when the Audit Commission slated it, saying it risked making the problems of abandoned housing in Newcastle's city center even worse, and in May 2004 the Labour-led Newcastle City Council was ousted by the Liberal Democrats, who in January 2005 replaced the Going for Growth strategy with a significantly scaled-back version, the Benwell Scotswood Area Action Plan, that seeks to extend prosperity westward in the urban core.

Cameron (2003) speculates whether Newcastle's Going for Growth strategy is akin to the Dutch policy of 'housing redifferentiation' (see Chapter 6) which adds more expensive dwellings to low-income areas to create a more socially diverse population in neighborhoods. He suggests that this term may be more appropriate than 'gentrification' for the Going for Growth strategy. However, he finds a key difference—the low-rent neighborhoods in the Netherlands all have some middle-class and even higher-income residents. The neighborhoods being targeted in Newcastle were low income only.

Cameron's (2003) paper is speculative, that is, it is not based on empirical evidence about gentrification but rather is a review of the Going for Growth strategy and a suggestion of what its impacts might be (or might have been if it had continued). Cameron emphasizes policy intertextuality: how the Going for Growth text either refers to or seems to draw on other policy texts, such as the Urban White Paper (DETR 2000a) and *Bringing Britain Together* (Social

Exclusion Unit 1998). Although Cameron makes reference to a number of newspaper journalist interviews with the people involved in the formulation of Going for Growth, he does not undertake any interviews himself. We could have learned more about Going for Growth if Cameron had included a discourse analysis (which is interested not just in the document but also in those who have produced it) alongside his textual analysis. This is something that Mills (1988) did. Rydin's (2005) discussion of the relevancy of discourse analysis to policy research provides a useful account of how such methods are useful to our understanding of, and engagement with, public policy:

> [A] discourse approach to policy in a substantive area allows the analyst to understand the different actors' perspectives and self-presentations of the policy process. It enables a fuller understanding of the engagement of actors within the policy process, an engagement that is fundamentally communicative and hence discursive. It can link the actors' use of discourses with societal discourses, suggesting how the discursive power of an actor's representations may draw on these broader social resources. At the same time it can identify how actors actively use language to pursue their interests. A discourse approach can reveal features of the policymaking organisation in terms of its prevailing norms and routines, which contribute to a mobilization of bias within the organization. Again this can help explain path dependency; it can also suggest discursive strategies for managing communication and the practices of policymakers in order to undermine such path dependency. (pp. 16–17)

Given the importance now of gentrification researchers looking carefully at the interplay between gentrification and public policy and between public policy and gentrification (Lees 2003c), a detailed investigation of how a New Labour–led Newcastle City Council came up with this (disturbing) strategy (and almost got away with it) would be most interesting.

*Case Study 3: London's Riverside Renaissance*

Davidson and Lees (2005) discuss brownfield new-build gentrification along the River Thames in London. They argue that recent new-build developments along the Thames are part and parcel of the maturation and mutation of the gentrification process in its third wave (for more detail on third-wave gentrification, see Chapter 5). Following Neil Smith (2002: 390–392), they argue that studies of gentrification have to date failed to 'problematize the locations of gentrification adequately' and that as such we need to widen the 'spatial lens' of gentrification studies (Phillips [2004] argues similarly). The lens needs to be widened because in its third wave, gentrification has mutated into different parts of the city, no longer always the central city, to rural locations, coastal locations, and outside of First World cities. For Davidson and Lees, an upsurge in state-led new-build gentrification is one of these mutations in the third wave. They discuss other authors who have found new-build gentrification to be important in third-wave gentrification. Hackworth (2001, 2002a), for example, identifies the presence of new-build corporate developments in marginal locations. By way of contrast, Rose (2002) discusses the construction of new-build infill housing in neighborhoods in Montréal that have already been gentrified.

Davidson and Lees's (2005) case study of London's riverside is an important one because London's riverside is changing out of all recognition. Large numbers of brownfield sites stretching the full length of the Thames are being redeveloped under policy initiatives designed by the Greater London Authority (GLA). The GLA's *London Plan* (2004: xii) wants to

> develop London as an exemplary, sustainable world city, based on three interwoven themes:
>
> - strong, diverse long term economic growth
> - social inclusivity to give all Londoners the opportunity to share in London's future success
> - fundamental improvements in London's environment and use of resources.

Later in the document, they demonstrate an implicit urban renaissance agenda, one tied to the British government's Social Exclusion Unit's promotion of social mixing and balanced communities (see Chapter 6 on 'positive gentrification' for more detail). There are some similarities between these riverside brownfield new-build developments and those of London's Docklands, but there are important differences too. As Davidson and Lees (2005: 1171) argue,

> The Docklands redevelopment concerned a relocation of business (the City) through (what eventually became) a publicly subsidized programme of large-scale redevelopment and in tandem underwent tremendous residential change in the classic Thatcher model of erasing the working-class history and geography of the city in order to make everyone middle class. ... In contrast, contemporary new-build developments along the Thames are not connected to the relocation of the City; they are smaller in scale, privately funded, tend to be located in the traditional retail and commercial core of the city, and are fundamentally tied to New Labour's attempts both to attract the middle classes back to the central city and, in so doing, to instigate social mixing in an attempt to defeat social exclusion and social malaise.

As is the case of new-build gentrification in Newcastle (above), social mixing is high on the local government agenda. But whereas Cameron's discussion is conjectural, Davidson and Lees (2005) provide empirical evidence that indicates that the new-build developments are not conducive to social mixing; rather, the result is gentrification, segregation, and social exclusion (for more detail, see Davidson 2006). Davidson and Lees (2005) use UK Census, survey, and interview data to back up their argument that these riverside new-build developments are gentrification. Although the 2001 census data (National Statistics 2001) only captures the early days of this process, it is clear that social upgrading is occurring along the Thames. Between 1991 and 2001, in the Thameside boroughs investigated, the number of professionals increased by 42.9 percent, the number of associate professional and technical residents by 44.5 percent, and the number of managers and senior officials by 20.9 percent. By way of contrast, lower-middle-income and lower-income occupational groups in the same Thameside boroughs decreased: administrative and secretarial by 11.4 percent, skilled trades by 12.8 percent, personal service by 29.5 percent, and process, plant, and machine workers by 6.9 percent. The corresponding increase in elementary workers (e.g., cleaners, kitchen staff, security guards, and porters) is, as Davidson and Lees (2005: 1184) argue, not surprising given these groups are those most likely to service the incoming middle classes. The survey and interview data reveal that long-term residents view this new gentrification as a negative thing—they see the redevelopment as being for younger, commuting people and little housing being built for the working class. Social mixing does not occur between the riverside new-build and adjacent neighborhood residents; if anything, there is fear from the new-build residents of their riverside neighbors. As such, the new-build developments have fostered social exclusion rather than social inclusion. In conclusion, Davidson and Lees (2005: 1187) state,

> Given the increasing middle-class recolonisation of central London, specifically along the River Thames, and the corresponding displacement of lower social classes, it would be folly to disavow new-build developments of the label "gentrification".

## Super-gentrification

Butler with Robson (2003) suggested that Barnsbury in London was 'witnessing second generation (re)gentrification' driven largely by finance and financial sector workers employed in the City of London. Lees (2000, 2003b), in the context of specific neighborhoods in Brooklyn, New York City, termed this process 'super-gentrification' or 'financification'. Super-gentrification is a further level of intensified gentrification that is happening in a few select neighborhoods in global cities like London and New York. More recently, Butler and Lees (2006) have worked together to provide detailed empirical evidence of a third wave of gentrification, super-gentrification, in Barnsbury, London. We outline that evidence in the next section, thus bringing up-to-date our story of gentrification in Barnsbury (see Chapter 1). Then, continuing with a trans-Atlantic comparison, we compare it with the case of super-gentrification in Brooklyn Heights, New York City.

In the term 'super-gentrification', the prefix 'super' is used to demonstrate that this is not only a higher level of gentrification, but also one superimposed on an already gentrified neighborhood; one that has global connections— social, economic, and cultural; and one that involves a higher financial or economic investment in the neighborhood than previous waves of gentrification, and as such requires a qualitatively different level of economic resource. The suffix 'gentrification' is used as a metaphor for social change; here a new, more elite, more globally connected gentry is moving into the neighborhood (Butler and Lees 2006). This argument revolves around Sassen's (1991) argument about the creation of a new class of financial engineers who have successfully commodified the financial services industries, creating new products and great wealth for themselves. The spread of this industry has been such that it has also included those in supporting industry sectors such as marketing, information technology, and, crucially, legal services.

Super-gentrification is an interesting phenomenon in that it goes against the grain of stage models of gentrification which assume an endpoint to the process, the endpoint being mature gentrification (see Chapter 1). As such, it poses important questions about the historical continuity of current manifestations of gentrification with previous rounds of neighborhood change. As Lees (2003b: 2491) argues,

> Like the now-discredited climax ecology models of vegetation invasion and succession on which they were predicated … gentrification stage models assume that the process of gentrification will eventually reach a stable and self-perpetuating final climax stage of "mature gentrification". The example of super-gentrification demonstrates the folly of this assumption about the stability both of the underlying processes and of the resulting patterns of gentrification.

It also stands against neo-Marxist, rent gap-type explanations (see Chapter 2) which focus on the dialectic of disinvestment and reinvestment, ignoring changes in neighborhoods that have already been gentrified. Whereas traditional work on gentrification has concentrated on the turn from a disinvested to a reinvested neighborhood, here an already gentrified, upper-middle-class neighborhood is transformed again into an even more exclusive and expensive enclave. There is no exploitation of a rent gap. Gentrification continues but takes a different form, we go from a state of supposedly mature gentrification to a state of super-gentrification. In this, certain neighborhoods have become the focus of intense investment and conspicuous consumption by a new generation of super-rich 'financiers' fed by the fortunes from the global finance and corporate service industries. Importantly, super-gentrification is different from re-gentrification, which may well happen to other neighborhoods, because super-gentrification is only likely to happen in neighborhoods in global cities that are easily commutable to global financial headquarters such as the City of London—the 'Golden Square Mile'—or Wall Street—or in cities such as San Franciso with very particular cirumstances, in this case the impact of Silicon Valley and IT (information technology) companies. Super-gentrification is not Dangschat's (1991) typology of 'ultra-gentrification'. 'Ultra-gentrification', however, might well be the fate of a number of success-ful inner-city gentrified neighborhoods the world over if the embourgeoise-ment of the central city continues. As Atkinson and Bridge (2005: 16) argue:

> As gentrification has become generalised so it has become intensified in its originating neighbourhoods, many of which have now moved into stellar price brackets and now resemble established elite enclaves rather than the ascetic pioneer gentrifier spirit of the 1960s and 1970s.

And, as Chris Hamnett (1984: 314) argued some time ago now,

> It should be clear that gentrification is merely another stage in a con-tinuing historically contingent sequence of residential area evolution. There are no universally and temporally stable residential patterns.

Neil Smith (2002: 441) argues that the hallmark of the latest phase of gentrification is the 'reach of global capital down to the local neighbourhood scale'. Atkinson and Bridge (2005: 7), however, argue that 'the literature on globalisation has not been geared towards the level of the neighbourhood' and that 'the neighbourhood has been under-recognised as the site of the repro-duction of a wider set of power relations and contacts which operate at local, urban, regional, and international levels'. The following case studies on super-gentrification make concrete the rather abstract claims about the relationships between global economic and urban-scale processes.

*Case Study 1: Barnsbury, London (Continued)*

Butler and Lees (2006) look at a global elite of gentrifiers who have chosen not to colonize, but to recolonize, an already gentrified neighborhood—Barnsbury (see Chapter 1). These super-gentrifiers, they argue, actively connect global capital flows to the neighborhood level. In contrast to Rofe's (2003) argument (with respect to gentrifying transnational elites) that in order to maintain a distinctive identity, the gentrifying class as an emergent elite projects their identity from the scale of the local onto the global, Butler and Lees (2006) demonstrate the opposite: elite super-gentrifiers projecting a global identity onto the local. Rather than the erosion of space by globalization (which much of the globalization literature suggests), here we see the reconstitution of (elite) space at the neighborhood level.

Butler and Lees (2006) reveal that a new group of super-wealthy professionals working in the City of London are slowly imposing their mark on this inner

London housing market in a way that differentiates it and them both from traditional professionals and from the traditional urban upper classes. This third generation of gentrifiers has, over the last decade, begun to displace some of the original middle-class gentrifiers. Butler and Lees argue that there is a close interaction between elite forms of education, particularly Oxbridge; work in the newly globalizing industries of the financial services economy; and residence in Barnsbury, which is very different from other areas of largely gentrified inner London. As McDowell (1997a) has shown, this new service class has had a major impact in shaping the inner London housing market. This group has been recruited disproportionately from the privileged upper ranks of British society through the public schools and its favored universities—Oxford, Cambridge, Bristol, Durham, and some University of London colleges (McDowell 1997b). As Massey (1993) argues, those social groups most empowered by globalization are often preexisting elite groups. In Butler and Lees's (2006) arguments about the pivotal importance of the occupations of super-gentrifiers, they follow on from earlier work by, for example, David Ley (1994, 1996) on liberal public sector workers, and Sharon Zukin (1982) on artists, as pioneer gentrifiers (see Chapter 3).

Butler and Lees (2006) argue that super-gentrification could not have happened in Barnsbury without the stabilizing influence of the second wave of gentrification which occurred in the 1980s. Second-wave gentrification (see Chapter 5) saw a much more visible upgrading of Upper Street, the main commercial street in Barnsbury. The redevelopment of the old Agricultural Hall into a Business Design Centre symbolized the more corporate gentrification that ensued. In this phase, although many gentrifiers still worked in the public sector, an increasing number of them worked in the private sector and particularly the City, where jobs had expanded due to deregulation. Butler and Lees (2006) discuss how and why both the number of jobs and the salaries and bonuses associated with these jobs increased significantly over this period, and even more so since the mid-1990s. (Ex-British Prime Minister) Tony Blair and Cherie Blair, who moved to Barnsbury towards the end of this second wave of gentrification in 1993, are good examples of the influx of City workers. Indeed, they benefited from the emerging third wave of super-gentrification in Barnsbury, for by the time they sold their Richmond Crescent home (see Plate 4.4) in 1997 (on moving to Downing Street), it had nearly doubled in price (to £615,000). It was sold again in 2001 for £1.25 million! When the Blairs moved in, it was still possible for successful but traditional professionals to buy a family property in Barnsbury. By the time they sold, it was really only those working in the top end of the legal professions and the financial services industries and the otherwise wealthy who could afford to buy such houses. It is this third generation of gentrifiers that Butler and Lees term 'super-gentrifiers' because their ability to operate in such a rarified housing market is almost entirely dependent on the financial revolution that took place from

**Plate 4.4** Tony Blair's Richmond Crescent Home

This house is probably worth over £2 million today despite its tiny back garden and the large pockets of social housing within a stone's throw from its front door!
*Source:* Photograph by Loretta Lees.

the mid-1990s onwards in the City of London. Few New Labour politicians would be able to buy in Barnsbury today without having to answer some very searching questions about their probity!

Butler and Lees (2006) use census data to show the growth in managerial and employed professionals in Barnsbury between 1991 and 2001, both of which cover the main top groups in the City of London. The data shows that there has been growth in the top groups in Barnsbury over recent years and a restructuring of its gentrification. Unlike in the case of Brooklyn Heights, below, where the middle-income professional groups are in decline, in

Barnsbury there is a large and continued expansion of Socio Economic Group 5.1, the group which has driven inner London's gentrification particularly in the boroughs to the north and south of Islington. This group continues to grow both in Barnsbury and in Islington as a whole, suggesting that the supergentrification thesis in Barnsbury is one of relative rather than absolute transformation and that we might be witnessing a tripartite class division between super-wealthy professionals and managers, middle-class professionals, and the working class or economically inactive. Such divisions raise interesting questions about social mixing in the neighborhood. In an innovative turn, Butler and Lees (2006) use data on Barnsbury from the geodemographic software package Mosaic to underline their evidence for class change. Two thirds of Barnsbury respondents were in Group A, Symbols of Success, and in two subgroups, Global Connections (51 percent) and Cultural Leadership (16 percent); the remainder (30 percent) were almost all in Group E, Urban Intelligence—which is normally associated with areas of inner London gentrification.

*Case Study 2: Brooklyn Heights, New York City*

Unusual in the gentrification literature, Lees (2003b) begins her story of super-gentrification in Brooklyn Heights using the biography of a brownstone. She elucidates the story of pioneer gentrification, as a young lawyer and his wife buy the brownstone with sitting tenants, only to evict these tenants over time, thus gaining control of the whole house and gradually renovating it in their spare time. She takes up the story of super-gentrification as the owner sells his brownstone in the mid-1990s and downsizes to a carriage house two streets away. The buyer of his brownstone was an Englishwoman working on Wall Street, a broker specializing in Japanese bonds and securities who wrote a personal check for the full price of the house—£595,000. As Lees (2003b: 2489) states, previous (first- and second-wave) gentrifiers needed mortgages:

> By contrast in New York there is now a new generation flush with the exorbitant rewards of the global finance and corporate service industries.... They are able to marshal previously unheard of sums to finance their domestic reproduction. It is not only the volume and source of the assets they mobilise that mark out these "financifiers" from previous generations of gentrifiers, but also, I would suggest, their lifestyles and values as well.

The lifestyles and values of super-gentrifiers are quite different from those of traditional gentrifiers. Rather than the piecemeal, sweat equity renovations that the previous owner had undertaken, the new owner hired contractors to gut the place and redo it (while she rented a very expensive apartment nearby). They completely changed the floor plan and put in a marble bathroom with a Jacuzzi. They ripped out the mature urban garden at the back of the house and

**Figure 4.1** Income Change in Brooklyn Heights, 1970–2000

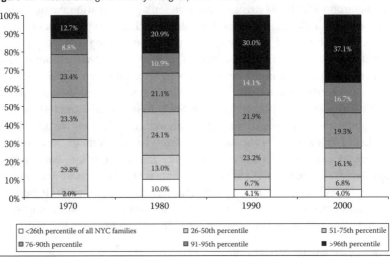

| | <26th percentile of all NYC families | 26-50th percentile | 51-75th percentile |
| 76-90th percentile | 91-95th percentile | >96th percentile |

This figure shows the distribution of families in Brooklyn Heights by annual income percentile categories for all New York City families. Note how in 2000, more than half of the families in Brooklyn Heights were among the wealthiest 10 percent of all families in the City of New York.
*Source:* Lees (2003b).

turfed it all over—in true suburban style. Her commitment to the neighborhood was such that after 4–5 months of moving in, she sold up and moved to Arizona!

In her analysis of census data from 1970 to 2000, Lees (2003b) found that Brooklyn Heights had experienced a dramatic increase in income and the progressive displacement of lower-income families by higher-income families. Significantly, over the past ten years the small number of low-income families left in the neighborhood has held steady, whilst the number of upper-middle-income families has fallen by 9.7 percent; at the same time, the number of families in the top 10 percent of all New York City families by income has increased by the same amount. As such, in this super-gentrified neighborhood now more than half of the families are in the top decile of wealthiest families in New York City (see Figure 4.1). Lees's survey results show that residents see this as a tidal wave of Wall Street money sweeping over their neighborhood.

### Definitional Overload and the Politics of Gentrification

The existence of such a welter of terms (and they cite—urban regeneration, urban revitalization, gentrification, neighborhood renewal, rehabilitation, renovation, back-to-the-city movement and urban reinvasion) to describe the very same phenomenon is not simply meaningless terminological entrepreneurship. One of the lessons of the sociology of knowledge is that words are not passive; indeed, they help to shape and create our perceptions of the world around us. The terms we choose to label or describe events, must, therefore, convey appropriate connotations or images of the phenomenon under consideration in order to avoid serious misunderstandings.

Palen and London (1984: 6)

In 1991 Saskia Sassen declared that 'new scholarship had developed a far broader meaning of gentrification, linking it with processes of spatial, economic, and social restructuring' (p. 255). Gentrification was a 'far broader process linked to the profound transformation in advanced capitalism' (p. 255). However, in recent years there have been calls from a number of quarters to drop the term 'gentrification' altogether. Bondi (1999a: 255), for example, warned of the dangers of trying to overload the concept with reconceptualizations:

I would argue that creative approaches to the production of academic knowledge entail cyclical processes of conceptualisation and reconceptualisation. In this context, Ruth Glass's (1964) coining of the term "gentrification" opened up new questions about urban change. But the more researchers have attempted to pin it down the more burdens the concept has had to carry. Maybe the loss of momentum around gentrification reflects its inability to open up new insights, and maybe it is time to allow it to disintegrate under the weight of these burdens.

We do not think that we should allow the term to disintegrate under the weight of these burdens. Of course, by encompassing all the mutations and derivatives listed above under the term 'gentrification', we do run the risk of undermining the 'usefulness, and distinction, of the concept for understanding urban change' (N.Smith 2002: 390–392). It is, however, a risk we must take.

One of the reasons why so many people have sought to keep new types of gentrification closely connected to the term 'gentrification' (e.g., greentrification and financification) is because of the politics of that term. Gentrification is, perhaps more than any other word in urban geography or urban studies, a political, politicized, and politically loaded word. The anti-gentrification groups discussed in Chapter 7 would have little political clout without being able to be against 'gentrification' and the class-based displacement and oppression that the word evokes. After all, as stated in the Preface, it is hard to be against revitalization, regeneration, or renaissance, but much easier to be against gentrification. The way that governments and municipalities deliberately avoid using the word 'gentrification' in their policy documents that promote revitalization, regeneration, or renaissance reveals this. As Davidson and Lees (2005: 1167) argue,

[D]efining new-build developments, such as those being constructed along London's riverfront, as gentrification is politically important if we seek to question the increasing middle-class recolonisation of the central city.

The Real Estate Board of New York City, who back in 1985 purchased space in the *New York Times* that devoted an entire page to 'Is Gentrification a Dirty Word?' (see Figure 4.2), were certainly clear about the political importance of the word 'gentrification'. As Neil Smith (1996a: 30-34) explains,

> On the morning of December 23, 1985, *New York Times* readers awoke to find the most prestigious advertising spot in their morning paper taken up by an editorial advert in praise of gentrification. Some years earlier the newspaper had begun to sell the bottom right quarter of its Opinion Page to the Mobil Corporation, which used to extol the social and cultural merits of organized global capitalism. By the mid-1980s, with the New York real estate market ablaze, gentrification was increasingly understood as a threat to people's rents, housing and communities, and the Mobil Corporation no longer had an exclusive claim to the purchased ideological ink of the *Times'* Opinion Page. It was the "Real Estate Board of New York, Inc." which now purchased the space to bring a defense of gentrification to the citizens of New York. "There are few words in a New Yorker's vocabulary that are as emotionally loaded as 'gentrification'", the advert began. Gentrification means different things to different people, the Real Estate Board conceded, but "In simple terms, gentrification is the upgrading of housing and retail businesses in a neighborhood with an influx generally of private investment". It is a contributor to the diversity, the great mosaic of the city, the advert suggested; "neighborhoods and lives blossom". If a modicum of displacement inevitably results from a neighborhood's private market "rehabilitation", suggests the Board, "We believe" that it "must be dealt with with public policies that promote low- and moderate-income housing construction and rehabilitation, and in zoning revisions that permit retail uses in less expensive, side street locations". It concludes: "We also believe that New York's best hope lies with families, businesses and lending institutions willing to commit themselves for the long haul to neighborhoods that need them. That's gentrification".

Indeed, because of the now well-recognized and political nature of the word, 'gentrification' is a term that the media now use to discuss middle-class colonization, whether of the central city or of rural areas.

However, if we are to retain the word (and its political purchase), as Davidson and Lees (2005: 1187) argue, '[G]entrification scholars need to allow the term gentrification enough elasticity to "open up to new insights" and indeed to reflect the mutations in the C21st of this increasingly active and somewhat different process'. They argue that Glass's (1964) definition of the process is

# IS GENTRIFICATION A DIRTY WORD?

There are few words in a New Yorker's vocabulary that are as emotionally loaded as "gentrification."

To one person, it means improved housing. To another, it means unaffordable housing. It means safer streets and new retail businesses to some. To others, it means the homogenization of a formerly diverse neighborhood. It's the result of one family's drive for home ownership. It's the perceived threat of higher rental costs for another family.

In simple terms, gentrification is the upgrading of housing and retail businesses in a neighborhood with an influx of private investment. This process and its consequences, however, are rarely simple.

### Neighborhoods and lives blossom.

Examples of gentrification are as varied and distinctive as New York itself and reflect the city's enduring vitality. That vitality is expressed in terms of change...for neighborhoods and people. We see immigrants from Asia transforming the Flushing community in Queens with their industriousness, while recent arrivals from Russia are bringing new flavor to the Brighton Beach area of Brooklyn. Over a decade ago, painters, sculptors and fledgling dance companies looking for loft space turned SoHo, then a manufacturing "ghost town" on Lower Manhattan's northern border, into a world-renowned artistic center. Today a new generation of artists is creating a similar colony in Greenpoint, Brooklyn. Elsewhere, middle class pioneers have bought brownstones in dilapidated areas and enlivened their districts—such as the portion of Columbus Avenue north of Lincoln Center for the Performing Arts—with energy and style.

Different neighborhoods throughout the city have undergone similar changes at different times: Park Slope, Chelsea and the Upper West Side, for example. In each case, neighborhoods that were under-populated and had become shabby and/or dangerous were turned into desirable addresses by families and merchants willing to risk their savings and futures there.

### Who has to make room for gentrification?

The greatest fears inspired by gentrification, of course, are that low-income residents and low-margin retailers will be displaced by more affluent residents and more profitable businesses.

The Department of City Planning's study of gentrified neighborhoods in Park Slope and on the Upper West Side concluded that some displacement occurs following a community's decline as well as after its rehabilitation. The study also found, however, that residential rent regulations gave apartment dwellers substantial protection against displacement. In addition, the study pointed out that the mix of retail stores and service establishments has remained the same in both areas since 1970.

In this regard, it should also be noted that tenants of residential rental buildings that are converted to cooperative ownership remain protected by non-eviction plans if they decide they don't want to buy their units. A survey conducted by the Real Estate Board of New York found that 85 percent of such tenants thought the conversion process had been a fair one.

### A role for public policy.

We believe that whatever displacement gentrification causes, though, must be dealt with with public policies that promote low- and moderate-income housing construction and rehabilitation, and in zoning revisions that permit retail uses in less expensive, side street locations.

We also believe that New York's best hope lies with families, businesses and lending institutions willing to commit themselves for the long haul to neighborhoods that need them.

That's gentrification.

 **The Real Estate Board of New York, Inc.**

---

**Figure 4.2** Is Gentrification a Dirty Word?
*Source: The New York Times,* December 23, 1985. Reprinted with permission of Real Estate Board of New York, Inc.

now a relic of its time, but that it is still useful 'as a spring board from which to open out the definition as opposed to something that restricts it' (Davidson and Lees 2005: 1187). They suggest that we hold onto the core elements of gentrification: (1) the reinvestment of capital, (2) the social upgrading of locale by incoming high-income groups, (3) landscape change, and (4) direct or indirect displacement of low-income groups; and that we do not attach it to a particular landscape or context. In this way, we should be able to 'keep hold of "gentrification" as an important term and concept for analyzing urban change in the 21st-century city' (p. 1187).

Back in the 1980s, a number of authors argued that gentrification was a chaotic concept describing the contingent and geographically specific results of different processes operating in different ways in different contexts. Rose (1984), for example, argued that gentrification was a chaotic concept that needed disaggregation. She urged researchers to question existing categories and to start to explore the actual processes through which groups subsumed under the category 'gentrifiers' were produced and reproduced: 'We ought not to assume in advance that all gentrifiers have the same class positions as each other and that they are "structurally" polarized from the displaced' (p. 67). Similarly, Beauregard (1986: 40) argued,

> "[G]entrification" must be recognized as a "chaotic concept" connoting many diverse if interrelated events and processes. ... Encompassed under the rubric of gentrification are the redevelopment of historic row houses in Philadelphia's Society Hill initiated by an urban renewal project ... the transformation of a working class neighborhood of Victorian houses in San Francisco by gay men ... the redevelopment of abandoned housing in the Fells Point area of Baltimore, and the conversion of warehouses along the Boston waterfront to housing for the affluent. Each of these instances not only involves different types of individuals, but also proceeded differently and had varying consequences. The diversity of gentrification must be recognized, rather then conflating diverse aspects into a single phenomenon.

He goes on to argue,

> Recognition of the complexity of processes involved furthers our sensitivity to "gentrification" as a chaotic concept. No one or even two factors are determinant. Conversely, the absence of any one factor does not mean that gentrification will not occur. (p. 53)

More recently, Clark (2005: 256–257) strongly refutes focusing on the chaos and complexity of gentrification. He argues,

> We wrongly assume that seeking to identify order and simplicity in gentrification is tantamount to reductionism and simplemindedness,

and that critical thinking requires us to stick to the lodestars of chaos and complexity. This overriding tendency in gentrification research is not unrelated to more general trends in social science where there has been a remarkable turnaround in radical political sensibilities which has seen the social construction of objects of study dominate over other discourses of understanding.

Clark (2005) is right to argue that Beauregard's (1986: 35–40) concern for 'the essence of gentrification', its 'essential meanings and underlying causes', its 'essential form', and the 'structural forces necessary for its general form' has been overlain by gentrification researchers focusing on the chaos and complexity of gentrification leading to narrow and quixotic definitions. He argues that we need a much broader definition of gentrification than is commonly found in the literature. In so doing, he also argues, like Lees (2000), for a more inclusive perspective on the geography and history of gentrification. Clark's (2005) definition of gentrification is indeed broad and loose; it includes the root causes of gentrification, which he sees to be 'commodification of space, polarised power relations, and a dominance of vision oversight characteristic of "the vagrant sovereign"' (p. 261). Clark (2005) makes some good points. If we are to retain the usefulness of the politicized term 'gentrification', then we must stick with a broad, simple, but loose definition and operationalization of the term. Like Davidson and Lees (2005), he argues that the term needs to be elastic enough to allow new processes of gentrification which may yet emerge to be drawn under its umbrella, and at the same time be able to make political statements. It needs to be 'an elastic yet targeted definition' (Clark 2005: 258).

## Summary

Gentrification has mutated over time, so that it now includes not just traditional, classical gentrification in the vein of Ruth Glass's (1964) definition but also rural gentrification, new-build gentrification, super-gentrification, and many other derivatives. As a result we seem to be moving towards a broader and more open definition of 'gentrification', one able to incorporate the more recent mutations of the process into its fold. David Ley (1996: 34), for example, argued for a broad definition of gentrification that included 'renovation and redevelopment on both residential and non-residential sites'; and Neil Smith (1996a: 39) defined gentrification as an all-encompassing middle-class restructuring of the central city. Clark (2005: 256) too argued for a broader definition of gentrification: 'Our overly narrow definitions render the concept genuinely chaotic by conflating contingent and necessary relations. This effectively interferes with probing underlying causes and slants our view towards particularities'. Clark (2005) came up with an 'elastic yet targeted definition' in which 'gentrification is a process involving a change in the population of land-users such that the new users are of a higher socio-economic status than the previous users, together with an associated change in the built environment through a reinvestment in fixed capital' (p. 258). It is this 'elastic yet targeted' definition that we would like to keep hold of. At the same time, we would like to leave this chapter calling for 'less definitional deliberation and more critical, progressive scholarship' (Slater, Curran, and Lees 2004: 1145).

**Activities and Exercises**

- Read Palen and London's (1984) discussion (and criticism) of the word 'gentrification' on pages 7–8.
- Find a newspaper article on gentrification. How is the term used, and what does it convey?
- Think about whether you agree with Clark (2005: 260) that 'Haussmannization' is an early form of gentrification.
- Try to visit an area of classical gentrification. Then, a few days later, try to visit an area of new-build gentrification. List the differences and similarities between the two.
- Visit an area of supposedly rural or coastal gentrification. Is this really 'gentrification'?
- Write down and compare different definitions of gentrification over time.
- Read Butler and Smith's (2007) special issue, 'Extending Gentrification', *Environment and Planning A*. Are some of these authors extending the term too far? Are others refusing to see the political purchase of the term?

**Further Reading**

Atkinson, R., and G. Bridge (2005) 'Introduction', in R. Atkinson and G. Bridge (eds.) *Gentrification in a Global Context: The New Urban Colonialism* (London: Routledge) 1–17.

Beauregard, R. A. (1986) 'The chaos and complexity of gentrification', in N. Smith and P. Williams (eds.) *Gentrification of the City* (Boston: Allen and Unwin) 35–55.

Butler, T., and L. Lees (2006) 'Super-gentrification in Barnsbury, London: Globalisation and gentrifying global elites at the neighbourhood level', *Transactions of the Institute of British Geographers* 31:467–487.

Butler, T., and D. Smith (guest eds.) (2007) 'Extending gentrification', *Environment and Planning A* 39, 1 (special issue).

Cameron, S. (2003) 'Gentrification, housing redifferentiation and urban regeneration: "Going for Growth" in Newcastle upon Tyne', *Urban Studies*, 40, 12: 2367–2382.

Clark, E. (2005) 'The order and simplicity of gentrification: A political challenge', in R. Atkinson and G. Bridge (eds.) *Gentrification in a Global Context: The New Urban Colonialism* (London: Routledge) 256–264.

Davidson, M., and L. Lees (2005) 'New-build "gentrification" and London's riverside renaissance', *Environment and Planning A*, 37, 7: 1165–1190.

Lees, L. (2003b) 'Super-gentrification: The case of Brooklyn Heights, New York City', *Urban Studies*, 40, 12: 2487–2510.

Mills, C. (1988) '"Life on the up-slope": The postmodern landscape of gentrification', *Environment and Planning D: Society and Space*, 6:169–189.

Mills, C. (1993) 'Myths and meanings of gentrification', in J. S. Duncan and D. Ley (eds.) *Place/Culture/Representation* (London: Routledge) 149–170.

Phillips, M. (2004) 'Other geographies of gentrification', *Progress in Human Geography*, 28:5–30.

Podmore, J. (1998) 'Re-reading the "loft-living" habitus in Montreal's inner city', *International Journal of Urban and Regional Research*, 22:285–302.

Rofe, M. (2003) '"I want to be global": Theorising the gentrifying class as an emergent elite global community', *Urban Studies*, 40, 12: 2511–2526.

**Plate 5.1** Gentrification in Ostozhenka, Moscow

Moscow: from socialist city to gentrified city.
*Source:* Photograph by Oleg Golubchikov.

# 5
# Contemporary Gentrification

In Chapter 1 we described pioneer or classical gentrification. In Chapters 2 and 3 we discussed gentrification theory, a body of theory that for the most part explains classical gentrification. In Chapter 4 we showed how gentrification has mutated over time and space. In this chapter we investigate contemporary gentrification in more detail. We look at the impacts of globalization, neoliberalism, and the changing role of the state; we assess the literature on the (re)scaling of gentrification; we draw on Hackworth and Smith's (2001) schematic history of gentrification in New York City to develop a new stage model or history of gentrification (for New York City, but with discussion about its wider applicability) that includes a fourth wave of gentrification; and we make some strong arguments about the necessity for a geography of gentrification. We conclude the chapter by asking whether the theories (based for the most part on first-wave or classical gentrification) in Chapters 2 and 3 have any purchase for analyzing and explaining gentrification today.

### Globalization, Neoliberalism, and the Changing Role of the State

Neil Smith (2002) was perhaps the first gentrification scholar to highlight the relationship between globalization, neoliberalism, and the changing role of the state in contemporary gentrification. He argues that gentrification is now a 'global urban strategy' linked to a new globalism and a related new urbanism. He makes two central arguments about the changing relationship between neoliberal urbanism and globalization: first, the neoliberal state is now the agent of, rather than the regulator of, the market. As such, a new revanchist urbanism (see Chapter 6 on the revanchist city thesis) has replaced the liberal (often welfare-orientated) urban policy of First World cities, and neoliberal urban policy now expresses the impulses of capitalist production rather than social reproduction. Second, he argues that gentrification has now gone global (see Chapter 4); it is no longer restricted to North America, Europe, or Oceania, but rather is a generalized strategy that is connected into the circuits of global capital and cultural circulation.

In popular discourse, the term 'neoliberalism' entered widespread usage in the 1980s to describe the harsh structural adjustment policies that First World institutions like the International Monetary Fund (IMF) and the World Bank imposed on the countries and cities of the Global South. These dictates slashed social spending and government regulations while favoring unimpeded trade and the unfettered right of foreign investors to repatriate profits. But it soon became clear that the cities of the Global North were experiencing many of the same political pressures, albeit in the very different industrial and spatial structures distinctive to First World urbanization. In the past decade or so, neoliberalism has become a widely recognized but often misunderstood term. Academics and policy analysts use it as a descriptive shorthand to summarize the prevailing trends towards deregulation, commercialization, privatization, labor-market flexibility, public–private partnerships, and the downsizing of those parts of government that help the poor, racial or ethnic minorities, and other groups marginalized by market processes. But the term has also become a rallying cry for activists who question the priorities of corporate globalization and the inequalities it unleashes. And so, in much the same way that 'globalization' became the keyword for the transnational flows and integrations that seemed to accelerate in the 1990s, in the 2000s 'neoliberalism' has become the flashpoint of political struggle and theoretical debate.

But this debate is not really so new. Although the word entered popular usage only twenty years ago, the philosophies it denotes go back much earlier. Just as 'neoclassical' economics refers to a twentieth-century incarnation of eighteenth- and nineteenth-century classical political economy, neoliberalism represents an effort to revive the purest, most brutal streams of political philosophy. As Neil Smith (2002: 429) puts it,

> By neoliberalism I mean something quite specific. Eighteenth-century liberalism, from John Locke to Adam Smith, pivoted on two crucial assumptions: that the free and democratic exercise of individual self-interest led to the optimal collective social good; and that the market knows best: that is, private property is the foundation of this self-interest, and free market exchange is its ideal vehicle. Twentieth-century American liberalism, from Woodrow Wilson to Franklin Roosevelt to John F Kennedy—emphasizing social compensation for the excesses of the market and private property—is not so much a misnomer, therefore—it by no means abrogated these axioms of liberalism—but it is an outlier insofar as, in a co-optive response to the challenge of socialism, it sought to regulate their sway. The neoliberalism that carries the twentieth into the twenty-first century therefore represents a significant return to the original axioms of liberalism, albeit one galvanized by an unprecedented mobilization not just of national state power but of state power organized and exercised at different geographical scales.

This mobilization of power at different geographical scales involved long-range strategic planning as well as short-run tactical sophistication. Jamie Peck (2006) traces the histories of powerful conservative business figures in Britain and the United States who began working as early as the 1950s to establish a network of right-wing think tanks to promote free-market philosophies and policies. Focusing on the United States, Peck (2006: 682–683) narrates the triumphs of an entire right-wing urbanism—a movement that began to achieve its first successes when Ronald Reagan (elected in 1980) moved quickly to dismantle major federal programs designed to help cities and the urban poor. And now, more than a quarter century later,

> ... it is difficult to dispute the contention that the "new urban right" has notched up some significant victories in the war of ideas—along the way, reframing the debate around America's cities, their alleged pathologies, and their putative salvation. Even though, a generation later, conservative intellectuals continue to portray themselves as lonely voices of reason, as principled outsiders in a corrupt, distracted, and wrongheaded world, both their circumstances and their traction have certainly changed. The ideational shift toward free-market strategies—which, beyond simple "deregulation" or marketization, licences new forms of state interventionism—has been a seismic one. ... If cities began this period as a policy category-cum-beneficiary, they ended it as an often-maligned political target; if urban policy once designated a set of programs for cities, conceived as centers of progressive reform and policy innovation, today the dominant view is that it is cities *themselves* that must be reformed.

All of these factors have transformed the context for gentrification. In the 1970s and 1980s, scholars debating the causes of gentrification could explore the dynamics of production and consumption with at least some comfort in the knowledge that there were still a few public policies in place to cushion the harsh injustices of rampant gentrification. More recently, public policy in many national contexts has shifted decisively. Gentrification is seen as a positive result of a healthy real estate market, and 'the market' is always understood as the solution, not a problem. Thanks to intense economic competition and policy directives from state and federal governments, cities now must be sophisticated entrepreneurs—doing whatever it takes to lure wealthy investors, residents, and tourists to town (Harvey 1989b, 2000). Nearly all major spending initiatives by city governments in the United States are scrutinized by investors (whose purchases of municipal bonds will finance school construction or other major capital expenditures) and bond-rating agencies that quite literally 'grade' city budgets and creditworthiness (Hackworth 2002b). And so gentrification has become a particularly attractive policy mechanism for more and more cities. It has been woven ever more tightly together with capital market processes, public sector privatization schemes, globalized city competition, welfare retrenchment and workfare requirements, and many other threads of the fabric of neoliberal urbanism.

*Contingent Geographies of Change*

All of these general tendencies are worked out differently in particular national, regional, and urban settings. At the interurban scale, the expansion of gentrification worldwide is tied to the rise of service-based economies and the shifting functions of central cities, as well as the enforced diffusion of neoliberal models of urban governance and redevelopment. Smith argues that gentrification has evolved from a marginal urban process in a few western cities during the 1960s to an increasingly popular and widespread 'global urban strategy' (N. Smith 2002). In the Global North, this urban strategy involves an innovative race to create attractive, novel, and interesting—but also safe and sanitized—playgrounds for the wealthy residents and visitors who work for (or receive interest and dividends from) the institutions of global capital (Mitchell 2003). In the process, the poor and disinvested territory of the as-yet ungentrified inner city becomes a battleground for a wider political struggle over neoliberal urbanism: large blocks of publicly assisted housing, for example, physically embody neoliberalism's antithesis—Keynesian egalitarian liberalism. As we shall see in Chapter 6, such public housing is now the target of 'positive gentrification policies' in a number of different countries.

But in the Global South, gentrification as an urban strategy is playing out in even more diverse ways. Although urban thinking in much of Europe and North America is obsessed with the contours of postindustrial society, urbanization in the Global South is driven by the simultaneous expansion of 'old' and 'new' spatial economic shifts; cities are being reshaped by the expansion of manufacturing and heavy industrial activities, as well as the growth of high-tech offshoring and outsourcing activities and smaller pockets of service-sector innovation. Increasingly, though, the class transformation of urban space in cities of the Global South involves systematic, large-scale reconstruction of large chunks of the urban fabric—backed by the financial support of transnational investors and the political support of state-led efforts to define indigenous populations as an undeserving poor.

Taken together, all of these trends hint at a complex geographical contingency to neoliberal urbanism. Neoliberalism appeals to a fundamentally universal notion of the individual, of private market relations, and of the proper role of the state. But this political movement varies widely in the way these principles are implemented in law and practice, and today's neoliberal policies are layered atop previous generations of political and economic rules, traditions, norms, and institutions. Contemporary geographies of gentrification, therefore, vary depending on national and regional context and the interaction of various components of neoliberal policy—aggressive urban entrepreneurialism, local government reorganization to create favorable business climates, public sector privatization schemes, the increasing number and power of professionals committed to neoliberal urban policies, and the increasingly sophisticated policing of urban space and activism itself.

*A New Colonialism?*

Recognizing complexity and contingency, however, does not mean ignoring common threads and similarities. Indeed, Rowland Atkinson and Gary Bridge (2005) offer an especially provocative analysis that gives some historical perspective to the way we understand today's many different expressions of gentrification. Atkinson and Bridge argue that the triumph of neoliberalism in urban life is nothing short of a latter-day, urban version of the massive social changes that followed the European 'Age of Discovery' of the sixteenth century. The subtitle to their edited collection *Gentrification in a Global Context* is quite explicit: *The New Urban Colonialism*. Atkinson and Bridge suggest that contemporary gentrification—based as it is on wide differences in wealth and power—resembles earlier waves of colonial and mercantile expansion that exploited national and continental differences in economic development. It has been exported from the metropoles of North America, Western Europe, and Australasia into new territories in former colonial possessions throughout the world. It privileges wealth and whiteness, and reasserts the white Anglo appropriation of urban space and historical memory (W. Shaw 2000, 2005). And it universalizes the neoliberal principles of governing cities that force poor and vulnerable residents to endure gentrification as a process of colonization by more privileged classes:

> Those who come to occupy prestigious central city locations frequently have the characteristics of a colonial elite. They often live in exclusive residential enclaves and are supported by a domestic and local service class. Gentrifiers are employed in ... "new class" occupations, and are marked out by their cosmopolitanism. Indeed, in many locations, especially in ex-communist European and east Asian countries, they often are western ex-patriots [sic] employed by transnational corporations to open up the markets of the newly emerging economies. (Atkinson and Bridge 2005: 3)

Badyina and Golubchikov (2005) demonstrate not just the global expansion of gentrification, but also the relationship between neoliberalism and gentrification in a nonwestern context. They focus on the gentrification of Ostozhenka, a residential neighborhood in central Moscow (see plate 5.1 at the begining of this chapter). They argue that although market forces have driven the process, Moscow's government has actively facilitated gentrification. They compare communist Moscow with neoliberal Moscow:

> The introduction of the market economy has unlocked the mismatch between, on the one hand, the function and the morphology of the socialist cities and, on the other, the logic of the market. A consequence has been a flood of new urban processes, which have rapidly changed the function and appearance of cities. (p. 114)

Moscow's city government facilitated the gentrification of Ostozhenka by assigning residential buildings in that neighborhood for demolition, due to their 'state of disrepair', and thus the households in them for resettlement:

> The city has either to rehouse the tenants in non-privatized (and therefore municipal) rooms in other apartments … or, in the case of privatized dwellings, to compensate the owners in kind or in cash. This resettlement mechanism has turned out to be an "effective" tool in authorizing an immediate displacement of a large number of residents. (p. 122)

But as Badyina and Golubchikov go on to reveal, as soon as corporate interest in the neighborhood was established, developers started to contribute to this compulsory rehousing through public–private partnerships in which they paid for the cost of resettlement in exchange for the sites. Most of the residents had not wanted to move.

They conclude,

> Whereas the physical improvement of the city centre signifies departing from the Soviet legacies of under-investment in the housing built environment, the growing socio-spatial polarization undermines the social achievements of the Soviet system and denotes the triumph of the neoliberal urban regime in Moscow. (Badyina and Golubchikov 2005: 113)

Badyina and Golubchikov's study is a revealing one, for it also points to the fact that different waves of gentrification have been active in Ostozhenka, and, like in Butler and Lees (2006) on Barnsbury, they point to philosophical/ideological conflicts between these different waves of gentrifiers. They also discuss neocolonialism:

> The promoters of Ostozhenka like to speak about what they call "Europeanization" of the neighbourhood. By "Europeanization" they imagine the ultimate manifestation of prosperity combined with a sort of disparagement of the rest of Russian society. (p. 124)

The cohort investing in, or buying and living in, these new gentrified properties shares its identity with the new upper classes colonizing the elite districts in major world cities—they are business executives, business elites, and media elites, along with foreign businesspeople and diplomats. The more expensive inner area is under the constant surveillance of closed-circuit television (CCTV), and Badyina and Golubchikov note the distinct possibility that the entire neighborhood will be gated and closed to general public access. However, unlike in Neil Smith's (2002) thesis in which neoliberalism seems to have won lock, stock, and barrel, Badyina and Golubchikov conclude that

> as the social and political context in the Russian state is changing, so the Moscow government's operational rhythm becomes increasingly challenged. It is likely that the present regime will be discontinued.

The contours of the coming order are not yet clearly identifiable, and whether it will offer a more emancipatory alternative remains to be seen. (p. 127)

**The (Re)scaling of Gentrification: Outwards and Downwards**

Gentrification is no longer confined to western metropolises, as we have seen in the case of Moscow; it has gone global (N. Smith 2002; Atkinson and Bridge 2005), and more recently researchers have argued that it has descended or cascaded down the urban hierarchy too (Dutton 2003; Atkinson and Bridge 2005). What these two scales of gentrification have in common is the fact that in both cases, gentrification is searching for a 'rent gap' (see Chapter 2; see also Chapter 4 on the other mutations of contemporary gentrification) in marginal locations previously untouched, or relatively untouched, by gentrification, whether that be in Moscow, Russia, or Burnley in Lancashire. Here we investigate the arguments around these two scales of gentrification in more detail. First, we investigate gentrification and globalization. Atkinson and Bridge (2005: 7) argue quite rightly that 'gentrification today must be seen in the context of globalisation'; however, they gloss over the causal links between globalization and gentrification. Like N. Smith (2002) (see above), they link globalization and gentrification by discussing neoliberal urban policy regimes, the hypermobility of global capital and workers, the expansion and increased wealth of the cosmopolitan class, and so on. But they provide little to no empirical or conceptual detail in their discussion. The challenge is made even more difficult by the fact that the globalization literature and the gentrification literature have, to date, paid little attention to each other (Butler and Lees 2006). It is evident now that this must change, and following Atkinson and Bridge (2005), we begin here to draw together these literatures. Second, we investigate the idea that gentrification is cascading down the urban hierarchy. Such a process has happened, and indeed is still happening, in the United Kingdom, but gentrification has been active in cities quite far down the urban hierarchy in the United States since its early days. As we mentioned in Chapter 4, in Portland, Maine, for example, gentrification began in the 1960s (Lees 2006). However, gentrification does seem to be cascading even further down the urban hierarchy in the United States today, to small towns like Fort Kent and Machias in Maine, which state and local officials hope to regenerate into mini creative class-led hubs. Context, time, and space are all important considerations, as our final section in this chapter, which seeks to think through a geography of contemporary gentrification, argues.

*The Nuances of Gentrification and Globalization*

In the literature on gentrification and globalization, gentrifiers are seen to be the emissaries of global capital flows. For example, Rofe (2003) positions the gentrifying class as an emergent elite global community, arguing that '[t]he spatial occurrence of the gentrifying class in a number of prominent cities around the globe lends this group a global geography' (p. 2512). Rofe (2003) argues that the duality of global–local is an artificial one, and he quotes M. Smith (2001: 157), who argues that this duality 'rests on a false opposition that equates the local with a ... space for stasis ... and the global as the site of dynamic change'. Instead, Rofe argues that the global and the local are mutually entwined and that the linking of distant local spaces through the auspices of globalization has enabled the 'jumping of scales' (N. Smith 2001: 5), creating transnational networks. On reading the gentrification and the globalization literatures, he finds a striking similarity between the transnational elite and the gentrifying class (both are highly educated, affluent professionals employed in high-status, white-collar professions), but divergences too (the transnational elite serves the interests of global expansion, whilst the gentrifying class is more interested in the inner city in which they have chosen to live; cf. Ley 1996). Rofe (2003) found that a significant number of the gentrifiers he surveyed, in the Australian cities of Sydney and Newcastle, self-identified as being global; as such, he concluded that they constituted an emerging elite global community.

Atkinson and Bridge (2005: 7) argue,

> The literature on globalization has not been geared towards the level of the neighbourhood. However, in the context of neighbourhood changes like gentrification it would seem increasingly important to acknowledge that neighbourhood scales may be an important locus of concentrations of professionals and managerial groups in networks of dialogue and co-ordination of state and sub-state governance structures. In short, the neighbourhood has been under-recognised as the site of the reproduction of a wide set of power relations and contacts which operate at local, urban, regional and international levels.

In response to this, and in an attempt to read both the gentrification and globalization literatures together, Butler and Lees (2006) studied the relationship between (super)gentrification, globalization, and global elites at the neighborhood level in Barnsbury, London (see also Chapter 4). In contrast to Rofe's (2003) study of a supermobile fraction of the cosmopolitan elite who framed their identities in a global context, Butler and Lees study a specific fraction of the global elite (super-gentrifiers) who are relatively immobile (e.g., do not jet around the world) and are relatively fixed in a particular residential neighborhood. As such, their study takes issue with a globalization literature (and, indeed, a good deal of the recent gentrification literature) that emphasizes (hyper)mobility, unfixity, flow, dislocation, transnationalism, and cosmopolitanism, for the super-gentrifiers who they study, who are part of the new global elite, do not share these characteristics. They have formed 'personal micro-networks' that center on residence and leisure space in

Barnsbury. They work in a contact-intensive subculture where co-location in the City and face-to-face meetings are very important, as is the need to socialize and live with their own cohort. As such, Butler and Lees (2006) draw a distinction between a genuinely transnational faction of the global elite (the super-rich), globally mobile managers, and those professionals who maintain the global finance machine from their fixed bases in Manhattan and the City of London and a very restricted list of B-grade cities. Their super-gentrifiers can be distinguished from the global managers restlessly roaming the world identified by Rofe (2003), who sees one of the major consequences of globalization as being the erosion of space. By way of contrast, in Barnsbury space is not being eroded by globalization; rather, it is being (re)produced through super-gentrification as a by-product of globalization. Butler and Lees (2006) agree with Rofe (2003: 2517), who argues that recognizing the 'spatially fragmented and socially fragmenting nature of globalisation is vital if balanced critiques of globalisation's impacts and the emergence of global elite communities are to be achieved'.

### Gentrification Cascading Down the Urban Hierarchy?

There has long been a bias towards research on large metropolitan cities in the gentrification literature. As Dutton (2003: 2558) argues, '[M]uch of the empirical and theoretical research in the 1980s and early 1990s, either explicitly or implicitly, considered gentrification in the context of cities occupying strategic positions in the international urban hierarchy'. But this is changing as 'a nascent body of gentrification research in provincial cities provides the beginnings of a much-needed empirical mapping of the development of gentrification beyond global cities' (Dutton 2005: 223; see also Bridge 2003). This is leading to research and discussion, especially in the United Kingdom, on the differences between gentrification in smaller, provincial cities and in larger, metropolitan cities. This research into gentrification further down the urban hierarchy is to be welcomed. However, the suggestion in some recent writings (e.g., on the cascade effect, see Atkinson and Bridge 2005: 2, 11; but see also Dutton 2003, 2005) that gentrification does not occur in cities further down the urban hierarchy until saturation occurs in high-order cities is a false one. Indeed, Dutton (2003) contradicts himself—in alternate pages, he argues that 'by the early 1980s, gentrification in Britain had already been observed in a number of cities outside London' (p. 2558), and he cites Williams (1984: 221), who observes gentrification in Bristol, Oxford, Bath, and so on. He then states on the adjacent page, 'Although the process commenced in the dynamic environments of a limited number of high-order global cities, suitable conditions for gentrification can now be found in many lower-tier provincial but globalising cities' (p. 2559). This suggests that disentangling the mechanisms and the contextual and temporal dimensions that are part of the so-called cascade effect is important.

Lees (2006) finds three possible mechanisms that are argued to cause the so-called cascade effect. The first is economic—the idea, as stated above, that the rent gaps are exhausted in metropolitan cities such as New York and London, so capital seeks out new frontiers lower down the urban hierarchy. The assumption here is that there is a unified real estate market and easy diffusion, nationally, of information about investment opportunities. Dutton (2003, 2005), for example, demonstrates the diffusion of gentrification from London and the South East of England to Leeds. This is something that more corporate investment is likely to take advantage of, as Dutton (2003: 2559) points out with respect to Leeds. The risk associated with gentrification is probably greater in smaller cities, and this is a risk that institutional/corporate actors who gentrify en masse are probably better able to bear than individual pioneer households. The second possible cascade mechanism is cultural—the diffusion of a gentrification lifestyle from center to periphery. Podmore (1998), for example, discusses the role of the mass media in reproducing the values and meanings of gentrification from one metropolitan context to another, the habitus of loft living from New York to Montréal. Indeed, as we have argued throughout this book, gentrification is now the blueprint for new urban living around the world; it is a 'gentrification generalised' (N. Smith 2002). Finally, a third mechanism is a policy one—small cities borrow regeneration policies, plans, and ideas from bigger ones. Think of the way that waterfront redevelopment, repackaged by those people who first did Faneuil Hall in Boston, then South Street in New York and the Inner Harbor Baltimore, sold the idea of putting the old commercial city back in touch with its waterfront. And even further down the urban hierarchy, as mentioned in Chapter 4, small towns like Burnley in Lancashire are trying to reinvent themselves by taking regeneration ideas from larger cities such as Seattle and Manchester.

Lees's (2006) case study of small-city gentrification in Portland, Maine, however, complicates the cascade idea in at least three ways. First, historically, as said before, Portland does not lag behind New York and Boston in the urban renaissance game but is right there with them, perhaps even ahead of them. Second, Portland, Maine, although not a high-order or first-tier city, has become the regeneration model for towns and cities elsewhere in New England. And third, Portland's success, however, in terms of its urban renaissance, is due to a series of historically and geographically contingent reasons—its place in the regional/state city hierarchy, its strong local entrepreneurial base, its success in the regional service economy and in attracting back office services from Boston, and its position as the State of Maine's only metropolis—that comprise a strong economic base on which to grow the arts. This case shows the real importance of studying the context, temporality, and scale of gentrification—in other words, the geography of gentrification (see later in this chapter).

The next section considers temporality in more detail, drawing on but also filling out (using other discussions of gentrification over time), expanding (making it more generalizable beyond New York City), and updating (identifying a fourth wave) Hackworth and Smith's (2001) schematic history of gentrification in New York City. We look at the progression of gentrification through four distinct waves.

## Towards a New Stage Model of Gentrification

> The insight that the stage model gives us of gentrification's progression should not be abandoned along with its evidently flawed prediction that all gentrifying areas will ultimately have reached the same end state.
>
> K. Shaw (2005: 172)

The early stage models of gentrification outlined at the end of Chapter 1 were designed before researchers knew enough about the unfolding of the process. These days, we know much more about the process, and contemporary models are much more useful than the early stage models. One of the best recent attempts to model gentrification has been that of Hackworth and Smith (2001), who following Lees (2000: 16) recognize that 'gentrification today is quite different to gentrification in the early 1970s, late 1980s, even the early 1990s'. Hackworth and Smith (2001) have drawn up a schematic history of gentrification in New York City that takes its impetus from neo-Marxist rent gap models (see Chapter 2). The schema or model they designed (see Figure 5.1) is divided into three distinct waves of gentrification separated by two transitional periods of recession-induced restructuring of the institutional context and mechanisms through which gentrification occurred. The model, however, is overreliant on neo-Marxist rent gap models, and as such it underplays the extraordinary range of people involved in the process of gentrification, people who Rose's (1996) stage model (see the conclusion to this chapter) and indeed the earlier stage models revealed well (see also Chapter 3 on agency). Furthermore, the model is now somewhat outdated, for we would argue that a fourth wave of gentrification has emerged in the United States since 2001.

Boxes 5.1, 5.2, and 5.3 outline first-, second-, and third-wave gentrification, providing some flesh for the bones of Figure 5.1. We suggest you read through them carefully before turning to our discussion below of a possible fourth wave of gentrification.

### A Fourth Wave of Gentrification?

It is six years now since Hackworth and Smith (2001) designed their schematic history of gentrification in New York City, and well over a decade since the third wave of postrecession gentrification first began. In their case studies of New York neighborhoods, Hackworth and Smith (2001: 475) emphasized that the local effects of increased state intervention in gentrification should be understood as part of a broader shift in the political economy of the

| Year | Wave | Description |
|------|------|-------------|
| 1999 | **Third-wave** | **Gentrification returns:** Prophesies of degentrification appear to have been overstated as many neighborhoods continue to gentrify while others, further from the city center begin to experience the process for the first time. Post-recession gentrification seems to be more linked to large-scale capital than ever, as large developers rework entire neighborhoods, often with state support. |
| 1998 | | |
| 1997 | | |
| 1996 | | |
| 1995 | | |
| 1994 | | |
| 1993 | | |
| 1992 | Transition | **Gentrification slows:** The recession constricts the flow of capital into gentrifying and gentrified neighborhoods, prompting some to proclaim that a 'degentrification' or reversal of the process was afoot. |
| 1991 | | |
| 1990 | | |
| 1989 | | |
| 1988 | | |
| 1987 | **Second-wave** | **The anchoring of gentrification:** The process becomes implanted in hitherto disinvested central city neighborhoods. In contrast to the pre-1973 experience of gentrification, the process becomes common in smaller, non-global cities during the 1980s. In New York City, the presence of the arts community was often a key correlate of residential gentrification, serving to smooth the flow of capital into neighborhoods like SoHo, Tribeca, and the Lower East Side. Intense political struggles occur during this period over the displacement of the poorest residents. |
| 1986 | | |
| 1985 | | |
| 1984 | | |
| 1983 | | |
| 1982 | | |
| 1981 | | |
| 1980 | | |
| 1979 | | |
| 1978 | Transition | **Gentrifiers buy property:** In New York and other cities, developers and investors used the downturn in property values to consume large portions of devalorized neighborhoods, thus setting the stage for 1980s gentrification. |
| 1976 | | |
| 1977 | | |
| 1975 | | |
| 1974 | | |
| 1973 | | |
| 1972 | **First-wave** | **Sporadic gentrification:** Prior to 1973, the process is mainly isolated in small neighborhoods in the north eastern USA and Western Europe. |
| 1971 | | |
| 1969 | | |
| 1968 | | |

**Figure 5.1** Hackworth and Smith's (2001) Stage Model of Gentrification
*Source:* Jason Hackworth and Neil Smith, The changing state of gentrification, *Tijdschrift voor Economische en Sociale Geografie*, 22:464–477. © 2001 Blackwell Publishing.

---

**Box 5.1**

**First-Wave Gentrification**

The first wave, beginning in the 1950s and lasting until the 1973 global economic recession, was 'sporadic and state-led'. Disinvested inner-city housing in the United States, Western Europe, and Australia became a target for reinvestment (Hackworth and Smith 2001: 466) largely as a result of the 'green-lining' activities of pioneer gentrifiers (see the detailed empirical case studies of first-wave gentrification in Chapter 1). These gentrifications were often funded by the public sector because gentrification was thought to be too risky for the private sector: 'Governments were aggressive in helping gentrification because the prospect of inner-city investment (without state insurance of some form) was still very risky ... state involvement was often justified through the discourse of ameliorating urban decline' (Hackworth and Smith 2001: 466). Gotham (2005) argues that in the United States, the first wave was an outgrowth of the 1949 and 1954 Housing Acts that provided federal funds for the redevelopment of blighted areas. Lees (1994b) notes the importance of both federal and local (e.g., the J-51 Program) state funds in the gentrification of Park Slope (see also Chapter 1). In the United Kingdom, home improvement grants (as discussed in the case study of Barnsbury in Chapter 1) were the British equivalent. The economic downturn that came with the global economic recession that affected various national economies between 1973 and 1977 then 'encouraged the shift of capital from unproductive to productive sectors, setting the stage for a reinvestment in central-city office, recreation, retail and residential activities (Harvey 1985)' (Hackworth and Smith 2001: 466).

---

**Box 5.2**

**Second-Wave Gentrification**

The second wave in the postrecession 1970s and 1980s, described as 'expansion and resistance', anchored and stabilized the gentrification process and resulted in an aggressive entrepreneurial spirit. It was characterized by the 'integration of gentrification into a wider range of economic and cultural processes at the global and national scales' (Hackworth and Smith 2001: 468; also Wyly and Hammel 2001).

In Barnsbury (see Chapter 1 and Chapter 4) during its second wave, the process of gentrification and the gentrifiers themselves became more corporate and the neighborhood more stable. The neighborhood changes occurring in Barnsbury were enframed by wider changes taking place in London as a whole. London emerged as a global city in the 1960s, slightly earlier than New York, a result of its milder regulatory climate that 'brought many financial operations from New York to London in the mid-1960s, and existing facilities for international currency trading helped London to become the centre of the eurodollar markets in the 1970s' (Zukin 1992: 196). The number of foreign banks in London increased from 163 in 1970 to 521 in 1989 (King 1990). During the period 1968–1987, the number of staff working in foreign banks and securities houses increased eightfold from 9,000 to 72,000. London became the main center for the international euro currency business, eurobond transactions, foreign exchange, insurance, fund management, and corporate financial advice (Pryke 1991: 205). The City of London's function as a banking and finance center became more pronounced with the deregulation of the London Stock Exchange in 1986 and the full internationalization of securities dealing:

> The City was to become the hub not of a culturally familiar, slow-paced, empire-orientated regime of trade finance but of a new fast-moving capitalism in which the City itself was to become equally international. As capital was expanding across the globe the financial system which was feeding that growth had to change too. (Pryke 1991: 210)

Accountancy, law, business, and the function of the general clearinghouse for information around the world were concentrated in the 'golden square mile' around the Bank of England, but since 1984 these functions have expanded west and east through the redevelopment of the Docklands. The development of London as a global city aided those areas near to the city such as Barnsbury by providing jobs and an excess of capital for property investment, much of it from overseas. The second generation of gentrifiers was in some respects a transitional group between the first- and third-generation gentrifiers. They were a wealthier group of professionals than the pioneer gentrifiers and were overwhelmingly represented in Socio Economic Group 1 (employers and managers in central and local government, industry and commerce – large establishments). As we said in Chapter 4, New Labour's Tony Blair was the epitome of a gentrifier who moved into Barnsbury in this second wave. The City types beginning to move in were drawn from the upper professionals that Sassen (1991: 265) noted:

> The most central areas of London have undergone a transformation that broadly parallels Manhattan's.... We see a parallel increase in the stratum of what Brint (1991) has described as upper professionals, a group largely employed in corporate services, including finance. The sharp growth in the concentration of the mostly young, new high-income

professionals and managers employed in central London represents a significant change from a decade ago.

Gotham (2005) argues that two features marked this second wave: first is the integration of gentrification with new cultural strategies of economic redevelopment, meaning new investments in museums and art galleries. For example, in the 1980s and 1990s, following the models designed in cities such as Pittsburgh in the United States, and Glasgow in Scotland, Bilbao in Spain used flagship property-led redevelopment projects, such as the Guggenheim Museum, as central ingredients in its urban regeneration. Its urban regeneration was based on six key elements: (1) a postindustrial vision for the city; (2) altering the city's image; (3) transforming its physical environment, focusing on symbols of renaissance (e.g., exhibition centers and concert halls); (4) an explicit focus on the downtown and its derelict areas; (5) the importance of urban leisure economies—the Guggenheim effect; and (6) a new urban governance system based on public-private partnerships (Vicario and Martinez Monje 2005). The case of Bilbao is in many ways emblematic of gentrification in its second wave.

Second is the increased connection between gentrification and global systems of real estate and banking finance. These changes led to developments such as Boston's Faneuil Hall, Baltimore's Inner Harbor, New York City's South Street Seaport, and the art-led gentrification of the Lower East Side (see Bowler and McBurney 1991; Deutsche and Ryan 1984; Lees and Bondi 1995). The second wave was characterized by public–private partnerships, the increasing role of developers in the process, and laissez-faire subsidies. In this second wave, globalization was in part responsible for the ushering in of a 'new urban politics' (Cox and Mair 1988) characterized by a shift away from an emphasis on the provision of welfare to a more proactive commitment to local economic development. The shift was characterized by Harvey (1989b) as being from 'urban managerialism' to 'urban entrepreneurialism'. For example, in the 1980s, Thatcherite urban regeneration focused on economic growth and used public funds to lever in largely undirected market investment, as exemplified by London's Docklands (see Brownill 1990; Ogden 1992). The result was a highly polarized landscape between an incoming affluent population and a disinherited working-class population. As Fyfe and Kenny (2005: 157) argue, 'The juxtaposition of rich and poor in Docklands is an important reminder that the local politics of growth cannot be separated from the local politics of welfare and social provision'. There was also growing resistance to gentrification (see Chapter 7) in New York City and elsewhere at this time, as Neil Smith's (1996a) discussion of the Tompkins Square riots in the Lower East Side demonstrates (see also Abu-Lughod 1994).

| Box 5.3 |
| --- |
| **Third-Wave Gentrification** |

The third wave of gentrification is characterized by interventionist governments working with the private sector to facilitate gentrification: quite a shift from the typical second-wave position of passive support.

K. Shaw (2005: 183)

Third-wave or postrecession gentrification, described as 'recessional pause and subsequent expansion', began in the mid-1990s. Following debates over whether gentrification was in decline during the worldwide economic recession of the early 1990s (Bourne 1993a; Badcock 1993; see Preface and Chapter 7), there was widespread agreement that the assumed demise of gentrification was premature and that the phenomenon had entered a third wave of postrecession gentrification. In their discussion of third-wave gentrification, Hackworth and Smith (2001) suggest that the evolution of gentrification into a generalized strategy of capital accumulation, as seen in the second wave, was extended and intensified in the third wave:

Post-recession gentrification—the third wave of the process—is a purer expression of the economic conditions and processes that made reinvestment in disinvested inner areas so alluring for investors. (Hackworth and Smith 2001: 468)

Gentrification became linked to large-scale capital more than ever. Hackworth (2002a) argues that four changes distinguish gentrification's third wave: (1) corporate developers became the leading initiators of gentrification, less so pioneer gentrifiers; (2) federal and local governments were more open and assertive in facilitating gentrification; (3) anti-gentrification movements became more marginalized; and (4) gentrification was diffusing into more remote neighborhoods. Hackworth (2002a: 839) argues that in its third wave, overall, gentrification became 'more corporate, more state facilitated, and less resisted than ever before'. In many ways the heightened role of the state in gentrification, in terms of both public policy and investment, was the most important of these changes. The state's affair with gentrification, however, is nothing new; it began almost as soon as the process of gentrification was realized, as is shown in the two case studies in Chapter 1. However, after subsequent years of laissez-faire gentrification, the state began assisting gentrification again in its third wave, and in a much more assertive way: 'The state, at various levels, is fuelling the process of gentrification more directly than in the past, largely due to increased devolution' (Powell and Spencer 2003: 450).

Third-wave gentrification has, however, played out differently in different neighborhoods. In specific neighborhoods in global cities like Brooklyn Heights and Barnsbury, it has taken the form of super-gentrification (see Chapter 4), whilst in most other gentrifying or gentrified neighborhoods the process has intensified, stabilized more thoroughly, and reached a state of saturation. In other marginal locations it has emerged, as we have seen with respect to the more recent new-build gentrification outlined in Chapter 4 and the provincial gentrification discussed earlier in this chapter.

process—and, indeed, 'a systemic change in the way that the state relates to capital' and urbanization itself. Several developments in the first half of this decade, however, suggest that we are seeing a new, distinctive fourth wave of gentrification in the United States (see Figure 5.2). This wave combines an intensified financialization of housing combined with the consolidation of pro-gentrification politics and polarized urban policies.

In the last few years, gentrification has been swept up in the general financial transformation of housing. When a recession began to hit the U.S. economy in early 2001, the standard response of the Federal Reserve System (the Fed)—a quick barrage of interest rate cuts—brought unexpected results. This recession was different: it was brought on by a collapse in business expenditures, and sustained consumer borrowing and spending helped to cushion the slowdown. And over the previous decade, financial services competition and public policy had altered mortgage lending practices by relaxing underwriting standards, reducing down payment requirements, and expanding the secondary market, where borrowers' debt obligations are traded much like stocks and bonds. As a result, the flows of capital in local neighborhoods became much more tightly integrated with the conditions of national and global capital markets. In contrast to the housing market collapse that accompanied the early 1990s recession with its predictions of 'de-gentrification', the years after 2001 funneled enormous flows of capital into housing. Mortgage debt mushroomed by $850 billion in only two years, and in a single year the Fed's interest rate cuts led to a doubling in the number of refinanced loans, to more than 11 million (Deep and Domanski 2002). Low interest rates and lenient underwriting allowed home buyers to bid prices up through the recession, and there were signs that an increasing number of wealthy households who had suffered stock market losses began to look at housing as an alternative means of speculation. From the end of 1999 through the first quarter of 2001, total household wealth in equities and mutual funds dipped from $12.3 trillion to $8.7 trillion, while housing equity jumped from $5.4 trillion to $6.2 trillion (Baker 2001). In the four years following the end of 1999, households withdrew a net sum of $1.02 trillion from corporate equities, while their net

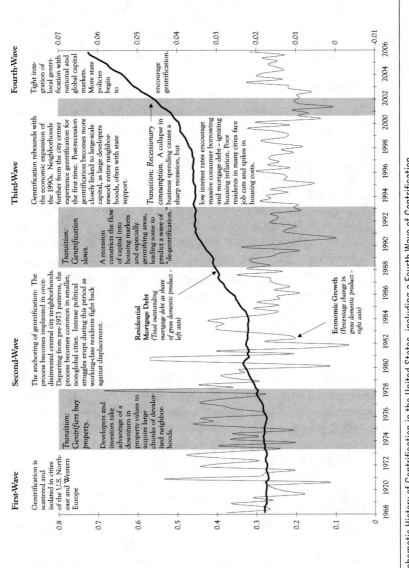

**Figure 5.2** A Schematic History of Gentrification in the United States, including a Fourth Wave of Gentrification

*Source:* Adapted from Hackworth and Smith (2001) U.S. Federal Reserve, Flow-of-Funds Accounts, National Bureau of Economic Research.

mortgage borrowing racked up an additional $3.30 trillion (see Figure 5.3). Analysts who had warned of a stock market bubble in the late 1990s now sounded the alarm for housing, and the growing practice of same-day house resales was dubbed 'an early 21st-century version of day trading. Buying stocks on margin has morphed into buying homes with no money down' (Rich and Leonhardt 2005). *The Economist*, not usually the place to look for dire predictions of crisis, estimated that the total value of residential property in all the world's developed economies shot up by more than $30 trillion over a five-year period, an increase equivalent to 100 percent of the combined GDP of these countries—an increase exceeding the stock market bubbles of the 1990s and the 1920s: 'In other words, it looks like the biggest bubble in history' (*The Economist* 2005). Various indicators point to a gentle cooling of the market beginning in late 2005, but years of heavy capital flows into housing have greatly worsened the affordability crises for low-income renters, with particularly severe stress for those living in gentrifying neighborhoods.

These broad economic trends have driven gentrification deeper into the heart of disinvested city neighborhoods. In contrast to earlier waves when financial institutions were risk averse (see Chapter 1 on red-lining in Barnsbury and Park Slope), lenders are now aggressively competing to make loans; moreover, new underwriting technologies now allow a much more precise separation of the risks of lending to particular borrowers in specific places. It is now common for qualified racial and ethnic minority applicants to be rejected for loans by mainstream banks, for wealthy gentrifiers to receive multiple competitive loan offers from big national lenders, and for low-income home owners to be targeted by risky, high-cost predatory lenders—often all in the same neighborhood (Howell 2006; Squires 2003, 2004). Disinvestment, reinvestment, and rent gap dynamics are now playing out in more geographically complex patterns, inscribing fine-grained inequalities of class and race in city neighborhoods. In the case of New York, total mortgage commitments for condos and single-family homes ballooned from $14 billion in 2000 to $46.9 billion three years later, and home buyers were moving into some of the last remaining concentrations of low-cost rental housing in the city's poor, racially marginalized communities—Harlem, the South Bronx, and even Bedford–Stuyvesant (see Figure 5.4). To be sure, the gentrification of Harlem is nothing new (see Freeman 2006)—more than twenty years ago, the German magazine *Der Spiegel* ran a piece on the neighborhood under the (translated) title 'Oh, Baby. Shit. How Did That Happen?' (Kruger 1985, quoted in Smith 1996a: 140). Even today, reinvestment is far from complete: central Harlem has 107,000 people and 53,000 housing units, and a poverty rate four times the national average; the darkest-shaded U.S. Census tracts in Harlem on Figure 5.4 saw only 190 purchase or refinance mortgages in 2003, with median loan amounts between $302,000 and $405,000 across the different tracts. In other words, the tensions of gentrification are likely to continue in neighborhoods like this for many years to come.

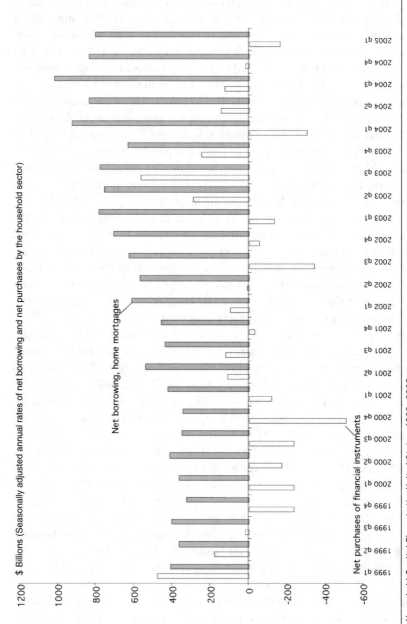

**Figure 5.3** Household Capital Flows in the United States, 1999–2005

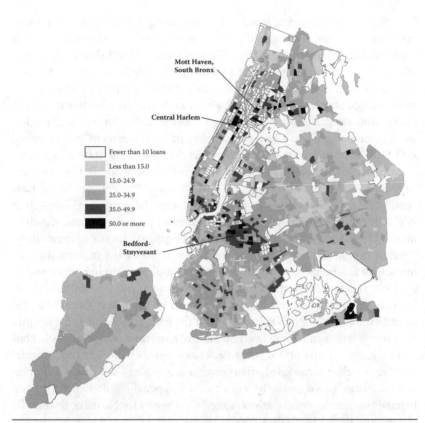

**Figure 5.4** Mortgage Capitalization Ratio for New York City Neighborhoods, 2003. This map shows the ratio of the median mortgage loan to the median annual rent for each census tract. The ratio is similar to the price-to-earnings ratios used to study stock markets. Census tracts with the highest ratios represent areas where low-cost rentals are surrounded by increasingly expensive home sales. In the darkest areas on this map, median mortgage loans are more than fifty times the corresponding local rent.
*Sources:* U.S. Bureau of the Census (2002), *Summary File 3, Census Tract Data, 2000* Census; FFIEC (2004), *2004 HMDA Raw Data.*

But if the stark polarization of places like Harlem is part of the long history of gentrification, the policy context does seem to have changed. The most distinguishing features of a new fourth wave involve the consolidation of a powerful national political shift favoring the interests of the wealthiest households (see Dumenil and Levy 2004; see also Chapter 6), combined with a bold effort to dismantle the last of the social welfare programs associated with the 1960s. The groundwork for this new phase was laid during the Clinton administration, when an ideology of 'reinventing government' drove the use of public–private partnerships and other market-oriented responses to urban problems—allowing private market gentrification to flourish while the state bore the costs of removing some of the remaining barriers (e.g., the poorest residents of government-owned public housing projects; Goetz 2003). This movement continues in the United Kingdom under New Labour, albeit with (somewhat ironically) the input of a social justice agenda (see Imrie and Raco 2003; also Chapter 6), but there has been a mixture of continuity and departure in the United States. George W. Bush's administration has continued many of the Clinton-era programs encouraging home ownership for low- and moderate-income households; Clinton's language of 'empowerment' has morphed into Bush's vision for an 'ownership society' in which the state recedes and individuals bear all the risks and rewards for their behavior. But Bush's overwhelming emphases on tax cuts for investors and the War on Terror have completely sidelined domestic policy—and especially urban policy—since late 2001. Local governments have continued to pursue economic development and housing policies that generally favor gentrification, but these efforts are now taking place in a national climate marked by the incidental urban impacts of federal policies on taxes, privatization, social welfare cuts, and so on. Gentrification is flourishing in this environment, and its manifestation in hundreds of neighborhoods across the country seems at first glance to be the same as it was in the 1990s third wave; but the political economy that justifies the process has been consolidated by years of hard work by operatives in conservative urban think tanks. Jamie Peck has diagnosed this as a fundamental shift from 'welfarist modes of urban governance' to a new dominant conservative urbanism 'based on the invasive moral and penal regulation of the poor, together with state-assisted efforts to reclaim the city for business, the middle classes, and the market' (Peck 2006: 681).

The identification of this fourth wave of gentrification in the United States reinforces the importance of considering the geography of gentrification, for this fourth wave is not readily identifiable outside of the United States. In the United Kingdom, for example, any suggestion of a fourth wave of gentrification is more about the extension and consolidation of national urban policy, as Davidson and Lees (2005) have demonstrated in terms of the extension and reinforcement of national urban policy into the recently published *Greater London Plan*. There are some similar trends in the United Kingdom, for example, the increase in buy-to-let (this scheme was introduced in 1996 and has revolutionized the provision of mortgage finance to the private rented sector; in mid-2006, there were £84 billion buy-to-let mortgages), the rise of the 120 percent mortgage, and the increase in mortgage indebtedness (in August 2006, gross mortgage lending reached £32.7 billion), but there is a danger of overstating the issues. Buy-to-let is a very small part of the market; it is quite stable and has helped sustain demand rather than drive up the market. The 120 percent mortgage is only one of approximately 4,000 products, and although market indebtedness has gone up, so has the value of homes. British banks and mortgage companies do not reject ethnic minority applicants for loans, and low-income home owners are not targeted by high-cost predatory lenders. Also, by way of contrast, the British government has been quite interventionist: for example, it aims to boost housing supply and curb house prices to stabilize an inflationary housing market. Readers interested in attaining more statistical information about the British housing market should look at the Council of Mortgage Lenders website, http://www.cml.org.uk.

*Katrina and the Fourth Wave in the United States*
The outlines of this regime in the United States became clear in the aftermath of Hurricane Katrina in August 2005, when conservative commentators and public officials moved quickly to redefine the problem—shifting the focus away from the inequalities of racism and urban poverty in order to blame the inherent failures of liberal, welfarist policies of assistance. The liberal welfare state was blamed for creating New Orleans' underclass and its 'dangerous criminal class—yes, likely the same African Americans we see looting now'— and helpless women, children, and elderly who showed up at the Louisiana Superdome 'expecting their government to take care of them' (Gelinas 2005: 2; see also Peck 2006). The conservative solution was to 'rebuild New Orleans' moral levees' (Sowell 2005) on a clean slate that would become a free-market city–state ruled by the principles of small government, low taxes, and a sacred commitment to property rights. Post-Katrina urban policies have thus presented an unprecedented opportunity for a more pure, harsh fourth wave of gentrification. Its principles were proclaimed most clearly by the widely read conservative columnist for the *New York Times*, David Brooks (2005: A29), who wrote a week after the storm about 'Katrina's Silver Lining':

> Katrina was a natural disaster that interrupted a social disaster. It separated tens of thousands of poor people from the run-down, isolated neighborhoods in which they were trapped. ... It has created as close to a blank slate as we get in human affairs, and given us a chance to rebuild a city that wasn't working.

Brooks argued in favor of 'cultural integration'—in order to 'integrate people who lack middle-class skills into neighborhoods with people who possess those skills and who insist on certain standards of behavior' (see Chapter 6 on gentrification as a 'positive public policy tool'; and British policy initiatives on transferring social capital through social mixing)—while giving the displaced the option 'to disperse into middle-class areas nationwide'. And for New Orleans, 'the key will be luring middle-class families into the rebuilt city, making it so attractive to them that they will move in, even knowing that their blocks will include a certain number of poor people' (Brooks 2005: A29).

These kinds of sentiments distorted and simplified an ongoing social science debate on the effects of income-mixing policies (see Chapter 6). But the conservative interpretation of the evidence represented the dominant policy consensus in Washington, with the Bush administration able to subvert, co-opt, and outflank its weak congressional opponents. And so, post-Katrina New Orleans is now serving as a policy laboratory and template for broader urban redevelopment priorities. The administration is very conscious of precedent, and therefore refused to use an existing program, the Housing Choice Voucher program (see Chapter 6), to assist the hundreds of thousands of displaced residents; the federal government chose to pay exorbitant rates to hotels and to contractors selling trailers, to avoid granting legitimacy to a voucher program that it would rather eliminate. Unfortunately, the harsh displacement and redevelopment realities of fourth-wave gentrification in New Orleans received considerable legitimacy when prominent sociologist and urban poverty expert William Julius Wilson led a petition signed by dozens of researchers advocating 'Moving to Opportunity in the Wake of Hurricane Katrina'. The dispersal- and mixed-income redevelopment policies supported by those who signed the petition—all with impeccable center–left politics and research credibility—are nearly identical to the policy mix favored by Washington in the 1990s. But the entire political environment of fourth-wave gentrification is different, and Reed and Steinberg (2006) point out that Wilson and his colleagues

> remain strangely oblivious of their potential for playing into the hands of the retrograde political forces that would use their call to justify displacement. … They provide liberal cover for those who have already put a resettlement policy into motion that is reactionary and racist at its core.

It may be too early for us to consider any kind of definitive judgment on post-Katrina New Orleans and its influence on gentrification in other cities, or even if there is a truly distinctive fourth wave that departs from the basic tendencies analyzed by Hackworth and Smith (2001). But the early indications are not encouraging. New Orleans' displaced renters have been almost completely ignored in the fanfare over what the chair of the Louisiana Recovery Authority suggests 'may be the biggest redevelopment project in history' (Eaton 2006: A1). Nearly $10 billion of federal aid is going directly to home owners, and subject to certain conditions, owners can decide whether and where to rebuild, or to leave the state and accept reduced compensation. One of the national figures invited to help lead local discussions about the design future of Gulf Coast communities and New Orleans neighborhoods is Andres Duany, who offered 'Three Cheers for Gentrification' in a right-wing think tank magazine in 2001. Five years later, Duany described his work in New Orleans to the *New York Times*:

> For a city to become a city that's planned, it has to destroy itself; the city literally has to molt. … Usually this takes 20 years, but after a hurricane,

it takes five years. The people can see the future in their own lifetime. (Quoted in Pogrebin 2006: B1)

## Towards a Geography of Contemporary Gentrification

This discussion of contemporary gentrification vis-à-vis neoliberalism, globalization, rescaling, and four waves of the process has also been something of a whistle-stop tour through a number of different geographical contexts in which gentrification has been occurring. We agree with Neil Smith (2002) that gentrification has become 'generalised' into a global urban strategy, but just as neoliberalism and globalization unfold in different ways in different places in a pattern of uneven development (Tickell and Peck 2003; Harvey 2006b), so too does gentrification. Given the massive literature on gentrification, the pace at which it expanded in the 1990s, and the fact that geographers have been the most common contributors, it may seem surprising that it is only recently that scholars have noted that building a geography of gentrification is important if we are to gain a more complete understanding of the process, particularly with respect to both space and time. David Ley (1996) made this important observation near the start of his book on gentrification:

> The embourgeoisement of the inner city … is incomplete even in those neighbourhoods where it has been most prominent, but none the less it has contributed to a significant reshaping in the housing market in cities with expanding downtown employment in advanced services. This qualifier immediately leads to the important recognition that there is a geography to gentrification, that the trends remaking the inner cities of Toronto, San Francisco, or London are not shared by Winnipeg, Detroit, or Liverpool. (p. 8)

Ley's major contribution towards explaining this geography was an assessment of inter-metropolitan and inter-neighborhood gentrification across Canada. The caveat with which Ley concludes his book is not just pertinent to his insistence that gentrification theory cannot ignore empirical trends in urban Canada, but also points to a new research avenue: '[T]he geographical specificity of gentrification should caution us from making arguments that are too binding from evidence that is limited to the United States' (p. 352). Reviewing much of the 1980s and 1990s literature on gentrification, Lees (2000) worked Ley's observations into a call for 'a geography of gentrification' which takes into account context, locality, and temporality in more detail— despite much analytical progress, theoretical tensions (which we explained in Chapters 2 and 3) were threatening explanatory closure when these tensions could be kept alive in new investigations focused on the geography of the process.

Lees argued that the geography of gentrification 'works on a number of different levels—international comparison, intranational, and citywide comparison' (p. 405). Ley was rather cautious with international comparisons, contending that 'internationally, no truly comparative data exist to permit an assessment of the variation of inner-city reinvestment by country' (p. 81). This might account for the fact that international comparisons are still something of a rarity (for the exceptions, see Cybriwsky, Ley, and Western 1986; Lees 1994b, 1996; Carpenter and Lees 1995; N. Smith 1996a; Eade and Mele 1998; Slater 2004a; Sýkora 2005; Krase 2005; Petsimeris 2005). It must be noted that Ley was arguing that no data exist for the purposes of rigorous statistical comparison; but there is no question that other sources of data allow for comparative assessments, as evidenced by the exceptions cited above. Intranational comparisons have been more common, especially in the United States, producing a range of conclusions depending on the methodology deployed and the perspective of the researcher (Nelson 1988; Wyly and Hammel 2004, 2005; Freeman 2005). At the citywide scale, Lees noted that within a single city, gentrification of a similar time period has a quite different geography depending on its site. This is particularly evident in the work of Tim Butler and Garry Robson, who have attempted to tease out the subtle differences in the ways in which the middle classes 'come to terms with London' in different London neighborhoods. The impetus for their research was clearly set out:

> One criticism of existing approaches to gentrification is that they tend to see gentrification as a more or less homogenous process. … Our hypothesis is that different middle-class groups would be attracted to different areas and this would be determined by a range of factors, in addition to what they might be able to afford in particular housing markets. (Butler and Robson 2001b: 2146–2148)

After testing this hypothesis by interviewing gentrifiers in Telegraph Hill, Battersea, and Brixton, they found that gentrification had consolidated very different forms of middle-class identity in each location. They concluded with the argument that '[g]entrification … cannot in any sense be considered to be a unitary phenomenon, but needs to be examined in each case according to its own logic and outcomes' (p. 2160). Their work illustrates that there is substantial differentiation in gentrification (or, more specifically, the experiences of gentrifiers) between London neighborhoods which are not separated by much physical distance—a major finding that moves away from earlier research which took a broader, quantitative view and thus tended to refer to 'London's gentrification' (e.g., Williams 1976; Hamnett and Randolph 1984; Munt 1987).

At first glance, calls for 'a geography of gentrification' may seem rather simple. Of course, the process is different in different places! While there may be common undercurrents of capital flows, real estate speculation, and professionalization, of course gentrification will be very different in, say, San Francisco than it is in, say, Seoul, and of course there will be neighborhoods in Paris that have different trajectories and experiences of gentrification! It is hardly a novel observation to claim that explanations and interpretations of gentrification cannot be divorced from the contexts in which they are formed, but this has received surprisingly little attention in the literature on gentrification (see Slater 2002). So, if calls for 'a geography of gentrification' seem simplistic, we argue that a purposeful simplicity is in fact necessary—only in this manner can researchers illustrate what Jacobs and Fincher (1998) call 'the complexity of spatial scales that flow through "place": the ways in which the local is always also a national or international space' (p. 21). Furthermore, a heightened sensitivity to the mutually constitutive local, national, and global aspects of urban change is important not just to gentrification but also to the study of all urban processes (Brenner 2001).

Building 'a geography of gentrification' requires attention to the contextual specificities of the gentrification process, with particular sensitivity to the ways in which the process is configured under interlocking geographical scales, whilst retaining a critical eye on the more general factors that constitute the engine behind the process. As Lees (2000) has noted, 'a geography of gentrification' is something that has policy relevance too:

> More detailed research into the geography of gentrification … would enable us to consider the merits or dangers of cities further down the urban hierarchy taking on board the gentrification practices of cities higher up the urban hierarchy, cities with a very different geography. (p. 405)

In this chapter, we have outlined the complexities and nuances of the process in its contemporary form—the uneven outwards and downwards rescaling of the process, the differences between a fourth wave of gentrification in the United States and not in the United Kingdom, and the contingent geographies of gentrification as an expression of neoliberal urbanism—all of which demonstrate the need for 'a geography of gentrification'.

In the next chapter, we examine the emancipatory and revanchist discourses on gentrification which have emerged from very different research contexts. As researchers have recently noted (e.g., Lees 2000; Slater 2002), perspectives on gentrification that are usually attributed to differences in theory, ideology, and methodology are equally attributable to geography—the places in which the process was researched. New York and the Lower East Side present a different landscape of gentrification from Vancouver and False Creek. We explore these important geographies in more depth in Chapter 6.

### Producing and Consuming the New Gentrification?

Contemporary geographies of gentrification seem to have become more complicated, involving intricate tensions between local and global, old versus new, and cultural versus economic. In light of this complexity, is there any contemporary use for the production and consumption perspectives described in Chapters 2 and 3? Or are these separate narratives entirely obsolete?

Today, most observers acknowledge that both production and consumption perspectives are crucially important in explaining, understanding, and dealing with gentrification. For many analysts, the acknowledgment ends there, with no serious effort to address the substantive differences between the two perspectives. But for many others, the production–consumption dichotomy has been set aside for very different reasons. This duality may have contributed to the advance of urban theory in the 1970s and 1980s, but in subsequent years it became clear that the differences between the two camps had been exaggerated. Even so, we cannot ignore fundamental incommensurability in the abstract concepts of the rent gap, cultural-lifestyle, and postindustrial economic base explanations (Clark 1994). The central elements of each of these narratives remain as important and relevant today as they did a quarter century ago. But these frameworks are no longer used in attempts to determine *the* ultimate cause of gentrification, or to illustrate the One Right Way to Do Gentrification Research. And fewer researchers feel the pressure to 'assume that we *can* synthesise or integrate them into a consistent unity, one grand coherent picture, and that we *should* of course put all our efforts into this noble task' (Clark 1994: 1040, emphasis in original).

But this is not simply about the postmodern recognition of indeterminacy and the inadequacy of representations of a supposedly stable, external 'reality.' In more practical terms, the questions have changed: more and more researchers have turned away from questions of *causality*—which lead almost invariably to contests between competing explanations—to examine *consequences*. What this means is that some of the fundamental theoretical tensions between production and consumption explanations have never really been resolved (see Clark 1994). But after forty years of sustained gentrification in many different kinds of cities around the world, we are no longer putting all our effort into painting the 'grand coherent picture' that answers the question of 'Why?' Instead, more researchers are concerned with the question of 'So what?' And with this shift, many researchers are less troubled by the real and apparent tensions between production and consumption narratives. Both provide crucially important, and quite different, ways of understanding the dimensions of contemporary gentrification.

And both require constant revision to keep up with changes in contemporary urbanism, while recognizing the enduring continuity of certain processes and practices. This balance between the old and the new applies to both the cultural and economic realms: the details of what kinds of occupations count as 'postindustrial' have changed considerably, for instance, as have the particular kinds of brands and styles favored by the new middle classes, and the innovations in financial instruments that link world financial markets to the operation of localized rent gaps. Atkinson and Bridge (2005: 8) describe how some of these familiar aspects of gentrification theory come together in new ways:

The explanation offered by Smith's rent gap formulation (1979, 1996) now seems to underpin an expanded cognitive map of search and relocation activities of elite social fractions, be they political, cultural or economic. In a sense the decision to locate in Seattle is no longer a world apart from London in its amenity or ambience, even less its distance by jet. At another level in the professional and urban hierarchy this might be a choice between Athens and Auckland, Madrid and Mumbai. International services, ICT linkages, increasing urban homogeneity of services and "feel", as well as rapid travel, mean that many more "new" neighbourhoods exist insulated from local poverty, wider systematic inequalities and public squalor. (Atkinson and Bridge 2005: 8)

Perhaps the most progressive way to deal with both production and consumption theories in the gentrification literature is to recognize the remarkable theoretical sophistication that has developed over three decades of research and debate, whilst at the same time acknowledging that the finer details of such theories can quite easily become victims of history, and need to be brought into contemporary geographies of gentrification. The least progressive way to deal with production and consumption theories is to perpetuate the series of hidden assumptions that crept into the gentrification literature in the early 1990s—assumptions that had begun to undermine our ability to make sense of what was happening in gentrifying neighborhoods. Production explanations were then seen as the mirror opposite of consumption theories. Thanks to Hamnett's (1991) influential review of the sophisticated work of Smith and Ley, many urbanists saw gentrification in terms of a stark 'either/or' choice: supply or demand, capital or culture, structure or agency. An entire generation of students, reading through equally compelling explanations under separate headings for 'production' and 'consumption', responded as best they knew how: both explanations matter, many students replied, while others embraced one side or another based on personal experience or the style of writing they found most convincing. The neoclassical view of gentrification was ignored, or treated as an historical approach that fell out of favor after the 1960s. Widespread discussion of the idea of a 'post-gentrification' era led many urbanists to turn their attention to other topics. Many of those who did continue to study the topic drew inspiration from the cultural turn then sweeping through human geography and related fields.

But the mid-1990s was precisely the wrong time to turn our attention away from what was happening on city streets, in boardrooms where corporate and development decisions are made, and in corridors and think tank seminar rooms where policies are conceived, negotiated, and justified. As we have seen in our discussion of third-wave gentrification, the process was about to undergo a resurgence that would accentuate all of the inequalities and tensions associated with the process a generation earlier; but the economic and political context of this resurgence had changed, making it much more difficult for neighborhood advocates and low-income residents to resist or adjust (see Chapter 7). Moreover, it became clear that the production–consumption dichotomy was fundamentally flawed and that it had obscured the ongoing influence of neoclassical urban thought on public policy. Throughout most of Europe, the United States, Canada, and Australia, neoclassical principles exerted a powerful influence on the way policy makers selectively used research on urban poverty and housing markets to justify sweeping shifts in urban policy. Important contextual differences certainly mattered in shaping varied trajectories of policy—but the general trend was to favor market processes and public interventions that encouraged gentrification. It is now clearly recognized that production and consumption cannot be understood in terms of simplistic dichotomies. But there is also a growing recognition that the political and economic developments of the last decade have accentuated many of the polarizing tendencies at the heart of both production and consumption theories. In response, a new generation of gentrification research has moved beyond these limited binaries to analyze the new patterns and processes sustaining inequality in cities around the world.

## Summary

In this chapter, we looked at the main features of contemporary gentrification, comparing them to earlier waves of gentrification. We looked at a more recent stage model of the process and tentatively identify a fourth wave of gentrification to add to this model. We discussed the roles of globalization and neoliberalism, and the changing role of the state in contemporary gentrification, and argue that moving towards an understanding of the geography of gentrification is a timely and relevant research direction. Gentrification today is a global phenomenon; in this chapter, we looked not just at its spread—across the globe and down the urban hierarchy—but also at the conceptual and empirical work on the links between gentrification and globalization. We conclude that the production and consumption explanations of gentrification outlined in Chapters 2 and 3 of the book, explanations based on classical or first-wave gentrification, still have resonance today, even if they need to be tweaked in places, and rigorously updated in others.

## Activities

- Design a stage model of gentrification for London, like Hackworth and Smith (2001) did for New York City, using the case study material throughout this book on Barnsbury and drawing also on Chris Hamnett's (2003a) book *Unequal City: London in the Global Arena*.
- Compare and contrast Rofe's (2003) arguments about gentrification and globalization with those of Butler and Lees (2006).

- Compare and contrast four or more studies of gentrification from around the world using Atkinson and Bridge (2005) and recent journal articles. How are they the same? How do they differ?
- Do some Internet (or documentary) research about contemporary urban regeneration in a small town or city near you. Can you see a 'gentrification blueprint' in action?
- Watch and compare the following American TV shows—*The Cosby Show* and *Frasier.* Can you see the subtext of gentrification in the lifestyles and residences of the main characters? Can you see 1980s and 1990s gentrification represented?
- Write down a list of neoliberal urban policies at both the state and city levels in your own country and for a chosen city in your own country. What do you think about these policies?
- Read the OpenCity repository at http://www.opencity.org.uk.

## Further Reading

Atkinson, R., and G. Bridge (eds.) (2005) *Gentrification in a Global Context: The New Urban Colonialism* (London: Routledge).

Brenner, N., and N. Theodore (eds.) (2003) *Spaces of Neoliberalism: Urban Restructuring in North America and Western Europe* (Oxford: Blackwell).

Butler, T., with G. Robson (2003) *London's Calling: The Middle Classes and the Remaking of Inner London* (Berg: London).

Davis, M. (1990) *City of Quartz: Excavating the Future in Los Angeles* (New York: Verso).

Hamnett, C. (1996) 'Social polarization, economic restructuring and welfare state regimes', *Urban Studies*, 33, 8: 1407–1430.

Hamnett, C. (2003a) *Unequal City: London in the Global Arena* (Routledge: London).

Harvey, D. (1989b) 'From managerialism to entrepreneurialism: The transformation in urban governance in late capitalism', *Geografiska Annaler*, 71B: 3–17.

Harvey, D. (2000) *Spaces of Hope* (Edinburgh: Edinburgh University Press).

Harvey, D. (2005) *A Brief History of Neo-liberalism* (Oxford: Oxford University Press).

Imrie, R., and M. Raco (eds.) (2003) *Urban Renaissance? New Labour, Community and Urban Policy* (Bristol: Policy Press).

Kearns, G., and C. Philo (eds.) (1993) *Selling Places: The City as Cultural Capital, Past and Present* (Oxford: Pergamon Press).

Raco, M., G. MacLeod, and K. Ward (guest eds.) (2003) 'Negotiating the contemporary city', *Urban Studies*, (special issue): 40, 8.

Sassen, S. (1991) *The Global City: New York, London and Tokyo* (Princeton, NJ: Princeton University Press).

Uitermark, J., J. Duyvendak, and R. Kleinhans (2007) 'Gentrification as a governmental strategy: Social control and social cohesion in Hoogvliet, Rotterdam', *Environment and Planning A* 39, 1: 125–141.

Wyly, E., and D. Hammel (2005) 'Mapping neoliberal American urbanism', in R. Atkinson and G. Bridge (eds.) *Gentrification in a Global Context: The New Urban Colonialism* (London: Routledge), 18–38.

**Plate 6.1** 'There Goes the Neighbourhood'; Toronto

This image was taken in Trinity-Bellwoods Park, Toronto, in 2001.
*Source:* Photograph by Tom Slater.

# 6

# Gentrification
*Positive or Negative?*

As new frontier, the gentrifying city since the 1980s has been oozing with optimism. Hostile landscapes are regenerated, cleansed, reinfused with middle-class sensibility; real estate values soar; yuppies consume; elite gentility is democratized in mass-produced styles of distinction. So what's not to like? The contradictions of the actual frontier are not entirely eradicated in this imagery but they are smoothed into an acceptable groove.

N. Smith (1996a: 13)

In this chapter we compare and contrast arguments that see (and public policies that promote) gentrification to be a positive neighborhood process with those that see it to be a negative neighborhood process. Gentrification, of course, has both positive and negative aspects to it; we weigh up these different aspects (see Box 6.1). We also outline and discuss the two main discourses that dominate the gentrification literature—what Lees (2000) calls the 'emancipatory city thesis' versus the 'revanchist city thesis'—for these discourses play off of the positive and negative aspects of gentrification respectively. There is a temporal dimension to all of this, for arguably pioneer gentrification ideologically and practically has more positive aspects associated with it than later waves of gentrification. For example, pioneer gentrifiers desired social mixing, whereas second- and especially third-wave gentrifiers are much more individualistic (see Butler and Lees [2006], who compare first-, second-, and third-wave gentrification in Barnsbury). However, arguably it is pioneer gentrifiers who initiate processes of displacement, even if this is not a deliberate behavior.

## A Positive Neighborhood Process?

In an essay titled 'Two Cheers for Gentrification', J. P. Byrne (2003: 405–406) of Capitol Hill, Washington, D.C., gentrifier and professor of law at Georgetown University Law Center, states,

This essay takes issue with this negative judgment about gentrification. That a number of individuals have lost affordable apartments that were home to them cannot be denied. Yet increases in the number of affluent and well-educated residents is plainly good for cities, on balance, by

**195**

| Box 6.1 | |
|---|---|
| The Positives and Negatives of Gentrification | |
| **Positive** | **Negative** |
| | Displacement through rent/price increases |
| | Secondary psychological costs of displacement |
| Stabilization of declining areas | Community resentment and conflict |
| Increased property values | Loss of affordable housing |
| | Unsustainable speculative property price increases |
| Reduced vacancy rates | Homelessness |
| Increased local fiscal revenues | Greater take of local spending through lobbying/articulacy |
| Encouragement and increased viability of further development | Commercial/industrial displacement |
| | Increased cost and changes to local services |
| Reduction of suburban sprawl | Displacement and housing demand pressures on surrounding poor areas |
| Increased social mix | Loss of social diversity (from socially disparate to rich ghettos) |
| Rehabilitation of property both with and without state sponsorship | Under occupancy and population loss to gentrified areas |
| *Source:* Rowland Atkinson and Gary Bridge, eds., *Gentrification in a Global Context: the New Urban Colonialism*, p. 5. © 2005 Routledge. | |

increasing the number of residents who can pay taxes, purchase local goods and services, and support the city in state and federal political processes. My contention here goes somewhat further: gentrification is good on balance for the poor and ethnic minorities. The most negative effect of gentrification, the reduction in affordable housing, results primarily not from gentrification itself, but from the persistent failure of government to produce or secure affordable housing more generally. Moreover, cities that attract more affluent residents are more able to aggressively finance affordable housing. Thus, gentrification is entitled to "two cheers", if not three, given that it enhances the political and economic positions of all, but exacerbates the harms imposed on the poor by the failures of national affordable housing policies.

Byrne (2003) cites a study of displacement in New York City in the 1990s by researchers Freeman and Braconi (2002) as support for his idea that gentrification is a positive process. Freeman and Braconi (2002) looked at surveys in the 1990s of persons who had recently moved into new units and found that 5.47 percent of them could be considered as displaced. When they compared movements by low-income people from gentrifying neighborhoods, as opposed to non-gentrifying neighborhoods, they found that poor households were less likely to move from gentrifying neighborhoods. Moreover, they found that increases in rents were associated with a lower, rather than higher, likelihood of moving out. They argued,

> Our research sheds new light on the gentrification process. Although it does not prove that secondary displacement [i.e., from rising rents] of the poor does not occur in gentrifying areas, it suggests that demographic transition is not predicated on displacement. Low-income households actually seem less likely to move from gentrifying neighbourhoods than from other communities. Improving housing and neighbourhood conditions appear to encourage the housing stability of low-income neighbourhoods to the degree that they more than offset any dislocation resulting from rising rent. (2002: 4)

Byrne (2003: 419–420) also argues, rather patronizingly (as we shall see later in this chapter, such a view is part of the ideology of pioneer gentrifiers and of policy makers' framing of 'gentrification as a positive public policy tool'), that gentrification can improve the economic opportunities for the urban poor:

> At the simplest level, existing residents should find expanding employment opportunities in providing locally the goods and services that more affluent residents can afford. Studies suggest that poor people can find better employment in the suburbs than in the city. The problem has been that inner city residents cannot reach these suburban jobs because of distance and the lack of a necessary automobile. While one may be concerned that local jobs generated by gentrifiers often will be low-paying, unskilled positions in restaurants and shops, existing residents may need opportunities that do not require much education.... Gentrification may also contribute to citywide enhancement of employment for low-income residents. Increases in urban populations will enhance demand for municipal services and thus the need for municipal employment. They will also increase municipal tax receipts, making possible increases in public employment.

He goes on to argue that 'gentrification creates urban political fora in which affluent and poor citizens must deal with each other's priorities in a democratic process' (p. 421), and that gentrification ameliorates the social isolation of the poor, reduces crime, and increases the educational attainments of the poor (pp. 422–424). As such, as a lawyer, he argues,

> My essentially rosy view of gentrification leads me to oppose most of the limits that several legal writers have wanted to place on it. They mistakenly seek to arrest a process that appears to be beneficial both

for the city as a whole and for its poor inhabitants. Prohibiting poor people from being succeeded by more affluent people dooms the neighborhood, and perhaps, the city to poverty. ... Urban policies should support gentrification generally, even as it addresses some of the harms to which gentrification may contribute. (pp. 424–425)

Such urban policies are already underway, but more often without the safeguards that Byrne mentions, such as protective policies against displacement, for example rent control, caps on annual increases in real property taxes, and effectively addressing affordable housing for the urban poor.

### Gentrification as a Positive Public Policy Tool

More than ever before, gentrification is incorporated into public policy—used either as a justification to obey market forces and private sector entrepreneurialism, or as a tool to direct market processes in the hopes of restructuring urban landscapes in a slightly more benevolent fashion. Trumpeted under the friendly banners of regeneration, renewal, or revitalization, many of these placebo policies fail in their boosterish goals: a solid consensus among mainstream economists and policy analysts holds that targeted revitalization strategies, ranging all the way from tax credits to tax increment financing to enterprise zones, have only marginal impacts on the overall structure of landmarkets shaped by ongoing metropolitan decentralisation forces. But gentrification policy can have substantial effects at the neighbourhood scale, and when it does succeed in leveraging private capital it worsens housing affordability in ways that increase the demands on the remnants of the redistributive local state. Wyly and Hammel (2005: 35)

In recent years in the United Kingdom, there is evidence of the neoliberal urban agenda outlined in Chapter 5: local urban regeneration initiatives have been seeking to entice more affluent, middle-class populations into low-income areas using policies of what Stuart Cameron (2003: 2373) calls 'positive gentrification' or 'gentrification as a positive public policy tool'. These locally based policies of 'positive gentrification' espouse the same discursive construction of gentrification and social mixing as the Urban Task Force report (DETR 1999) and the Urban White Paper (DETR 2000a) (see the Preface). The idea is to diversify the social mix and dilute concentrations of poverty in the inner city through gentrification.

The Urban Task Force report states,

Without a commitment to social integration, our towns and cities will fail. We can, however, establish certain principles to ensure that wealth and opportunity are spread more evenly among urban neighbourhoods.

...

In responding to social problems we must avoid repeating the mistakes of the past. Developing large amounts of social housing in one location does not work. Many existing social housing estates have a strong sense of community—often more so than wealthier neighbourhoods—but there is not the economic capacity to make these neighbourhoods work over the long term. As a result, jobs and investment go elsewhere, exacerbating the physical isolation of many of these estates. In future, we must develop on the basis of a mix of tenures and income groups. (DETR 1999: 45)

And New Labour's Urban White Paper (the current national urban policy document for England and Wales) argues,

Our aim is to make urban living a positive experience for the many, not the few, to bring all areas up to the standard of the best, and to deliver a lasting urban renaissance. (DETR 2000a: foreword by John Prescott)

Moving towards more mixed and sustainable communities is important to many of our plans for improving the quality of life. (DETR 2000a: 8)

The British government's stated intention to bring the middle classes back to the central city (read 'gentrification') is therefore motivated by, and indeed sold to us as, an attempt to reduce sociospatial segregation and strengthen the 'social tissue' of deprived neighborhoods. Selling gentrification to us as something 'positive', that has a social-mixing or social inclusion agenda, is quite canny in that it neutralizes the negative image that the process of gentrification brings with it. Social mixing and improved social balance are viewed as key to reducing what they term 'neighbourhood effects'—the spatial concentration of disadvantaged populations in local areas, creating a social milieu that reinforces aspects of disadvantage and actively reduces an individual's ability to move out of poverty or disadvantage. The British government's Social Exclusion Unit argues that social capital in excluded communities can be rebuilt if they socially mix, because social mixing brings people into contact with those outside their normal circle, broadening horizons and raising expectations. As Canadian geographer Damaris Rose (2004: 281) states,

[S]ince the image of the "livable city" has become a key aspect of a city's ability to compete in a globalized, knowledge-based economy (Florida 2003), post-industrial cities have a growing interest in marketing themselves as being built on a foundation of "inclusive" neighbourhoods capable of harmoniously supporting a blend of incomes, cultures, age groups and lifestyles".

Cameron (2003) talks about Newcastle City Council's citywide regeneration policy, adopted in 1999, called Going for Growth (discussed in Chapter 4). This was probably the first large-scale example in the United Kingdom of a policy of so-called positive gentrification—its explicit objective being to rebalance the population of disadvantaged and stigmatized central-city neighborhoods in inner-city Newcastle by the introduction of a more affluent population. As Cameron (2003: 2369) states, the strategy linked 'economic development, urban renaissance and the retention and growth of population within the city to the future of deprived and stigmatised neighbourhoods characterised by population loss and low housing demand'. In many ways, Newcastle (like other cities in the North East and the North West of England) is the kind of city (unlike, say, London) that the Urban White Paper (DETR 2000a) and much British New Labour urban policy prescription has been written for—a city characterized by socioeconomic polarization, regional economic weakness, population out-migration, and low housing demand in its inner-city areas. In Newcastle, the middle classes have sought to distance themselves from stigmatized inner-city areas and crowded into a small number of neighborhoods regarded as safer and higher status. In response to this, the (then) New Labour–run Newcastle City Council decided to bulldoze a selection of low-income neighborhoods in the inner city and build new housing on these sites, housing designed specifically to attract the middle classes. Cameron (2003) argued that the Going for Growth strategy would actively displace existing low-income residents, not all of whom would be rehoused readily (see Chapter 4 for a more detailed discussion).

A smaller-scale example of such a policy of 'positive gentrification' is the Elephant Links regeneration program at Elephant and Castle in central London in which residents have had to fight a hidden social-cleansing agenda. In the 1990s the borough of Southwark was seen to be suffering from having too many socially excluded people with low aspirations and low social capital. In a now infamous remark, Southwark's then Director of Regeneration Fred Manson said,

> We need to have a wider range of people living in the borough ... social housing generates people on low incomes coming in and that generates poor school performances, middle class people stay away. (DeFilippis and North 2004: 79)

The council's answer with respect to the regeneration of Elephant and Castle was

> managed but inclusive gentrification to bring in more wealthy residents with higher levels of social capital and labour market involvement and paying higher levels of local tax, which could be used to benefit local

residents (provided they were not displaced in the process). (DeFilippis and North 2004: 79)

The two main estates—the Heygate (see Plate 6.2) and the Aylesbury (the largest public housing estate in Europe)—are to be demolished. The center-piece of the £1.5 billion plan is a forty-two-story residential tower with only 30 percent affordable housing; it will be a mixed-use development with a hotel, cinema, 219 homes, restaurants, shops, and a bustling market square. Due to the public participation now required by law before any regeneration plan can go ahead, the council boasts that the regeneration plan has the support of 80 percent of the local community (but see DeFilippis and North [2004], who discuss the complexities of public participation and anti-gentrification activism in this case).

Most recently, *The London Plan* (Greater London Authority [GLA] 2004) has gotten on board the 'positive gentrification' bandwagon. It promotes an urban renaissance and social-mixing agenda in a similar vein to the Urban White Paper:

> New housing development, including additional provision arising from conversions, should ... help to promote mixed and balanced communi-ties. (GLA 2004: 59)

**Plate 6.2** Elephant and Castle in London

The Heygate Estate, an enormous 1960s council estate and one of the two main estates in Elephant and Castle, is to be demolished as part of the urban regeneration program Elephant Links.
*Source:* Photograph by Loretta Lees.

London's riverside and urban waterways, labeled the 'Blue Ribbon Network' by the GLA, have been given a spatial strategy all of their own. There are two main aims:

> To promote social inclusion and tackle deprivation and discrimination, policies should ensure that the Blue Ribbon Network is accessible for everyone as part of London's public realm and that its cultural and environmental assets are used to stimulate appropriate development in areas of regeneration and need. (GLA 2004: 194)

and

> The Blue Ribbon Network should not continue to be developed as a private resource or backdrop, which only privileged people can afford to be near or enjoy. (GLA 2004: 207)

One can see here the imprint of London's mayor, Ken Livingstone, for the GLA's *London Plan* has a much clearer social justice agenda than the Urban White Paper. However, despite the rhetoric, in a detailed study of social mixing, Mark Davidson (2006) found no social mixing between the new-build (see Chapter 4 on new-build gentrification) residents along the Thames and those lower-income groups living in the adjacent communities. As such, there was no transference of social capital from high- to low-income groups, or any of the other desired outcomes from the introduction of a middle-class population into these central-city riverside locations. In part this was due to the transitory nature of the new-build residents, and in part it was due to the spatially segregated nature of the new-build developments with respect to the adjacent low-income communities. The new-build developments did allow access to the Thames for the adjacent low-income communities, but those communities rarely went there because the imposing nature of the new-builds and their security put them off. As Damaris Rose (2004: 280) states, there is an 'uneasy cohabitation' between gentrification and social mix.

And it is not just the United Kingdom that is promoting a process of 'positive gentrification' in this way, for this notion of gentrification and social mixing is at the leading edge of neoliberal urban policy (see Chapter 5) around the world. In the Netherlands a policy of 'housing redifferentiation' (see Hulsbergen and Stouten 2001; Musterd, Priemus, and van Kempen 1999; Priemus 1995, 1998, 2001; Salet 1999; Uitermark 2003; van Kempen and van Weesep 1994), as they call it, has been underway since 1996 (the British Urban Task Force was especially excited by this policy). This is a policy of adding more expensive dwellings to low-income areas by removing inexpensive dwellings through demolition, together with the sale and upgrading of existing dwellings—the idea being to create a more socially diverse population in neighborhoods via gentrification. The ideas about social mixing have gained new intensity since 2002 related to the political turbulence due to the rise of the Pim Fortuyn Party and its 'Leefbaar Rotterdam' (Livable Rotterdam). There are now strong calls in the Netherlands for the dispersal of the poor and immigrant inhabitants and the creation of mixed communities. In Rotterdam, Uitermark, Duyvendak, and Kleinhans (2007:129) argue,

> The city now actively markets itself as a good place for affluent residents and especially targets the so-called creative class (see Florida, 2005). The city has boosted both the construction of owner-occupied dwellings and the demolition of social rented housing. Each year, developers add about 3,000 new owner-occupied dwellings to the total of 250,000 dwellings, while demolishers destroy about 4,000 social houses. ... In language that hardly requires textual deconstruction, the government of Rotterdam declares that it aims to attract "desired households" to "problem areas" ... therefore reinforcing and politicizing the connection between owner-occupied housing and liveability. This discourse no longer only involves the right-wing parties that were in office since 2002. The Labour Party that won the local elections of February 2006 supports similar policies. A document produced by top civil servants to articulate a new vision after Labour's victory explicitly argues that gentrification needs to be "enhanced". ...

And in the United States, HUD's Hope VI (Home Ownership and Opportunity for People Everywhere) Program has been used to socially mix (read 'gentrify') public housing in order to break down the culture of poverty and the social isolation of the poor:

> While debate on these questions persists, the consensus among policy makers is that poverty is fundamentally transformed by its spatial concentration: When [*sic*] neighborhood poverty rates exceed some critical threshold, contagion effects spread behavioral pathologies through peer groups, while collective socialization erodes because children no-longer see adults in positive role models as educated workers and married parents. (Wyly and Hammel 1999: 740)

The current trend in U.S. housing redevelopment is to replace existing high-rise, high-density 'projects' with new lower-density mixed-income communities, for example, Cabrini–Green in Chicago. Despite being located next to some of the most expensive real estate in Chicago, in 1994 Cabrini–Green (see Plate 6.3) qualified as the worst case of public housing in the United States under HUD guidelines and received $50 million to redevelop a portion of the site. The reduction of densities from demolition of units and the 'vouchering out' (where residents are usually given vouchers that subsidize the cost of privately rented accommodation) of public housing tenants led to significant displacement of low-income tenants and gentrification (see J. Smith 2001).

**Plate 6.3** Cabrini–Green, Chicago

Look now before this well-known pocket of public housing in Chicago is completely gentrified.
*Source:* Photograph by Elvin Wyly.

In cities that are highly dependent on property taxes as a source of revenue, such as those in the United States, seeking to increase your tax base by increasing the percentage of middle-class home owners in the central city is seen to be fiscal pragmatism. By 'manufacturing' a socially mixed community, it is thought that gentrification

> can ameliorate the social isolation of the poor. New more affluent residents will rub shoulders with poorer existing residents on the streets, in shops, and within local institutions, such as public schools. Such newcomers may exhibit possibilities of social mobility and a determination to secure adequate public services that provide existing residents with the kind of role models and contacts the absence of which Wilson [W .J. Wilson 1987] finds debilitating in the ghetto. (Byrne 2003: 422)

Cunningham (2001), however, has criticized the use of HOPE VI in Washington, D.C., arguing that placing HOPE VI projects in gentrifying neighborhoods does not aid the revitalization of depressed neighborhoods; rather, it reduces affordable housing in areas with spiraling rents and prices:

> From the perspective of the approximately 20,000 low income households on the waiting list for DCHA housing or Section 8 vouchers, it looks like another tool in the hands of the area's gentrifiers to reduce the number of affordable housing units. (p. 357)

Despite not spurring the revitalization of depressed neighborhoods, Wyly and Hammel (1999) do concede that the replacement of a traditional large public housing project may permit otherwise existing market demand to prompt investment in the area. And, as Byrne (2003: 429) asserts,

> The success of HOPE VI in a gentrifying neighborhood actually represents the first successful government program to integrate residential neighbourhoods by income, a startling contrast to the patterns that have typified metropolitan development for 100 years.

Gotham (2001: 437), however, disagrees; he argues,

> [T]he redevelopment of public housing is a form of "exclusive" development that is designed to exclude the very poor from the revitalized spaces and render them safe for resettlement by the wealthy and affluent.

In fact, Wyly and Hammel (2001) note the now severe housing affordability problems in Capitol Hill, Washington, D.C., calling it 'one of the most intensely gentrified neighbourhoods in the country' (p. 24). The Ellen Wilson Dwellings public housing complex subjected to HOPE VI demolition was followed by gentrification in the form of 'a complete [mixed-income] redevelopment of the site with 153 townhouse units designed to resemble mews typical of the historic district of which the complex is part' (p. 240). Byrne (2003), however, appears delighted at this development, rounding off his essay with this happy tale of social mixing:

> On a recent Saturday, I attended a multi-family yard sale at the nearby Townhomes on Capitol Hill with my wife and teenage daughter. The member co-op that manages the project had organized the sale as a 'community day.' We strolled along the sidewalks chatting with the residents about how they enjoyed living there and examining their modest wares. We bought a number of paperbacks, many of which were by black authors. My daughter bought a remarkable pink suitcase, rather beat up, which perfectly met her sense of cool. My wife, being who she is, reorganized several residents' display of goods to show them off to better effect, to the delight of the sellers. I bought and devoured a fried fish sandwich that Mrs. Jones was selling from her apartment. Such a modest event hardly makes news and certainly does not cancel the injustices of our metropolitan areas. No public officials attended nor made claims for what it promised for the future. Yet it was a time of neighbourly intercourse, money circulation and mutual learning. If multiplied many times, it promises a better future for our communities. (p. 431)

Lance Freeman (2006: 2) argues similarly that gentrifiers do bring benefits to indigenous residents, 'but in ways more limited than the poverty deconcentration thesis would suggest'. He is clear that income mixing is no guarantee of upward mobility.

In a study of Vancouver's Downtown Eastside (see also Chapter 7), Nick Blomley (2004) has commented on just how 'morally persuasive' the concept of social mix can be in the face of addressing long-term disinvestment and poverty:

> Programs of renewal often seek to encourage home ownership, given its supposed effects on economic self-reliance, entrepreneurship, and community pride. Gentrification, on this account, is to be encouraged, because it will mean the replacement of a marginal anticommunity (nonproperty owning, transitory, and problematized) by an active, responsible, and improving population of homeowners. (p. 89)

But Blomley's work helps us to think more in terms of who has to move on to make room for a social mix:

> The problem with "social mix" however is that it promises equality in the face of hierarchy. First, as often noted, it is socially one-sided. If social mix is good, argue local activists, then why not make it possible for the poor to live in rich neighbourhoods? ... Second, the empirical evidence suggests that it often fails to improve the social and economic

conditions for renters. Interaction between owner-occupiers and renters in "mixed" neighbourhoods seems to be limited. More importantly, it can lead to social segregation and isolation. (p. 99)

Creating social mix, however, invariably involves the movement of the middle class into working-class areas, not vice versa, working on the assumption that a socially mixed community will be a socially 'balanced' one, characterized by positive interaction between the classes. Although gentrifiers are 'presumably more amenable than the suburban middle class to having the poor as neighbors' (Freeman 2006: 206), there are very few examples of government support to allow the poor to move into affluent suburban communities: the widely-discussed 'Moving to Opportunity' program in the United States, for example, is not a housing program but rather a tiny demonstration and research experiment involving about 5,000 families in five large metropolitan areas, each with populations of at least 1.5 million. The planning and policy optimism that surrounds social mixing, however, rarely translates into a happy situation in gentrifying neighborhoods, not least in South Parkdale, Toronto, where a deliberate policy of social mixing initiated in 1999 exacerbated home owner NIMBYism (NIMBY stands for 'not in my backyard') and led to rent increases and tenant displacement (Slater 2004b). Uitermark, Duyvendak, and Kleinhans (2007) argue that an influx of middle-class residents into a disadvantaged neighborhood does not increase social cohesion; rather, the contacts between low-income and higher-income households tend to be superficial at best and downright hostile at worst.

Gentrification disguised as 'social mix' serves as an excellent example of how the rhetoric and reality of gentrification have been replaced by a different discursive, theoretical, and policy language that consistently deflects criticism and resistance. In the United Kingdom, social mix (particularly tenure mix) has been at the forefront of "neighborhood renewal" and "urban regeneration" policies for nearly a decade now, but with one or two well-known exceptions (N. Smith 2002; Lees 2003a; Davidson and Lees 2005), there is still not much of a critical literature that sniffs around for gentrification amidst the policy discourse. In order to grasp the specifics of state-led gentrification, it is necessary for future research to study the evolution and nature of the governance networks that promote urban restructuring/gentrification in disadvantaged neighborhoods.

*Gentrification as an Emancipatory Social Practice*

The notion of gentrification as a positive process is not, however, confined to the policy arena. Pioneer gentrification (see Chapter 1) was associated with the same appeals to diversity, difference, and social mixing found above in our discussions of gentrification as a 'positive public policy tool' (see also Chapter 5). Indeed, the birth of gentrification is synonymous with social mixing. In Barnsbury, Islington, London (as we saw in Chapter 1), pioneer gentrifiers were part of a left-liberal new middle class who actively sought social mixing. They were champions of the comprehensive school revolution of which Margaret Malden's Islington Green was a prototype. As one Barnsbury gentrifier—Mary Hall—said in a letter to the *Times* (Letters to the Editor' 1977),

> Sir, the Socialists are determined that we should sit side by side to be educated and lie side by side when ill. Why on earth, then, should we not also live side by side?

And another, architect Ken Pring, said (also cited in Chapter 1),

> The present trend towards a rising proportion of the middle classes in the population will continue. This will help create a better social balance in the structure of the community, and the professional expertise of the articulate few will ultimately benefit the underprivileged population. (Quoted in Pitt 1977: 1)

Irving Allen (1984: 31–32) sums up and explains this desire for social and cultural diversity:

> Sociocultural diversity is a leitmotif in the new tastes for central city housing and neighborhood. One of the great amenities of dense city living, it is said, is exposure to such social and cultural diversity as ethnicity. A composite statement of the idea made up from many fragments is as follows: A milieu of diversity represents a childrearing advantage over "homogeneous suburbs", because children are exposed to social "reality" and to the give and take of social and cultural accommodation with those who are different. For adults the urban ambience of diversity is a continual source of stimulation and renewal and a reminder of the cultural relativity of one's own style of life. It is said to be a relief from the subcultural sameness and "boredom" of many suburban communities.

Some early writers on gentrification, however, questioned whether the gentrifying middle classes and the preexisting low-income communities could live side by side, and

> whether policy can promote population mixes of different socioeconomic and racial groups while simultaneously enhancing the civil class domination of the neighbourhood. In the past new people and incumbents have often not mixed well when they were of different races or socioeconomic statuses. The normative integration that is a prerequisite for upgrading does not develop. ... This probably becomes more serious when racial mix is combined with socioeconomic mix. (Clay 1979: 70)

In large measure a reflection of the ideologies associated with pioneer gentrification, there is a significant body of writing on gentrification that frames it as a positive, 'emancipatory process'. Lees (2000) lumps these writings together under the label 'emancipatory city thesis' in contrast to the 'revanchist city thesis' which we will discuss in the next section. In many ways, the emancipatory city thesis and the revanchist city thesis reflect the dichotomy in the gentrification literature between demand- versus supply-side explanations (see Chapters 2 and 3), but they are not simply a mirror image of this.

The emancipatory city thesis is implicit in much of the gentrification literature that focuses on the gentrifiers themselves and their forms of agency—for example, David Ley (1980, 1994, 1996) and Tim Butler (1997)—but it is in Canadian sociologist Jon Caulfield's (1989, 1994) work that the thesis is most explicit. In his thesis, gentrification is seen to be a process which unites people in the central city, and creates opportunities for social interaction, tolerance, and cultural diversity. Gentrification is seen to be a liberating experience for both gentrifiers and those who come into contact with them. Caulfield's (1994) analysis of pioneer gentrification in Toronto, Canada, focuses on the inner city as an emancipatory space and gentrification as a 'critical social practice', which he defines as 'efforts by human beings to resist institutionalised patterns of dominance and suppressed possibility' (p. xiii). For Caulfield, then, (pioneer) gentrification is a reaction to the repressive institutions of the suburbs, and it is a process that creates tolerance (cf. the quotation by Irving Allen [1984: 31–32], above). By resettling old inner-city neighborhoods, Caulfield argues that gentrifiers subvert the dominance of hegemonic culture and create new conditions for social activities, leading the way for the developers who follow. For Caulfield, old city places offer 'difference' as seen in the diversity of gentrifiers: '[G]ays may be lawyers or paperhangers, professors may live in shabby bungalows or upmarket townhomes, feminists may or may not have children' (1989: 618). Lees (2000; see also Lees 2004), however, is critical of his thesis on the inner city as an emancipatory social space. She asks, 'What is it about old buildings in inner-city neighborhoods that makes people supposedly tolerant?' 'Is there some kind of link between the new uses of these old inner-city buildings and social diversity?' Whereas Caulfield argues that encounters between 'different' people in the city are enjoyable and inherently liberating, Lees finds other authors who argue differently. Young (1990), for example, argues that the interaction between strangers is often disinterested, and Merry (1981) argues that far from being liberating, the anonymity of urban life is often viewed as threatening. In fact, Zukin (1995) has argued that such anxieties about strangers have spurred the growth of private police forces and gated communities. In conclusion, Lees (2000: 393) argues,

> The emancipatory inner city of Toronto thus appears as a rose-tinted vision as much as a description of contemporary urban experience. The actual encounter with social difference and strangers, so often referred to as a source of emancipation in the city by many authors, needs to be evaluated in more depth.

She goes on to surmise that Caulfield's celebration of social diversity and freedom of personal expression in the inner city inadvertently privileges particular subject positions, cultural practices, and class fractions (see Pratt and Hanson [1994] on the importance of a geography of placement):

> Although Caulfield is under no illusions about gentrifiers, his thesis obscures the fact that anti-gentrification groups, often largely composed of working class and/or ethnic minorities, do not always share the same desires as gentrifiers. The dream of gentrifying tolerance and equality has struggled to accommodate people who do not accept the idea that all values deserve equal protection. (p. 393)

This is particularly so in global cities like London and New York, where gentrifiers are rubbing shoulders with people from radically different cultural backgrounds. As Jane Jacobs (1996) has argued with respect to the competing visions for the rehabilitation of Spitalfields in the East End of London, '[T]he co-presence of Bengali settlers, home-making gentrifiers and megascale developers activated an often conflictual politics of race and nation' (p. 72). Lees (2000: 394) concludes,

> By abstractly celebrating formal equality under the law, the rhetoric of the emancipatory city tends to conceal the brutal inequalities of fortune and economic circumstance that are produced through the process of gentrification.

In similar vein to Jon Caulfield, in their respective writings on gentrification David Ley (1996) and Tim Butler (1997) argue that one of the hallmarks of the 'new' middle class is their ability to exploit the emancipatory potential of the inner city, and indeed to create a new, culturally sophisticated, urban class fraction, less conservative than the 'old' middle class (see Chapter 3). Gentrification is deemed to be a spatial manifestation of these new cultural values. Ley (1980) argues that gentrification in Canadian cities was initiated by a marginal counterculture that sought inner-city spaces in an 'expressive ideology' against the dominant 1950s and 1960s 'instrumentalist ideology' (p. 242). As discussed in Chapter 3, in more recent work Ley (1994) demonstrated that the principal gentrifying districts in the three largest Canadian cities, Toronto, Montréal, and Vancouver, had an electorate that predominantly sided with more liberal, socially inclusive, reform politics. For Ley (1994: 59–60), such reform politics exhibit

> closer management of growth and development, improved public services, notably housing and transportation, more open government with various degrees of neighbourhood empowerment, and greater attention to such amenity issues as heritage, public open space, and cultural and leisure facilities.

In *The New Middle Class and the Remaking of the Central City*, Ley (1996) argues that Canadian pioneer gentrifiers saw inner-city neighborhoods to be sites of resistance: 'oppositional spaces: socially diverse, welcoming difference, tolerant, creative, valuing the old, the hand-crafted, the personalized, countering hierarchical lines of authority' (p. 210). While Ley is not unaware of the realities of displacement, the Canadian inner city is represented as 'a place of sensuous encounter, to be experienced and possessed' (p. 208), where a 'remarkable pot-pourri of artistic, spiritual and social science fragments' (p. 182) collide in a 'feast of conviviality' which thrives on 'the sharpening of the moment, the will-to-immediacy through sensation, tactile, visual, aural' (p. 338). This language does tend to have the unintended effect of embracing gentrification, when more time could have been spent documenting how these urban values and experiences are not shared by all residents.

Tim Butler's (1997) research on gentrifiers in Hackney, inner London, follows a similar, if less sensuous and spiritual, line of argument. He explains the differences between the middle class in Hackney and elsewhere by their choice of residence in a deprived inner London borough. He argues that Hackney's gentrifiers sought out people with similar cultural and political values, ones attuned to what inner-city living had to offer, such as cultural infrastructure, social and cultural diversity, and old, Victorian terraced houses. As his interviewees said,

> There's a great social mix here, we've got an orthodox Jewish family that side, an English family two doors down who have become great mates. We've got a black family this side who we are very friendly with and an Anglo–French family the other side up there, a New Zealander over there and there's no tension at all in the street. ... I don't like to be set in an enclave of all middle class or all anything because I think that as soon as you get all anything the same frictions start, you get the "one upmanships", the silly, petty "I have got to be better than the next door". (p. 117)

> I would hate to have a [modern] Georgian townhouse: I could never see myself living in that sort of thing because it was something that was imposed upon me, there's something about [a north London terrace] that was here before me. There's something about the way that it's laid out and the way it's built that I find empathetic. I don't find empathetic the imposition of a Barratt's "Georgian style" on me. Why can't they just build something new that is designed, why are they harking back? (p. 128)

But Butler (1997) points to some interesting contradictions. He argues that 'there appears to be an increasing tendency towards spatial segmentation within the middle class both occupationally and residentially' (p. 161). So despite the Hackney 'new' middle class' desire for diversity and difference, they tend to self-segregate! Notions of diversity are more in the minds of these gentrifiers than in their actions, reflecting one way in which they define themselves as a specific class faction, and in particular as cosmopolitan citizens (Butler and Robson 2001b).

As Lees (2000) points out, much of the literature on gender, sexuality, and gentrification can also be grouped under the emancipatory city thesis (see also Ray and Rose 2000), for the central city is seen to be an emancipatory space for both women and gays, as Ley (1996: 208) points out:

> The remaking of gender and family relations has been one of the proj-
> ects facilitated by an inner-city location which encourages alternative
> and plural ways of living.

The inner city facilitates some negotiation of the model of the patriarchal family among heterosexual households (see Chapter 3). The inner city allows more flexible family identities for middle-class women, as well as men. Damaris Rose's (1984) concept of the 'marginal gentrifier' was very much influenced by the changes in gender relations and social reproduction that took place in the 1970s:

> [S]ome of the changes which are usually subsumed within the concept
> "gentrification" can bring into existing neighbourhoods intrusions of
> alternative ways of living, which would never be tolerated if they were
> not being introduced by "middle-class" and "professional" people in the
> first instance. (p. 68)

As we saw in Chapter 3, Rose (1984) argued that single professional women, with or without children, and restricted by marginal positions in the labor force, found the inner city to offer a range of useful support services and networks. Also, following Ann Markusen (1981), she pointed out that women in dual-earner households may find inner-city areas more suitable for working out equitable divisions of domestic labor (Mills's 1989 research on the 'post-patriarchal gentrifier household' found this to be true). We also looked at the work of Robert Beauregard (1986) on the consumption practices of gentrifiers (often single individual households and childless couples) being linked to their decisions on biological reproduction, and the work of Briavel Holcomb (1984) and Peter Williams (1986), who pointed to the inner city as a site of women's education, liberation, and expression. If we consider all this research as a collective, there is no question that a central theme is how gentrification is playing a positive, emancipatory role in the lives of middle-class women who have physically and mentally rejected the oppressive, patriarchal conditions of suburbia. Yet while the breaking down of any sexual apartheid separating women from the rights and privileges enjoyed by men is encouraging, it says a lot about the capitalist conditions under which gentrification thrives that it is almost exclusively and selectively well-educated, professional, middle-class women who have benefited from gentrification. In fact, the lives of working-class and/or ethnic minority women living in gentrifying neighborhoods is a massively underresearched area—only one study, that of Vicky Muniz (1998) in Sunset Park, Brooklyn, on the lives of Puerto Rican women resisting gentrification and displacement, exists to address this issue. If research on gender and gentrification is to advance, perhaps a key question to ask alongside Bondi's (1999b) insistence that we research gender and the life course is 'Does the gentrifying inner city act as an emancipatory space for *all* women?'

Researchers have also noted the emancipatory qualities of the inner city for the gay community. As Ley (1996: 208) argues,

> The studied, often self-conscious, tolerance of these inner-city districts provides an enabling environment for the construction of homosexual identities.

Ley continues by quoting a respondent in Jon Caulfield's (1994) study of Toronto:

> Suburbs are sexually policed; that's what they're for—institutionalized heterosexuality. ... [But in the inner city,] lesbian women can connect up with organizations that represent their kind of life-style, and they can live as lesbians without feeling surveilled or threatened. ... There's a wider range of acceptable behaviours here. (p. 188)

Gay men are often seen to be pioneer gentrifiers, along with artists (see Chapter 3). Gay gentrification is seen to be an emancipatory, critical social practice, and the gay gentrified neighborhood is constructed by various authors to be an oasis of tolerance that satisfies the need for a sense of place and belonging (see Forest 1995; Knopp 1992, 1997; Lauria and Knopp 1985). Anonymity in the city is useful, and city dwellers have come to expect a certain amount of interaction with, and toleration of, 'alien' groups. Gay gentrified neighborhoods are also seen to be spaces from which the gay community can combat oppression, develop economic and political clout, and gain access to the state apparatus. This is the central theme of Manuel Castells's (1983) work on gay gentrification in San Francisco, where the process is viewed in a positive light:

> They have paid for their identity, and in doing so have most certainly gentrified their areas. They have also survived and learnt to live their real life. At the same time they have revived the colors of the painted façades, repaired the shaken foundations of buildings, lit up the tempo of the street and helped make the city beautiful and alive, all in an age that has been grim for most of urban America. (p. 161)

The fact that gays desire to live in socially and culturally diverse inner-city neighborhoods is important because, first, these are the types of neighborhoods that, as we saw earlier in the discussion of 'gentrification as a positive

**Plate 6.4** Child on His Bike in a Gentrifying Lane in Brooklyn Heights, New York City, 2001

This child is on his bike riding past both derelict and multimillion-dollar properties in this lane of carriage houses (called 'mews houses' in the United Kingdom) in Brooklyn Heights. He is the child of a gentrifying family. What must it be like for this child to grow up in this physical and social environment?

*Source:* Photograph by Loretta Lees.

public policy tool', policy makers are promoting; and, second, Richard Florida (2003) has pointed to the gay community as an instigator of economic growth and a measure, through the gay index, of a city's creativity (see Chapters 3 and 5).

Interestingly, there has been little to no work done to date on gentrification and age (for an exception, see D. Smith and Holt 2007), and no doubt age would affect one's ideological stance towards living in the inner city. Is the inner city an emancipatory space for children (see Plate 6.4) or the elderly, for example? Only recently have policy makers in the United Kingdom and elsewhere realized that they cannot continue to just attract young, middle-class people into central cities; they also need to attract families and the elderly to create sustainable communities (see also Karsten [2003] on the Netherlands). Furthermore, on the issue of young people, despite a rhetoric of 'diversity' that seeks a mix of age groups, children and youth are often seen to be 'undesirable', as Lees's (2003d) research into planning for diversity in Portland, Maine, reveals.

### A Negative Neighborhood Process?

In contrast to Byrne (2003), who they see as defending the market, in their reply to him Powell and Spencer (2003) argue that gentrification is a negative neighborhood process. They begin by citing University of Chicago policy analyst John Betancur (2002), who, in a study of gentrification in West Town, Chicago, argues that gentrification is really a struggle between community and accumulation, a struggle for which we must assume responsibility:

> There is an aspect of gentrification that mainstream definitions ignore. Descriptions of gentrification as a market process allocating land to its best and most profitable use, or a process of replacing a lower for a higher income group, do not address the highly destructive processes of class, race, ethnicity, and alienation involved in gentrification. ... [T]he right to community is a function of a group's economic and political power. ... [T]he hidden hand is not so hidden in the process of gentrification and ... in fact, it has a face—a set of forces manipulating factors such as class and race to determine a market outcome. ... The most traumatic aspect ... is perhaps the destruction of the elaborate and complex community fabric that is crucial for low-income, immigrant, and minority communities—without any compensation. (p. 807)

Betancur's analysis of the racial injustice of gentrification is especially helpful to Powell and Spencer (2003), who reject the claims of Byrne that the process is good for poor and ethnic minorities, and instead argue that any definition 'must take whiteness and white privilege into account. ... [B]eing white contributes to and draws benefits from the privileges and entitlements associated with the "white face" of gentrification' (p. 439). For Betancur, gentrification is not about social mix, emancipation, creativity, and tolerance; it is about arson, abandonment, displacement, 'speculation and abuse', ethnic minority tenant hardships, and class conflict, all of which are woven into a mournful account of struggle, loss, and, above all, 'the bitterness of the process and the open hostility/racism of gentrifiers and their organizations toward Puerto Ricans' (p. 802):

> Much of West Town is now gentrified. Even entrenched minority, low-income clusters have seen gentrification push through their borders. Churches, service organizations, schools and institutions have been affected by it. Their numbers have dwindled or their constituencies changed. Many small churches have closed; public school enrolment has decreased in the most gentrified sections, and higher income children are taking over local private schools. (p. 792)

Betancur's assault on the process rises to a crescendo near the end of his paper, where the current situation is a depressing state of affairs:

> The ethnic enclaves that managed to hold on through the years are also falling prey to gentrification—especially as their now senior population dies. As gentrification advances, the community continues resisting the ever-stronger blows coming from the forces of gentrification. (p. 805)

Powell and Spencer (2003) also argue that this is not a 'natural' process—the state also fuels gentrification through 'inaction' and 'court sanction'; for example,

> under a short lived Seattle ordinance, any landlord in the city who demolished low-income housing was required to replace the same number or contribute to the State Housing Trust Fund; but the ordinance was struck down by the state supreme court in 1992. And most recently in HUD v. Rucker [2002], the Supreme Court ruled that local housing authorities could evict tenants of public housing when household members or guests were in violation of anti-drug policies, even if the tenant was unaware of drug activity.
>
> Moreover, since there are fewer easily gentrified neighbourhoods left, the state directly assists in gentrification by removing barriers to redevelopment in mixed-use land parcels, remote locations, and public housing projects. These state-sanctioned shifts now expose "a broad swath of the inner city to gentrification pressures in new and troubling ways". (pp. 450–451)

For so many scholars, gentrification is not, as one might be encouraged to think from reading so many positive media reports and the work of Byrne, the savior of our cities. Abu-Lughod's richly detailed (1994) narrative of the East Village in New York is a case in point. Bringing together several essays on the neighborhood in an edited collection, her somber conclusions lament the difficulty of resistance, the destruction of community, and the loss of place under the revengeful gentrification that occurred there in the 1980s:

> Not every defense of a neighborhood succeeds and, we must admit, not every successful defense succeeds in all ways. ... [I]f the attacks against it are too powerful, the community can eventually lose its vitality and verve. ... [I]t is also easier for government to destroy community than to nurture this intangible element of the human spirit. To some extent, while the developers and most particularly, the long arm of the law of the City of New York that aided and abetted them, failed to convert this portion of an old quarter into a paradise for yuppies, they succeeded, at least for the time being, in killing much of the precious spirit of the neighborhood. The funeral pall that in 1991 hung over the community is the legacy of their efforts. (Abu-Lughod 1994: 340)

Associated skepticism about the voyeuristic and appropriative relationship of gentrification to social difference by authors such as Jon May (1996) and Andy Merrifield (2000) has been given new impetus by recent empirical research into the social interactions of actual gentrifiers. The middle-class gentrifiers interviewed by Tim Butler and Garry Robson (2001a; Butler with Robson

2003) in London engaged in little social mixing with local low-income groups. Social interaction by gentrifiers was greatest in areas where other groups had been largely pushed aside, and where they had not, gentrification tended to result in 'tectonic' juxtapositions of polarized socioeconomic groups rather than in socially cohesive communities. With their focus on middle-class reproduction, Butler and Robson did not consider the experiences of non-gentrifiers; nevertheless their findings raise important questions about the role of gentrification in fostering an inclusive urban 'renaissance'.

It is worth remembering that the term 'gentrification' was coined by Ruth Glass with critical intent, intended to capture the disturbing effects of the middle classes arriving in working-class neighborhoods, and was researched in that critical spirit for many years. One negative effect in particular, the displacement of the working class and/or ethnic minorities, was (and still is) of serious concern, as Powell and Spencer (2003) show in Chicago:

> [W]e note that reversals in racial compositions of gentrifying neighborhoods in Chicago between 1980 and 1990 show white residents are gaining, while black residents are losing. The Near West Side's black–white ratio, for example, fell from 6:1 to 3:1; the number of childless young professionals increased; the proportion of residents under age twenty-five declined; and the higher average levels of education increased. While crime rates have declined significantly and the number of retail establishments grown, the residents of color are being pushed out. Who will be left to enjoy these opportunities as gentrifying forces proceed? (pp. 432–433)

Let us take a closer look at displacement and some recent work on this major issue in gentrification research.

*Displacement*

> Displacement from home and neighborhood can be a shattering experience. At worst it leads to homelessness, at best it impairs a sense of community. Public policy should, by general agreement, minimize displacement. Yet a variety of public policies, particularly those concerned with gentrification, seem to foster it. Marcuse (1985a: 931)

There are long-standing claims that gentrification leads to displacement, as working-class and minority residents are steadily priced out of gentrified areas (e.g., LeGates and Hartman 1986; Marcuse 1986; N. Smith 1996a; Wyly and Hammel 2004). Many of the articles in early collections on gentrification such as Laska and Spain (1980), Schill and Nathan (1983), Palen and London (1984), and N. Smith and Williams (1986) were concerned with displacement, and, indeed, much greater attention was paid to the effects of gentrification on the working class than to the characteristics of the new middle class who were moving in. Although there was no real agreement on the severity and extent of the problem (Sumka 1979), displacement was undoubtedly a major theme. Even scholars associated with a less critical take on the process were concerned about displacement:

> The magnitude of dislocation is unknown … though the scale of renovation, demolition, deconversion, and condominium conversion noted … implies that tens of thousands of households have been involuntarily displaced through various forms of gentrification over the past twenty-five years in Toronto, Montréal, Vancouver, and Ottawa alone. (Ley 1996: 70)

Displacement is, however, extremely difficult to quantify. Atkinson (2000) has called measuring displacement 'measuring the invisible', whereas Newman and Wyly (2006) sum up the quantification problem as follows:

> In short, it is difficult to find people who have been displaced, particularly if those people are poor. … By definition, displaced residents have disappeared from the very places where researchers and census-takers go to look for them. (p. 27)

In the 1990s, especially, these significant barriers to undertaking quantitative or indeed other research on displacement steered researchers away from displacement altogether. In the neoliberal context of public policy being constructed on a 'reliable' (i.e., quantitative) evidence base, no numbers on displacement meant no policy to address it. It was almost as if displacement didn't exist. This is in fact the conclusion of Chris Hamnett (2003b) in his paper on London's rampant gentrification from 1961 to 2001; in the absence of data on the displaced, he reasserts his thesis that London's labor force has 'professionalized':

> The transformation which has taken place in the occupational class structure of London has been associated with the gradual replacement of one class by another, rather than large-scale direct displacement. (p. 2454)

But when reading these words, we must wonder whether it is precisely a sign of the astonishing scale of gentrification and displacement in London that there isn't much of a working class left in the occupational class structure of that inner city! Hamnett's conclusion also sits uneasily with work by Michal Lyons (1996) and Rowland Atkinson (2000), who both used the longitudinal survey and found evidence suggesting gentrification-induced displacement in London. Davidson and Lees (2005) also found evidence of gentrification-induced displacement in riverside wards along the Thames that had experienced new-build gentrification (see Chapter 4).

The lack of attention to displacement in the 1990s, however, has recently changed—dramatically—with the work of Lance Freeman and Frank Braconi (2002, 2004), whose work we mentioned briefly earlier in this chapter. These scholars have been seen by the media and, worryingly, policy makers as putting forward the 'definitive verdict' on gentrification and displacement (see Newman and Wyly 2006: 29)—the verdict being that displacement is negligible and gentrification therefore isn't so bad after all. Their work has been summarized at length elsewhere (Newman and Wyly 2006), but briefly, Freeman and Braconi (2002) examined the triennial New York City Housing and Vacancy Survey (which contains questions pertaining to demographic characteristics, employment, housing conditions, and mobility), and found that between 1996 and 1999, lower-income and lesser-educated households were 19 percent less likely to move in the seven gentrifying neighborhoods studied than those elsewhere, and concluded that displacement was therefore limited. They suggested that such households stay put because they appreciate the public service improvements taking place in these neighborhoods and thus find ways to remain in their homes even in the face of higher rent burdens. This was the main reason that *USA Today*, on April 20, 2005, decided to feature their work with the headline 'Gentrification: A Boost for Everyone' (see Plate 6.5).

More recently, however, Freeman has backpedaled somewhat and written this:

> The chief drawback [of gentrification] has been the inflation of housing prices on gentrifying neighbourhoods. ... Households that would have formerly been able to find housing in gentrifying neighbourhoods must now search elsewhere. ... Moreover, although displacement may be relatively rare in gentrifying neighbourhoods, it is perhaps such a traumatic experience to nonetheless engender widespread concern. (Freeman 2005: 488)

On the point of shrinking the pool of low-rent housing, it is important to return to Peter Marcuse's identification of 'exclusionary displacement' under gentrification, referring to households unable to access property because it has been gentrified:

> When one household vacates a unit voluntarily and that unit is then gentrified ... so that another similar household is prevented from moving in, the number of units available to the second household in that housing market is reduced. The second household, therefore, is excluded from living where it would otherwise have lived. (Marcuse 1985b: 206)

As Marcuse (2005) has recently pointed out, the Freeman and Braconi work only touches on this crucial question: are people not moving not because they like the gentrification around them, but rather because there are no feasible

**Plate 6.5** Media Coverage of Freeman and Braconi's (2002, 2004) Gentrification Research

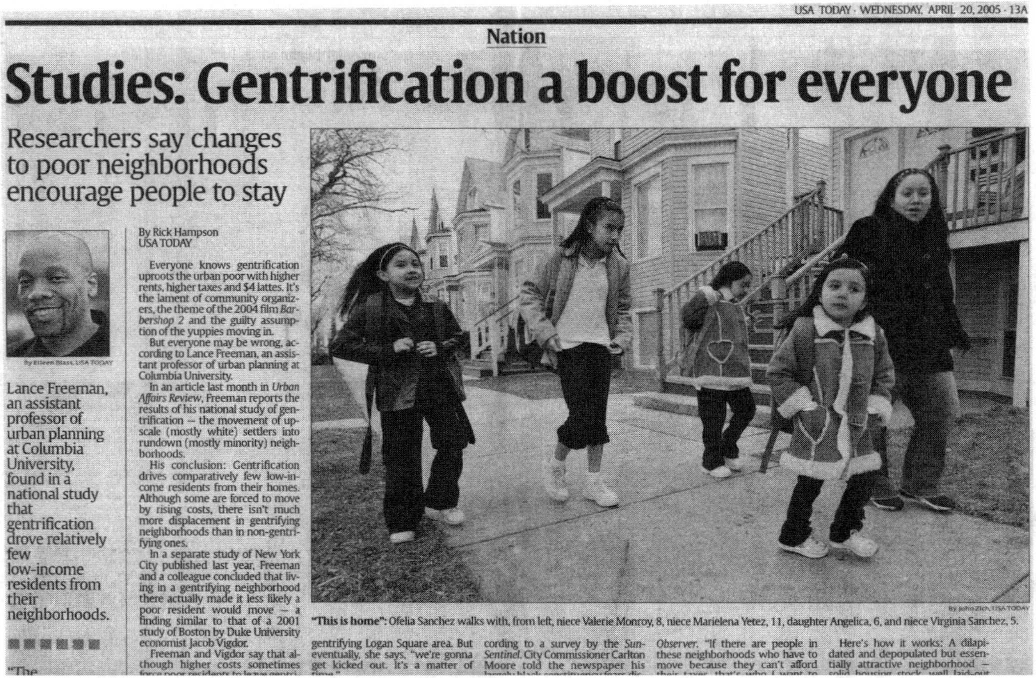

USA TODAY · WEDNESDAY, APRIL 20, 2005 · 13A

Nation

# Studies: Gentrification a boost for everyone

## Researchers say changes to poor neighborhoods encourage people to stay

By Eileen Blass, USA TODAY

Lance Freeman, an assistant professor of urban planning at Columbia University, found in a national study that gentrification drove relatively few low-income residents from their neighborhoods.

"The

By Rick Hampson
USA TODAY

Everyone knows gentrification uproots the urban poor with higher rents, higher taxes and $4 lattes. It's the lament of community organizers, the theme of the 2004 film *Barbershop 2* and the guilty assumption of the yuppies moving in.

But everyone may be wrong, according to Lance Freeman, an assistant professor of urban planning at Columbia University.

In an article last month in *Urban Affairs Review*, Freeman reports the results of his national study of gentrification – the movement of upscale (mostly white) settlers into rundown (mostly minority) neighborhoods.

His conclusion: Gentrification drives comparatively few low-income residents from their homes. Although some are forced to move by rising costs, there isn't much more displacement in gentrifying neighborhoods than in non-gentrifying ones.

In a separate study of New York City published last year, Freeman and a colleague concluded that living in a gentrifying neighborhood there actually made it less likely a poor resident would move – a finding similar to that of a 2001 study of Boston by Duke University economist Jacob Vigdor.

Freeman and Vigdor say that although higher costs sometimes

By John Zich, USA TODAY

**"This is home":** Ofelia Sanchez walks with, from left, niece Valerie Monroy, 8, niece Marielena Yetez, 11, daughter Angelica, 6, and niece Virginia Sanchez, 5.

gentrifying Logan Square area. But eventually, she says, "we're gonna get kicked out. It's a matter of

cording to a survey by the *Sun-Sentinel*. City Commissioner Carlton Moore told the newspaper his

*Observer*. "If there are people in these neighborhoods who have to move because they can't afford

Here's how it works: A dilapidated and depopulated but essentially attractive neighborhood –

Freeman and Braconi found that lower-income and lesser-educated households were less likely to move in the gentrifying neighborhoods that they studied than those elsewhere, and concluded that displacement was therefore limited. This optimistic picture of gentrification has given fuel to the neoliberal agenda of state-led gentrification in the United States and attracted a lot of media attention.

*Source: USA Today*. April 20, 2005. Reprinted with permission.

alternatives available to them in a tight/tightening housing market (i.e., that so much of the city has gentrified that people are trapped)? This is the carefully considered conclusion of a paper on the gentrification of Brussels by Mathieu van Criekingen:

> [E]vidence highlighted in Brussels strongly suggests that poorly-resourced households are less likely to move away from marginal gentrifying districts because they are "trapped" in the lowest segment of the private rental housing market, with very few alternatives outside deprived neighbourhoods, even in those areas experiencing marginal gentrification. (van Criekingen 2006: 30)

The traumatic experiences of displacement (see Chapter 1 on winkling and Rachmanism in Barnsbury) have been documented recently in New York City by Curran (2004), Slater (2004a), and particularly Newman and Wyly (2006), who as well as conducting interviews with displaced tenants, used the same data set as Freeman and Braconi to demonstrate that displacement is not 'relatively rare' but occurs at a significantly higher rate than Freeman and Braconi imply. This points to the absolute necessity of mixing methods in the study of displacement:

> The difficulties of directly quantifying the amount of displacement and replacement and other "noise" in the data are hard to overcome. It may be that further research at a finer spatial scale using a more qualitative approach could usefully supplement this work. (Atkinson 2000: 163)

On reviewing the evidence from a survey of the gentrification literature, Atkinson (2004) found that, whether displacement is involved or not, gentrification was viewed overwhelmingly as a 'negative neighbourhood process' (see Box 6.1). Unfortunately, the policy makers and local governments discussed in the previous section who are promoting gentrification as a public policy tool have not read or listened to this critical gentrification literature (cf. Lees 2003a). Atkinson and Bridge (2005) sum this up well:

> At the neighbourhood level itself poor and vulnerable residents often experience gentrification as a process of colonisation by the more privileged classes. Stories of personal housing dislocation and loss, distended social networks, "improved" local services out of sync with local needs and displacement have always been the underbelly of a process, which, for city boosters, has represented something of a saviour for postindustrial cities. (p. 2)

One renowned scholar has taken this further and argued that gentrification is a process of revenge against poor populations seen to have 'stolen' urban neighborhoods from the middle classes. This has proved to be a very influential thesis, to which we now turn.

*The Revanchist City*

> Previously accepted notions of social justice and an explicit concern
> with injustice, so central to the progressive urban ambitions of the
> 1960s and 1970s, have been flushed away with the remains of liberalism.
> In the same period, the narrowest visions derived from Marxism have
> also proven bankrupt. The new urbanism results from the political and
> cultural rush to fill this vacuum. Neil Smith (1996c: 117)

In June 1989, Bruce Bailey, a longtime low-income tenant organizer in
Manhattan, was found murdered and dismembered in several garbage bags in
the Bronx. Bailey was especially feared by rapacious landlords of large apartment buildings in the city's poorer neighborhoods, and whilst police sus-
pected landlords of his murder, no one was ever formally charged. In 1995, it
transpired that two brothers with Mafia connections, Jack and Mario Ferranti,
who regularly intimidated and terrorized tenants (with the use of large dogs
and occasionally guns) in the numerous buildings that they owned, and who
were serving long sentences for arson and attempted murder, were implicated
in the crime. Bailey was murdered simply because he was involved in organizing tenants—something he was very good at—in four of Jack Ferranti's
buildings. According to prosecutors, Bailey's actions contravened an alleged
'understanding' between Jack Ferranti and Bailey—cemented by bribery—
that Bailey would not organize Ferranti's buildings. Jack Ferranti ordered
his brother to terrorize and kill Bailey, and Mario Ferranti allegedly claimed
credit for mutilating the corpse.

What does this crime have to do with the gentrification of New York City
in the 1990s? Everything, according to Neil Smith, who in the 1990s, clearly
disturbed by what he had seen on the streets of that city since the end of the
1980s, switched his attention from explaining the causes of gentrification to
accounting for the violence of the process. Rounding off the opening chapter
of *The New Urban Frontier*, which concentrates on the battle for Tompkins
Square Park in the Lower East Side, Smith saw the Bailey murder as indicative
of what was happening to the city where he lived and worked. His argument,
in short, was that right-wing middle- and ruling-class whites were seeking
revenge against people who they perceived had 'stolen' the city from them,
and gentrification had become an integral part of this strategy of revenge. Bailey was organizing and advocating for low-income tenants, one of the groups
seen to have stolen the city, and for Smith, his murder was just one of many
incidents through which we could detect the emergence of what he called 'the
revanchist city'.

This troublesome word has its roots in late nineteenth-century France—
revanchists (from the French word *revanche*, meaning revenge) were a group
of bourgeois nationalist reactionaries opposed to the liberalism of the Second
Republic, the decadence of the monarchy, the defeat by Otto von Bismarck in

the Franco–Prussian War, and especially the socialist uprising of the Paris Commune, where Paris' working classes took over from the defeated government of Napoleon III and controlled the city for months. The revanchists, led by poet-turned-soldier Paul Deroulede and the Ligue des Patriotes, were determined to reinstate the bourgeois order with a strategy that 'mixed militarism and moralism with claims about public order on the streets as they flailed around for enemies' (N. Smith 1999: 185). This was a right-wing movement intent on taking revenge (*revanche*) on all those who had 'stolen' their vision of France from them.

Smith identified a striking similarity between the revanchism of late nineteenth-century France and the political climate of New York City which emerged in the early 1990s from the disintegration and vilification of liberal urban policy. Whereas the liberal era of the post-1960s period was characterized by redistributive policy, affirmative action, and antipoverty legislation, the era of neoliberal revanchism (see Chapter 5 on neoliberalism), which arrived in the early 1990s, was characterized by a public discourse of

> [r]evenge against minorities, the working class, women, environmental legislation, gays and lesbians, immigrants … [a]ttacks on affirmative action and immigration policy, street violence against gays and homeless people, feminist bashing and public campaigns against political correctness and multiculturalism. (N. Smith 1996a: 44–45)

Smith argues that this was all 'a reaction against the supposed "theft" of the city, a desperate defense of a challenged phalanx of privileges, cloaked in the populist language of civic morality, family values and neighbourhood security' (1996a: 211). Just as the bourgeois order was perceived as under threat by the revanchists of 1890s France, in 1990s New York, Smith explained that 'white middle-class assumptions about civil society retrench as a narrow set of social norms against which everyone else is found dangerously wanting' (p. 230). A particular, exclusionary vision of 'civil society' was being reinstated with a vengeance, and Smith introduced us to this contemporary revanchism and its geography of exclusion.

Two important factors fueled the fire of revanchism; first was the rapid collapse of 1980s optimism into the bleak prospects of the early 1990s recession (see Chapter 5 between second- and third-wave gentrification), which triggered unprecedented anger amongst the white middle classes. Smith demonstrates that such anger needed a target on which to exercise revenge, and the easiest target was the subordinated, marginalized populations of the inner city. The following sentence explains,

> More than anything the revanchist city expresses a race/class/gender terror felt by middle- and ruling-class whites who are suddenly stuck in place by a ravaged property market, the threat and reality of unemployment,

the decimation of social services, and the emergence of minority and immigrant groups, as well as women, as powerful urban actors. (p. 211)

Second, Smith states that revanchism is 'screamingly reaffirmed' by symbolic representations of urban malaise in television and the media in 'an obsessive portrayal of the violence and danger of everyday life' in the city (p. 211). Such is the influence of these anti-urban (re)productions of paranoia and fear that they have amplified and aggravated the paranoia and fear among large swathes of middle-class urban and suburban voters seeking scapegoats for their unease in public spaces and city streets. It came as no surprise to many that, in 1993, Rudolph Giuliani was elected mayor on the promise to offer a better 'quality of life' for 'conventional members of society'. As Smith pointed out in later works (N. Smith 1998, 1999, 2001), neoliberal revanchism in the 1990s under Mayor Giuliani was consolidated by blaming the failures of earlier liberal policy on the disadvantaged populations such policy was supposed to assist:

> Rather than indict capitalists for capital flight, landlords for abandoned buildings, or public leaders for a narrow retrenchment to class and race self-interest in the assertion of budget priorities, Giuliani led the clamor for a different kind of revenge. He identified homeless people, panhandlers, prostitutes, squeegee cleaners, squatters, graffiti artists, "reckless bicyclists", and unruly youth as the major enemies of "public order and public decency", the culprits of urban decline for generating widespread fear. (Smith 2001: 73)

A particularly mean-spirited and repressive attitude towards these 'culprits', as exemplified by the well-publicized 'zero-tolerance' policies (see Fyfe 2004) of Giuliani's police force, has been playing out in particularly racist and classist ways in New York City. As the city's economy recovered in the 1990s, the crime rate dropped, and public spaces such as Times Square (see Reichl 1999) and Bryant Park were privatized and commodified, New York City became a major tourist destination, an arena for lavish middle-class consumption—yet the people who had to be swept away and/or incarcerated to allow this to happen were sidelined by the fanfare of success attributed to a charismatic mayor.

Where does all this fit in with the gentrification of New York City? In an angry and gripping analysis of the gentrification of the Lower East Side, and particularly the conflict over Tompkins Square Park (see Plate 6.6), Neil Smith urges his readers to consider gentrification as a spatial expression of revanchist anti-urbanism. He peels back the rhetorical gloss of urban 'pioneering' (omnipresent in media representations) and dispels the mythology of the urban 'frontier' constructed by both the real estate and the art industries to make the argument that the middle-class movement into the Lower East Side

**Plate 6.6** 'Class War' and 'Rich Pigs Go Away' Graffiti, Lower East Side, 1988

During the summer of 1988, such graffiti was rife in the Lower East Side, especially around the hotspots of Tompkins Square Park into Alphabet City.
*Source:* Photograph by Loretta Lees.

is part of a plan by the collective owners of capital to retake the neighborhood from those they feel have stolen it:

> The poor and working-class are all too easily defined as "uncivil", on the wrong side of a heroic dividing line, as savages and communists. The substance and consequence of the frontier imagery is to tame the wild city, to socialize a wholly new and therefore challenging set of processes into safe ideological focus. As such, the frontier ideology justifies monstrous incivility in the heart of the city. (1996a: 17–18)

Smith's point is that the Lower East Side was sold to the white middle classes as a place devoid of history and geography, a wild, dangerous place lost to a horde of undesirables, and now awaiting an advancing frontier of 'brave' urban pioneers to save it from 'decay' and make it 'livable' again. The gentrification of that neighborhood did not happen without a fight, (see Abu-Lughod 1994), but the political drive to turn it into a bourgeois playground is, for Smith, a consummate expression of the shift from a liberal urbanism to a revanchist anti-urbanism: 'The rallying cry of the revanchist city might well be: "Who lost the city? And on whom is revenge to be exacted?"' (N. Smith 1996a: 227).

One of the more troubling aspects of revanchism for Smith is the fact that it knows no party lines, and in fact began in New York City under the supposedly liberal mayoral administration of David Dinkins (the more conservative administration of Rudy Giuliani that followed simply pushed extant revanchism into overdrive). As Don Mitchell (2003) has pointed out, Dinkins's particularly tough stance on homeless encampments in Tompkins Square Park was mirrored by liberal mayors in other cities such as Paul Schell in Seattle and Willie Brown in San Francisco. The failure of 1960s-style liberal urban policy led to the far-from-liberal erosion of compassion and tolerance. Mitchell explains this as follows:

> [W]hat is at work is the implementation, at the urban scale, of a regulatory regime—and its ideological justification—appropriate to the globalizing neoliberal political economy that developed out of the global recessions of the 1970s, the debt crisis of the early 1980s, the economic crises of the late 1980s (and 1990s, for Asia), and the implosion of the Soviet Union and its satellites. ... "Revanchism" describes an urban regime that cuts across mainstream party lines and has even taken on the cast of common sense. (p. 164)

Mitchell (1997) has researched the municipal laws against begging, panhandling, and sleeping or urinating on sidewalks and in other public spaces, linking contemporary homelessness with the material and rhetorical imperatives of globalization. He has argued that many of the laws and police practices affecting the homeless are increasingly used to cleanse the public spaces used by tourists, the middle class, and wealthy residents and visitors. As cities aggressively compete to make themselves attractive places to live in and for investors, they are more willing to impose harsh penalties on those people seen as undesirable by wealthy visitors, tourists, shoppers, commuters, and investors. Municipal ordinances are mobilized to criminalize behavior that is offensive or unpleasant to the resident and visiting middle classes. Wyly and Hammel (2005) have attempted to classify cities according to the injustices imposed on the poor and the homeless, looking for connections between the treatment of the homeless and the creation of new landscapes of wealth and privilege in the gentrifying inner city. We have updated this 'revanchist urban hierarchy' and tallied it with Richard Florida's creativity index (see Figure 6.1).

Note in particular how San Francisco and Seattle, two of the cities with the 'meanest' policies towards the homeless and marginal populations, come second and third, respectively, on Richard Florida's creativity index. This raises the crucial issue of the disturbing ordinances deployed to make way for the influx of his 'creative class'. As Tickell and Peck (2003) have shown, when 1980s 'roll-back' neoliberalism collapsed, what came in its place in the 1990s was not a new ideology but a new 'roll-out' stage of neoliberalism, with the same free market imperatives but now with far greater emphasis on regulating

**Prohibited Activities†**

| | Share of affluent central-city homebuyers choosing gentrified neighborhoods, 1995–2002 | Hourly wage required to afford the median metropolitan rent for a 2-bedroom apartment, 2001 | curfew for minors | spitting | urination or defecation | begging | "aggressive" panhandling | sleeping | camping | loitering, loafing, or vagrancy | obstruction of sidewalks or public places | Ranked as "meanest city" | Richard Florida's Creativity Index Rank |
|---|---|---|---|---|---|---|---|---|---|---|---|---|---|
| Boston | 49.9% | $18.80 | x | | | | x | x | | | x | | 5 |
| Philadelphia | 23.9% | $14.52 | x | x | x | | x | | | | x | | 35 |
| Chicago | 22.5% | $15.15 | | | | | | | | x | x | 2002 | 39 |
| Milwaukee | 18.8% | $12.17 | | | | | | | | | x | | 124 |
| Washington, DC | 17.5% | $16.60 | x | | | | x | | | x | | | 11= |
| San Francisco | 16.5% | $33.60 | x | | | x | x | | | x | x | 1996, 2002 | 2 |
| Seattle | 14.8% | $15.56 | | | x | | x | | | | x | 1996 | 3 |
| Baltimore | 13.3% | $12.71 | | x | x | | x | | | x | x | 2002 | 11= |
| Minneapolis-St. Paul* | 11.7% | $13.50 | x | x | | x | | | | | x | | 10 |
| St. Louis | 9.7% | $12.02 | x | x | | | x | | x | x | x | | 113 |
| Detroit | 5.7% | $12.81 | | | | x | | | | x | x | | 68= |
| Cincinnati | 4.9% | $10.71 | | | x | | | | | x | | | 68= |
| Dallas | 4.5% | $15.02 | x | | | | x | | | | x | | 21 |
| New Orleans | 3.6% | $10.13 | | | | | x | x | | | | | 147 |
| San Diego | 3.5% | $19.46 | | | | x | x | x | | | | | 19 |
| Atlanta | 3.4% | $15.29 | x | x | x | x | x | | x | | x | | 15 |
| Oakland | 2.5% | $23.90 | | x | x | | | x | x | | x | | n/a |
| Denver | 2.3% | $14.71 | | x | | | | | x | | x | | 14 |
| Kansas City** | 1.1% | $11.48 | x | x | | x | x | | | | | | 32 |
| Indianapolis | 1.1% | $10.75 | | x | | x | x | | | x | x | | 98 |
| San Jose | 0.6% | $30.60 | | x | x | | | | | | x | | n/a |
| Phoenix | 0.1% | $14.62 | x | | x | | x | | x | | x | | 28 |

†Bans on begging, sleeping, camping, and loitering/loafing/vagrancy include only city-wide ordinances.
*Prohibited activities refer only to Minneapolis; St. Paul was not included in NCH/NLCHP survey.
**Prohibited activities refer only to Kansas City, MO; Kansas City, KS was not included in NCH/NLCHP survey.

**Figure 6.1** A Revanchist Hierarchy of U.S. Cities and Florida's Creativity Index

*Sources:* Federal Financial Institutions Examination Council (1994–2001); National Coalition for the Homeless / National Law Center on Homeless and Poverty (2002); Wyly and Hammel (2005).

and punishing those suddenly scapegoated for earlier economic and social failures:

> The contemporary neoliberal state is a facilitative, market-managerial presence in matters of capital regulation, but adopts an ever more aggressive, invasive, and neopaternalist attitude towards the regulation of the poor. (Tickell and Peck 2003: 178)

Mitchell's point about 'common sense' is crucial in this regard, for what we have seen in a number of cities (more especially in the United States) since the early 1990s recession is a discourse of competitive progress and rapid economic recovery that ostracizes people who cannot take greater 'personal responsibility' for their own well-being. Welfare payments are practically consigned to history; the unemployed have become 'job seekers' regardless of skills, education, or training; poverty is often attributed to fecklessness and deviance; and if the market cannot take care of 'troublesome' groups, then the penal system will:

> Reduced welfare expenditures are not indicative of a shift towards reduced government intervention in social life ... but rather a shift toward a more exclusionary and punitive approach to the regulation of social marginality. (Beckett and Western 2001: 47)

Many commentators have lamented the fact that the much lauded welfare 'safety net' of the Keynesian welfare state, designed to protect vulnerable citizens during times of economic insecurity, has been removed by a neoliberal 'postwelfare' ethos that attributes economic insecurity to those same vulnerable citizens. Furthermore, the punitive, revengeful strategies to deal with those citizens are put forward by their architects as common sense, not a matter for discussion or resistance (Keil 2002).

As the Giuliani administration gathered vengeful steam in New York during the 1990s (building on the platform laid by the Dinkins administration), Neil Smith advanced his revanchist thesis further. In one of his more scathing pieces of writing, Smith (1998) revealed that Giuliani had

> a vendetta against the most oppressed—workers and "welfare mothers", immigrants and gays, people of color and homeless people, squatters, anyone who demonstrates in public. (p. 1)

Using the example of the famous and remarkably (many would say depressingly) influential 'zero-tolerance' policing strategy advanced by Giuliani and his onetime police commissioner William Bratton, Smith accounted for the existence of this extreme strategy of revenge against oppressed groups:

> This visceral revanchism is no automatic response to economic ups and downs but is fostered by the same economic uncertainties, shifts, and insecurities that permitted the more structured and surgical abdication

of the state from many tasks of social reproduction. Revanchism is in every respect the ugly cultural politics of neoliberal globalization. At different scales it represents a response spearheaded from the standpoint of white and middle-class interests against those people who, they feel, stole their world (and their power) from them. (p. 10)

It is worth recognizing that there is a significant literature on zero-tolerance policing, 'broken windows' criminology, and the rise and fall of the crime rate in New York City (for a good overview, see Bowling 1999; see also Fyfe 2004, who explores the tensions and anxieties around the interplay of deviance, difference, and crime control), but covering this literature is beyond the focus of this book. Our purpose here has been to explain how gentrification was viewed by Smith as one of the ways in which Giuliani attempted to 'recapture' the streets of the city from those who he saw as the enemy within (see also N. Smith and DeFilippis 1999; Papayanis 2000).

*The Geography of Revanchism*

Visiting Malmö, Neil Smith asked me to show him the battlefields of gentrification. At the time, I was at a loss to explain that there were processes of gentrification in Malmö, but no battlefields. Conflicting interests, displacement, personal tragedies, yes, but not the desperation behind battlefields. Clark (2005: 263)

Smith's revanchist city thesis has proved to be one of the more influential and powerful in urban studies in recent years. Just as he did with his rent gap thesis in 1979, Smith introduced something completely new and exciting to the gentrification debate (and debates beyond gentrification). So persuasive and evocative were Smith's arguments that they seemed to invite other researchers to see if revanchism was empirically accountable in their cities—all the more so when one considers that Smith stated that revanchism was not something just observable in New York or American cities, but all late capitalist cities:

[I]f the US in some ways represents the most intense experience of a new urban revanchism, it is a much more widespread experience ... gentrification and the revanchist city find a common conjuncture in the restructured urban geography of the late capitalist city. The details of each conflict and of each situation may be different, but a broad commonality of contributing processes and conditions set the stage. (N. Smith 1996a: 46–47)

There is some respect here for local and national differentiation, but the argument is very clearly made that revanchism is not confined to the United States. However, it is possible to detect a degree of inconsistency in *The New Urban Frontier*. In the introduction to the book, Smith argues,

> While I accept the admonition that radically different experiences of gentrification obtain in different national, regional, urban and even neighbourhood contexts, I would also hold that among these differences a braid of common threads ripples through most experiences of gentrification. (p. xix)

Later in the book, comparing gentrification in three European cities (Paris, Amsterdam, and Budapest), he argues that

> general differences really do not gel into a sustainable thesis that these [instances of gentrification] are radically different experiences. ... [T]he existence of difference is a different matter from the denial of plausible generalization. I do not think that it makes sense to dissolve all these experiences into radically different empirical phenomena. (pp. 185–186)

So, puzzlingly, he accepts 'radical differences' in the introduction, but then rejects their existence later on, saying that it is nonsensical to draw out such differences. He also rejects Lees's (1994b) empirically substantiated concept of an 'Atlantic Gap' in the process of gentrification (between London and New York, in case studies of Barnsbury and Park Slope; cf. Chapter 1), dismissing it as 'a false dichotomy' (N. Smith 1996a: 185). While there may indeed be, as Smith says, 'as much differentiation of the gentrification experience within Europe or North America as between them' (p. 185), he is most definitely of the view that there is no significant differentiation between them at all. While prioritizing what is general about gentrification reminds us that gentrification is both a theoretically coherent category and a widespread urban phenomenon, and is politically important if we are to contest the process, Smith is less willing to pay attention to the particularities of gentrifying neighborhoods in their geographical contexts, which, as a number of scholars have argued, can help us to understand the implications of the process. Indeed, it might be a more important geographical project to reveal the context and contingency of gentrification by looking for what might be 'plausibly general' and 'radically different' between two or more cases of gentrification.

The issue of the applicability of revanchism to other urban contexts has been taken up empirically in a paper by Gordon MacLeod (2002), who traced the extent to which revanchism has permeated the place marketing and entrepreneurialism behind the recent 'renaissance' of central Glasgow in Scotland. MacLeod argues that the dismissive treatment of Glasgow's homeless during its 1990s economic recovery suggests that the city 'bears the imprints of an emerging politics of revanchism' (p. 615), but stops short of saying that fully fledged New York–style revanchism is present there:

> I fully acknowledge the need for caution when comparing Glasgow with a city like New York. For while Glasgow may be witnessing the

routine arrest of so-called "aggressive beggars", in contrast to New York and indeed certain British cities … the Strathclyde Police Force has concluded that zero tolerance offers an inappropriately "short-term" approach to crime prevention. Instead, it has introduced a Street Liaison Team, which, rather than immediately criminalizing street people and prostitutes, aims to cultivate improved relations between those "on the margins of society", the police, and the wider public. (p. 616)

Further to this marked contrast in policing, MacLeod argues that a range of policy schemes designed to assist marginalized populations in Glasgow

appear to be at odds with the repressive moments of vengeance inscribed into New York's local state strategy. Stretching this a little further, can we point to Glasgow's gentrification wars (police militia, sweeping helicopters), or its military-style sweeps on quality-of-life offenders and its vengeful political attacks on the city's universities? As yet, the answer to these questions remains a tentative "no". (p. 616)

Above all, MacLeod urges us to acknowledge that 'revanchist political economies will assume different forms in different contexts' (p. 617). The case of Glasgow demonstrates what MacLeod calls 'a selective appropriation of the revanchist political repertoire … minor-league in comparison to the perspective's "home-base" of New York' (p. 603). He does not therefore reject the revanchist city thesis—in fact, he views it as 'a deeply suggestive heuristic with which to reassess the changing geographical contours of a city's restless urban landscape' (p. 616). But in contrast to Smith, MacLeod is cautious when commenting on the broader applicability of revanchism.

A much broader geographical lens was adopted by Rowland Atkinson (2003b) in a paper attempting to reveal whether a vengeful public policy is emerging in Britain's public spaces. Atkinson is from the outset very suspicious of the broader applicability of revanchism:

[C]an we really talk of the emergence of vengeful or revanchist programmes emerging in the British context? It is likely that part of the reality behind these programmes is mundane; organisations and people simply doing their job and trying to make places safer for their users, even if this means the exclusion of certain groups on the utilitarian grounds that doing so enables the majority to use those spaces. (p. 1830)

In thinking about the revanchist city, Atkinson discerned four competing strands of revanchism which, when separated, might help us analyze the control and management of public spaces in different national contexts (see Box 6.2). Atkinson takes two extreme cases of public policy with a specific emphasis on controlling public spaces, the Hamilton (Scotland) Child Safety Initiative (effectively a curfew aimed at youth living in deprived housing

---

**Box 6.2**

**Four Competing Strands of Revanchism**

1. A mode of governance expressing connections between a number of different agencies at different levels that seek to control the public realm and to dictate recognized or approved uses for such space
2. A set of programs designed to secure public space or the behavior of users of space, such as zero-tolerance policing or anti-begging drives by government
3. A prophetic and dystopian image of a downward spiral of social relations in which public spaces and the city are seen, in themselves, to represent a form of urban malaise and distress from which vengeful policies may act as an ameliorative
4. A reference to economic objectives seen in the connection between economic development and the need to secure capital investment, increasingly seen as being footloose, by beautifying and securing city spaces in order to market the quality of living in such locations

*Source:* Atkinson (2003b: 1833).

---

estates) and 'zero-tolerance' policing in Scotland, both of which have been influential across British cities, and looks for strands of revanchism in both cases. His conclusion is as follows:

> Is a revanchist strand observable in policies directed at British urban spaces? An unequivocal response to this question is hard to produce. ... It may be possible to assert that revanchist threads are shared in responses to social disorder in British cities. This view must be tempered by the fact that this is only an exploratory and extreme case analysis. (p. 1840)

Atkinson argues that far more research is needed to reveal the extent to which revanchism has influenced public policy, so the real contribution of the paper lies not in its geographical focus but in the way the author carves a path for future projects assessing the existence or extent of revanchism beyond New York City. Nevertheless, throughout his paper, Atkinson is clearly concerned that vengeance is increasingly perceived in Britain as a way to capture public spaces for consumers. On this spreading geography of revanchism, Wyly and Hammel (2005) sum up the worrying implications, particularly for the homeless:

> In short, the triumph of neoliberalism has altered the context and consequences of gentrification, creating new inequalities and locally-distinctive strands of revanchism. But if local variations do matter, the underlying dilemma remains the same. The gentry want nice, attractive

cities free of homeless people begging, sleeping, urinating, defecating in public—living in public—and in today's political climate, wealthy urbanites are increasingly willing to support policies that criminalize the activities that homeless people must do in order to live. (p. 36)

However, it is not just from American research that gentrification is portrayed as revengeful. While researchers in the United States present the most disturbing accounts of exclusionary inner-city reinvestment, academic accounts of gentrification from cities in other countries, including Canada, exhibit much in the way of revanchism. For example, few, if any, scholars researching gentrification in Vancouver's Downtown Eastside have ever spoken of gentrification as anything other than a serious problem created by revengeful urban policy (e.g., Sommers 1998; H. Smith 2003; N. Smith and Derksen 2003; Blomley 2004), and more recently, displacement in London has been blamed partly on tenant harassment of 'undesirables' that goes unreported (Atkinson 2000). The literature is too vast to summarize here, but when considered as a collective, Atkinson (2002) elaborates,

> On the issue of neighbourhood impacts it can be seen that the majority of research evidence on gentrification points to its detrimental effects. ... [R]esearch which has sought to understand its impacts has predominantly found problems and social costs. This suggests a displacement and moving around of social problems rather than a net gain either through local taxes, improved physical environment or a reduction in the demand for sprawling urban development. Even where positive effects have been identified, these are widely considered to be relatively small compared to the downside. (pp. 20-21)

Finally, in a recent account of gentrification that explicitly seeks to weigh up the positive and negative impacts of the process, Freeman (2006) reaches similar conclusions to Atkinson's (2002) and our own. Focusing on the indigenous residents in two gentrifying neighborhoods, Clinton Hill and Harlem in New York City, Freeman argues,

> Gentrification can bring benefits that the indigenous residents of these neighbourhoods are appreciative of. There are, however, significant potential downsides to this revitalization, including the loss of affordable housing, conflict between newcomers and more established residents, and resentment stemming from feelings of irrelevance; the neighbourhood improvements are for "them". (p. 207)

He finds ample reason to be wary of the negative impacts of gentrification beyond displacement and is skeptical of poverty deconcentration/social-mixing policies as the cure-all for urban ills. For Freeman, the pertinent debate seems to be how to dampen gentrification's harms and identify its benefits. As he says,

It might seem paradoxical to affirm both the emancipatory and revanchist view of gentrification. But ... gentrification is a complex process that can mean different things depending on one's vantage point. (p. 201)

## Summary

In this chapter, we have outlined those arguments that view gentrification to be a positive process and those that view it to be a negative process. Gentrification is promoted positively by policy makers who ignore the less desirable effects of the process. Their promotion of gentrification as a way to socially mix, balance, and stabilize neighborhoods has connections with the ideologies of pioneer gentrifiers who seek/sought both residence in the inner city and sociocultural diversity. Many of these pioneer gentrifiers were women (including lesbians) and gay men. These 'marginal' groups chose to live in the inner city to avoid the institutionalized heterosexuality and nuclear family units of the suburbs. The inner city for them was an emancipatory space. By way of contrast, many more authors view gentrification to be a negative process, one that causes direct or indirect displacement, and that purifies and sanitizes the central city. Some see it to be a visceral and revanchist process of capitalist appropriation. Of course, both the positive and negative takes on gentrification have validity, but the review here suggests that the negative impacts have not been considered seriously, or indeed have been ignored, by policy makers. As Atkinson and Bridge (2005: 16–17) argue,

It remains important for policy-makers and academics to try and understand how equitable development can be achieved without the stark problems associated with unchecked gentrification, itself symptomatic of a middle-class and self-serving process of investment. In short, gentrification as a process of investment and movement by the wealthy may have modified or positive effects in cities characterised by strong welfare regimes, enhanced property rights and mediation, and low competition for housing resources.

## Activities

- Read the exchange between Byrne (2003) and Powell and Spencer (2003) in the *Howard Law Journal* (http://www.law.howard.edu/dictator/media/229/huljvol46_3.pdf). Byrne sees gentrification to be predominantly a positive process, whereas Powell and Spencer rebuke his analysis as a 'defense of the market' and see gentrification to be a predominantly negative process. Which set of arguments do you find most persuasive?
- Read Neil Smith's (1996a) book *The New Urban Frontier* and compare it to David Ley's (1996) book *The New Middle Class and the Remaking of the Central City*. Consider how both authors write about

gentrification: one frames it positively, whereas the other frames it negatively.

- What might the point of view of a pioneer gentrifier be in regard to gentrification, as opposed to that of a non-gentrifier?
- Read the first half of *The Fortress of Solitude*, a novel by Jonathan Lethem (2003) set in the predominantly Puerto Rican but gentrifying neighborhood of Boerum Hill in Brooklyn in the 1970s. The novel tells the story of two boys who are friends, one black and one white. Focus on the scene of abandoned buildings, racial interactions, and the white gentrifier boy Dylan Ebdus's feelings of difference. Ask yourself, 'Was the gentrifying Boerum Hill emancipatory for Dylan Ebdus at that time?'
- Read Lance Freeman's (2006) *There Goes the 'Hood: Views of Gentrification from the Ground Up*. This is a book that explicitly sets out to weigh up the differential impact of gentrification on indigenous residents. Do you think 'he sits on the fence' in terms of his conclusions?

## Further Reading

Atkinson, R. (2003a) 'Introduction: Misunderstood saviour or vengeful wrecker? The many meanings and problems of gentrification', *Urban Studies*, 40, 12: 2343–2350.

Atkinson, R. (2004) 'The evidence on the impact of gentrification: New lessons for the urban renaissance?' *European Journal of Housing Policy*, 4, 1: 107–131.

Caulfield, J. (1994) *City Form and Everyday Life: Toronto's Gentrification and Critical Social Practice* (Toronto: University of Toronto Press).

Freeman, L., and F. Braconi (2002) 'Gentrification and displacement', *The Urban Prospect: Housing, Planning and Economic Development in New York* 8, 1 (January/February): 1–4.

Gotham, K. (2001) 'Redevelopment for whom and for what purpose', in K. Fox Gotham (ed.) *Critical Perspectives on Urban Redevelopment*, vol. 6 of *Research in Urban Sociology* (Oxford: Elsevier) 429–452.

*Howard Law Journal* (2003) 46, 3 (http://www.law.howard.edu/dictator/media/229/huljvol46_3.pdf).

Johnstone, C., and M. Whitehead (eds.) (2004) *New Horizons in Urban Policy: Perspectives on New Labour's Urban Renaissance* (Aldershot, UK: Ashgate).

Lees, L. (2000) 'A reappraisal of gentrification: Towards a "geography of gentrification"', *Progress in Human Geography*, 24, 3: 389–408.

Ray, B., and D. Rose (2000) 'Cities of the everyday: Socio-spatial perspectives on gender, difference and diversity', in T. Bunting and P. Filion (eds.) *Canadian Cities in Transition: The Twenty-First Century* 2nd ed. (Oxford: Oxford University Press) 507–512.

Rose, D. (2004) 'Discourses and experiences of social mix in gentrifying neighbourhoods: A Montréal case study', *Canadian Journal of Urban Research* 13, 2: 278–316.

Slater, T. (2004a) 'North American gentrification? Revanchist and emancipatory perspectives explored', *Environment and Planning A* 36: 1191–1213.

Smith, N. (1996a) *The New Urban Frontier: Gentrification and the Revanchist City* (London: Routledge).

Uitermark, J. (2003) '"Social mixing" and the management of disadvantaged neigh-bourhoods: The Dutch policy of urban restructuring revisited', *Urban Studies* 40, 3: 531–549.

Wyly, E., and D. Hammel (1999) 'Islands of decay in seas of renewal: Housing policy and the resurgence of gentrification', *Housing Policy Debate*, 10, 4: 711–771.

**Plate 7.1** 'Cooper Square Is Here to Stay—Speculators Keep Away', Lower East Side, 1988

Anti-gentrification activists, community activists, and groups of people and individuals under threat of displacement were very active in trying to combat gentrification during the 1980s in the Lower East Side.

*Source:* Photograph by Loretta Lees.

# 7
# The Future of Gentrification?

## Gentrifying the Future

> If present trends accelerate, the social geography of the nineteenth century industrial city may appear to urban scholars as a temporary interlude to a more historically persistent pattern of higher status segregation adjacent to the downtown core. Ley (1981: 145)

> In some corners of the city, the experts say, gentrification may be remembered, along with junk bonds, stretch limousines, and television evangelism, as just another grand excess of the 1980s.... As the dust settles, we can see that the areas that underwent dramatic turnarounds had severe limitations. Rich people are simply not going to live next to public housing. Lueck (1991: 1)

> [T]he extent and impacts of gentrification have been exaggerated in the urban literature of the 1970s and 1980s, and ... the process itself will be of decreasing importance as we move beyond the recession of the early 1990s. Bourne (1993b: 183)

> [N]either the memory nor the profits of gentrification are likely to be erased so quickly. Indeed, it may not be too much of an exaggeration to surmise that proclaiming the end of gentrification today may be akin to anticipating the end of suburbanization in 1933. N. Smith (1996a: 230)

Futurism is notoriously hazardous, particularly in the humanities and social sciences. Yet it has been at the heart of academic and popular interest in gentrification since the 1960s. The very existence of gentrification contradicted the implicit future projections of then dominant urban models—neighborhood life-cycle theories that were given material expression when accepted and implemented by public institutions (Metzger 2000), and the Alonso–Muth transportation–land price trade-off model now described as 'the masterpiece of urban theory' (Glaeser, Kahn, and Rappaport 2000: 7) predicting inexorable upper-income suburbanization. We should not be surprised, then, that the future of gentrification is as hotly contested as are its causes, dimensions, and consequences.

Will gentrification continue? Will it grow more important or fade from the scene as an obsolete concern of a previous era? These questions have persisted for two generations, and they are unlikely to be settled now with clarity or consensus. Peering ahead in the future of gentrification offers a compelling case for the notion that the questions we ask are just as important as any answers we might offer: it should be clear from our tour of the intellectual and policy landscapes of gentrification in this book, and it is obvious in the streets of protest and everyday life, that to even utter the word is to raise questions of class, culture, inequality, and social justice. The fact that so many people use the word 'gentrification' in debates and struggles over neighborhood life is thus quite remarkable. Indeed, it may not be too much of an exaggeration to suggest that forty years of debate over the causes and consequences of gentrification have made the word a signature call to arms in urban discourse—a term that is almost as familiar as politically charged words like 'globalization', 'neoliberalism', '(neo)colonialism', and 'imperialism' (see Chapter 4 on the politics of definition). For anyone concerned with the future of poor and working-class lives and communities, 'gentrification' mobilizes, organizes, and catalyzes social movements that can sometimes succeed in creating small-scale utopian spaces of hope (Harvey 2000). In this sense, we may be able to find unexpected possibilities amidst the slippery conceptual definitions and empirical measurements that (quite understandably) frustrate Larry Bourne and many others. Perhaps gentrification, like space, may qualify as a new *keyword*:

> [I]t turns out to be an extraordinarily complicated keyword. It functions as a compound word and has multiple determinations such that no one of its particular meanings can properly be understood in isolation from all the others. But that is precisely what makes the term, particularly when combined with time, so rich in possibilities. (Harvey 2006a: 293)

Despite this complexity, there are several ways to answer the simple questions regarding its future magnitude and relevance. First, we can follow the empirical path of researchers who develop baseline measures and pursue subsequent follow-up analysis. In one of the earliest examples of this 'empirical-extrapolation approach', in 1975 the Urban Land Institute (ULI) surveyed officials in all central cities in the United States with populations over 50,000, and found that nearly half saw evidence of 'private-market housing renovation in older, deteriorated areas'; a follow-up four years later documented a pronounced expansion in the number of city officials reporting activity—from 65 percent to 86 percent for cities with more than 150,000 residents—but the total number of homes affected in each city remained infinitesimal (Black 1980). The ULI survey was widely interpreted as describing a future of dramatic growth rates based on very small numbers, but there have been very few subsequent efforts to devise systematic projections. Developing baseline measures of the magnitude of gentrification is difficult as it is; doing so in a way that provides comparable measures over time is even more challenging (Bourne 1993a, 1993b; Hammel and Wyly 1996; Wyly and Hammel 1998). Recently, however, Meligrana and Skaburskis (2005) combined an analysis of census population and housing variables for ten Canadian metropolitan areas between 1971 and 2001 with key informant interviews for each city; they were thus able not only to develop estimates of the total population and housing units encompassed by gentrified neighborhoods, but also to match their findings with earlier pioneering work by Ley (1988, 1992). They estimate that 11.9 percent of the occupied housing units in Montréal's inner city were gentrified between 1971 and 2001, 21.1 percent of those in Toronto, and 19.9 percent in Vancouver. If the definition was broadened to consider neighborhoods identified by statistical thresholds but not cited by key informants, these figures rise to 23.4 percent, 40.5 percent, and 34.5 percent respectively. These figures confirm that gentrification 'has made major changes to these inner cities' (p. 1581) and suggest a future expansion as demographic trends (rising housing consumption even with falling household sizes) and land-market processes push inner-city boundaries farther outwards; and yet the process remains very limited when viewed in the context of continued metropolitan decentralization and suburbanization (Kasarda 1999; Berry 1999). The most generous estimates suggest that 6.4 percent of the population of metropolitan Montréal lives in gentrified or potentially gentrifying neighborhoods, 7.1 percent in greater Toronto, and 7.3 percent in metropolitan Vancouver. Sohmer and Lang (2001) use a different set of methods to measure population changes in the downtown cores of two dozen U.S. cities in the 1990s. They find especially rapid increases in downtown residential densities (increases of more than 1,000 people per square mile) in Seattle, Chicago, Houston, Portland, Denver, and Atlanta. Moreover, just over half of all cities in their study posted increases in the downtown's share of total metropolitan population; but nearly all central cities decreased their share of metropolitan population, casting doubt on the prospects for downtown growth to drive any dramatic expansion in the scale of gentrification. Still, Sohmer and Lang (2001: 9) believe, 'The unique history of downtown areas in combination with their central location and proximity to mass transit, work, and amenities offers potential for the growth of the 1990s to continue into the next decade'.

A second approach involves a much more explicit theoretical consideration of future trends associated with gentrification. Not surprisingly, this 'theoretical projection approach' is intertwined with differences between production and consumption explanations. Larry Bourne's (1993a) prediction of a 'post-gentrification' era, for example, relied on a primarily demand-side, consumption view of the process: Bourne foresaw weakening demand in tandem with shifts in demography, economic growth, educational levels, living arrangement preferences, and public sector spending priorities. Of course, Bourne did consider some supply-side processes—projecting that a 'shift of capital into urban real estate' in the gentrification era would give way to a post-gentrification era in which the 'balloon has shrunk' and a 'switch of capital out of property' would bring a period of stable or declining prices, high vacancies, and rising foreclosures (1993a: 104). But production explanations have shown how local and regional capital flows into real estate have been interwoven with increasingly transnational flows and secondary market institutions—while ongoing devalorization and rent gap processes create ever stronger incentives (although not the absolute certainty) for profitable gentrification in an ever-expanding disinvested urban fabric. Jason Hackworth's (2002a) theoretical and empirical analysis of third-wave reinvestment points to continued strength in the processes driving gentrification, and our consideration of a possible fourth wave extends this logic (see Chapter 6).

Yet some of the most intriguing theoretical projection evidence comes from housing demographers and urban economists attempting to rework the classical locational choice and bid-rent models. Dowell Myers and his colleagues (2001) combine survey results with demographic projections to chart the future demand for dense, walkable living environments in the United States—environments which include not only gentrified inner-city neighborhoods but also suburban areas built on 'smart growth' or 'new urbanist principles'. They find an increasing preference for density among older households, with the effect magnified by the size of the aging baby boom cohort: in the United States, total households are expected to grow by 1.11 percent per year in the 2000–2010 period, but

> the number of owners age 45 and older likely to change residence and who prefer denser neighborhoods will increase by 2.46% per year. This market segment will account for 31.0% of all the growth in owners likely to change residence during the 2000–10 period. The same segment drew only 15.4% of growth in the 1990s. (Myers et al. 2001: 1)

A more direct assessment of gentrification comes from Jan Brueckner and Stuart Rosenthal, urban economists working to refashion bid-rent models in ways that offer a neoclassical route to the political–economy conclusions of Neil Smith's devalorization cycle. Brueckner and Rosenthal (2005) are mistaken in their belief that they've found something *conceptually* new—'This paper identifies a new factor, the age of the housing stock, that affects where high and low-income neighborhoods are located' (p. i)—but their model and empirical results do offer certain new insights, evaluating changes in average income for all neighborhoods (measured by U.S. Census tracts) as a function of the predominant preference for new housing for all U.S. metropolitan areas between 1980 and 1990. Their projections to 2020 suggest that the continued aging of the housing stock (which production theorists would set in the context of devalorization and disinvestment processes) will lead to a modest relative decline of central cities in small metropolitan areas; but for larger metropolitan areas, if present housing-age preferences remain the same,

> central-city economic status is expected to rise relative to that of the suburbs by up to 20 percent of MSA mean income, a large effect. Nevertheless, while this shift implies ongoing gentrification in the central cities of larger metropolitan areas, those neighborhoods are expected to remain poor, on average, relative to the suburbs. (Brueckner and Rosenthal 2005: 29)

Gentrification will continue, in other words, along with uneven development, disinvestment, and persistent central-city poverty.

### 'It Was Right before My Eyes'

Neither empirical extrapolations nor theoretical projections capture the full significance of a gentrified future, however. Discourse also matters. The material realities of gentrification will continue to shape the lives of new generations of urban residents—rich, poor, and middle class—in cities and urban regions throughout the world. New cities and new neighborhoods are confronting the tensions of gentrification, while other neighborhoods that first experienced the process a quarter century ago are still being transformed today. And so a new generation enters the conversation over its causes and consequences. Not long ago, Higher Achievement, a private after-school program that operates in many of the schools of Washington, D.C., sponsored a citywide essay contest about gentrification. One of the winners was twelve-year-old Monique Brevard, who said, 'Gentrification is really happening in my neighborhood. ... It was right before my eyes; I just didn't know what it's called' (quoted in Layton 2006: B1). Monique recalled classmates who had to move away because their families could not afford the escalating rents of Columbia Heights, but on the other hand, she liked the renovations in the neighborhood, and wrote, 'Now there are Asians, Hispanics, and a few Caucasians on my block, whereas before it was predominantly African American.... So it's brought more diversity into the neighborhood' (quoted in Layton 2006: B1).

Monique's voice is one among many in an enormous societal conversation on the meaning of home and community, and there is every indication that the discursive facets of gentrification are growing quite steadily—in part because of the struggles over definition we explored in earlier chapters. As of September 2006, the Google Scholar search engine turned up only 793 academic books and articles with 'gentrification' in the title. But an open search of Google ferrets out about 3,090,000 web pages. And a more systematic search documents substantial growth in major press coverage (see Figure 7.1). In 1985–1986, 'gentrification' appeared in the headline, lead paragraph, or subject terms for only 37 articles in the general news category for major newspapers; another 10

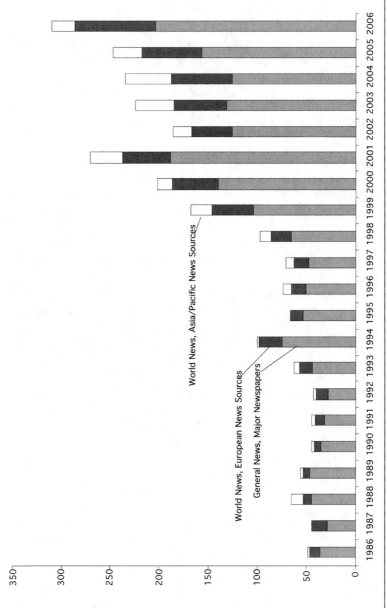

**Figure 7.1** Gentrifying the Headlines. Number of articles with 'gentrification' in the headline, lead paragraph, or subject term. Years are measured from July 1 to June 30 (such that the count for 2006 refers to July 1, 2005 through June 30, 2006).
*Source:* Reed Elsevier, Inc. (2006).

articles in the world news category carried the term as reported in European news sources, and 2 in Asia–Pacific news sources. Between July 2005 and July 2006, the corresponding figures were 204, 82, and 24 respectively. In 2005–2006, the number of general news articles focused on gentrification exceeded those devoted to another term of theory with its own theoretical and political heritage: 'underclass'. It's worth recalling the very real policy shifts that came with sustained press attention to the 'underclass problem' as framed by neoliberal and conservative attacks on welfare-state dependency, mythical welfare mothers driving Cadillacs, and draconian workfare schemes premised on the supposed need to encourage 'personal responsibility' (see Peck 2006). 'Gentrification' is still understood as a term of class conflict that raises questions of equity and fairness; and so it is crucial that we challenge the political campaigns of those who are trying to displace the term in favor of soft euphemisms (regeneration, revitalization, renaissance, reurbanization, residentialization, etc.) and those such as Andres Duany trying to redefine the term as a badge of honor for gentrifiers.

*'Rich People Move In, Poor Move Out, Rents Go Up'*

But even this cartography of journalism and popular discourse underestimates the future of gentrification, because in so many cases the term is absent from discussion of the more interesting landscapes of reinvestment, redevelopment, and socio-cultural change. One example might include New York's Co-Op City, the huge middle-income development built in the northern Bronx in 1966 that even today 'is the largest cooperative housing complex in America, possibly the world' (Frazier 2006: 54). Conceived initially as a way to keep middle-class city residents (mostly whites) from moving further out to the suburbs, Co-Op City has subsequently become three quarters black and Latino, has aged into what the board president calls 'the largest naturally occurring retirement community in the world' (p. 64), and, with the expiration of restrictions tied to city government affordable-housing subsidies, is now free to consider privatization. In 2005, the co-op residents voted 55 percent to 45 percent in favor of investigating the issue, with a final decision to come in several years. One retired resident lamented, 'We would lose the senior-citizen benefits, then rich people move in, poor move out, rents go up. I get eighty-six dollars a month in pension!' (quoted in Frazier 2006: 65). But a former board president offered a more ambivalent view:

> It's interesting, though, that if privatization went through, you're talking about seventy-two thousand rooms at an estimated fifty thousand dollars a room. With the people who are living here now that would be the largest transfer of real-estate wealth to people of color in US history. (Frazier 2006: 65)

Co-Op City looks nothing like the classical gentrified environments of the Village, Chelsea, Williamsburg, or newer frontiers of gentrification in Harlem and elsewhere. But no one concerned with gentrification can ignore the growing number of urban, suburban, and rural areas where 'rich people move in, poor move out, rents go up'.

Or consider another example where 'gentrification' never appears anywhere in the article. In mid-2006, the *New York Times* carried a front-page article on the real estate boom transforming Mitchell's Plain and other South African townships, where FNB Bank of South Africa undertook a survey and found that each township home offered for sale attracted seven potential buyers in Johannesburg, eight in Cape Town, and twice that many in Durban. Two of the country's largest real estate firms have moved aggressively into the township market, in part because of a sustained run of price escalation in existing elite areas: 'Now that those prices are reaching their potential, investors are seeking the next bargain. Some find it at the other end of the income spectrum' (Wines 2006: A14). All the elements of production and consumption narratives of gentrification seem to be in place: an agent for a firm that built its reputation with luxury-home transactions proclaims, 'It's a gold mine, Mitchell's Plain, a gold mine. You've got more buyers than stock', and the *Times* correspondent concludes, 'Urban townships have something else in their favor: among the nation's rising black middle class, they are becoming preferred places to live, especially as shopping and other services take root. In short, they are becoming hip' (Wines 2006: A14).

Is this gentrification? Is the possible future privatization of Co-Op City equivalent to gentrification? The questions matter more than the answers. And these questions are being asked in more places, by more people concerned about the ways that culture and capital interact to remake home and community in once neglected neighborhoods. Gentrification will continue, and so will the scholarly analyses, policy symposia, organizing campaigns, and street protests. Contra Bourne (1993a), the 'gentrification era' has just begun.

### Social Justice and Resistance

Moving people involuntarily from their homes or neighbourhoods is wrong. Regardless of whether it results from government or private market action, forced displacement is characteristically a case of people without the economic and political power to resist being pushed out by people with greater resources and power, people who think they have a "better" use for a certain building, piece of land, or neighbourhood. The pushers benefit. The pushees do not. Hartman, Keating, and LeGates (1982: 4)

If ... gentrification is becoming a widespread trend that represents the future of many cities, we should be thinking about how to manage the process to help us achieve a more equitable and just society. Freeman (2006: 186)

The two quotations above capture just how far the debate over the effects of gentrification has shifted since the early 1980s, particularly in the United States. Back then, the tone was more often than not one of outrage, of urgency, and of struggle—indeed, the publication from where the first quotation is taken is entitled *Displacement: How to Fight It*. But now, we have Lance Freeman, a high-profile researcher (due to media coverage of his earlier work with Braconi), saying that gentrification is likely to be the future, and instead of fighting it, we need to manage it (and through the policy of social mixing, which as we have seen in Chapter 6, is hardly something leading us on a smooth path to a more equitable and just society). Despite Freeman's major mixed-methods contribution to the literature and his empirically informed arguments that gentrification has some positive benefits, we see his words as somewhat troubling. This is, after all, a process which has caused major upheaval and loss, as many of the quotations in his book (and so many elsewhere) illustrate, and indeed as we have argued in several chapters in this book. How can such a polarizing process be managed? By way of corollary, one could argue that apartheid in South Africa had 'positive benefits' in terms of economic growth—but did the African National Congress wish to manage that process? This is not to draw an inappropriate equivalence with gentrification and apartheid, but merely to state that something so often portrayed as unjust is not really something that we should consider 'managing', but rather resisting.

In the Preface to this book, we argued for a critical geography of gentrification, one that follows a social justice agenda and one that is focused on resisting gentrification where necessary. We supported the arguments of Holcomb and Beauregard (1981), who argued that research into gentrification must be motivated by concerns to address its unjust and unequal outcomes; indeed, this is why all three of us began researching gentrification. We also noted in the Preface that we have all been involved in anti-gentrification activities, mainly in North America; as such, we have had firsthand experience of the complexities of resisting something so often viewed as the natural outcome for urban neighborhoods, and increasingly viewed as the way things 'should' be. Neil Smith (1996a) has written in detail about the battle for Tompkins Square Park in the Lower East Side, a battle that was symbolic both of his notion of a revanchist city and of class war. But the latter, despite its renown, is just one in a number of stories of resistance to gentrification. This chapter focuses on some different efforts that have been made by people and community organizations to resist gentrification, to protect against displacement, and to encourage a more socially just form of neighborhood change not geared to the interests of those who benefit financially from such changes.

Before we summarize some examples of resistance to gentrification, we must be aware that resistance continues to change over time in both tactics and intensity. In recent years, academics at the forefront of gentrification debates have been reflecting on why the widespread resistance to gentrification's second wave has diminished with its third wave. In a fairly recent commentary lamenting the absence of effective 'urban redevelopment movements' (which we can read as a pseudonym for community organizing) in the United States, Wilson and Grammenos (2000) offer an explanation why the activism and 'group consciousness' of the 1960s have been eroded:

> [T]oday the mix of postindustrialism and globalization has devastated urban redevelopment movements. Organising people has reached a new low, real estate capital has shown itself resistant to grassroots social pressures, investors flaunt their mobility and leverage vast amounts of municipal resources, the motors that propel accumulation now operate at an international scale, and people struggle to understand a hyper-fast and complexly signified and ascripted world. (p. 361)

There can be little doubt that the dominance of neoliberal urbanism has made for frustrating times among community activists, anchored around their ability to remain in the gentrifying city. Over fifteen years ago, two well-known voices in urban studies explained that

> [t]he effectiveness of neighborhood organizations depends on the entrepreneurial abilities and political connections of their leaders. It depends also on general community characteristics to the extent that a particular district has a population containing activists. (Fainstein and Fainstein 1991: 321)

It is worth putting these words in the context of third-wave gentrification in New York City, where Hackworth (2002a) pointed out the following:

> Compounding the tricky political position of community-based opposition are the aggregate spatial effects of continued reinvestment in the inner city. As gentrification continues and the working class is less able, as a whole, to afford rents in neighborhoods close to the central business district (CBD), prospects of an oppositional collective consciousness are reduced. (p. 824)

So, if Hackworth is correct, the outlook for effective resistance to gentrification in New York does not look promising. Furthermore, if we look at the words of Neil Smith, this is a problem not just confined to New York:

> From Amsterdam to Sydney, Berlin to Vancouver, San Francisco to Paris, gentrification's second wave was matched by the rise of myriad homeless, squatting, housing, and other anti-gentrification movements and organizations that were loosely linked around overlapping issues. These rarely came together as citywide movements, but they did challenge gentrification sufficiently that, in each case, they were targeted by

city politicians and police forces. Apart from anything else, the heightened levels of repression aimed at anti-gentrification movements in the 1980s and 1990s testified to the increasing centrality of real estate development in the new urban economy. ... The emergence of the revanchist city was not just a New York phenomenon: it can be seen in the anti-squatter campaigns in Amsterdam in the 1980s, attacks by Parisian police on homeless (largely immigrant) encampments, and the importation of New York's zero tolerance techniques by police forces around the world. ... The new authoritarianism both quashes opposition and makes the streets safe for gentrification. (2002: 442)

Writing together, Hackworth and Smith (2001) noted that 'a palpable decline of community opposition' (p. 475) characterized the 1990s resurgence of gentrification, in marked contrast to the 'intense political struggles' (p. 467) over displacement that characterized the 1970s and 1980s. In sum, important statements about the recent and current nature of gentrification have claimed that resistance has diminished due to the twin factors of (1) continued working-class displacement robbing a city of activists, and (2) the authoritarian (neoliberal) governance of urban places making challenges to gentrification extremely difficult to launch.

We do not doubt the difficulties of progressive and effective community organization in the neoliberal age. The devolution of social welfare functions from the federal to the city level, and the growing tendency of city governments to contract with nonprofits, charities, and community development corporations, means that more and more community activists are doing the work of the local state, and cannot therefore risk protesting as much as in previous decades (DeFilippis 2004; Newman and Lake 2006). We also do not doubt that the struggles that took place over gentrification all over the world in the 1980s are less prevalent today. We do feel, however, that caution must be taken when commenting on the decline of resistance, as this is only a short step away from saying that gentrification is not resisted at all, and thus by implication not a problem. This is not to argue that Hackworth and Smith are sending us down that path, but simply to point out that observations of the decline of resistance can so easily be appropriated by agents of gentrification and used to justify the process with rhetoric such as 'Nobody is objecting to what is going on here!' The lack of overt conflict over space in a number of cases does not mean that gentrification is somehow 'softer' or less feared by low-income and working-class people—as we shall see shortly, it still provides a strong focus for politicization.

Today the struggles remain on the creative/destructive edge of gentrification, however muted they might be in some places and however different in form from one place to the next. We must also question whose interests it serves if we forget or refuse to recognize these class struggles that are part of

the definition of gentrification. It is precisely a sign of the success of gentrification (and now-historical struggles over urban space) that there is hardly
a working class left in many neighborhoods. But the struggles themselves
transform with the process. Today, the sharpest social contests can be seen
in places like London's East End, which is currently the subject of a comprehensive redevelopment plan for the 2012 Olympics, or indeed in downtown
Los Angeles, where gentrification is pressing on the homeless encampments
of 'Skid Row' from all sides, with revanchist Police Chief William Bratton
(of 'zero-tolerance' fame) and local property owners wanting to 'clean up' the
encampments, to the delight of waiting-in-the-wings developers and loft con-
verters. These struggles are still occurring and await the attention of future
analysts; in what follows, we summarize some other recent struggles over the
process and see what strategies and tactics were adopted, what was achieved,
and what lessons have been learned.

*Case 1: Lower Park Slope, Brooklyn, New York City: The Fifth
Avenue Committee and the 'Displacement Free Zone'*

> Recently, I was talking with one of the doormen on my block. ... I asked
> him where he lived.
> "Brooklyn", he said. "Park Slope".
> "Where in Park Slope?"
> "Fourth Avenue and 23rd Street", he said.
> "That's not Park Slope. That's Sunset Park".
> "No", he said. "They call it Park Slope now".
> Park Slope has now come to extend from Prospect Park, as a friend of
> mine says, "all the way to Egypt".
>                    Vince Passaro, *New York Times Magazine*, November 11, 2001

> The issue for community groups is not simply coming out for or
> against growth but getting the right kind of growth. Fainstein and
> Fainstein (1991: 317)

In Chapter 1 we summarized the gentrification of Park Slope in Brooklyn,
New York City, closing with the observation that the section of the neighborhood earliest to gentrify has recently been experiencing super-gentrification,
leading to rampant gentrification of the lower section of the neighborhood
too. As we shall see in this first case study, gentrification in the latter has not
happened without a fight—a fight that has become one of the most high-profile
and influential anti-gentrification campaigns anywhere. Before discussing
this, however, a little more contextual background is needed.

Lower Park Slope (see Map 7.1) experienced only sporadic gentrification
when Upper Park Slope was gentrifying intensely in the 1960s, 1970s, and
1980s (Gelb and Lyons 1993; Lees 1994b; Carpenter and Lees 1995; Lees
and Bondi 1995). However, from the mid-1990s onwards, sales and rental

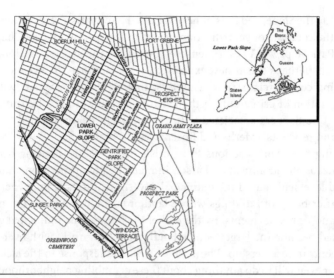

**Map 7.1** Lower Park Slope, Brooklyn, New York City

prices have become so prohibitively high in gentrified Park Slope that the middle classes are now finding that the only affordable accommodation is in Lower Park Slope. The term 'overspill gentrification' has been noted elsewhere (Dantas 1988), and it is a useful image to apply to Lower Park Slope and also to many other previously non-gentrified New York City neighborhoods—they have become 'reservoirs of gentrification overflow' (*New York Magazine*, March 12, 2001: 51). Overspill in Brooklyn has been intensified by the 1997 New York State Rent Regulation Reform Act, which introduced 'high-rent vacancy decontrol', meaning that any rent-stabilized apartment renting above $2,000 per month leaves the rent regulation system completely, enabling landlords to charge whatever they like to new tenants once these apartments become vacant. This has 'whittled away the stock of rent regulated apartments' (Hevesi 2002) in Manhattan, where the majority of these expensive apartments are located, and pushed young stockbrokers, publishers, and dot-com and new media entrepreneurs from Manhattan's 'Silicon Alley', and even young lawyers and doctors, out into more affordable, gentrifying neighborhoods in the outer boroughs of Brooklyn, Queens, and the Bronx (Phillips-Fein 2000: 29).

Lower Park Slope's current gentrification is quite a turnaround from its condition in the 1970s and 1980s, when three decades of disinvestment had culminated in serious dilapidation and abandonment of some of its housing stock, and the erosion of its economic and tax base—a neighborhood 'ravaged by decay', as one assessment put it (Lawson 1984: 248), with little political bargaining power to attract the kind of reinvestment it needed for its residents. Its housing stock, whilst attractive, was and remains not as magnificent as that further up the Slope, and thus none of it gained Landmark Preservation status, one of the catalysts of gentrification nearer to Prospect Park (see Chapter 1). Lower Park Slope was in every sense left behind by the 'success' of Upper Park Slope, and perhaps this is best expressed by the fact that 7th Avenue became a bustling commercial strip during this time, whilst 5th Avenue 'witnessed a proliferation of crime during the 1970s as a result of narcotic trafficking', where '[t]he dangers associated with this problem nearly vacated the retail stores and residents' (Merlis and Rosenzweig 1999: 13).

During New York's serious fiscal crisis of the 1970s, housing became a key issue, as abandonment and arson in many neighborhoods on an unprecedented level had caused the municipal government to take up ownership of block after block of buildings whose landlords could not meet the maintenance and/or tax payments. By the end of the decade, the municipal government had become the largest single landlord in New York, with over 40,000 apartments in receivership (Plunz 1990: 325). The response to the lack of city policy or even will to do anything about these crumbling neighborhoods aside from owning property in them has been documented as follows:

> As landlords abandoned their buildings, the City took ownership but failed miserably to keep the buildings up. Many were condemned, while others were effectively abandoned. All over the city, community organizations organized rent strikes, squatting and building takeovers, protests and sit-ins at city agencies, demanding that the City resolve the disastrous conditions in the enormously expanding stock of low-income housing coming into City ownership. The City responded by turning much of that housing over to community based organizations. (Lander 1997: 8)

It was in 1977, during this era of crisis, disinvestment, and neglect, that a nonprofit community group called the Fifth Avenue Committee (FAC) was founded in Lower Park Slope by local residents. 1977 perhaps represents the deepest trough of disinvestment in Lower Park Slope, a time when sustained red-lining and abandonment had resulted in over 200 vacant buildings and 159 vacant lots in the neighborhood, many city-owned (Slater 2004a), and a time when something had to be done to improve both the physical and social conditions of a place that was basically left to its own devices by a city administration with neither the money nor the will to take steps towards positive change. Unlike the community development corporations that were concerned almost exclusively with grassroots (re)development, the FAC was formed to act as convenors and advocates, organizers and sources of technical assistance, and packagers and developers—certainly ambitious considering the long-standing conflict of interests between organizing and development in community politics (Katznelson 1981), but such ambition was perhaps needed in the aftermath of New York's devastating 1970s fiscal retrenchment.

Funded since its inception by a mix of public and private sources, the initial activities of the FAC were somewhat pedestrian, involving the establishment of community gardens, sporadic renovations of neighborhood buildings and façade improvements to local businesses, lobbying for better sanitation services, and creating a neighborhood family center. These development processes gathered steam in the 1980s, particularly in the form of a 'sweat equity program' aimed at renovating the dilapidated housing stock, and the 'Park Slope Village' plan, which saw the construction of forty-four affordable three-family homes on a massive vacant block. Organization took the form of marches against harassment practices by landlords and against unscrupulous real estate tactics which led to tenant evictions, and employment programs were initiated to get youth off the streets and into work.

The most significant development advances since 1977 have been in housing provision. For more than two decades, the FAC has raised millions of dollars to build or rehabilitate over 600 housing units in over 100 buildings in the neighborhood and its environs, making it the largest provider of affordable housing in South Brooklyn. When considering the substantial impact of the FAC's development initiatives on the physical (and, to a lesser extent, social) improvements in the neighborhood since the 1970s, there arises a fairly obvious contradiction with their current organizing initiatives. As the neighborhood improved, it made gentrification a more likely scenario, because Lower Park Slope was no longer lying in such stark contrast to Upper Park Slope. While the conditions which led to overspill gentrification described earlier are the principal reasons behind the current gentrification of Lower Park Slope, they are not entirely sufficient for it to proceed. In an unfortunate yet not unrecognized irony, the FAC were, unwittingly, a major institutional force in establishing the preconditions for the gentrification of Lower Park Slope— yet today they are a major institution attempting to resist gentrification! As the FAC's former director of organizing wrote, '[A] disinvestment problem became an overinvestment and gentrification problem' (Dulchin 2003: 29). The more they improved the neighborhood for current residents, the more attractive it became to new residents frozen out of higher-end, gentrified neighborhoods by impossible sale and rental prices. With their arrival, the previously low rents in Lower Park Slope escalated, and existing residents who were supposed to be benefiting from the improvements undertaken by the FAC ended up being indirectly threatened by these improvements as landlords realized that after a barren spell of profitability, they could now cash in on the neighborhood.

The current mission of the Fifth Avenue Committee is

> to advance social and economic justice principally by developing and managing affordable housing, creating employment opportunities, organizing residents and workers, providing adult-centered education

opportunities, and combating displacement caused by gentrification. (Fifth Avenue Committee, 2007)

The threat of displacement in Lower Park Slope is compounded by the fact that the neighborhood contains many apartment buildings built before 1947 with fewer than six units, which are thus exempt from New York State's rent stabilization laws. In 1999, the FAC undertook a survey of how many small buildings had changed hands in the neighborhood between 1996 and 1999. They were concerned about the fact that a change in ownership in unregulated small buildings leads to significant increases in rents as new landlords seek to claim back on their mortgage and maintenance payments, and seek to profit from overspill gentrification by attracting wealthier tenants. They found that 21 percent of buildings had changed hands—a remarkable pace of turnover indicating booming real estate activity.

To combat the change from a trickle of tenant evictions into a flood, they devised a strategy in 1999 called a Displacement Free Zone (DFZ), where a territory was marked out in which the FAC claimed there would be 'no evictions' of low- and moderate-income tenants. Initially a thirty-six-block area, the zone was extended in 2002 north and south to cover the entire neighborhood, 108 square blocks, crossing the southern border of the neighborhood and into Sunset Park. The purpose of the DFZ is to preserve the ethnic and class diversity of the neighborhood, to keep its housing stock affordable and residents stable in their homes, and to respect the needs of its long-term (particularly ethnic minority) residents and senior citizens. It actively aims to discourage anyone from what they call 'profiteering at the expense of our community'—a reference to people buying a building and then evicting the long-term, low-rent-paying tenants either to attract new tenants who can afford much higher rents, or to claim the building back for themselves. The FAC considers the case of any tenant who meets the criteria set out in Figure 7.2, and relies on tenants to come forward, as they have no way of tracking large rent increases or incidents of tenants being served eviction notices. If they hear about a rent increase which threatens displacement, they will work with religious leaders to appeal to the landlord's 'conscience'. If this fails, and the case goes to court, they have the support of the local Legal Services to defend the tenant, who will prolong the case, making it more expensive for the landlord to proceed. If this fails, the FAC attempts to hold the landlord publicly accountable for his or her actions. This could take the form of demonstrating in front of the landlord's home or business, or generating media attention about the unfairness of the eviction—all intended to bring the landlord to a negotiating table and reach a compromise that allows the tenant to stay.

The great strength of the strategy is that it increases the visibility of displacement and draws marginalized community members into organizing, and extremely vocal and public resistance to displacement may discourage

- The tenant lives within the DFZ area
- The tenant lives in a small building that is not protected by rent stabilization
- The tenant is low-income
- The tenant is being evicted because the landlord wants to increase the rent dramatically

Priority is given to tenants in the following situations:

- The landlord has other housing and financial options, and is raising the rent simply to increase profits
- The landlord is an absentee owner
- The tenant is a long-time resident of the neighbourhood and/or senior citizen
- The tenant is facing a housing emergency and has no other housing options

**Figure 7.2** Criteria for Eligibility to Receive Assistance from Fifth Avenue Committee's Displacement Free Zone Campaign

landlords from buying houses in the neighborhood solely for investment purposes. On the other hand, the strategy could be accused of alienating owner-occupiers or incoming higher-income tenants who may be 'community minded', and also the FAC may be targeting the wrong people, when it is the statewide lack of rent stabilization permitting landlords to behave in the ways that they do which seems to be the most pressing problem. It is encouraging, however, to see the reduction in evictions achieved by this campaign:

> We looked at court-supplied eviction records from the year before the campaign began and the year after the campaign began and compared the area of the DFZ to a demographically similar area next to the DFZ. We found that while both areas experienced a decline in evictions, the DFZ area experienced a decline in evictions more than double that of the non-DFZ area. (Dulchin 2003: 31)

Difficulties in measuring displacement make it unclear precisely how much of this decline is due to activism, but as Dulchin says, '[S]ome part of the decrease had to do with the work of the DFZ' (p. 31).

The Fifth Avenue Committee learned a lot from this high-profile campaign, and offers advice for neighborhood organizers resisting gentrification (see Box 7.1). Perhaps the most important lesson of the FAC and its DFZ is that it is possible to fight the free market by insisting on the moral right to adequate and affordable housing, and that a community can defend against gentrification if it can get the message across that landlords will be met with a determined campaign of protest if they seek unreasonable profits at the expense of some community members.

*Case 2: Gentrification Dot-Com: Boom and Bust in San Francisco's Mission District*
(Note to readers: an excellent online discussion of gentrification in the Mission District [see Map 7.2], with a timeline, an analysis, and photography, has

| Box 7.1 |
|---|
| **The Fifth Avenue Committee's Advice On Resisting Gentrification** (Adapted from Dulchin 2003: 31–3) |
| 1) *Have fun with a purpose, and build community.* Demonstrations should not be angry, but rather carnival-themed, inviting onlookers to join in on the 'party with a purpose.'<br>2) *Tell stories.* Build a campaign around the individual cases of tenants whose stories personify the injustice of gentrification. This humanises the problem more than any real estate data ever could.<br>3) *Celebrate the community, take the moral high ground.* Do not use anti-landlord rhetoric, but rather pro-community rhetoric. A sense of community pride is less likely to alienate anyone who is vital to the struggle.<br>4) *Let the local leadership lead.* An organizing campaign cannot work unless it is in sync with the culture and values of the community.<br>5) *Recruit wholesale, not retail.* The best way to achieve widespread support is to tap into informal social networks of people who already know each other (through, for example, churches, schools, senior citizens organisations). |

been put together by local resident Tom Wetzel and can be found at http://www.uncanny.net/~wetzel/macchron.htm.)

> For decades San Francisco was considered a hotbed of political activism, artistic expression, and diversity. As rents and salaries have skyrocketed, many political activists, artists and people of color have been forced to leave the city. Similarly, as the cost of retail space continues to escalate local business people have been priced out of business and cannibalised by chain stores. Previously interesting neighbourhoods like Haight Ashbury, the Inner Sunset, and the Mission District are becoming bland reflections of corporatist culture. Sadly, the increased cost of living in San Francisco has meant the inability to support the rich diversity of protest activity, artistic development, and immigrant culture that once made the city famous. (Roschelle and Wright 2003: 164–165)

Reading this mournful commentary, one could be forgiven for assuming that gentrification has not been resisted in San Francisco in recent years. But as Roschelle and Wright note, there have been contestations, perhaps the best-known of which is the fight against gentrification in the Mission District. One of the more memorable moments of Francine Cavanaugh, A. Mark Liiv, and

## INNER MISSION DISTRICT
### San Francisco, California

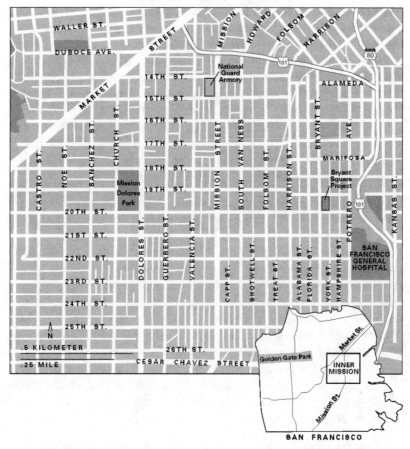

**Map 7.2** The Mission District, San Francisco

Adams Wood's stunning documentary *Boom! The Sound of Eviction*, a film about that fight, occurs when a local artist, Gordon Winiemko, frustrated at the displacement of artists from that neighborhood by incoming beneficiaries of the late 1990s dot-com boom, decides to reinvent himself as 'E. Victor'. Wearing a suit and carrying a briefcase, he issues eviction papers to startled gentrifiers at restaurants and bars in the Mission, to make the point that the consumption practices they are enjoying have come at too high a price for many of the people living in the neighborhood before their arrival. Here is how Winiemko described the local changes that led to the birth of E. Victor:

> It's hard not to notice ... when a new restaurant opens up seemingly every day, replacing a small grocery store or auto body shop ... when

snow white, picture-perfect Buffy and Ken come out to play at night, their shiny new luxury tanks lining the middle of the street ... when you can't walk ten feet without tripping over yet another "artist loft" development without any artists in it ... or when all your friends and the community organizations that support you are being evicted or can't afford to stay here anymore. In San Francisco these days, it seems like every third person has an eviction story. And it's particularly bad in the Mission district, for decades home to small, funky businesses of every stripe, nonprofits, Latino families, and artists. One day you wake up and realize that the city is being white-washed, its polyglot bohemia surgically replaced by a corporate, consumption-loving monoculture. One day you decide to do something about it. (http://cometmagazine. com/cometsite4/cometsite3/comet2/artstrikes.html)

This wonderfully vivid description of gentrification, however, needs an explanation. What happened in the Mission, how was gentrification contested, and with what results?

The Mission is named after Mission Dolores, a makeshift chapel and the first building in San Francisco, founded in 1776 by Father Palou, a Spanish priest (the building moved to its current location on 16th and Dolores Streets in 1783). It is interesting to note that displacement has a long history in this part of the world—the founding of Mission Dolores marked the first time a population was displaced from the Mission, for Costanoan Indians inhabited the area before being uprooted by Spanish colonialists (Alejandrino 2000: 16). With the Gold Rush and transportation advances, such as the horse-drawn streetcar and San Francisco's Municipal Railway (otherwise known as MUNI, which began carrying passengers in 1851), more residents and businesses came to the neighborhood, so that by 1890,

> most of the Inner Mission was built up, and the basic land-use pattern, still existing today, was established. Mixed-use buildings lined Mission, 16th, and Valencia Streets, and single- and multi-family residences for middle-class San Franciscans developed throughout the neighbour-hood, except in the district's northeast industrial corner. (Alejandrino 2000: 16)

Following the devastating 1906 earthquake and fire in San Francisco, the Mission received large numbers of suddenly homeless citizens from damaged parts of the city, and soon became home to many working-class Irish and Italian families. The 1950s and 1960s federal housing subsidies saw many of these families leave the Mission for the suburbs, to be replaced by an influx of immigrants from Central and South America. The Latino community grew very quickly, served by a fledgling network of immigrant services, community organizations, and local businesses—at precisely the same time as systematic disinvestment and discrimination accelerated. By the late 1960s, the Mission District experienced poverty, crime, and a deteriorating housing stock, making the threat of 'urban renewal' the central political issue of the time. Renewal was successfully resisted, however, by the Mission Coalition Organization, a coalition of community groups which 'established a legacy of grassroots organizing and community action' (Alejandrino 2000: 17) in the Mission (see also Castells 1983: 106–137). Today, the Mission remains the symbolic core of San Francisco's working-class Latino community (home to around one third of all Latinos in the city), and it is also a focal point of urban artistic expression; during the 1970s, a community of artists also began to develop there, attracted by cheap studio and warehouse space in the neighborhood's northeast section.

The 1990s saw another group of settlers—gentrifiers—arriving in the Mission, leading to huge local conflicts and tensions. A booming regional economy anchored around the high-tech industries in Silicon Valley to the south of the city began to affect San Francisco's housing market dramatically. Rebecca Solnit (2000) captures these changes as follows:

> [G]entrification is just the fin above the water. Below is the rest of the shark: a new American economy in which most of us will be poorer, a few will be far richer, and everything will be faster, more homogenous and more controlled or controllable. The technology boom and the accompanying housing crisis have fast-forwarded San Francisco into the newest version of the American future. (p. 14)

For Solnit and many low- to moderate-income tenants in the city—particularly in the Mission—this future is not a pretty sight. Employment growth (half a million jobs were created in San Francisco's Bay Area from 1995 to 2000) massively outstripped housing production in the city—only one housing unit was created for every 3.14 jobs from 1990 to 2000 (Alejandrino 2000: 14). An informative report by the city's Urban Habitat Program (2000) explained the consequences:

> The growing gap between low wage and high wage workers and the scarcity of housing, especially affordable housing for low income households, is resulting in the displacement of low income people by middle and high income households in historically urban communities of color. (p. iii)

One of these communities was the Mission. Its relatively affordable housing became irresistible to young middle-class professionals (many of whom were profiting from the 'dot-com' explosion of the late 1990s) attracted by the area's unique cultural identity, transit access, proximity to downtown, and increasingly hip nightlife scene. Trendy restaurants, bars, and clubs began to price out local serving businesses and the nonprofit organizations supporting the neighborhood's immigrant population. On Valencia Street, a major artery of the Mission, over 50 percent of the businesses there in 1990 had vanished by 1998, and neighborhood commercial rents jumped by 42 percent in just two years (1997–1999; Solnit 2000: 62). Many longtime Latino tenants were evicted as new housing developments raised property values, and as landlords looked to capitalize on the growing popularity of the Mission by raising rents.

Between 1997 and 1999, the average rent of a two-bed unit in the Mission increased by 26 percent, 10 percent more than across the city as a whole (Alejandrino 2000: 21). Furthermore, a large number of recent immigrants were renters, and less familiar with tenant rights due to language or other cultural barriers, making quick evictions easier to accomplish. Also in this short time period, the Mission experienced over 16 percent of San Francisco's 'owner move-in evictions', which, until 1998, allowed building owners to evict tenants so long as they resided in the building for twelve months after the eviction, after which they could return it to the market and escape rent control (after 1998, that time period was extended to thirty-six months). Together with a massive increase in Ellis Act evictions, a California state law which allows property owners to remove their property from the rental market and evict all the tenants (so long as paltry sums of money are given to each evictee—$4,500 for low-income persons, and $3,000 to elderly or disabled persons), the Mission experienced an epidemic of evictions in the late 1990s.

Another major contributor to 1990s gentrification in the Mission was the mushrooming of 'live–work' loft developments in the more industrial northeast corner of the neighborhood. Back in 1988, city artists lobbied successfully for a municipal 'live–work' ordinance to legalize the conversion of industrial space into live-in studios. Two key features of this ordinance were exemption from affordable housing quotas (as live–work developments are not technically 'housing', they are released from the citywide requirement that 10 percent of the units within housing developments must be affordable), and a lower rate of contribution to school taxes. At the time, artists did not know how this ordinance was creating a bonanza for developers, led by the Residential Builders Association, that would eventually lead to their eviction from their live–work studios, not to mention the eviction of their neighbors in the Mission. Developers marketed the live–work lifestyle to young urban home buyers, and the 1990s saw construction of live–work developments in vacant lots, but particularly prolific conversion of existing buildings—housing small businesses, low-income tenants, and/or artists—into a high-end form of live–work:

> Live/work spaces have become infamous as cheaply built condominiums at sky-high prices almost no artist can afford. From near downtown to the city's poorest southern reaches, these angular modernist structures with glaring walls of glass pop up between industrial buildings, old Victorians and other older buildings, directly displacing numerous

small businesses. … Several hundred jobs already lost can be traced directly to the replacement of work-places by live/work condos; many other small businesses have been forced to relocate or close because the new neighbors just wanted their neighbourhood to *look* industrial, not *be* industrial. (Solnit 2000: 103)

Particularly upsetting for many Mission residents was the fact that live–work developments were increasingly and illegally inhabited by dot-com businesses looking for affordable commercial space, at the expense of vital local businesses serving a well-established community. In sum, the Mission in the 1990s was characterized by frighteningly rapid commercial and residential gentrification, with a flood of evictions and displacement of small businesses, artists, and pre-dominantly Latino low-income tenants. In the latter part of that decade, local people against these changes decided to get together and fight both the developers and the legislation that was proving propitious for gentrification.

Initial efforts by a newly formed Coalition for Jobs, Arts and Housing (CJAH) were focused on getting the city's Board of Supervisors to close loopholes in the live–work ordinance, thus preventing further development. In August 1999, CJAH held a No More Lofts! rally at city hall to back these efforts, but they were eventually thwarted by the prodeveloper bias of the majority of supervisors and the intimidation tactics of the Residential Builders Association (Wetzel 2001). A more direct and angry form of protest came in the form of the Mission Yuppie Eradication Project (MYEP) founded and led by local activist Kevin Keating. MYEP put up a series of six posters in the Mission (which can be viewed at http://www.infoshop.org/myep/cw_posters.html) advocating, among other things, the vandalism of 'yuppie cars', squatting in newly built loft units, and 'attacking and destroying' various 'yuppie bars and restaurants in the Mission'. When Keating was arrested for 'late night postering', a number of local people turned out in support of him and the anti-gentrification message he was trumpeting, even if many disagreed with the threatening tactics. While Keating himself maintained that it was all a publicity stunt intended to raise awareness of gentrification, the influence of MYEP may have led to the 1999 torching of two live–work buildings under construction (Wetzel 2001), and more broadly to the aggressive 'dot-commie' rhetoric pervading the neighborhood at that time. But as Wetzel argued, this tag, and that of 'yuppie', 'obscures distinctions of income and power. The people who simply work in the industry weren't calling the shots. The venture capitalists, dot-com CEOs, office developers, landlords of commercial buildings and top city leaders were making the relevant decisions' (2001: 52).

It was those decision makers who became subject to a sustained challenge by anti-gentrification activists in 2000, following the emergence of two large development projects in the Mission. The first was the Bryant Square project— 160,000 square feet of multimedia and high-tech office space in a retrofitted factory building (evicting a sweater factory that employed thirty people, mostly Mission residents), and the demolition of an artist loft structure for a five-story office monolith. Nearly fifty artists (animators, filmmakers, and photographers) were evicted to make way for this project. The second was the transformation of an empty former National Guard Armory into 300,000 square feet of dot-com office space. Both these projects provoked a stern reaction from all sections of the Mission community. Staff from local Mission nonprofits, small business owners, artists, and other activists came together to form the Mission Anti-Displacement Coalition (MAC) to fight these two projects. Interestingly, this is a rare case of artists in a gentrifying neighborhood uniting with working-class families and tenants to protest against gentrification.

The largest community meeting in two decades, organized by the MAC, took place in June 2000, where the head of San Francisco's planning department and three of the planning commissioners faced an angry crowd of over 500 people chanting 'moratorium' in response to the MAC demand for an immediate ban on live–work and office development in the Mission. This was followed a few weeks later by a *caminata* (street protest) of over 1,000 people walking 'to defend the right to live in the Mission', and then by roughly 2,000 people attending an 'eviction party' for a dance group unable to afford their rehearsal space (Wetzel 2001: 53–54). These anti-displacement protests resulted in a victory when the developer proposing the Armory office space pulled out, citing community pressure and conflict as the key reasons. Yet in the face of the resilience of prodevelopment Mayor Willie Brown, activists realized that more work had to be done and that they had to adopt legislative as much as direct, vocal tactics. The CJAH in particular, led by Debra Walker, a local artist, was instrumental in the writing of a citizens' initiative, Proposition L, which would

1. end the live–work loophole by making lofts subject to the same rules as other housing construction,
2. ban office projects larger than 6,000 square feet in the Mission, and
3. ensure all office developers provide some below-market-rate space for nonprofits.

Prop. L was effectively the culmination of all the anti-displacement efforts in the Mission that had taken place in the previous two years. Thirty thousand signatures were gathered in two weeks to ensure that Prop. L had a place on the local elections ballot. Not surprisingly, developers and their political allies poured millions of dollars into campaigns against Prop. L, distributing propaganda claiming that it was harmful to 'economic development'. The proposition was narrowly defeated in November 2000, but a partial victory was gained the following month in the election to powerful Board of Supervisors positions of seven out of eight pro–Prop. L candidates in the running—a major shift to the left in city politics, which immediately had the effect of reforming a prodevelopment planning department and implementing some Prop. L measures on a temporary basis. The intense activism that sprouted from the context of endemic evictions in the Mission led to a change in politics at a citywide level—an extraordinary achievement. Voters realized that prodevelopment and proeconomic growth interests were a threat to the cultural diversity, the progressive countercultural activism, and the character of historic inner-urban neighborhoods which have for generations been a hallmark of San Francisco's identity.

In 2001 the dot-com industry went bust as quickly as it had boomed, and the gentrification pressures in the Mission began to dissipate as commercial rents and housing prices began to stabilize (see Graham and Guy 2002). Vacant storefronts now dot some of the Mission's main retail corridors, and vacancy rates are rising—yet it would be unwise to claim that San Francisco's housing market has crashed. It is still too early to assess the long-term effects of the dot-com boom, but if anything, activists in San Francisco and elsewhere have learned that gentrification and displacement can be challenged, which is perhaps the most important long-term effect of all.

*Case 3: 'Raising Shit': The Downtown Eastside, Vancouver, Canada*

But in whose image is space created?

David Harvey (1973)

raise shit
against the kind of "urban cleansing"
gentrification unleashes…

to raise shit is to actively resist
and we resist with our presence…

we resist
person by person
square foot by square foot
room by room
building by building
block by block

Bud Osborn (1998: 287-288)

Vancouver has a reputation for liveability, beauty, and tranquility—a reputation that is occasionally warranted (depending on one's ability to consume it), but mostly one constructed by 'residents, the media, real estate developers, and government officials' (Lees and Demeritt 1998: 339). In tandem with tourist board employees, these groups spend much of their time selling Vancouver as some sort of paradise on the Pacific—the very essence of multicultural harmony in a veritable smorgasbord of mountains, towering fir trees, and orca-filled oceans and inlets, where fresh salmon cooks on sidewalk grills in front of latte-fueled outdoor-types wearing wraparound shades, sitting atop gleaming new mountain bikes, all speaking passionately about environmental issues whilst eagerly anticipating the 2010 Winter Olympics (and the regular rainfall in the city is all part of the fun). Just to the east of downtown, however, and just south of the ultra-touristy Gastown district, where Cowichan sweaters, moose antlers, and maple syrup are sold in shops below swanky loft apartments, is a neighborhood which few city boosters would like visitors to experience—the Downtown Eastside (see Map 7.3). Vancouver as a bastion of liberal tolerance and cycle-path hedonism is suddenly disrupted in a place where 'one hundred years of struggle' (Hasson and Ley 1994) have left a landscape of agony and addiction, for which the frequent remedial prescription is gentrification in the guise of 'revitalization'. As we write, the fight over the Downtown Eastside's future is far from over, but what has happened so far, and especially in recent years, serves as an excellent example of what DeFilippis (2004) and Slater (2006) have called the 'false choice' facing low-income communities of either long-term disinvestment and neglect or gentrification and displacement. Realizing that this choice is a false one is absolutely crucial if a more progressive and socially just form of urban development is to be pursued in a place which has been under severe gentrification pressures for over two decades.

As the Downtown Eastside is one of the poorest neighborhoods in Canada, and certain sections of it are such a sudden jolt to the senses and so glaringly at odds with much of the rest of Vancouver, it is easy to treat it as a place independent from its wider urban context or, worse, as a place that has developed separately because of the 'self-destructive' behavior of the people living there. But as numerous scholars have noted (Sommers 1998; Shier 2003; Sommers and Blomley 2003; Blomley 2004), this division is artificial, and the struggles over the Downtown Eastside are a direct consequence of generations of powerful material and representational practices that have constructed this part of Vancouver as a 'foreign land', when in fact it is a local expression of the uneven geographical development that results from the commodification of housing under capitalism (Harvey 2006b). This is a place with a complex history of settlement and dispossession, of ruin and renovation, where conflicting claims to the ownership of land and property jostle with shifting public policy priorities. Such complexity cannot be unveiled in this book, but a very condensed history is important if we are to understand the struggle taking place there today.

Just as the early years of San Francisco's Mission District were characterized by displacement and upheaval, so indeed were the early years of an urbanizing Downtown Eastside. The large fishing, hunting, and gathering First Nations population which originally settled this part of Canada were from the 1870s onwards displaced by waves of European and East Asian (especially Chinese and Japanese) migration in an episode of colonial dispossession beyond the scope of this book—here, it is important to realize that 'such struggles cast

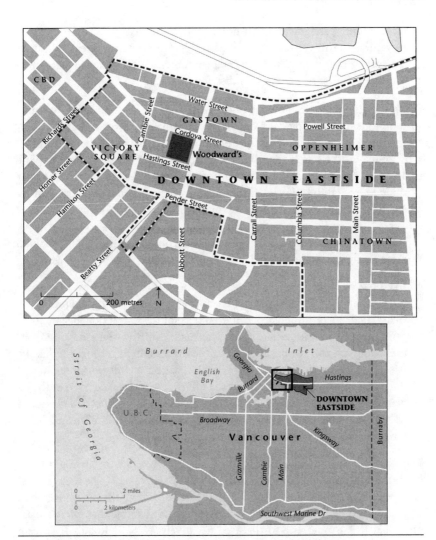

**Map 7.3** The Downtown Eastside, Vancouver

complicated shadows over contemporary contests over property and land'
(Blomley 2004: 34). In the early years of the twentieth century, the area became
known as the East Side, and was promptly vacated by the middle class and
property-owning working class moving outwards in search of more space, leav-
ing it to immigrants, the unemployed poor, and seasonal workers (such as loggers, miners, and railroad and construction laborers) who found cheap lodging
housing in the area. Sommers (1998) describes the landscape in detail:

> The condition of the housing that they occupied, some of the earli-
> est built in the city, and its cheek-by-jowl proximity to the complex of

lumber mills, freight and fish docks and canneries, rail yards, grain elevators, clothing sweatshops, and warehouses extending east along the waterfront from downtown helped constitute the place as part of Vancouver's first so-called slum district. (p. 292)

Sommers also discusses at length how this was a place dominated by single men, not just demographically but also culturally—pre–World War II downtown Vancouver became a 'masculine space' where red-light districts, bootlegging joints, brothels, and gambling establishments served a transient, mobile male population perceived by the authorities as a threat to the social order of the city, partaking in a less 'proper' form of manhood than the family-oriented, stable, and self-supporting form common to bourgeois (suburban) circles.

Following World War II, this part of Vancouver and the male seasonal workers living in it were hit hard by wider economic changes:

[A] slow decline began in the neighbourhood as its central role in warehousing, transportation, and a host of manufacturing operations that relied on or supported hinterland resource extraction began to dim. Over the same period, there was also a shift in the structure of the labour market. Consolidation in the ownership of resource industries, on one hand, and increasing unionization of the workforce, on the other, reduced the demand for the migrant workers who lived in the neighbourhoods around the downtown waterfront. At the same time, waterfront industries began to relocate to cheaper land far from the downtown core. (Sommers and Blomley 2003: 31)

The numerous single-room occupancy hotels (SROs) in the neighborhood became the permanent homes to many unemployed, older single men, as well as the discharged psychiatric patients of the deinstitutionalization movement, who had few alternative housing options. It was at this time that middle-class observers began referring to the area negatively as 'Skid Road'. This term emerged from late nineteenth-century Seattle (Morgan 1981; Allen 1993) to describe the greased corduroy tracks of saplings over which logs were skidded towards the water to be floated to sawmills. 'Skid Road' later came to refer to the area of a town where out-of-work loggers congregated in bars, hotels, and bordellos; arrival there signified that one was sliding downwards in society, or 'going on the skids.' During the Depression, the phrase expanded to denote the rundown section of any city in North America where homeless and unemployed people clustered (in many cities, this has changed to a generic 'skid row'). Journalists in the early 1950s described the East Side of Vancouver as 'Skid Road' in order to feed the wider perception that this was a neighborhood 'no longer identified through work, but rather in terms of the morally dubious nature of other activities that took place in the area' (Sommers and Blomley

2003: 32–33). Sommers (1998) has shown to whom blame was attributed for the deteriorating condition of the area:

> Since the early 1950s, when Vancouver's skid road was "discovered" and labelled a "scar" on the city's landscape, the presence of large numbers of single men and their problematic conduct had been treated as primary causal factors in the deterioration of the built environment. ...
> [T]he skid road's inhabitants were considered to be the *cause* of urban blight and decay. The skid road was distinguished precisely by its lack of both families and the respectability that somehow accompanied them. (p. 296)

These pathological constructions added fuel to the fire of urban renewal plans in the 1960s, which were gathering serious momentum until it was pointed out by academics and activists that urban renewal and displacement via freeway construction would simply recreate another Skid Road elsewhere, and until the countercultural uprising in Canada in the late 1960s (which we described in detail in Chapters 3 and 6), where modernist urban planning came under sustained and ultimately successful opposition (even today, there are no freeways in Vancouver).

An outcome of the reform-era social movement in Canada, and particularly of its broader background of an expanding welfare state, was the outcropping of neighborhood organizations representing community demands for services and political representation (Hasson and Ley 1994). One such organization, the Downtown Eastside Residents Association (DERA), formed in 1973 to insist that this area be recognized as a community, and one that was not isolated from but tied together with the history of the Vancouver waterfront. DERA fought hard to challenge the lack of local services, the inadequate housing provision, and particularly the negligent and dismissive attitude of planners, politicians, businesses, and the media towards local residents. Skid Road became the 'Downtown Eastside', and people 'who were once seen as derelicts and deviants were now being recognized as former loggers, miners, seamen, railroad workers, waitresses, cooks, longshoremen, mill workers, and others associated with the economic expansion of the west' (Sommers and Blomley 2003: 39). Yet this major progress for the Downtown Eastside was at the same time challenged by the 'historic preservation' of the Old Granville Townsite, which was renamed 'Gastown' in a property development strategy masked as a model vision of democratic public space, setting off the first set of gentrification pressures in the area. Four hundred SRO rooms were lost between 1968 and 1975, displacing large numbers of low-income residents (p. 41).

A drive east along Hastings Street from downtown Vancouver will quickly reveal a very wide rent gap (see Chapter 2), where decades of disinvestment have depressed land values in the area. The fact that this rent gap has not yet been comprehensively closed would seem to be a major empirical challenge to

Neil Smith's theorizations—but because of sustained resistance, gentrification there remains a major threat, rather than something that is actually marching along this important thoroughfare. The first attempt to exploit this rent gap was in the early 1980s, when Vancouver got ready for the 1986 World's Fair (EXPO '86). The anticipated demand for hotel rooms encouraged a number of SRO hotel owners to upgrade their properties and convert them from residential to tourist use. Several hundred long-term residents were evicted and displaced, many of whom were elderly, mentally ill, and in poor health—approximately 2,000 low-income housing units were lost in the process (Olds 1989). Blomley (2004) has pointed out that this horrendous episode is now seen as a 'political touchstone' in the Downtown Eastside, forming a convincing moral critique both of capitalist property relations and of Vancouver's integration into global capitalist networks (p. 51). When development pressures intensify, local activists draw on this event to highlight the importance of retaining affordable housing, and also the community's 'moral right not only to continue as an entity, but to remain *in situ*' (p. 52). From the 1990s onwards, there has been strong activism along these lines as gentrification and displacement loom ever larger:

> In the past few years, a number of megaprojects on the periphery of the area … combined with more recent incursions by loft developers into the neighbourhood have occurred. Social polarization has increased. Combined with residential gentrification in Strathcona, in the east, the effect is to create a property frontier that encircles the area. Real estate in the most depressed areas of the neighbourhood is cheap. (p. 35)

Lying in one of these most depressed areas is a building which N. Smith and Derksen (2003) believe could be, symbolically and materially, the 'Tompkins Square Park of Vancouver' (p. 87); although Lees (1999) prefers to think of it as the 'Christodora House' of Vancouver (the Christodora House, converted into condominiums, in the Lower East Side, was targeted by anti-gentrification activists as a symbol of gentrification in that neighborhood). This is the Woodward's building on the north side of Hastings Street—the former home of the Woodward's department store, which closed in 1993 after serving the community for almost a century (see Plate 7.2). Nobody did much about it for two years until local activists decided to counter claims that the presence of poor people was responsible for its abandonment by cleaning the sidewalks and painting community ownership slogans on the vacant storefront. These actions intensified after it was revealed that a local developer, Kassam Aghtai, had submitted an application that same year (1995) to turn Woodward's into 350 condominium units. These proposals were met with support from local speculators, merchants, and loft dwellers, and with anger and horror from activists representing the neighborhood's low-income population, who quickly mobilized into an organized campaign of anti-gentrification flier

**Plate 7.2** Woodward's Department Store, Vancouver

The boarded-up Woodward's, awaiting redevelopment or, more correctly, gentrification. Most of this structure has been demolished to make way for the construction of new condo towers, but a small corner of the facade of the old building in the far right will be integrated into the new design. The pre-sale marketing campaign launched in early 2006 seemed to be written as the latest text-book illustration of Neil Smith's rent gap and new urban frontier. A lavish two-page color spread in the local Georgia Straight newspaper emphasized investment: 'The smart money gets in early. Vancouver can only grow in one direction — East. Invest in Woodward's District, downtown's most extraordinary new address. In the tradition of fine universities like NYU, Woodward's offers a collection of modern living environments, connected to the city and Simon Fraser University. This is true urban living at the centre of a cutting edge, creative community'. The development's Web site (http://www.woodwardsdistrict.com) is even more revealing, as it reassures local residents that rent gaps are closing fast as global-city gentrification intensifies: 'If you've lived in Vancouver all your life you may think of Woodward's as edgy. But if you moved to Vancouver in the last 10 to 15 years, or have resided in any other major city in the world like New York or London, you will recognize the incredible potential. This is an emerging area, not a sanitized environment. Neighbourhoods like this are rare and offer an authentic mix of cutting-edge culture, heritage and character. That's why the intelligent buyer will get in early. This is the future. This is your neighbourhood. BE BOLD OR MOVE TO SUBURBIA.'
*Source:* Photograph by Elvin Wyly.

distribution (see Lees [1999] on how critical geographers became involved). So great was the pressure on Aghtai that he was forced to rework his proposal into a mixed-income development in tandem with both provincial and city administrations. But in April 1997, he pulled out altogether, saying that everything had become 'too bureaucratic' (cited in Blomley 2004: 41), and went back to his original condominium plan, which, astonishingly, was approved by the City of Vancouver. The inevitable protests that did follow were intense and were organized around the theme of community ownership—activists painted boarded-up windows with stencilled graffiti saying 'give it back', '100% ours', 'community property' and 'our community, our building'. In addition, protestors attempted to encircle the building with a human chain and surveyor's tape. This sustained opposition to gentrification was successful, as the building was taken from the hands of the developer by the outgoing provincial government.

In 2001, the newly elected (neoliberal) provincial government was less sympathetic to community activists' concerns, again showing interest in private bids for the building. The anti-gentrification response the following year (September 2002) came in the form of a squat of the building, until squatters were evicted by the police yet permitted to camp outside the building. This encampment became a high-profile embarrassment to the city (at the time of its 2010 Winter Olympics bid), and was only disbanded when protestors (all of them homeless, having been evicted from SRO hotels) were offered alternative accommodation (in December 2002) by the city government. In March 2003, the right-wing provincial government sold the building to the left-of-center city government—a huge victory for the protestors. The city immediately initiated a 'public consultation process' over the future of the building, and a summary of the responses can be viewed at http://www.city.vancouver.bc.ca/ corpsvcs/realestate/woodwards/ideas.htm. These responses are organized into several themes—residential, health, recreation, cultural, commercial and retail, employment, social, institutional, and general design—reflecting the policy wish to create a mixed-use development. The city invited proposals for a development along such lines, and in September 2004 chose Westbank Projects/Peterson Investment Group as the developer. The project is a mix of up to 536 market and 200 nonmarket housing units (a combination of both family and singles units). Also included are shops and services, community nonprofit space, public green space, a day care, and a postsecondary education facility.

Situating this winning proposal in the context of recent research into gentrification and social mixing, we can see that the resistance to exclusive development, however impressive the achievement, is something of a partial victory. It is partial because Woodward's is now a socially mixed development—and we have seen how such social mixing can amount to gentrification in the previous chapter. Furthermore, there are considerably more market than nonmarket units in the development, in a neighborhood which continues to lose SRO housing to gentrification (N. Smith and Derksen 2003), and the language of the entire project pivots around 'revitalization', which, as David Ley (1996) has pointed out, is 'objectionable, implying a sense of moral superiority in the process of residential succession, and imparting a mantle of less vitality on previous land uses and users' (pp. 33–34). These are worrying words when considering that one of the guiding principles of Woodward's is that it will be 'an urban revitalization catalyst'. It comes as no surprise to learn that on April 22, 2006, when the residential market units in the Woodward's development went on sale, all 536 units were sold by April 23, representing over $200 million in sales.

The Downtown Eastside is a complex place confronting a complex situation, where in the words of Heather Smith (2003), '[I]ntra-neighbourhood polarisation is identified by the simultaneous occurrence of upgrading *and* downgrading' (p. 506). Some further explanation explains the consequences:

> The designation of certain portions of the Downtown Eastside as official heritage or revitalization areas promotes gentrification in precisely the same neighbourhood spaces where the demand for assisted housing and services is most intense, and in some cases where drug and associated criminal activity continue to entrench. The government's oversight of other neighbourhood spaces facilitates deepening commercial and residential decline immediately adjacent to or enmeshed with gentrification. Further compounding polarisation in the neighbourhood has been the delay in protecting, both from deterioration and revitalisation, the area's SRO stock—one of the most important sources of truly affordable housing left in the city. (p. 506)

With these words, we can conclude that it would be naïve to assume that 'social mixing' will actually take place in a tortured neighborhood with such strong local polarization. Life courses, life chances, and lifestyles within this neighborhood, and especially within the new Woodward's, could not be more different; is it sensible even to suggest that the occupiers of the 536 market units will 'socially mix' with the occupiers of the 200 nonmarket units? The project is, of course, undoubtedly a better scenario than entirely exclusive market units, but if we consider things in terms of strength in numbers, over two times as many market units than nonmarket units does not bode well for those who have for years battled for a more equitable form of development than gentrification.

## What Property Ought to Be

Commenting on the conflict over the Woodward's building, Nick Blomley (2004) wrote these powerful words:

> [W]hen activists encircle the Woodward's building and say "it's ours" they do more than complicate the question of what property *is*. … [T]hey raise moral questions of what property *ought* to be. By saying "it's ours", activists challenge the legitimacy of other claimants, worry about the ethical consequences of those private claims, and imply that a collective

claim has an inherent value. The redevelopment of the inner city, here and elsewhere, concerns contending moral visions. (p. 74)

The three case studies described above all raise these moral questions of what property ought to be, and demonstrate that private development geared to the interests of certain privileged groups can be challenged, with varying degrees of success. They also demonstrate that property is much more than a financial asset—it is a home, the place we belong to and the place which belongs to us, and therefore has a critically important use value which far outweighs its exchange (market) value. As Squires (1992) has pointed out, anti-gentrification activists wish for housing to be 'treated as a public need and entitlement rather than as a private good to be obtained by the market' (p. 30). They put under a moral spotlight those for whom a building's exchange value is irrelevant and its commodification harmful, thus increasing awareness that there is more to housing than its sale price, and that low-income people have what Hartman (1984) famously called 'the right to stay put'.

Twenty years ago, in an essay entitled 'Towards the Decommodification of Housing', Achtenberg and Marcuse (1986) pointed out the need for

a program that can alter the terms of existing public debate on housing, that challenges the commodity nature of housing and its role in our economic and social system, and demonstrates how people's legitimate housing needs can be met through an alternative approach. (p. 475)

That same year, N. Smith and Williams (1986) concluded their seminal edited collection on gentrification with these words:

In the long run, the only defence against gentrification is the "decommodification" of housing. ... Decent housing and decent neighbourhoods ought to be a right, not a privilege. That of course is unlikely to be achieved through a series of reforms; rather, it will take a political restructuring even more dramatic than the social and geographical restructuring we now see. (p. 222)

The obstacles to the Marxist-inspired decommodification of housing are enormous, for such an approach 'clearly contradicts the strong ideological beliefs that have shaped public policy generally and housing policy in particular' (Squires 1992: 30) throughout the history of capitalist urbanization. Furthermore, the deepening neoliberalization that underpins the policy approach to urban neighborhoods across the entire planet (Brenner and Theodore 2002) hardly represents an about-turn in the attitude towards the rights of low-income and working-class people to remain in the places they call home.

In response to the march of global capital, and as people discover that commodified property markets are exclusive and displacing, and rent controls far from permanent, low-income communities have recently attempted to gain more control over, and ownership of, housing. These issues have recently been explored by James DeFilippis (2004) in his work on limited equity housing cooperatives (LEHCs), community land trusts (CLTs), and mutual housing associations (MHAs) in the United States. This passage explains what led to these forms of collective housing ownership:

> [R]einvestment needs to be understood through the lens of questions such as: What kind of investment? For whom? Controlled by whom? These processes have left residents of low-income neighborhoods in a situation where, since they exert little control over either investment capital or their homes, they are facing the "choices" of either contin- ued disinvestment and decline in the quality of the homes they live in, or reinvestment that results in their displacement. The importance of gentrification, therefore, is that it clearly demonstrates that low-income people, and the neighborhoods they live in, suffer not from a lack of capi- tal but from a lack of power and control over even the most basic compo- nents of life—that is, the places called home. (DeFilippis 2004: 89)

Briefly condensed from DeFilippis's (2004) work (see pp. 89–111), LEHCs are similar to other housing co-ops in North America in that the corporation owns and controls the housing development and residents are shareholders of that corporation, but different in that the price of the owners' shares is not determined by the wider real estate market, but by a set formula determined by the particular co-op's bylaws. This means that the resale price of the shares is restricted and the household's equity thus limited, ensuring that the co-op's housing units remain permanently affordable. Examples of this can be found in the Lower East Side of New York City, where long-term squatters eventually gained control of their squats and turned them into viable afford- able housing through the LEHC route. CLTs are another form of preserving affordable housing—a community organization owns and manages the land, while the residents own only the housing units located on the land. There are strict limitations on housing costs and the resale price, and people can only collect on investments they make in the units—any rise in housing value is socially created and not something that belongs to any individual. Examples are the CLT described by DeFilippis in Burlington, Vermont, and famously in the context of resisting real estate speculation and gentrification, the Dudley Street Neighborhood Initiative in Roxbury, Boston (http://www.dsni.org). MHAs are somewhat similar to LEHCs, but residents do not own shares in their cooperative—the housing is entirely free from the market, and a mix- ture of collective and individual ownership is within the hands of the MHA. Residents both rent their units from and constitute the MHA, and commu- nity and resident participation is written into the governance of each asso- ciation. Residents undertake mandatory maintenance work and pay monthly housing charges to the MHA, either fixed with periodic adjustments to keep pace with inflation, or paid as a percentage of the residents' income (less than 30 percent, which is substantially lower than in many gentrifying neighbor-hoods!). The example provided by DeFilippis is from Stamford, Connecticut, but there are at least thirty MHAs in the United States, and furthermore these are expansionist organizations, seeking to take more and more housing out of the private market.

What can we make of these collective ownership forms in the context of resistance to gentrification? This is obviously not militant resistance, but rather a 'soft' form of organizing in concert with Hackworth and Smith's (2001) claims that the most angry and disruptive forms of protest against gen-trification and displacement have all but disappeared. DeFilippis's verdict is mixed—they have unquestionably improved the lives of people living within them and given them a degree of control over their housing that otherwise would not be possible, but at the same time this control is perhaps more lim-ited than each MHA and CLT would imply; increasing property costs beyond the portfolio of each collective makes it harder to acquire more property; and the meanings of housing, property, and ownership in each collective are still the dominant, hegemonic, capitalist ones (p. 110), hardly disrupting the prevailing orthodoxy on profiting from property. But we include discussion of them here because currently these collective forms of ownership, given the decline of militant opposition to gentrification, are perhaps the best possi-bilities we have for something other then gentrification—something other than the false choice of disinvestment or displacement. There is also much to learn from the efforts of community organizations such as, inter alia, the Logan Square Neighborhood Association in Chicago, who have spent much of the last decade fighting for affordable housing quotas during a tidal wave of gentrification and luxury condo development in Uptown Chicago (Aardema and Knoy 2004), and also the Pilsen Alliance in the lower West Side of the same city, which has achieved some success in protecting the neighborhood's low-income Mexican American population from both residential and indus-trial displacement brought about by gentrification (Wilson, Wouters, and Grammenos 2004; Curran 2006).

Perhaps the most important lesson of all coming from numerous attempts to resist gentrification is that if you can't decommodify housing, then at the very least, you can defend it in many ways. Despite the many protestations to the contrary that we have discussed in this book, we feel that gentrifica-tion cannot be considered a process that is to be managed, harnessed, or twisted into a positive form of urban development. The difficulty in measur-ing displacement and finding conclusive evidence that it has been widespread does not mean we should deny its existence; and furthermore, displacement doesn't have to occur for affordable housing to be permanently removed by gentrification. Cities are at their least healthy, least diverse, and least interesting when they become bourgeois playgrounds, as Iain Borden (2003) has shown in a scathing critique of the gentrification agenda of Lord Richard Rogers, whose influence on the 'renaissance' of UK cities we discussed in the Preface:

> [Rogers's city] is the city of mocha, big Sunday papers, designer lamps, fresh pasta, and tactile fabrics. It is not, however, the city of all the disparate activities that people do in cities. It is not the city of sex, shouting, loud music, running, pure contemplation, demonstrations, subterranean subterfuges. It is not the city of intensity, of bloody-minded determination, of getting out-of-hand; nor is it the city of cab ranks, boot sales, railway clubs or tatty markets; nor is it the city of monkish seclusion, crystal-clear intellectualism or lonely artistic endeavour. (p. 114)

As Borden points out, what may be Rogers's vision of the city is not one shared by everyone, and as we have asked in this book, at what price does Rogers's city appear? The creation of 'cities for the few' results in loss of place for the many (Amin, Massey, and Thrift 2000). We leave the last words to a tireless social justice advocate to sum up the spirit in which we have written this book:

> [T]o deprive people of their territory, their community or their home, would seem at first sight to be a heinous act of injustice. It would be like taking away any other source of basic need-satisfaction, on which people depend absolutely. … But this experience is not simply deprivation: there is a literal necessity to be re-placed. People who have lost their place, for one reason and another, must be provided with or find another. There is no question about it. People need it. They just do. (D. M. Smith 1994: 152)

## Summary

In this chapter we have peered toward the future of gentrification, looking at its future magnitude and relevance. The chapter describes the empirical-extrapolation and theoretical projection that researchers have used to inform questions about the future of cities. We reviewed the discursive nature of gentrification and the societal conversations and confrontations that continue to swirl around the meaning of the term, particularly in media accounts. But the main focus of the chapter illustrated the difficulties and the possibilities that face contemporary movements in resisting gentrification, protecting against displacement, and encouraging a more socially just form of neighborhood change not geared to the interests of those who benefit financially from such changes. The chapter presented a series of case studies of recent struggles over gentrification, examining the variety of strategies and tactics

276 • Gentrification

adopted, including what was achieved and what lessons have been learned. The case studies highlighted the ways in which the history of different places affects current rounds of gentrification, and some of the commonalities between legal strategies, shaming tactics, popular protest, and their real, though partial, victories in resisting gentrification. Finally, the chapter turned to other strategies that low-income communities have developed to gain more control over, and ownership of, housing through limited equity housing cooperatives (LEHCs), community land trusts (CLTs), and mutual housing associations (MHAs). We conclude the chapter by reiterating a critical geography of gentrification that has a social justice agenda.

**Activities and Exercises**

- Read Neil Smith's (1996a) discussion of the battle for Tompkins Square Park in the Lower East Side. Read also Krzystzof Wodiczko and Rudolph Luria, 'The Homeless Vehicle Project', *Journal of Architectural Education* (1990) 43, 4: 37–42; and Neil Smith (1992b) 'Contours of a Spatialized Politics of Homeless Vehicles and the Production of Geographical Scale', *Social Text*, 33:54–81. What do you think about the different forms of resistance discussed?
- Find and examine newspaper articles on a celebrated 'reinvestment' or 'revitalization' project in a low-income neighborhood near you. Ask, 'Is this gentrification?'
- Read Hari Kunzru, 'The Battle for Tony's Café: An Everyday Tale of Gentrification' (an article about the battle over the commercial gentrification of Broadway Market just north of Hoxton in London), *The Guardian* g2, December 7, 2005, 8–11. Is resistance to commercial gentrification different from resistance to residential gentrification?
- Watch *Where Can I Live*, directed by Erik Lewis (1984). This program examines gentrification, focusing on three tenant groups in Brooklyn, New York City. It demonstrates how the threat of displacement led community residents to organize in defense of their homes and community.
- Review the case studies presented in this chapter. Make a list of the various tactics—from legal to artistic—that communities have engaged in to challenge prodevelopment forces and gentrification.
- In your own words, prepare a short definition and provide an example of what DeFilippis (2004) and Slater (2006) call the 'false choice' that low-income residents face in gentrifying communities.

**Further Reading**

Achtenberg, E. P., and P. Marcuse (1986) 'Toward the decommodification of housing', in R. Bratt, C. Hartman, and A. Meyerson (eds.) *Critical Perspectives on Housing* (Philadelphia: Temple University Press), 474–483.

Amin, A., D. Massey, and N. Thrift (2000) *Cities for the Many Not the Few* (Bristol: Policy Press).

Blomley, N. (2004) *Unsettling the City: Urban Land and the Politics of Property* (New York: Routledge).

Brownill, S., and J. Darke (1998) *Rich Mix: Inclusive Strategies for Regeneration* (Bristol: Policy Press).

Butler, T., C. Hamnett, and M. Ramsden (forthcoming) 'Inward and upward: Marking out social class change in London', *Urban Studies*.

DeFilippis, J. (2004) *Unmaking Goliath: Community Control in the Face of Global Capital* (New York: Routledge).

Harvey, D. (2000) *Spaces of Hope* (Edinburgh: Edinburgh University Press).

Lees, L. (1999) 'Critical geography and the opening up of the academy: Lessons from "real life" attempts', *Area*, 31, 4: 377–383.

Lees, L. (ed.) (2004) *The Emancipatory City: Paradoxes and Possibilities?* (London: Sage).

Meligrana, J., and A. Skaburskis (2005) 'Extent, location and profiles of continuing gentrification in Canadian metropolitan areas', *Urban Studies* 42: 1569–1592.

Mitchell, D. (2003) *The Right to the City: Social Justice and the Fight for Public Space* (New York: Guilford).

Myers, D., E. Gearin, T. Banerjee, and A. Garde (2001) *Current Preferences and Future Demand for Denser Residential Environments* (Coral Gables, FL: Funders' Network for Smart Growth and Livable Communities).

Newman, K. (2004) 'Newark, decline and avoidance, renaissance and desire: From disinvestment to reinvestment', *Annals of the American Academy of Political and Social Research* 594: 34–48.

Newman, K., and E. K. Wyly (2006) 'The right to stay put, revisited: Gentrification and resistance to displacement in New York City', *Urban Studies* 43: 23–57.

Slater, T. (2004b) 'Municipally managed gentrification in South Parkdale, Toronto', *The Canadian Geographer* 48: 303–325.

Sohmer, R. R., and R. E. Lang (2001) *Downtown Rebound*, Census Notes Series (Washington, DC: Fannie Mae Foundation, Brookings Institution).

Squires, D. (ed.) (1992) *From Redlining to Reinvestment: Community Responses to Urban Disinvestment* (Philadelphia: Temple University Press).

Wilson, D., J. Wouters, and D. Grammenos (2004) 'Successful project-community discourse: Spatiality and politics in Chicago's Pilsen neighbourhood', *Environment and Planning A* 36, 7: 1173–1190.

# Bibliography

Aardema, N., and S. J. Knoy (2004) 'Fighting gentrification Chicago style', *Social Policy* 34, 4: 1–6.

Abercrombie, P. (1944) *Greater London Plan 1944* (London: H.M.S.O.).

Abu-Lughod, J. (ed.) (1994) *From Urban Village to East Village: The Battle for New York's Lower East Side* (Oxford: Blackwell).

Achtenberg, E. P., and P. Marcuse (1986) 'Toward the decommodification of housing', in R. Bratt, C. Hartman, and A. Meyerson (eds.) *Critical Perspectives on Housing* (Philadelphia: Temple University Press) 474–483.

Alejandrino, S. V. (2000) *Gentrification in San Francisco's Mission District: Indicators and Policy Recommendations* (San Francisco: Mission Economic Development Association).

Allen, I. (1984) 'The ideology of dense neighbourhood redevelopment: Cultural diversity and transcendant community experience', *Urban Affairs Quarterly* 15: 409–428.

Allen, I. L. (1993) *The City in Slang: New York Life and Popular Speech* (Oxford: Oxford University Press).

Alonso, W. (1964) *Location and Land Use* (Cambridge, MA: Harvard University Press).

Amin, A., D. Massey, and N. Thrift (2000) *Cities for the Many Not the Few* (Bristol: Policy Press).

Amin, A., and N. Thrift (2002) *Cities: Reimagining the Urban* (Cambridge: Polity Press).

Andersson, R., and A. Samartin (1985) 'An extension of Mohring's model for land rent distribution', *Journal of Urban Economics* 18: 143–160.

Ash, M. (1972) 'Social London', in P. Murray (ed.) 'Invisible London', *Time Out*, issue 116, May 5–11.

Ashton, P. S. (2005) *Advantage or Disadvantage? The Changing Institutional Landscape of Central City Mortgage Markets*, Ph.D. thesis (New Brunswick, NJ: Urban Planning and Policy Development, Rutgers University).

Atkinson, R. (2000) 'Measuring gentrification and displacement in Greater London', *Urban Studies* 37: 149–166.

Atkinson, R. (2002) 'Does gentrification help or harm urban neighbourhoods? An assessment of the evidence-base in the context of the new urban agenda', ESRC Centre for Neighbourhood Research paper 5 (http://www.neighbourhoodcentre.org.uk/research/cnrpaperspdf/cnr5paper.pdf).

Atkinson, R. (2003a) 'Introduction: Misunderstood saviour or vengeful wrecker? The many meanings and problems of gentrification', *Urban Studies* 40, 12: 2343–2350.

Atkinson, R. (2003b) 'Domestication by cappuccino or a revenge on urban space? Control and empowerment in the management of public spaces', *Urban Studies* 40, 9: 1829–1843.

Atkinson, R. (2004) 'The evidence on the impact of gentrification: New lessons for the urban renaissance?' *European Journal of Housing Policy* 4, 1: 107–131.

Atkinson, R., and G. Bridge (eds.) (2005) *Gentrification in a Global Context: The New Urban Colonialism* (London: Routledge).

Badcock, B. (1989) 'An Australian view of the rent gap hypothesis', *Annals of the Association of American Geographers* 79, 1: 125–145.

Badcock, B. (1993) 'Notwithstanding the exaggerated claims, residential revitalization really is changing the form of some western cities: A response to Bourne', *Urban Studies* 30, 1: 191–195.

Badcock, B. (2001) 'Thirty years on: Gentrification and class changeover in Adelaide's inner suburbs, 1966–96', *Urban Studies* 38: 1559–1572.

Badyina, A., and O. Golubchikov (2005) 'Gentrification in central Moscow: A market process or a deliberate policy? Money, power and people in housing regeneration in Ostozhenka', *Geografiska Annaler B* 87: 113–129.

Baker, G. (2001) 'The American economy, remortgaged', *Financial Times*, August 17: 11.

Ball, M. (1985) 'The urban rent question', *Environment and Planning A* 17: 503–525.

Barnes, T. J. (2000) 'Political economy', in R. J. Johnston, D. Gregory, G. Pratt, and M. Watts (eds.) *The Dictionary of Human Geography* 4th ed. (Oxford: Blackwell) 593–594.

Barry, J., and J. Derevlany (eds.) (1987) *Yuppies Invade My House at Dinnertime: A Tale of Brunch, Bombs, and Gentrification in an American City* (Hoboken, NJ: Big River Publishing).

Beauregard, R. A. (1986) 'The chaos and complexity of gentrification', in N. Smith and P. Williams (eds.) *Gentrification of the City* (London: Allen and Unwin) 35–55.

Beauregard, R. A. (1990) 'Trajectories of neighbourhood change: The case of gentrification', *Environment and Planning A* 22: 855–874.

Beauregard, R. A. (1993) *Voices of Decline: The Postwar Fate of U.S. Cities* (Oxford: Blackwell).

Beauregard, R. A. (1994) 'Capital switching and the built environment: the United States, 1970–89', *Environment and Planning A* 25, 5: 715–732.

Beauregard, R. A. (2003a) 'Positioning urban theory', *Antipode* 35, 5: 999–1007.

Beauregard, R. A. (2003b) *Voices of Decline: The Postwar Fate of U.S. Cities* 2nd ed. (Oxford: Blackwell).

Beckett, K., and B. Western (2001) 'Governing social marginality: Welfare, incarceration, and the transformation of state policy', *Punishment and Society* 3, 1: 43–59.

Bell, D. (1973) *The Coming of Postindustrial Society: A Venture in Social Forecasting* (New York: Basic Books).

Berger, J. (2005a) 'Goodbye South Bronx blight, hello trendy SoBro', *New York Times*, June 24: A1.

Berger, J. (2005b) 'Gentrification moves in on Gowanus', *New York Times*, November 28: A19.

Berry, B. (1980) 'Inner city futures: An American dilemma revisited', *Transactions of the Institute of British Geographers* 5, 1: 1–28.

Berry, B. (1999) 'Comments on Elvin K. Wyly and Daniel J. Hammel's "'Islands of Decay in Seas of Renewal: Housing Policy and the Resurgence of Gentrification"—gentrification resurgent?' *Housing Policy Debate* 10, 4: 783–788.

Betancur, J. (2002) 'The politics of gentrification: The case of West Town in Chicago', *Urban Affairs Review* 37: 780–814.

Bhalla, C. K., I. Voicu, R. Meltzer, I. G. Ellen, and V. Been (2004) *State of New York City's Housing and Neighborhoods* (New York: Furman Center for Real Estate and Urban Policy, New York University School of Law).

Black, J. T. (1980) 'Private-market housing renovation in central cities: An urban land institute survey', in S. B. Laska and D. Spain (eds.) *Back to the City: Issues in Neighborhood Renovation* (New York: Pergamon) 3–12.

Blackburn, R. (2006) 'Finance and the fourth dimension', *New Left Review* 39, May/June: 39–70.

Blanton, K. (2006) 'Property-values website lets everyone compare', *Boston Globe*: March 17.

Blomley, N. (2004) *Unsettling the City: Urban Land and the Politics of Property* (New York: Routledge).

Boddy, M. (2007) 'Designer neighbourhoods: New-build residential development in non-metropolitan UK cities—the case of Bristol', *Environment and Planning A* 39, 1: 86–105.

Bondi, L. (1991) 'Gender divisions and gentrification: A critique', *Transactions of the Institute of British Geographers* 16: 290–298.

Bondi, L. (1999a) 'Between the woof and the weft: A response to Loretta Lees', *Environment and Planning D: Society and Space* 17, 3: 253–255.

Bondi, L. (1999b) 'Gender, class and gentrification: Enriching the debate', *Environment and Planning D: Society and Space* 17, 3: 261–282.

Borden, I. (2003) 'What is radical architecture?' in M. Miles and T. Hall (eds.) *Urban Futures: Critical Commentaries on Shaping the City* (London: Routledge) 111–121.

Bostic, R., and R. Martin (2003) 'Black homeowners as a gentrifying force? Neighborhood dynamics in the context of minority home-ownership', *Urban Studies* 40, 12: 2427–2449.

Bourassa, S. C. (1990) 'Another Australian view of the rent gap hypothesis', *Annals of the Association of American Geographers*, 80: 458–459.

Bourassa, S. C. (1993) 'The rent gap debunked', *Urban Studies* 30, 10: 1731–1744.

Bourne, L. S. (1993a) 'The demise of gentrification? A commentary and prospective view', *Urban Geography* 14, 1: 95–107.

Bourne, L. S. (1993b) 'The myth and reality of gentrification: A commentary on emerging urban forms', *Urban Studies* 30, 1: 183–189.

Bowler, A., and B. McBurney (1991) 'Gentrification and the avant-garde in New York's East Village: The good, the bad and the ugly', *Theory, Culture and Society* 8: 49–77.

Bowling, B. (1999) 'The rise and fall of New York murder: Zero tolerance or crack's decline?' *British Journal of Criminology* 39, 4: 531–554.

Boyd, M. (2000) 'Reconstructing Bronzeville: Racial nostalgia and neighbourhood redevelopment', *Journal of Urban Affairs* 22, 2: 107–122.

Boyd, M. (2005) 'The downside of racial uplift: The meaning of gentrification in an African–American neighborhood', *City & Society* 17: 265–288.

Brenner, N. (2001) 'World city theory, globalization and the comparative-historical method: Reflections on Janet Abu-Lughod's interpretation of contemporary urban restructuring', *Urban Affairs Review* 37, 1: 124–147.

Brenner, N., and N. Theodore (eds.) (2002) *Spaces of Neoliberalism: Urban Restructuring in North America and Western Europe* (Oxford: Blackwell).

Brethour, P. (2006) 'All aboard Alberta's real estate express: Where to go after Calgary and Edmonton?' *Globe and Mail*, June 28: B1, B9.

Bridge, G. (1994) 'Gentrification, class and residence: A reappraisal', *Environment and Planning D: Society and Space* 12: 31–51.

Bridge, G. (1995) 'The space for class? On class analysis in the study of gentrification', *Transactions of the Institute of British Geographers* 20, 2: 236–247.

Bridge, G. (2001a) 'Estate agents as interpreters of economic and cultural capital: The gentrification premium in the Sydney housing market', *International Journal of Urban and Regional Research* 25: 87–101.

Bridge, G. (2001b) 'Bourdieu, rational action and the time–space strategy of gentrification', *Transactions of the Institute of British Geographers* 26: 205–216.

Bridge, G. (2003) 'Time-space trajectories in provincial gentrification', *Urban Studies* 40, 12: 2545–2556.

Bridge, G., and R. Dowling (2001) 'Microgeographies of retailing and gentrification', *Australian Geographer* 32, 1: 93–107.

Brint, S. (1991) 'Upper professionals: A high command of commerce, culture, and civic regulation', in J. Mollenkopf and M. Castells (eds.) *Dual City: Restructuring New York* (New York: Russell Sage Foundation) 155–176.

Brooks, D. (2005) 'The bursting point', *New York Times*, September 4, A29.

Brownill, S. (1990) *Developing London's Docklands* (London: Paul Chapman).

Brownill, S., and J. Darke (1998) *Rich Mix: Inclusive Strategies for Regeneration* (Bristol: Policy Press).

Brueckner, J. K., and S. S. Rosenthal (2005) 'Gentrification and neighborhood housing cycles: Will America's future downtowns be rich?' Working paper (Irvine: University of California, Irvine, Department of Economics).

Brueckner, J. K., J. F. Thisse, and Y. Zenou (1999) 'Why is central Paris rich and downtown Detroit poor? An amenity-based theory', *European Economic Review* 43: 91–107.

Bugler, J. (1968) 'The invaders of Islington', *New Society*, August 15: 226–228.

Butler, T. (1997) *Gentrification and the Middle Classes* (Aldershot, UK: Ashgate).

Butler, T. (2003) 'Living in the bubble: Gentrification and its "others" in London', *Urban Studies* 40, 12: 2469–2486.

Butler, T., and C. Hamnett (1994) 'Gentrification, class and gender: Some comments on Warde's gentrification as consumption', *Environment and Planning D: Society and Space* 12: 477–493.

Butler, T., C. Hamnett, and M. Ramsden (2008, forthcoming) 'Inward and upward: Marking out social class change in London', 1981–2001, *Urban Studies*.

Butler, T., and L. Lees (2006) 'Super-gentrification in Barnsbury, London: Globalisation and gentrifying global elites at the neighbourhood level', *Transactions of the Institute of British Geographers*, 31: 467–487.

Butler, T., and G. Robson (2001a) 'Negotiating the new urban economy—work, home and school: Middle class life in London', paper presented at the Royal Geographical Society—Institute of British Geographers Conference, Plymouth, UK, January 2–5.

Butler, T., and G. Robson (2001b) 'Social capital, gentrification and neighbourhood change in London: A comparison of three south London neighbourhoods', *Urban Studies* 38: 2145–2162.

Butler, T., with G. Robson (2003) *London Calling: The Middle Classes and the Remaking of Inner London* (London: Berg).

Buzar, S., R. Hall, and P. Ogden (2007) 'Beyond gentrification: The demographic reurbanisation of Bologna', *Environment and Planning A* 39, 1: 64–85.

Byrne, J. P. (2003) 'Two cheers for gentrification', *Howard Law Journal* 46, 3: 405–432.

Cameron, S. (1992) 'Housing, gentrification and urban regeneration', *Urban Studies* 29, 1: 3–14.

Cameron, S. (2003) 'Gentrification, housing redifferentiation and urban regeneration: "Going for Growth" in Newcastle upon Tyne', *Urban Studies* 40, 12: 2367–2382.

Cameron, S., and J. Doling (1994) 'Housing, neighbourhoods and urban regeneration', *Urban Studies* 31, 7: 1211–1223.

Carpenter, J., and L. Lees (1995) 'Gentrification in New York, London and Paris: An international comparison', *International Journal of Urban and Regional Research* 19, 2: 286–303.

Carson, A. (1965) 'Islington Village', *New Statesman*, September 17: 395–396.

Carter, H. (2005) 'Stacks of potential', *The Guardian*, June 15.

Caruso, D. B. (2006) 'Officials envision gentrified jail for resurgent Brooklyn', *Associated Press*, March 25.

Castells, M. (1977) *The Urban Question: A Marxist Approach* (Cambridge, MA: MIT Press).

Castells, M. (1983) *The City and the Grassroots: A Cross-Cultural Theory of Urban Social Movements* (Berkeley: University of California Press).

Caulfield, J. (1989) 'Gentrification and desire', *Canadian Review of Sociology and Anthropology* 26:617–632.

Caulfield, J. (1994) *City Form and Everyday Life: Toronto's Gentrification and Critical Social Practice* (Toronto: University of Toronto Press).

Charney, I. (2001) 'Three dimensions of capital switching within the real estate sector: A Canadian case study', *International Journal of Urban and Regional Research* 25, 4: 740–758.

Charney, I. (2003) 'Spatial fix and spatial substitutability practices among Canada's largest office development firms', *Urban Geography* 24, 5: 386–409.

City of Vancouver (n.d.) Woodward's: A new beginning (http://www.city.vancouver. bc.ca/corpsvcs/realestate/woodwards/ideas.htm).

*Civic News* (1969) issue 32: 9.

*Civic News* (1972) 'Cinderella of Prospect Place' March 5: 3, 10–13.

*Civic News* (1973) 'Brownstone films' June 6: 4.

Clark, E. (1987) *The Rent Gap and Urban Change: Case Studies in Malmö, 1860–1985* (Lund, Sweden: Lund University Press).

Clark, E. (1988) 'The rent gap and transformation of the built environment: Case studies in Malmö, 1860–1985', *Geografiska Annaler B* 70, 2: 241–254.

Clark, E. (1991) 'Rent gaps and value gaps: Complementary or contradictory?' in J. van Weesep and S. Musterd (eds.) *Urban Housing for the Better Off: Gentrification in Europe* (Utrecht, the Netherlands: Stedelijke Netwerken) 17–29.

Clark, E. (1992) 'On blindness, centrepieces, and complementarity in gentrification theory', *Transactions of the Institute of British Geographers* 17: 358–362.

Clark, E. (1994) 'Toward a Copenhagen interpretation of gentrification', *Urban Studies* 31, 7: 1033–1042.

Clark, E. (1995) 'The rent gap re-examined', *Urban Studies* 32, 9: 1489–1503.

Clark, E. (2005) 'The order and simplicity of gentrification: A political challenge', in R. Atkinson and G. Bridge (eds.) *Gentrification in a Global Context: The New Urban Colonialism* (London: Routledge) 256–264.

Clark, K. (1964) *Dark Ghetto: Dilemmas of Social Power* (New York: Harper & Row).

Clay, P. (1979) *Neighborhood Renewal: Middle-Class Resettlement and Incumbent Upgrading in American Neighborhoods* (Lexington, MA: D.C. Heath).

Cloke, P., and N. Thrift (1987) 'Intra-class conflict in rural areas', *Journal of Rural Studies* 3: 321–333.

Cosgrove, D., and P. Jackson (1987) 'New directions in cultural geography', *Area* 19: 95–101.

Counter Information Services (1973) *The Recurrent Crisis of London* (London: CIS Anti-Report on the Property Developers).

Cowley, J., A. Kay, M. Mayo, and M. Thompson (1977) *Community or Class Struggle?* (London: Stage 1 Books).

Cox, K., and A. Mair (1988) 'Locality and community in the politics of local economic development', *Annals of the Association of American Geographers* 78: 307–325.

Cunningham, L. E. (2001) 'Islands of affordability in a sea of gentrification: Lessons learned from the DC Housing Authority's HOPE VI projects', *Journal of Affordable Housing and Community Development Law* 10, 4: 353–371.

Curran, W. (2004) 'Gentrification and the nature of work: Exploring the links in Williamsburg, Brooklyn', *Environment and Planning A* 36, 7: 1243–1258.

Curran, W. (2006) 'Gentrification: A case study', in R. Greene, M. Bouman, and D. Grammenos (eds.) *Chicago's Geographies: Metropolis for the 21st Century* (Washington, DC: Association of American Geographers) 259–263.

Cybriwsky, R., D. Ley, and J. Western (1986) 'The political and social construction of revitalized neighbourhoods: Society Hill, Philadelphia, and False Creek, Vancouver', in N. Smith and P. Williams (eds.) *Gentrification of the City* (Boston: Allen and Unwin) 92–120.

Dangschat, J. (1991) 'Gentrification in Hamburg', in J. van Weesep and S. Musterd (eds.) *Urban Housing for the Better-off: Gentrification in Europe* (Utrecht, the Netherlands: Stedelijke Netwerken) 63–88.

Dansereau, F., J. Godbout, J-P. Collin, D. L'Écuyer, M-J. Lessard, G. Larouche, and L. Chabot (1981) 'La transformation d'immeubles locatifs en copropriete d'occupation', Rapport presente au Gouverment du Quebec, May (Montréal: INRS-Urbanisation, Universite du Quebec).

Dantas, A. (1988) 'Overspill as an alternative style of gentrification: The case of Riverdale, Toronto', in T. Bunting and P. Filion (eds.) *The Changing Canadian Inner City*, Publication Series 31 (Waterloo, Ontario: Department of Geography, University of Waterloo) 73–86.

Darling, E. (2005) 'The city in the country: Wilderness gentrification and the rent-gap', *Environment and Planning A* 37, 6: 1015–1032.

Davidson, M. (2006) *New-Build Gentrification and London's Riverside Renaissance*, Ph.D. thesis (London: Department of Geography, King's College London).

Davidson, M., and L. Lees (2005) 'New-build "gentrification" and London's riverside renaissance', *Environment and Planning A* 37, 7: 1165–1190.

Davis, M. (1990) *City of Quartz: Excavating the Future in Los Angeles* (New York: Verso).

De Bartolome, C. A. M., and S. L. Ross (2002) 'The location of the poor in a metropolitan area: Positive and normative aspects', Department of Economics Working Paper Series, working paper 2002-02 (Storrs: University of Connecticut).

Deep, A., and D. Domanski (2002) 'Housing markets and economic growth: Lessons from the U.S. refinancing boom', *Bank for International Settlements Quarterly Review*, September: 37–45.

DeFilippis, J. (2004) *Unmaking Goliath: Community Control in the Face of Global Capital* (New York: Routledge).

DeFilippis, J., and P. North (2004) 'The emancipatory community? Place, politics and collective action in cities', in L. Lees (ed.) *The Emancipatory City? Paradoxes and Possibilities* (London: Sage) 72–88.

Dench, G., N. Gavron, and M. Young (2006) *The New East End: Kinship, Race and Conflict* (London: Profile Books).

Department of Environment (1977) *Policy for the Inner Cities* (London: H.M.S.O.).

Department of the Environment, Transport and the Regions (DETR) (1999) *Towards an Urban Renaissance* (London: DETR).

Department of the Environment, Transport and the Regions (DETR) (2000a) *Our Towns and Cities—the Future: Delivering an Urban Renaissance* (London: DETR).

Department of the Environment, Transport and the Regions (DETR) (2000b) *State of the English Cities* (London: H.M.S.O.).

DeRocker, R. (1981) 'Thousands of jobs lost in 70s: New figures add hope', *The Phoenix*, April 16: 3.

DeSalvo, J. S., and M. Huq (1996) 'Income, residential location, and mode choice', *Journal of Urban Economics* 40: 84–99.

Deutsche, R., and C. Ryan (1984) 'The fine art of gentrification', *October* 31: 91–111.

Drake, S., and H. Cayton (1945) *Black Metropolis: A Study of Negro Life in a Northern City* (Chicago: University of Chicago Press).

Draper, S. (1991) *A House Is on the Outside: A Home Is on the Inside: Gentrification as a Social Movement*, Ph.D. thesis (New York: Department of Anthropology, New York University).

Duany, A. (2001) 'Three cheers for gentrification', *The American Enterprise*, April/May: 36–39.

Dudley Street Neighborhood Initiative (2007) DSNI (http://www.dsni.org).

Dulchin, B. (2003) 'Organizing against gentrification, fighting the free market: The displacement-free zone campaign', *Social Policy* 34, 2: 29–34.

Dumenil, G., and D. Levy (2004) 'Neoliberal income trends: Wealth, class, and ownership in the USA', *New Left Review* 30: 105–133.

Duncan, J., and D. Ley (1982) 'Structural Marxism and human geography: A critical assessment', *Annals of the Association of American Geographers* 72, 1: 30–59.

Dutton, P. (2003) 'Leeds calling: The influence of London on the gentrification of regional cities', *Urban Studies* 40, 12: 2557–2572.

Dutton, P. (2005) 'Outside the metropole: Gentrification in provincial cities or provincial gentrification?' in R. Atkinson and G. Bridge (eds.) *Gentrification in a Global Context: The New Urban Colonialism* (London: Routledge) 209–224.

Eade, J., and C. Mele (1998) 'The Eastern promise of New York and London', *Rising East* 1, 3: 52–73.

Eaton, L. (2006) 'Hurricane aid finally flowing to homeowners', *New York Times*, July 17: A1, A14.

Elevate East Lancashire (2007) Building a better quality of life in Lancashire (http://www.elevate-eastlancs.co.uk).

Engels, B. (1994) 'Capital flows, redlining and gentrification: The pattern of mortgage lending and social change in Glebe, Sydney, 1960–1984', *International Journal of Urban and Regional Research* 18, 4: 628–657.

Engels, F. (1872/1975) *The Housing Question* (Moscow: Progress Publishers).

*enRoute* (2002) 'Canada's top ten coolest neighbourhoods', April: 37.

Fabozzi, F. (2001) *The Handbook of Mortgage-Backed Securities* (New York: McGraw-Hill).

Fainstein, S., and N. Fainstein (1991) 'The changing character of community politics in New York City: 1968–1988', in J. Mollenkopf and M. Castells (eds.) *Dual City: Restructuring New York* (New York: Russell Sage Foundation) 315–332.

Ferris, J. (1972) *Participation in Urban Planning: The Barnsbury Case* (London: Bell and Hyman).

Field, M., and M. Irving (1999) *Lofts* (London: Laurence King).

Fifth Avenue Committee (2007) Our community: Our future (http://www.fifthave.org).

Firey, W. (1947) *Land Use in Central Boston* (Cambridge, MA: Harvard University Press).

Florida, R. (2003) *The Rise of the Creative* Class (New York: Basic Books).

Florida, R. (2005) *Cities and the Creative Class* (New York: Routledge).

Forest, B. (1995) 'West Hollywood as symbol: The significance of place in the construction of a gay identity', *Environment and Planning D: Society and Space* 13: 133–157.

Frazier, I. (2006) 'Utopia, the Bronx', *The New Yorker*, June 26: 54–65.

Freeman, L. (2005) 'Displacement or succession? Residential mobility in gentrifying neighborhoods', *Urban Affairs Review* 40: 463–491.

Freeman, L. (2006) *There Goes The 'Hood: Views of Gentrification from the Ground Up* (Philadelphia: Temple University Press).

Freeman, L., and F. Braconi (2002) 'Gentrification and displacement', *The Urban Prospect: Housing, Planning and Economic Development in New York* 8, 1: 1–4.

Freeman, L., and F. Braconi (2004) 'Gentrification and displacement: New York City in the 1990s', *Journal of the American Planning Association* 70, 1: 39–52.

Fried, J. P. (1978) 'Demands for strong measures to combat redlining are growing', *New York Times*, January 1: 23.

Fyfe, N. (2004) 'Zero tolerance, maximum surveillance? Deviance, difference and crime control in the late modern city', in L. Lees (ed.) *The Emancipatory City? Paradoxes and Possibilities* (London: Sage) 40–56.

Fyfe, N., and J. Kenny (eds.) (2005) *The Urban Geography Reader* (London: Routledge).

Gale, D. E. (1979) 'Middle class resettlement in older urban neighborhoods: The evidence and the implications', *Journal of the American Planning Association* 45: 293–204.

Gale, D. E. (1984) *Neighborhood Revitalization and the Postindustrial City: A Multinational Perspective* (Lexington, MA: D.C. Heath).

Geertz, C. (1973) *The Interpretation of Cultures* (New York: Basic Books).

Gelb, J., and M. Lyons (1993) 'A tale of two cities: Housing policy and gentrification in London and New York', *Journal of Urban Affairs* 15, 4: 345–366.

Gelinas, N. (2005) 'A perfect storm of lawlessness', *City Journal*, September 1.

Gershun, M. (1975) 'Financing a brownstone: With luck you can come out ahead of the game', *The Phoenix*, October 2: 28.

Ghose, R. (2004) 'Big sky or big sprawl? Rural gentrification and the changing cultural landscape of Missoula, Montana', *Urban Geography* 25, 6: 528–549.

Gibson-Graham, J. K. (1993) 'Waiting for the revolution, or how to smash capitalism while working at home in your spare time', *Rethinking Marxism* 6, 2: 10–24.

Glaeser, E. L., M. E. Kahn, and J. Rappaport (2000) 'Why do the poor live in cities?' Working Paper 7636 (Cambridge, MA: National Bureau of Economic Research).

Glass, R. (1964) 'Introduction: Aspects of change', in Centre for Urban Studies (ed.) *London: Aspects of Change* (London: MacKibbon and Kee).

Glass, R. (1989) *Clichés of Urban Doom* (Oxford: Blackwell).

Goetz, E. G. (2003) *Clearing the Way: Deconcentrating the Poor in Urban America* (Washington, DC: Urban Institute Press).

Goodno, J. (1982) 'Owners forbidden to coop', *The Phoenix*, May 27: 1.

Gotham, K. F. (2001) 'Redevelopment for whom and for what purpose?' in K. Fox Gotham (ed.) *Critical Perspectives on Urban Redevelopment*, vol. 6 of *Research in Urban Sociology* (Oxford: Elsevier) 429–452.

Gotham, K. F. (2005) 'Tourism gentrification: The case of New Orleans' Vieux Carre (French Quarter)', *Urban Studies* 42, 7: 1099–1121.

Graham, J. (1990) 'Theory and essentialism in Marxist geography', *Antipode* 22: 53–66.

Graham, S., and S. Guy (2002) 'Digital space meets urban place: Sociotechnologies of urban restructuring in downtown San Francisco', *City* 6, 3: 369–382.

Greater London Authority (GLA) (2004) *The London Plan: Spatial Development Strategy for Greater London* (http://www.london.gov.uk).

Green, S. (1979) *Rachman* (London: Michael Joseph).

Griffin, G. (1982) 'Park Slope: Designs for living', *New Brooklyn* 4, 2: 22–27.

Griffith, D. (2000) 'Social capital and economic apartheid along the coasts of the Americas', *Urban Anthropology* 29, 3: 255–284.

Hackworth, J. (2000) 'State devolution, urban regimes, and the production of geographic scale: The case of New Brunswick, NJ', *Urban Geography* 21: 450–458.

Hackworth, J. (2001) 'Inner-city real estate investment, gentrification, and economic recession in New York City', *Environment and Planning A* 33: 863–880.

Hackworth, J. (2002a) 'Post recession gentrification in New York City', *Urban Affairs Review* 37: 815–843.

Hackworth, J. (2002b) 'Local autonomy, bond-rating agencies, and neoliberal urbanism in the United States', *International Journal of Urban and Regional Research* 26, 4: 707–725.

Hackworth, J., and N. Smith (2001) 'The changing state of gentrification', *Tijdschrift voor Economische en Sociale Geografie* 22: 464–477.

Hammel, D. J. (1999a) 'Re-establishing the rent gap: An alternative view of capitalized land rent', *Urban Studies* 36, 8: 1283–1293.

Hammel, D. J. (1999b) 'Gentrification and land rent: A historical view of the rent gap in Minneapolis', *Urban Geography* 20, 2: 116–145.

Hammel, D. J., and E. K. Wyly (1996) 'A model for identifying gentrified areas with census data', *Urban Geography* 17, 3: 248–268.

Hamnett, C. (1973) 'Improvement grants as an indicator of gentrification in Inner London', *Area* 5, 4: 252–261.

Hamnett, C. (1984) 'Gentrification and residential location theory: A review and assessment', in D. T. Herbert and R. J. Johnston (eds.) *Geography and the Urban Environment: Progress in Research and Applications* (London: Wiley & Sons) 283–319.

Hamnett, C. (1991) 'The blind men and the elephant: The explanation of gentrification', *Transactions of the Institute of British Geographers* 16, 2: 173–189.

Hamnett, C. (1992) 'Gentrifiers or lemmings? A response to Neil Smith', *Transactions of the Institute of British Geographers* 17, 1: 116–119.

Hamnett, C. (1994a) 'Socio-economic change in London: Professionalisation not polarization', *Built Environment* 20, 3: 192–203.

Hamnett, C. (1994b) 'Social polarisation in global cities: Theory and evidence', *Urban Studies* 31, 3: 401–424.

Hamnett, C. (1996) 'Social polarisation, economic restructuring and welfare state regimes', *Urban Studies* 33, 8: 1407–1430.

Hamnett, C. (2000) 'Gentrification, postindustrialism, and industrial and occupational restructuring in global cities', in G. Bridge and S. Watson (eds.) *A Companion to the City* (Oxford: Blackwell) 331–341.

Hamnett, C. (2003a) *Unequal City: London in the Global Arena* (London: Routledge).

Hamnett, C. (2003b) 'Gentrification and the middle-class remaking of inner London, 1961–2001', *Urban Studies* 40, 12: 2401–2426.

Hamnett, C., and B. Randolph (1984) 'The role of landlord disinvestment in housing market transformation: An analysis of the flat break-up market in Central London', *Transactions of the Institute of British Geographers* 9: 259–279.

Hamnett, C., and B. Randolph (1986) 'Tenurial transformation and the flat break-up market in London: The British condo experience', in N. Smith and P. Williams (eds.) *Gentrification of the City* (London: Allen and Unwin) 121–152.

Harris, R. (1987) 'A social movement in urban politics? A reinterpretation of urban reform in Canada', *International Journal of Urban and Regional Research* 11: 363–381.

Hartman, C. (1984) 'The right to stay put', in C. Geisler and F. Popper (eds.) *Land Reform, American Style* (Totowa, NJ: Rowman and Allanheld) 302–318.

Hartman, C., D. Keating, and R. LeGates (1982) *Displacement: How to Fight It* (Washington, DC: National Housing Law Project).

Hartshorn, T. (1992) *Interpreting the City: An Urban Geography* 2nd ed. (New York: John Wiley & Sons).

Harvey, D. (1973) *Social Justice and the City* (London: Edward Arnold).

Harvey, D. (1974) 'Class monopoly rent, finance capital, and the urban revolution', *Regional Studies* 8: 239–255.

Harvey, D. (1978) 'The urban process under capitalism: A framework for analysis', *International Journal of Urban and Regional Research* 2: 101–131.

Harvey, D. (1982) *The Limits to Capital* (Chicago: University of Chicago Press).

Harvey, D. (1985) *The Urbanization of Capital* (Baltimore: Johns Hopkins University Press).

Harvey, D. (1989a) *The Condition of Postmodernity* (Oxford: Blackwell).

Harvey, D. (1989b) 'From managerialism to entrepreneurialism: The transformation in urban governance in late capitalism', *Geografiska Annaler B* 71: 3–17.

Harvey, D. (2000) *Spaces of Hope* (Edinburgh: Edinburgh University Press).

Harvey, D. (2003) *The New Imperialism* (Oxford: Oxford University Press).

Harvey, D. (2005) *A Brief History of Neo-liberalism* (Oxford: Oxford University Press).

Harvey, D. (2006a) 'Space as a keyword', in N. Castree and D. Gregory (eds.) *David Harvey: A Critical Reader* (Oxford: Blackwell) 270–293.

Harvey, D. (2006b) *Spaces of Global Capitalism: Towards a Theory of Uneven Geographical Development* (London: Verso).

Hasson, S., and D. Ley (1994) *Neighbourhood Organizations and the Welfare State* (Toronto: University of Toronto Press).

Helms, A. C. (2003) 'Understanding gentrification: An empirical analysis of the determinants of urban housing renovation', *Journal of Urban Economics* 54: 474–498.

Hevesi, D. (2002) 'Skirmishes signal rent law countdown', *New York Times*, July 7.

Hiebert, D. (2000) 'The social geography of immigration and urbanization in Canada: A review and interpretation', Research on Immigration and Integration in the Metropolis, Working Paper Series no. 00-12, September (Vancouver, BC: Vancouver Centre).

Hodenfield, J. (1986) 'The sunny side of the street', *Daily News Magazine*, May 25: 6–9.

Holcomb. H. B. (1984) 'Women in the city', *Urban Geography* 5, 3: 247–254.

Holcomb, H. B., and R. A. Beauregard (1981) *Revitalizing Cities* (Washington, DC: Association of American Geographers).

Holton, P. (1968) 'New brownstone breed enlivens urban life', *The Brownstoner* 1, 1 (1st ed.).

*Howard Law Journal* (2003) 46, 3 (http://www.law.howard.edu/dictator/media/229/huljvol46_3.pdf).

Howell, B. (2006) 'Exploiting race and space: Concentrated subprime lending as housing discrimination', *California Law Review* 94: 101–147.

Hoyt, H. (1933) *One Hundred Years of Land Values in Chicago* (Chicago: University of Chicago Press).

Hoyt, H. (1939) *The Structure and Growth of Residential Neighbourhoods in American Cities* (Washington, DC: Federal Housing Administration).

*HUD v. Rucker*, 545 U.S. 125, 122 S.Ct. 1230 (2002).

Hulsbergen, E., and P. Stouten (2001) 'Urban renewal and regeneration in the Netherlands: Integration lost or subordinate?' *City* 5, 3: 325–337.

Imbroscio, D. L. (2004) 'Can we grant a right to place?' *Politics & Society* 32: 575–609.

Imrie, R. (2004) 'Urban geography, relevance, and resistance to the "policy turn"', *Urban Geography* 25, 8: 697–708.

Imrie, R., and M. Raco (eds.) (2003) *Urban Renaissance? New Labour, Community and Urban Policy* (Bristol: Policy Press).

Jackson, K. T. (1985) *Crabgrass Frontier: The Suburbanization of the United States* (Oxford: Oxford University Press).

Jackson, K., and J. Manbeck (eds.) (1998) *The Neighborhoods of Brooklyn* (New Haven, CT: Yale University Press).

Jacobs, J. (1996) *Edge of Empire: Postcolonialism and the City* (London: Routledge).

Jacobs, J. M., and R. Fincher (1998) 'Introduction', in R. Fincher and J. M. Jacobs (eds.) *Cities of Difference* (New York: Guilford) 1–25.

Jager, M. (1986) 'Class definition and the aesthetics of gentrification: Victoriana in Melbourne', in N. Smith and P. Williams (eds.) *Gentrification of the City* (London: Unwin Hyman), 78–91.

Jessop, B. (2002) 'Liberalism, neoliberalism, and urban governance: A state-theoretical perspective', *Antipode* 34, 3: 452–472.

Johnstone, C., and M. Whitehead (eds.) (2004) *New Horizons in Urban Policy: Perspectives on New Labour's Urban Renaissance* (Aldershot, UK: Ashgate).

Julian, K. (2006) 'Big houses', *The New Yorker*, May 29: 27.

Justa, F. (1984) *Effects of Housing Abandonment, Resettlement Processes and Displacement on the Evolution of Voluntary Community Organizations in Park Slope, Brooklyn, New York*, Ph.D. thesis (New York: City University of New York).

Karsten, L. (2003) 'Family gentrifiers: Challenging the city as a place simultaneously to build a career and to raise children', *Urban Studies* 40, 12: 2573–2584.

Kasarda, J. D. (1999) 'Comments on Elvin K. Wyly and Daniel J. Hammel's "Islands of Decay in Seas of Renewal: Housing Policy and the Resurgence of Gentrification"', *Housing Policy Debate* 10, 4: 773–781.

Kasinitz, P. (1988) 'The gentrification of "Boerum Hill": Neighborhood change and conflicts over definitions', *Qualitative Sociology* 11, 3: 163–182.

Katznelson, I. (1981) *City Trenches: Urban Politics and the Patterning of Class in the United States* (New York: Pantheon Books).

Kearns, G., and C. Philo (eds.) (1993) *Selling Places: The City as Cultural Capital, Past and Present* (Oxford: Pergamon Press).

Keating, K. (2007) Class war poster campaigns in San Francisco 1993–2001 (http://www.infoshop.org/myep/cw_posters.html).

Keil, R. (2002) '"Common-sense" neoliberalism: Progressive conservative urbanism in Toronto, Canada', *Antipode* 34, 3: 578–601.

Kern, C. R. (1981) 'Upper-income renaissance in the city: Its sources and implications for the city's future', *Journal of Urban Economics* 9: 106–124.

King, A. (1990) *Global Cities* (London: Routledge).

Knopp, L. (1990) 'Some theoretical implications of gay involvement in an urban land market', *Political Geography Quarterly* 9: 337–352.

Knopp, L. (1992) 'Sexuality and the spatial dynamics of capitalism', *Environment and Planning D: Society and Space* 10:651–669.

Knopp, L. (1997) 'Gentrification and gay neighborhood formation in New Orleans: A case study', in A. Gluckman and B. Reed (eds.) *Homo Economics: Capitalism, Community, Lesbian and Gay Life* (London: Routledge) 45–63.

Knox, P., and L. McCarthy (2005) *Urbanization* 2nd ed. (Englewood Cliffs, NJ: Prentice Hall).

Kodras, J. E. (2002) 'With liberty and justice for all: Negotiating freedom and fairness in the American income distribution', in J. A. Agnew and J. M. Smith (eds.) *American Space/American Place: Geographies of the Contemporary United States* (New York: Routledge) 187–230.

KQED (2007) *Castro* resource guide (http://www.kqed.org/w/hood/castro/resource-guide/index.html).

Krase, J. (2005) 'Poland and Polonia: Migration, and the re-incorporation of ethnic aesthetic practice in the taste of luxury', in R. Atkinson and G. Bridge (eds.) *Gentrification in a Global Context: The New Urban Colonialism* (London: Routledge) 185–208.

Krueckeberg, D. A. (1995) 'The difficult character of property: To whom do things belong?' *Journal of the American Planning Association* 61, 3: 301–309.

Kruger, K. H. (1985) 'Oh, baby. Schiesse. Wie ist das gekommen?' *Der Spiegel*, March 11 (quoted in Smith 1996a: 140).

Krugman, P. (2006) 'Coming down to Earth', *New York Times*, May 19: A23.

Kunzru, H. (2005) 'The battle for Tony's Café: An everyday tale of gentrification', *The Guardian* g2, December 7: 8–11.

Kwon, Y. (2005) 'Urban comparative statistics when commuting cost depends on income', *Journal of Housing Economics* 14: 48–56.

Lake, R. W. (1983) *Readings in Urban Analysis: Perspectives on Urban Form and Structure* (New Brunswick, NJ: Center for Urban Policy Research, Rutgers University).

Lake, R. W. (1995) 'Spatial fix 2: The sequel', *Urban Geography* 16, 3: 189–191.

Lake, R. W. (2002) 'Bring back big government', *International Journal of Urban and Regional Research* 26, 4: 815–822.

Lambert, C., and M. Boddy (2002) 'Transforming the city: Post-recession gentrification and re-urbanisation', paper presented at 'Upward Neighbourhood Trajectories: Gentrification in the New Century', University of Glasgow, Scotland, September 26–27.

Lander, B. (1997) 'Communities creating change? Development, organizing and social change', *Another Side: The Journal of the Michael Harrington Center* 5, 1: 5–16.

Laska, S. B., and D. Spain (eds.) (1980) *Back to the City: Issues in Neighborhood Renovation* (New York: Pergamon Press).

Lauria, M., and L. Knopp (1985) 'Towards an analysis of the role of gay communities in the urban renaissance', *Urban Geography* 6: 387–410.

Lawson, R. (1984) 'Tenant responses to the urban housing crisis, 1970–1984', in R. Lawson (ed.) *The Tenant Movement in New York City, 1904–1984* (New Brunswick, NJ: Rutgers University Press) 209–276.

Layton, L. (2006) 'Contest winners bear witness to a shifting Washington', *Washington Post*, May 8: B1.

Lee, S. (dir.) (1991) *Jungle Fever* (film).

Lees, L. (1994a) *A Pluralistic and Comparative Analysis of Gentrification in London and New York*, Ph.D. thesis (Department of Geography, University of Edinburgh, Scotland).

Lees, L. (1994b) 'Gentrification in London and New York: An Atlantic gap?' *Housing Studies* 9, 2: 199–217.

Lees, L. (1994c) 'Rethinking gentrification: Beyond the positions of economics and culture', *Progress in Human Geography*, 18, 2: 137–150.

Lees, L. (1996) 'In the pursuit of difference: Representations of gentrification', *Environment and Planning A* 28: 453–470.

Lees, L. (1998) 'Book review: "The new urban frontier: Gentrification and the revanchist city" by N. Smith and "Gentrification and the middle classes" by T. Butler', *Environment and Planning A* 30, 12: 2257–2260.

Lees, L. (1999) 'Critical geography and the opening up of the academy: Lessons from "real life" attempts', *Area* 31, 4: 377–383.

Lees, L. (2000) 'A reappraisal of gentrification: Towards a "geography of gentrification"', *Progress in Human Geography* 24, 3: 389–408.

Lees, L. (2003a) 'Visions of "urban renaissance": The Urban Task Force report and the Urban White Paper', in R. Imrie and M. Raco (eds.) *Urban Renaissance? New Labour, Community and Urban Policy* (Bristol: Policy Press) 61–82.

Lees, L. (2003b) 'Super-gentrification: The case of Brooklyn Heights, New York City', *Urban Studies* 40, 12: 2487–2509.

Lees, L. (2003c) 'Policy (re)turns: Urban policy and gentrification, gentrification and urban policy', *Environment and Planning A* 35, 4: 571–574.

Lees, L. (2003d) 'The ambivalence of diversity and the politics of urban renaissance: The case of youth in downtown Portland, Maine, USA', *International Journal of Urban and Regional Research* 27, 3: 613–634.

Lees, L. (2006) 'Gentrifying down the urban hierarchy: "The cascade effect" in Portland, Maine, USA', in D. Bell and M. Jayne (eds.) *Small Cities: Urban Experience beyond the Metropolis* (London: Routledge) 91–104.

Lees, L. (ed.) (2004) *The Emancipatory City? Paradoxes and Possibilities* (London: Sage).

Lees, L., and L. Bondi (1995) 'De-gentrification and economic recession: The case of New York City', *Urban Geography* 16, 3: 234–253.

Lees, L., and D. Demeritt (1998) 'Envisioning the livable city: The interplay of "Sin City" and "Sim City" in Vancouver's planning discourse', *Urban Geography* 19: 332–359.

Lefebvre, H. (1991) *The Production of Space*, trans. Donald Nicholson-Smith (Oxford: Blackwell).

LeGates, R., and C. Hartman (1986) 'The anatomy of displacement in the US', in N. Smith and P. Williams (eds.) *Gentrification of the City* (London: Unwin Hyman) 178–200.

LeRoy, S. F., and J. Sonstelie (1983) 'Paradise lost and regained: Transportation innovation, income, and residential location', *Journal of Urban Economics* 13: 67–89.

Lethem, J. (2003) *The Fortress of Solitude* (New York: Doubleday).

Ley, D. (1980) 'Liberal ideology and the postindustrial city', *Annals of the Association of American Geographers* 70: 238–258.

Ley, D. (1981) 'Inner-city revitalization in Canada: A Vancouver case study', *The Canadian Geographer* 25: 124–148.

Ley, D. (1986) 'Alternative explanations for inner-city gentrification: A Canadian assessment', *Annals of the Association of American Geographers* 76, 4: 521–535.

Ley, D. (1987a) 'The rent gap revisited', *Annals of the Association of American Geographers* 77, 3: 465–468.

Ley, D. (1987b) 'Styles of the times: Liberal and neo-conservative landscapes in inner Vancouver, 1968–1986', *Journal of Historical Geography* 13, 1: 40–56.

Ley, D. (1988) 'Social upgrading in six Canadian inner cities', *The Canadian Geographer* 32, 1: 31–45.

Ley, D. (1992) 'Gentrification in recession: social change in six Canadian inner cities, 1981–1986', *The Canadian Geographer* 13, 3: 230–256.

Ley, D. (1994) 'Gentrification and the politics of the new middle class', *Environment and Planning D: Society and Space* 12:53–74.

Ley, D. (1996) *The New Middle Class and the Remaking of the Central City* (Oxford: Oxford University Press).

Ley, D. (2003) 'Artists, aestheticisation and the field of gentrification', *Urban Studies* 40, 12: 2527–2544.

Ley, D. (2004) 'Transnational spaces and everyday lives', *Transactions of the Institute of British Geographers* 29, 2: 151–164.

Ley, D., and C. Mills (1993) 'Can there be a postmodernism of resistance in the urban landscape?' in P. Knox (ed.) *The Restless Urban Landscape* (Englewood Cliffs, NJ: Prentice Hall) 255–278.

Lipton, S. G. (1977) 'Evidence of central city revival', *Journal of the American Institute of Planners*, 43: 136–147.

Little, J. (1987) 'Gentrification and the influence of local-level planning', in P. Cloke (ed.) *Rural Planning: Policy into Action?* (London: Harper & Row) 185–199.

Logan, W. (1985) *The Gentrification of Inner Melbourne* (St. Lucia, Australia: University of Queensland Press).

London Borough of Islington (1966) *Barnsbury Environmental Study: Interim Report*, August (London: London Borough of Islington).

London Borough of Islington (1969) 'Planning and the public: A novel approach', press release, February 4 (London: London Borough of Islington).

Lueck, T. J. (1991) 'Prices decline as gentrification ebbs: The future is uncertain in areas that bloomed too late in the 1980s', *New York Times*, September 29, sec. 10: 1.

Lyons, M. (1996) 'Gentrification, socio-economic change and the geography of displacement', *Journal of Urban Affairs* 18: 39–62.

Lyons, M., and J. Gelb (1993) 'A tale of two cities: Housing policy and gentrification in London and New York', *Journal of Urban Affairs* 15, 4: 345–366.

MacLeod, G. (2002) 'From urban entrepreneurialism to a "revanchist city"? On the spatial injustices of Glasgow's renaissance', *Antipode* 34, 3: 602–624.

MacLeod, G., M. Raco, and K. Ward (guest eds.) (2003) 'Negotiating the contemporary city', *Urban Studies* 40, 8 (special issue).

Maine Arts Commission (2004) *Proceedings from the Blaine House Conference on Maine's Creative Economy*, August (http://www.mainearts.maine.gov/mainescreativeeconomy/conference/Proceedings).

Marcuse, P. (1985a) 'To control gentrification: Anti-displacement zoning and planning for stable residential districts', *Review of Law and Social Change* 13: 931–945.

Marcuse, P. (1985b) 'Gentrification, abandonment and displacement: Connections, causes and policy responses in New York City', *Journal of Urban and Contemporary Law* 28: 195–240.

Marcuse, P. (1986) 'Abandonment, gentrification and displacement: The linkages in New York City', in N. Smith and P. Williams (eds.) *Gentrification of the City* (London: Unwin Hyman) 153–177.

Marcuse, P. (2005) 'On the presentation of research about gentrification', unpublished manuscript, Department of Urban Planning, Columbia University, New York (available from author).

Markusen, A. (1981) 'City spatial structure, women's household work, and national urban policy', in C. Stimpson, E. Dixler, M. J. Nelson, and K. B. Yatrakis (eds.) *Women and the American City* (Chicago: University of Chicago Press) 20–41.

Maruca, J. (1978) 'Stalking the elusive city home mortgage', *The Brownstoner* 9 (February): 3.

Massey, D. (1993) 'Power-geometry and a progressive sense of place', in J. Bird, B. Curtis, T. Putnam, and G. Robertson (eds.) *Mapping the Futures: Local Cultures, Global Change* (London: Routledge) 59–69.

Massey, D. S. (2002) 'Comments on Jacob Vigdor's "Does Gentrification Harm the Poor?"' *Brookings-Wharton Papers on Urban Affairs*: 174–176.

May, J. (1996) 'Globalization and the politics of place: Place and identity in an inner London neighbourhood', *Transactions of the Institute of British Geographers* 21: 194–215.

McCall, B. (2004) 'Top brokers spot the hot new neighborhoods', *The New Yorker*, December 6: 128.

McDowell, L. (1997a) *Capital Culture: Gender at Work in the City* (Oxford: Blackwell).

McDowell, L. (1997b) 'The new service class: Housing consumption and lifestyle among London bankers in the 1990s', *Environment and Planning A* 29: 2061–2078.

Meligrana, J., and A. Skaburskis (2005) 'Extent, location and profiles of continuing gentrification in Canadian metropolitan areas', *Urban Studies* 42: 1569–1592.

Merlis, B., and L. A. Rosenzweig (1999) *Brooklyn's Park Slope: A Photographic Retrospective* (New York: Sheepshead Bay Historical Society).

Merrifield, A. (2000) 'The dialectics of dystopia: Disorder and zero tolerance in the city', *International Journal of Urban and Regional Research* 24: 473–489.

Merrifield, A. (2002a) *Dialectical Urbanism* (New York: Monthly Review Press).

Merrifield, A. (2002b) *Metromarxism: A Marxist Tale of the City* (New York: Routledge).

Merry, S. (1981) *Urban Danger: Life in a Neighborhood of Strangers* (Philadelphia: Temple University Press).

Metzger, J. (2000) 'Planned abandonment: The neighborhood life-cycle theory and national urban policy', *Housing Policy Debate* 11, 1: 7–40.

Milkowski, B. (1981) 'Land of the brownstones', *Antiques and Collectibles* November: 8–9, 11–12.

Millard-Ball, A. (2000) 'Moving beyond the gentrification gaps: Social change, tenure change and gap theories in Stockholm', *Urban Studies* 37, 9: 1673–1693.

Mills, C. (1988) 'Life on the upslope: The postmodern landscape of gentrification', *Environment and Planning D: Society and Space* 6: 169–189.

Mills, C. (1989) *Interpreting Gentrification: Postindustrial, Postpatriarchal, Postmodern?* Ph.D. thesis (Vancouver: Department of Geography, University of British Columbia).

Mills, C. (1993) 'Myths and meanings of gentrification', in J. Duncan and D. Ley (eds.) *Place/Culture/Representation* (London: Routledge) 149–170.

Milner Holland, Sir (1965) *Report of the Committee on Housing in Greater London*, Government White Paper, Cmnd. 2605 (London: H.M.S.O.).

Mitchell, D. (1997) 'The annihilation of space by law: The roots and implications of anti-homeless laws in the United States', *Antipode* 29: 303–335.

Mitchell, D. (2003) *The Right to the City: Social Justice and the Fight for Public Space* (New York: Guilford Press).

Monaghan, C. (1966) 'Park Slope group presses renewal', *New York Times*, July 10, sec. 8: 1, 9.

Morgan, M. (1981) *Skid Road: An Informal Portrait of Seattle* (Seattle: University of Washington Press).

Muir, J. (ed.) (1977) *Walk Park Slope: A Guide Book*, for the May 8, 1977, Walk Park Slope Day. New York : Park Slope Civic Council.

Mullins, P. (1982) 'The "middle-class" and the inner city', *Journal of Australian Political Economy* 11: 44–58.

Muniz, V. (1998) *Resisting Gentrification and Displacement: Voices of the Puerto Rican Woman of the Barrio* (New York: Garland).

Munt, I. (1987) 'Economic restructuring, culture, and gentrification: A case study in Battersea, London', *Environment and Planning A* 19: 1175–1197.

Musterd, S., H. Priemus, and R. van Kempen (1999) 'Towards undivided cities: The potential of economic revitalization and housing redifferentiation', *Housing Studies* 14, 5: 573–584.

Muth, R. (1969) *Cities and Housing* (Chicago: University of Chicago Press).

Myers, D., E. Gearin, T. Banerjee, and A. Garde (2001) *Current Preferences and Future Demand for Denser Residential Environments* (Coral Gables, FL: Funders' Network for Smart Growth and Livable Communities).

National Statistics (2001) Census 2001: The most comprehensive survey of the UK population (http://www.statistics.gov.uk/census2001/census2001.asp).

Nelson, K. (1988) *Gentrification and Distressed Cities: An Assessment of Trends in Intrametropolitan Migration* (Madison: University of Wisconsin Press).

Newman, K. (2004) 'Newark, decline and avoidance, renaissance and desire: From disinvestment to reinvestment', *Annals of the American Academy of Social and Political Sciences* 594: 34–48.

Newman, K., and R. Lake (2006) 'Democracy, bureaucracy and difference in US community development politics since 1968', *Progress in Human Geography* 30, 1: 44–61.

Newman, K., and E. Wyly (2006) 'The right to stay put, revisited: Gentrification and resistance to displacement in New York City', *Urban Studies* 43, 1: 23–57.

New York City Department of City Planning (1985) *Private Reinvestment and Neighborhood Change*, NYCDCP 85-25 (New York: New York City Department of City Planning).

*New York Magazine* (2001) Real estate 2001: Is there life beyond the boom? Volume 34, Issue 10, March 12.

Niedt, C. (2006) 'Gentrification and the grassroots: Popular support in the revanchist suburb', *Journal of Urban Affairs* 28, 2: 99–120.

Ogden, P. (ed) (1992) *London Docklands: The Challenge of Development* (Cambridge: Cambridge University Press).

O'Hanlon, T. (1982) *Neighborhood Change in New York City: A Case Study of Park Slope 1850 through 1980*, Ph.D. thesis (New York: Department of Environmental Psychology, City University of New York).

Olds, K. (1989) 'Mass evictions in Vancouver: The human toll of Expo '86', *Canadian Housing* 6: 49–52.

Osborn, B. (1998) '"raise shit": Downtown eastside poem of resistance', *Environment and Planning D: Society and Space* 16: 280–288.

O'Sullivan, D. (2002) 'Toward micro-scale spatial modeling of gentrification', *Journal of Geographical Systems*, 4, 3: 251–274.

Pacione, M. (1984) *Rural Geography* (London: Harper & Row).

Palen, J., and B. London (eds.) (1984) *Gentrification, Displacement and Neighborhood Revitalization* (Albany: State University of New York Press).

Papayanis, M. (2000) 'Sex and the revanchist city: Zoning out pornography in New York', *Environment and Planning D: Society and Space* 18: 341–353.

Park, R., E. Burgess, and R. McKenzie (1925) *The City* (Chicago: University of Chicago Press).

Parsons, D. (1980) 'Rural gentrification: The influence of rural settlement planning policies', Department of Geography Research Paper 3 (Brighton, UK: University of Sussex).

Passaro, V. (2001) 'The view from out here', *New York Times Magazine*, November 11.

Peck, J. (2005) 'Struggling with the creative class', *International Journal of Urban and Regional Research* 29, 4: 740–770.

Peck, J. (2006) 'Liberating the city: From New York to New Orleans', *Urban Geography* 27, 8: 681–713.

Petsimeris, P. (2005) 'Out of squalor and towards another urban renaissance? Gentrification and neighbourhood transformations in Southern Europe', in R. Atkinson and G. Bridge (eds.) *Gentrification in a Global Context: The New Urban Colonialism* (London: Routledge) 240–255.

Phillips, M. (1993) 'Rural gentrification and the processes of class colonization', *Journal of Rural Studies* 9: 123–140.

Phillips, M. (2002) 'The production, symbolisation and socialisation of gentrification: A case study of a Berkshire village', *Transactions of the Institute of British Geographers* 27, 3: 282–308.

Phillips, M. (2004) 'Other geographies of gentrification', *Progress in Human Geography* 28, 1: 5–30.

Phillips-Fein, K. (2000) 'The richer they get in Manhattan, the more poor people are evicted in Brooklyn', *The American Prospect*, December 4.

Pitt, J. (1977) *Gentrification in Islington* (London: Barnsbury People's Forum)

Plunz, R. (1990) *A History of Housing in New York City: Dwelling Type and Structural Change in the American Metropolis* (New York: Columbia University Press).

Podmore, J. (1998) '(Re)reading the "loft living" habitus in Montreal's inner city', *International Journal of Urban and Regional Research* 22: 283–302.

Pogrebin, R. (2006) 'An architect with plans for a new Gulf Coast', *New York Times*, May 24: B1, B8.

Powell, J., and M. Spencer (2003) 'Giving them the old "one-two": Gentrification and the K O of impoverished urban dwellers of color', *Howard Law Journal* 46, 3: 433–490.

Power, A. (1972) *A Battle Lost: Barnsbury 1972* (London: Friends House).

Power, A. (1973) *David and Goliath: Barnsbury 1973* (London: Holloway Neighbourhood Law Centre).

Pratt, G., and S. Hanson (1994) 'Geography and the construction of difference', *Gender, Place and Culture* 1: 5–29.

Priemus, H. (1995) 'How to abolish social housing: The Dutch case', *International Journal of Urban and Regional Research* 19: 145–155.

Priemus, H. (1998) 'Redifferentiation of the urban housing stock in the Netherlands: A strategy to prevent spatial segregation', *Housing Studies* 13, 3: 301–310.

Priemus, H. (2001) 'Social housing as a transitional tenure? Reflections on the Netherlands' new Housing Memorandum 2000–2010', *Housing Studies* 16, 2: 243–256.

Pring, K. (1968/1969) *Barnsbury Explored: Some Exercises in Exploiting the Townscape Potential of an Inner Urban Twilight Area in London* (London: Department of Architecture and Town Planning, The Polytechnic, Regent Street).

Pryke, M. (1991) 'An international city going "global": Spatial change in the City of London', *Environment and Planning D: Society and Space* 9: 197–222.

Raban, J. (1974) *Soft City* (London: Fontana).

Ray, B., and D. Rose (2000) 'Cities of the everyday: Socio-spatial perspectives on gender, difference and diversity', in T. Bunting and P. Filion (eds.) *Canadian Cities in*

*Transition: the Twenty-First Century* 2nd ed. (Oxford: Oxford University Press) 507–512.

Redfern, P. (1997) 'A new look at gentrification: 1. Gentrification and domestic technologies', *Environment and Planning A* 29: 1275–1296.

Reed, A., and S. Steinberg (2006) 'Liberal bad faith in the wake of New Orleans', *Black Commentator* 182, May 5.

Reed Elsevier, Inc. (2006) *LexisNexis Academic* (http://www.lexisnexis.com).

Reichl, A. (1999) *Reconstructing Times Square: Politics and Culture in Urban Development* (Lawrence: Kansas University Press).

Rich, M., and D. Leonhardt (2005) 'Trading places: Real estate instead of dot-coms', *New York Times*, March 25: A1, C2.

Rivlin, A. M. (2002) 'Comments on Jacob Vigdor's "Does Gentrification Harm the Poor?"' *Brookings-Wharton Papers on Urban Affairs*: 176–179.

Rofe, M. (2003) '"I want to be global": Theorising the gentrifying class as an emergent elite global community', *Urban Studies* 40, 12: 2511–2526.

Roschelle, A., and T. Wright (2003) 'Gentrification and social exclusion: Spatial policing and homeless activist responses in the San Francisco Bay Area', in M. Miles and T. Hall (eds.) *Urban Futures: Critical Commentaries on Shaping the City* (London: Routledge) 149–166.

Rose, D. (1984) 'Rethinking gentrification: Beyond the uneven development of Marxist urban theory', *Environment and Planning D: Society and Space* 1: 47–74.

Rose, D. (1989) 'A feminist perspective of employment restructuring and gentrification: The case of Montreal', in J. Wolch and M. Dear (eds.) *The Power of Geography: How Territory Shapes Social Life* (Boston: Unwin Hyman) 118–138.

Rose, D. (1996) 'Economic restructuring and the diversification of gentrification in the 1980s: A view from a marginal metropolis', in J. Caulfield and L. Peake (eds.) *City Lives and City Forms: Critical Research and Canadian Urbanism* (Toronto: University of Toronto Press) 131–172.

Rose, D. (2002) 'Gentrification through "infill-tration"? New condo owners' relationships to neighbourhood in a gentrifying economy', paper presented to the Annual Meeting of the Association of American Geographers, Los Angeles, March 19–23.

Rose, D. (2004) 'Discourses and experiences of social mix in gentrifying neighbourhoods: A Montréal case study', *Canadian Journal of Urban Research* 13, 2: 278–316.

Rose, D., and C. LeBourdais (1986) 'The changing conditions of female single parenthood in Montréal's inner city and suburban neighbourhoods', *Urban Resources* 3, 2: 45–52.

Rothenberg, T. (1995) '"And she told two friends": Lesbians creating urban social space', in D. Bell and G. Valentine (eds.) *Mapping Desire: Geographies of Sexualities* (London: Routledge) 165–181.

Rutheiser, C. (1996) *Imagineering Atlanta: The Politics of Place in the City of Dreams* (New York: Verso).

Rydin, Y. (2005) 'Geographical knowledge and policy: The positive contribution of discourse studies', *Area* 37, 1: 73–78.

Salet, W. (1999) 'Regime shifts in Dutch housing policy', *Housing Studies* 14, 4: 547–558.

Sassen, S. (1991) *The Global City: New York, London and Tokyo* (Princeton, NJ: Princeton University Press).

Saulhy, S. (2006) 'Investors lead home sale boom in New Orleans', *New York Times*, July 9.

Savage, M. (1991) 'Making sense of middle-class politics: A secondary analysis of the 1987 general election survey', *Sociological Review* 39: 26–54.

Savage, M., G. Bagnall, and B. Longhurst (2005) *Globalization and Belonging* (London: Sage).

Savage, M., J. Barlow, P. Dickens, and A. Fielding (1992) *Property, Bureaucracy and Culture: Middle Class Formation in Contemporary Britain* (Andover, MA: Routledge, Chapman and Hall).

Schaffer, R., and N. Smith (1986) 'The gentrification of Harlem?' *Annals of the Association of American Geographers* 76: 347–365.

Schill, M., and R. Nathan (1983) *Revitalizing America's Cities: Neighborhood Reinvestment and Displacement* (Albany: State University of New York Press).

Schumpeter, J. (1934) *The Theory of Economic Development* (Cambridge, MA: Harvard University Press).

Seiden Miller, R. (ed.) (1979) *Brooklyn USA: The Fourth Largest City in America* (New York: Brooklyn College Press).

Shaw, K. (2002) 'Culture, economics and evolution in gentrification', *Just Policy* December 28: 42–50.

Shaw, K. (2005) 'Local limits to gentrification: Implications for a new urban policy', in R. Atkinson and G. Bridge (eds.) *Gentrification in a Global Context: The New Urban Colonialism* (London: Routledge) 168–184.

Shaw, W. (2000) 'Ways of whiteness: Harlemising Sydney's aboriginal Redfern', *Australian Geographical Studies* 38, 3: 291–305.

Shaw, W. (2005) 'Heritage and gentrification: Remembering "the good olde days" in colonial Sydney', in R. Atkinson and G. Bridge (eds.) *Gentrification in a Global Context: The New Urban Colonialism* (London: Routledge) 57–71.

Shier, R. (2003) 'Introduction', in R. Shier (ed.) *Stan Douglas: Every Building on 100 West Hastings* (Vancouver: Contemporary Art Gallery) 10–17.

Short, J. R. (1989) 'Yuppies, yuffies and the new urban order', *Transactions of the Institute of British Geographers* 14, 2: 173–188.

Showley, R. M. (2006) 'Click and miss? Not everyone is thrilled with "zestimating" property values', *San Diego (CA) Union-Tribune*, March 19: I-1.

Slater, T. (2002) 'Looking at the "North American city" through the lens of gentrification discourse', *Urban Geography* 23, 2: 131–153.

Slater, T. (2004a) 'North American gentrification? Revanchist and emancipatory perspectives explored', *Environment and Planning A* 36, 7: 1191–1213.

Slater, T. (2004b) 'Municipally-managed gentrification in South Parkdale, Toronto', *The Canadian Geographer* 48, 3: 303–325.

Slater, T. (2006) 'The eviction of critical perspectives from gentrification research', *International Journal of Urban and Regional Research*, 30, 4: 737–757.

Slater, T., W. Curran, and L. Lees (2004) 'Guest editorial. Gentrification research: New directions and critical scholarship', *Environment and Planning A* 36, 7: 1141–1150.

Smith, D. (2002) 'Patterns and processes of "studentification" in Leeds', *Regional Review* 11: 17–19.

Smith, D. (2005) '"Studentification": The gentrification factory', in R. Atkinson and G. Bridge (eds.) *Gentrification in a Global Context: The New Urban Colonialism* (London: Routledge) 72–89.

Smith, D., and T. Butler (guest eds.) (2007) 'Extending gentrification', *Environment and Planning A* 39, 1 (special issue).

Smith, D., and L. Holt (2007) 'Studentification and "apprentice" gentrifiers within Britain's provincial urban locations: Extending the meaning of gentrification?' *Environment and Planning A* 39, 1: 142–161.

Smith, D., and D. Phillips (2001) 'Socio-cultural representations of greentrified Pennine rurality', *Journal of Rural Studies* 17: 457–469.

Smith, D. M. (1994) *Geography and Social Justice* (Oxford: Blackwell).

Smith, H. (2003) 'Planning, policy and polarisation in Vancouver's Downtown East-side', *Tijdschrift voor Economische en Sociale Geografie* 94, 4: 496–509.

Smith, J. (2000) 'The space of local control in the devolution of US public housing policy', *Geografiska Annaler B* 82, 4: 221–234.

Smith, J. (2001) 'Mixing it up: Public housing redevelopment in Chicago', paper presented at 'Area-Based Initiatives in Contemporary Urban Policy' conference, Danish Building and Urban Research/European Urban Research Association, Copenhagen, 17–19 May.

Smith, M. P. (2001) *Transnational Urbanism: Locating Globalization* (Oxford: Blackwell).

Smith, N. (1979) 'Toward a theory of gentrification: A back to the city movement by capital, not people', *Journal of the American Planning Association* 45, 4: 538–548.

Smith, N. (1982) 'Gentrification and uneven development', *Economic Geography* 58, 2: 139–155.

Smith, N. (1984) *Uneven Development: Nature, Capital, and the Production of Space* (Oxford: Blackwell).

Smith, N. (1986) 'Gentrification, the frontier, and the restructuring of urban space', in N. Smith and P. Williams (eds.) *Gentrification of the City* (London: Allen and Unwin) 15–34.

Smith, N. (1987) 'Gentrification and the rent gap', *Annals of the Association of American Geographers* 77, 3: 462–478.

Smith, N. (1992a) 'Blind man's bluff, or Hamnett's philosophical individualism in search of gentrification?' *Transactions of the Institute of British Geographers* 17, 1: 110–115.

Smith, N. (1992b) 'Contours of a spatialized politics of homeless vehicles and the production of geographical scale', *Social Text*, 33: 54–81.

Smith, N. (1996a) *The New Urban Frontier: Gentrification and the Revanchist City* (London: Routledge).

Smith, N. (1996b) 'Of rent gaps and radical idealism: A reply to Steven Bourassa', *Urban Studies* 33, 7: 1199–1203.

Smith, N. (1996c) 'Social justice and the new American urbanism: The revanchist city', in A. Merrifield and E. Swyngedouw (eds.) *The Urbanization of Injustice* (New York: New York University Press).

Smith, N. (1998) 'Giuliani time', *Social Text* 57: 1–20.

Smith, N. (1999) 'Which new urbanism? New York City and the revanchist 1990s', in R. Beauregard and S. Body-Gendrot (eds.) *The Urban Moment: Cosmopolitan Essays on the Late 20th Century City* (Thousand Oaks, CA: Sage) 185–208.

Smith, N. (2000) 'Gentrification', in R. J. Johnston, D. Gregory, G. Pratt, and M. Watts (eds.) *The Dictionary of Human Geography* 4th ed. (Oxford: Blackwell) 294–296.

Smith, N. (2001) 'Giuliani space: Revanchist city', in I. Miyares, M. Pavlovskaya, and G. Pope (eds.) *From Hudson to the Hamptons: Snapshots of the New York Metropolitan Area* (Washington, DC: Association of American Geographers) 70–78.

Smith, N. (2002) 'New globalism, new urbanism: Gentrification as global urban strategy', *Antipode* 34, 3: 427–450.

Smith, N., P. Caris, and E. Wyly (2001) 'The Camden syndrome: The menace of suburban decline. Residential disinvestment and its discontents in Camden County, New Jersey', *Urban Affairs Review* 36, 4: 497–531.

Smith, N., and J. DeFilippis (1999) 'The reassertion of economics: 1990s gentrification in the Lower East Side', *International Journal of Urban and Regional Research* 23: 638–653.

Smith, N., and J. Derksen (2003) 'Urban regeneration: Gentrification as global urban strategy', in R. Shier (ed.) *Stan Douglas: Every Building on 100 West Hastings* (Vancouver: Contemporary Art Gallery) 62–95.

Smith, N., B. Duncan, and L. Reid (1989) 'From disinvestment to reinvestment: Tax arrears and turning points in the East Village', *Housing Studies* 4, 4: 238–252.

Smith, N., and P. Williams (1986) 'Alternatives to orthodoxy: Invitation to a debate', in N. Smith and P. Williams (eds.) *Gentrification of the City* (London: Allen and Unwin) 1–10.

Smith, N., and P. Williams (eds.) (1986) *Gentrification of the City* (London: Allen and Unwin).

Social Exclusion Unit (1998) *Bringing Britain Together: A National Strategy for Neighbourhood Renewal* (London: H.M.S.O.).

Sohmer, R. R., and R. E. Lang (2001) *Downtown Rebound*, Brookings Institution Census Notes Series (Washington, DC: Fannie Mae Foundation).

Solnit, R. (2000) *Hollow City: The Siege of San Francisco and the Crisis of American Urbanism* (London: Verso).

Sommers, J. (1998) 'Men at the margin: Masculinity and space in downtown Vancouver, 1950–1986', *Urban Geography* 19: 287–310.

Sommers, J., and N. Blomley (2003) '"The worst block in Vancouver"', in R. Shier (ed.) *Stan Douglas: Every Building on 100 West Hastings* (Vancouver: Contemporary Art Gallery) 18–61.

Sorkin, M. (ed.) (1992) *Variations on a Theme Park: The New American City and the End of Public Space* (New York: Hill and Wang).

Sowell, T. (2005) 'Who will rebuild New Orleans' moral levees?' *Investors Business Daily*, September 7: A14.

Squires, G. (ed.) (1992) *From Redlining to Reinvestment: Community Responses to Urban Disinvestment* (Philadelphia: Temple University Press) 1–37.

Squires, G. (ed.) (2003) *Organizing Access to Capital* (Philadelphia: Temple University Press).

Squires, G. (ed.) (2004) *Why the Poor Pay More: How to Stop Predatory Lending* (London: Praeger).

Sugrue, T. J. (2005) *The Origins of the Urban Crisis: Race and Inequality in Postwar Detroit* 2nd ed. (Princeton, NJ: Princeton University Press).

Sumka, H. (1979) 'Neighborhood revitalization and displacement: A review of the evidence', *Journal of the American Planning Association* 45: 480–487.

Sýkora, L. (1993) 'City in transition: The role of the rent gap in Prague's revitalization', *Tijdschrift voor Economisce en Sociale Geografie* 84, 4: 281–293.

Sýkora, L. (2005) 'Gentrification in post-communist cities', in R. Atkinson and G. Bridge (eds.) *Gentrification in a Global Context: The New Urban Colonialism* (London: Routledge) 90–105.

Taylor, M. (1992) 'Can you go home again? Black gentrification and the dilemma of difference', *Berkeley Journal of Sociology* 37: 121–138.

Taylor, M. (2002) *Harlem: Between Heaven and Hell* (Minneapolis: University of Minnesota Press).

*The Brownstoner* (1981) 'Renaissance breaks more ground' September 12: 4.

*The Brownstoner* (1984) 'Gentrification: Genesis not genocide' July 15: 2.

*The Brownstoner* (1991) 'How to love a brownstone (eyes open but half closed too)' Fall, 6 [reprint from April 1969 edition of the *Brownstoner*].

*The Economist* (2005) 'The global housing boom', June 16.

*The Economist* (2006) 'Goldman Sachs and the culture of risk', April 29.

*The Times* (1977) 'Letters to the editor: Gentrification in Islington', August 22: 13.

Thrift, N. (1987) 'The geography of late twentieth-century class formation', in N. Thrift and P. Williams (eds.) *Class and Space: The Making of Urban Society* (London: Routledge and Kegan Paul) 207–253.

Tickell, A., and J. Peck (2003) 'Making global rules: Globalisation or neoliberalisation?' in J. Peck and H. Yeung (eds.) *Remaking the Global Economy* (London: Sage) 163–181.

Uitermark, J. (2003) '"Social mixing" and the management of disadvantaged neighbourhoods: The Dutch policy of urban restructuring revisited', *Urban Studies* 40, 3: 531–549.

Uitermark, J., J. Duyvendak, and R. Kleinhans (2007) 'Gentrification as a governmental strategy: Social control and social cohesion in Hoogvliet, Rotterdam', *Environment and Planning A* 39, 1: 125–141.

Urban Habitat Program (2000) *There Goes the Neighborhood: A Regional Analysis of Gentrification and Community Stability in the San Francisco Bay Area* (San Francisco: Urban Habitat Program; available from Urban Habitat Program, P.O. Box 29908, Presidio Station, San Francisco, CA 94129).

U.S. Bureau of the Census (2002) *New York City Housing and Vacancy Survey* (Washington, DC: U.S. Department of Commerce).

U.S. Bureau of the Census (2006). U.S. Census Bureau's guide to census tract resources (http://www.census.gov/geo/www/tractez.html).

U.S. Department of Housing and Urban Development (1999) *State of the Cities Report*, June (Washington, DC: U.S. Department of Housing and Urban Development).

van Criekingen, M. (2006) 'Migration and the effects of gentrification: A Brussels perspective', Working paper (Brussels: Department of Human Geography, Université Libre de Bruxelles, Belgium).

van Kempen, R., and H. Priemus (1999) 'Undivided cities in the Netherlands: Present situation and political rhetoric', *Housing Studies* 14, 5: 641–658.

van Kempen, R., and J. van Weesep (1994) 'Gentrification and the urban poor: Urban restructuring and housing policy in Utrecht', *Urban Studies* 31, 7: 1043–1056.

van Weesep, J. (1994) 'Gentrification as a research frontier', *Progress in Human Geography* 18: 74–83.

van Weesep, J., and S. Musterd (eds.) (1991) *Urban Housing for the Better-Off: Gentrification in Europe* (Utrecht, the Netherlands: Stedelijke Netwerken).

Vicario, L., and P. Martinez Monje (2005) 'Another "Guggenheim effect"? Central city projects and gentrification in Bilbao', in R. Atkinson and G. Bridge (eds.) *Gentrification in a Global Context: The New Urban Colonialism* (London: Routledge) 151–167.

Vigdor, J. (2002) 'Does gentrification harm the poor?' *Brookings-Wharton Papers on Urban Affairs*: 133–173.

von Thünen, J. (1966) *The Isolated State and Its Relation to Agriculture and National Economy*, ed. P. Hall (Oxford: Pergamon Press).

Walker, R. (1981) 'A theory of suburbanization: Capitalism and the construction of urban space in the United States', in M. Dear and A. J. Scott (eds.) *Urbanization and Urban Planning in Capitalist Society* (New York: Methuen), 383–429.

Walker, R., and D. Greenberg (1982) 'Post-industrialism and political reform in the city: A critique', *Antipode* 14, 1: 17–32.

Warde, A. (1991) 'Gentrification as consumption: Issues of class and gender', *Environment and Planning D: Society and Space* 9: 223–232.

Watkins, R. (1984) '"Quality of life" crimes have been a fact of life here for over 2 decades', *The Phoenix*, January 12: 7–9.

Watts, M. (2001) '1968 and all that. ...' *Progress in Human Geography* 25, 2: 157–188.

Webber, M. J., and D. L. Rigby (1996) *The Golden Age of Illusion: Rethinking Postwar Capitalism* (New York: Guilford Press).

Wetzel, T. (2000). A year in the life of the anti-displacement movement (http://www.uncanny.net/~wetzel/macchron.htm).

Wetzel, T. (2001) 'San Francisco's space wars', *Processed World* 2, 1: 49–57.

Wheaton, W. (1977) 'Income and urban residence: An analysis of consumer demand for location', *American Economic Review* 67: 620–631.

White, G. (1972) 'Geography and public policy', *The Professional Geographer* 24, 2: 101–104.

Williams, P. (1976) 'The role of institutions in the inner London housing market: The case of Islington', *Transactions of the Institute of British Geographers* 1: 72–82.

Williams, P. (1978) 'Building societies and the inner city', *Transactions of the Institute of British Geographers* 3: 23–34.

Williams, P. (1984) 'Gentrification in Britain and Europe', in J. Palen and B. London (eds.) *Gentrification, Displacement and Neighbourhood Revitalization* (Albany: State University of New York Press) 205–234.

Williams, P. (1986) 'Class constitution through spatial reconstruction? A re-evaluation of gentrification in Australia, Britain and the United States', in N. Smith and P. Williams (eds.) *Gentrification of the City* (London: Unwin Hyman) 56–77.

Wilson, D., and D. Grammenos (2000) 'Spatiality and urban redevelopment movements', *Urban Geography* 21, 4: 361–370.

Wilson, D., J. Wouters, and D. Grammenos (2004) 'Successful protect community discourse: Spatiality and politics in Chicago's Pilsen neighbourhood', *Environment and Planning A* 36, 7: 1173–1190.

Wilson, W. J. (1987) *The Truly Disadvantaged: The Inner City, the Underclass, and Public Policy* (Chicago: University of Chicago Press).

Wilson, W. J. (1996) *When Work Disappears: The World of the New Urban Poor* (New York: Random House).

Wines, M. (2006) 'A shack, be it ever so humble, gets a fancy South Africa price', *New York Times*, June 7: A1, A14.

Wodiczko, K., and R. Luria (1990) 'The homeless vehicle project', *Journal of Architectural Education* 43, 4: 37–42.

Wyly, E., and D. Hammel (1998) 'Modeling the context and contingency of gentrification', *Journal of Urban Affairs* 20, 3: 303–326.

Wyly, E., and D. Hammel (1999) 'Islands of decay in seas of renewal: Housing policy and the resurgence of gentrification', *Housing Policy Debate* 10, 4: 711–771.

Wyly, E., and D. Hammel (2000) 'Capital's metropolis: Chicago and the transformation of American housing policy', *Geografiska Annaler B* 82, 4: 181–206.

Wyly, E., and D. Hammel (2001) 'Gentrification, housing policy, the new context of urban redevelopment', in K. Fox Gotham (ed.) *Critical Perspectives on Urban Redevelopment*, vol. 6 of *Research in Urban Sociology* (London: Elsevier) 211–276.

Wyly, E., and D. Hammel (2004) 'Gentrification, segregation, and discrimination in the American urban system', *Environment and Planning A* 36, 7: 1215–1241.

Wyly, E., and D. Hammel (2005) 'Mapping neoliberal American urbanism', in R. Atkinson and G. Bridge (eds.) *Gentrification in a Global Context: The New Urban Colonialism* (London: Routledge) 18–38.

Young, I. M. (1990) *Justice and the Politics of Difference* (Princeton, NJ: Princeton University Press).

Zillow (2006) *CityHeatMaps* (http://www.zillow.com/heatmaps/CityHeatMaps.htm).

Zukin, S. (1982) *Loft Living: Culture and Capital in Urban Change* (Baltimore: Johns Hopkins University Press).

Zukin, S. (1989) *Loft Living: Culture and Capital in Urban Change* 2nd ed. (New Brunswick, NJ: Rutgers University Press).

Zukin, S. (1990) 'Socio-spatial prototypes of a new organization of consumption: The role of real cultural capital', *Sociology* 24: 37–56.

Zukin, S. (1991) *Landscapes of Power: From Detroit to Disney World* (Berkeley: University of California Press).

Zukin, S. (1992) 'The city as a landscape of power: London and New York as global financial capitals', in L. Budd and S. Whimster (eds.) *Global Finance and Urban Living: A Study of Metropolitan Change* (London: Routledge) 195–223.

Zukin, S. (1995) *The Cultures of Cities* (Oxford: Blackwell).

Zukin, S. (2006) 'David Harvey on cities', in N. Castree and D. Gregory (eds.) *David Harvey: A Critical Reader* (Oxford: Blackwell) 102–120.

# Index